# Paying for College

## 2020 Edition

By Kalman A. Chany with Geoff Martz

PrincetonReview.com

Penguin
Random
House

The Princeton Review
110 East 42nd St., 7th Floor
New York, NY 10017
Email: editorialsupport@review.com

## Editorial

Rob Franek, Editor-in-Chief
David Soto, Director of Content Development
Stephen Koch, Student Survey Manager
Deborah Weber, Director of Production
Gabe Berlin, Production Design Manager
Selena Coppock, Managing Editor
Aaron Riccio, Senior Editor
Meave Shelton, Senior Editor
Chris Chimera, Editor
Eleanor Greene, Editor
Orion McBean, Editor
Brian Saladino, Editor

## Random House Publishing Team

Tom Russell, VP, Publisher
Alison Stoltzfus, Publishing Director
Amanda Yee, Associate Managing Editor
Ellen Reed, Production Manager
Suzanne Lee, Designer

ISBN: 978-0-525-56879-7
eBook ISBN: 978-0-525-56883-4
ISSN: 1944-3781

The Princeton Review is not affiliated with
Princeton University.

Editor: Aaron Riccio
Production Editor: Lee Elder
Production Artist: Deborah Weber

Printed in the United States of America.

10 9 8 7 6 5 4 3 2 1

2020 Edition

# Acknowledgments

Geoff Martz and I are most grateful to those who have helped with this and prior editions of the book.

We would first like to thank Robert Franek, Deborah Weber, and Aaron Riccio at The Princeton Review and Tom Russell and Alison Stoltzfus at Penguin Random House.

Special thanks to Jeanne Krier, who has served as our publicist for more than twenty-five years. Her understanding of the many complex issues surrounding financial aid and college funding as well as her keen suggestions for future editions have been an ongoing source of help and support. Her skill as a public relations expert and the high regard that many members of media have for her professionalism have also contributed significantly to the success of this project.

We are also grateful to Victoria Malone, Michele Brown, Anita Gross, Daria Adams, and Jeanne Saunders at the U.S. Department of Education as well as Susan McCrackin, Ami Boshardt, and Jessica Bernier at the College Board who have been a tremendous source of help for many editions of this book.

I would also like to thank Isidore Matalon, my longtime friend and a constant source of new ideas; Steven Levine of the accounting firm of Lederer & Levine in Lyndhurst, New Jersey, for his helpful suggestions regarding tax law; Catherine O'Connor, my associate at Campus Consultants without whom I could never have managed; my friends Stuart Foisy and John Brubaker for their assistance with the worksheets at the back of this book; the high school counselors and independent college consultants who have entrusted students and their parents to me over the years; and my own parents, who somehow managed to pay for my college education without the benefit of having read a book like this.

Last but not least, I would like to thank my clients who have provided me with the opportunity to prove that financial aid planning really works.

—Kal Chany

# Contents

Get More (Free) Content ................................................................................ vi

Introduction ............................................................................................... 1

**Part One: Understanding the Process** ............................................................ **9**
   Chapter One: Overview ........................................................................... 11

**Part Two: How to Take Control of the Process** ............................................. **19**
   Chapter Two: Long-Term Strategies for Paying for College .......................... 23
   Chapter Three: Short-Term Strategies for Receiving More Financial Aid .............. 53
   Chapter Four: How to Pick Colleges ....................................................... 127
   Chapter Five: What the Student Can Do ................................................. 137
   Chapter Six: State Aid .......................................................................... 143

**Part Three: Filling Out the Standardized Forms** .......................................... **153**

**Part Four: The Offer and Other Financial Matters** ....................................... **217**
   Chapter Seven: Innovative Payment Options ............................................ 235
   Chapter Eight: Managing Your Debt ....................................................... 245
   Chapter Nine: Special Topics ................................................................ 255
   Chapter Ten: Less Taxing Matters .......................................................... 279
   Chapter Eleven: Looking for a Financial Aid Consulting Service .................. 287
   Chapter Twelve: Looking Ahead ............................................................ 291

**Part Five: Worksheets and Forms** ............................................................. **295**
Sample Forms ......................................................................................... 323

**Appendices** ............................................................................................. **335**
   Glossary ............................................................................................. 336
   Institutional Methodology Comments and Case Studies ............................. 342
   Key Things To Know About the IRS Data Retrieval Tool and the
     IRS Transcript Verification Requirement ............................................. 347

About the Authors .................................................................................... 351

# Get More (**Free**) Content
## at **PrincetonReview.com/cracking**

## As easy as **1•2•3**

**1** Go to PrincetonReview.com/cracking and enter the following ISBN for your book:
**9780525568797**

**2** Answer a few simple questions to set up an exclusive Princeton Review account. *(If you already have one, you can just log in.)*

**3** Enjoy access to your **FREE** content!

# Once you've registered, you can...

- Take a full-length practice SAT or ACT.

- Get valuable advice about the college application process

- If you're still choosing between colleges, use our searchable rankings of *The Best 385 Colleges* to find out more information about your dream school.

- Check to see if there have been any corrections or updates to this edition.

## Need to report a potential **content** issue?

Contact **EditorialSupport@review.com** and include:

- full title of the book
- ISBN
- page number

## Need to report a **technical** issue?

Contact **TPRStudentTech@review.com** and provide:

- your full name
- email address used to register the book
- full book title and ISBN
- Operating system (Mac/PC) and browser (Firefox, Safari, etc.)

# Introduction

The college application process has been described as the closest thing America has to a "savage puberty rite." In fact, entire books have been written about the traumatic effect the application process has on students. Much less attention has been paid to another group of unsung heroes who are going through a similar ordeal all their own: the parents who are supposed to pay for all this.

# If This Is So Good for Me, Why Does It Feel So Bad?

The cost of a four-year private college education has passed the $250,000 mark at some schools, which is enough to cause even the most affluent parent to want to sit down and cry. The public Ivies—state schools with excellent reputations—have been raising their tuition even faster than the privates. This year, an out-of-state student will have to pay more than $63,000 to attend the University of Michigan for one year.

Meanwhile, stagnating university endowments caused by the stock market slump along with cuts to the education budgets of state governments have combined to create a crisis in higher education. Some colleges have had to slash their budgets, lay off professors, even consolidate with other schools. And even when you factor in the new educational tax benefits, the financial aid available per student has shrunk as rising tuition has forced more and more parents to apply for assistance.

## The Joy of Aid

If there is a bright side to all this it is that in spite of all the bad news, there is still a great deal of financial aid available—and we are talking *billions* of dollars. At these prices, almost every family now qualifies for some form of assistance. Many parents don't believe that a family that makes over $150,000 a year, owns their own home, and holds substantial assets could possibly receive financial aid. These days, that family—provided it is presented in the right light—almost certainly does. Many parents who make $50,000, rent their home, and have no assets, don't believe they can afford to send their child to any type of college at all. They almost certainly can—in fact, they may find to their surprise that with the financial aid package some schools can put together for them, it may cost less to attend an "expensive" private school than it would to go to a "cheap" state school.

## Who Gets the Most Financial Aid?

You might think that the families who receive the most financial aid would be the families with the most need. In fact, this is not necessarily true. The people who receive the most aid are the people who best understand the aid process.

Some years ago, we had a client who owned a $1 million apartment in New York City and a stock portfolio with a value in excess of $2 million. Her daughter attended college—with a $4,000-a-year need-based grant.

## Is This Fair?

No. But lots of things in life aren't fair. In that particular case, we were able to take advantage of a financial aid loophole involving the way state aid is computed in New York. There are lots of financial aid loopholes.

## Is This Legal?

You bet. All of the strategies we are going to discuss in this book follow the law to the letter.

## Is This Ethical?

Let us put a hypothetical question to you: If your accountant showed you a legal way to save $4,000 on your income tax this year, would you take it?

The parallels between taxes and financial aid are interesting. Both have loopholes that regularly get exploited by the people who know about them. But more important, both also involve adversarial relationships. In the case of your taxes, the IRS wants as much money from you as it can get. You, in turn, want to give the IRS as little as possible. This pas de deux is a time-honored tradition, a system of checks and balances that everyone understands and accepts. And as long as both sides stick to the rules, the system works as well as anyone can expect.

In the case of college, it is the job of the financial aid officer (known in college circles as the FAO) to get as much money from you as he can. In the pursuit of this task, he will be much more invasive than the IRS ever is, demanding not just your financial data but intimate details of your personal life such as medical problems and marital status. He wants to protect the college's assets and give away as little money as possible. Let the financial aid officer do *his* job—believe us, he's very good at it. In the meantime, you have to do *your* job—and your job is to use the rules of financial aid to make your contribution to college as small as possible.

Parents who understand these rules get the maximum amount of financial aid they are entitled to under the law. No more, and no less.

## Besides, You've Already Paid for Financial Aid

Whether you know it or not, you've been contributing to financial aid funds for years. Each April 15, you pay federal taxes, a piece of which goes straight to the federal student aid programs. You pay state taxes, part of which goes directly to state schools and to provide grant programs for residents attending college in-state. You may even make contributions to the alumni fund-raising campaign at your own college.

Your son or daughter may not go to your alma mater, may not attend a school in your state, may not even go to college, but you have paid all these years so that *someone's* son or daughter can get a college education.

You may now have need of these funds, and you should not be embarrassed to ask for them.

## Is This Only for Rich People?

Many people think that tax loopholes and financial strategy are only for millionaires. In some ways, they have a point: certainly it is the rich who can reap the greatest benefits.

But financial aid strategy is for everyone. Whether you are just getting by or are reasonably well off, you still want to maximize your aid eligibility.

## A College Is a Business

Despite the ivy-covered walls, the slick promotional videos, and a name that may intimidate you, a college is a business like any other. It provides a service and must find customers willing to buy that service.

You may have heard of an education scam that's been cropping up in different parts of the country in which bogus "trade schools" provide valueless educational courses to unwary consumers. While not to be confused with legitimate trade schools that have been providing valuable educational training to students for years, these so-called "beauty academies," "computer programming schools," "truck driver schools," etc., talk students into paying for their "courses" by taking out government-guaranteed student loans. The schools pocket the money, the student receives very little in the way of education, and then must spend the next ten years paying off the loan. Or not paying off the loan, in which case the taxpayer must pick up the tab.

Higher education sometimes seems like a slightly more genteel version of the bogus "trade school" scam. The colleges need warm bodies to fill their classrooms. Many of these warm bodies qualify for federal aid (including student loans), which helps keep the colleges afloat. Meanwhile, the financial aid officers do their bit by trying to get as much money from the student and her family as possible.

Indeed, an article in *Money* magazine some years ago reported that 65% of private institutions and 27% of public universities now engage in financial aid leveraging. This is a process used to determine how little aid needs to be awarded to still get the student to enroll.

## The Ivy-Covered Bottom Line

Of course there is a great deal more to college than merely a business selling a service—there is the value of tradition, the exploration of new ideas, the opportunity to think about important issues, the chance to develop friendships that will last for the rest of a student's life—but do not lose sight of the bottom line. Colleges stand accused by many experts of wasting a good part of their endowment through sloppy management, misguided expansion, and wasteful expenditures. A college tuition would cost much less today if the colleges had been run in a businesslike manner over the past twenty-five years.

If colleges are in trouble right now, there are many who would say it is their own doing, and that they will be better off once they have lost some of the excess fat they allowed themselves to gain during the past few decades. Certainly it is not your responsibility to pay for their mistakes if you don't have to.

But the FAOs have their own bottom line to consider.

## An Uneducated Consumer Is Their Best Customer

It is not in the FAO's best interest for you to understand the aid process. The more you know about it, the more aid they will have to give you from the school's own coffers. You can almost *feel* the FAO's reluctance to let the consumer know what's going on when you look at the standardized financial aid applications (known as need analysis forms), which are constructed in consultation with the colleges. These forms (unlike the federal tax forms that allow you to calculate your own taxes) require you to list your information but do not allow you to calculate the amount of money you will be required to pay to the college. This calculation is done by the need analysis company. Mere parents are not allowed to know how the formula is constructed.

We are going to show you that formula and much more.

## Understanding and Taking Control of the Process

In this book we will first give you an overview of the process of applying for aid, and then show you how to begin to take control of that process. We will discuss long-term investment strategies for families that have time to plan, and short-term financial aid strategies for families about to begin the aid process. We have devoted an entire chapter to a step-by-step guide to filling out the standardized need analysis forms, because the decisions the colleges will make on the basis of these forms are crucial to your ability to pay for college. Once you have received your aid packages from the schools, you will want to compare them. Part four of this book, "The Offer", shows you how to do that, as well as discussing how to negotiate with the colleges for an improved package.

The majority of our readers are parents planning for their children's education, but this book is also for older students who are continuing their own studies.  Most of the financial aid strategies to increase your eligibility for aid are essentially the same.

## A Word of Caution

Some of the aid strategies we will discuss in this book are complicated, and because we do not know the specifics of your financial situation, it is impossible for us to give anything but general advice. Nor can we cover every eventuality. We recommend that you consult with a competent professional about your specific situation before proceeding with a particular strategy. In Chapter 11, we discuss how to find a good financial aid consulting service.

Unfortunately, because of the volume of correspondence, we can't answer individual mail or give specific advice over the telephone. If we did, we'd have no time for our private clients—or for the daunting task of preparing next year's edition of *Paying for College*.

## Keeping You Up-to-Date

One reason we initially resisted writing this book was our reluctance to put out a book that might be bought after it was out of date. In the world of financial aid, things change rapidly. We agreed to do this book only after getting a commitment from our publisher that there would be a new edition every year.

However, even within the space of a year, things can change: tax laws can be amended, financial aid rules can be repealed. By consulting the (free) online student tools included with this book, you will be able to keep up-to-date on the very latest changes until the 2021 edition of this title becomes available in the fall of 2020. In response to many requests from our readers, you'll also be able to access an index there. If you are not connected to the information superhighway, be aware that most public libraries and educational institutions offer Internet access.

# A Final Thought

Depending on which survey you read, between 70% and 80% of all college-bound high school students were accepted by their first-choice college last year. Except for a handful of schools, selectivity has gone by the board. Nowadays, the problem is not so much how to get into college, but how to pay for it once you are there.

In the following pages we will show you how to pay for college. This is not about ripping off the system, or lying to get aid you don't deserve. This is about empowering students and parents with the information they need to get the maximum amount of aid they are entitled to receive under the law and to minimize their out-of-pocket costs.

# Part One

## Understanding the Process

# Chapter One

Overview

# How the Aid Process Works: Paying for College in a Nutshell

Ideally, you began this process many years ago when your children were quite small. You started saving, at first in small increments, gradually increasing the amounts as your children got older and your earning power grew. You put the money into a mixture of growth investments like stock funds, and conservative investments like treasury bonds, so that now as the college years are approaching you are sitting pretty, with a nice fat college fund, a cool drink in your hand, and enough left over to buy a vacation home in Monte Carlo.

However, if you are like most of us, you probably began thinking seriously about college only a few years ago. You have not been able to put away large amounts of money. Important things kept coming up. An opportunity to buy a home. Taxes. Braces. Soccer camp. Taxes.

If you are foresighted enough to have bought this book while your children are still young, you will be especially interested in our section on long-term planning. If your child is already a senior in high school just about to apply for college, don't despair. There is a lot you can do to take control of the process.

Most people cannot afford to pay the full cost of four years of college. Financial aid is designed to bridge the gap between what you can afford to pay for school and what the school actually costs. Parents who understand the process come out way ahead. Let's look at the aid process in a nutshell and see how it works—or at least how it's supposed to work. Later on, we will take you through each step of this process in greater detail.

## The Standardized Need Analysis Forms

While students start work on their admissions applications, parents should be gathering together their records in order to begin applying for financial aid.

At a minimum, you need to fill out a standardized need analysis form called the Free Application for Federal Student Aid (FAFSA). This form, which is available in either a paper version, a PDF version, or an online version, can be filled out only after October 1 of the student's senior year in high school.

Many private colleges and some state-supported institutions may require you to electronically complete the CSS/Financial Aid PROFILE Form as well. This form is developed and processed by the same organization that brings you the SAT—The College Board.

A few schools will require other forms as well—for example, the selective private colleges often have their *own* financial aid forms. For students whose two biological or adoptive parents are no longer living together, the situation gets more complicated. To find out which forms are required by a particular college, consult the individual school's financial aid office website or printed information. All of the forms ask the same types of questions.

These questions are invasive and prying. How much did you earn last year? How much money do you have in the bank? What is your marital status? A hundred or so questions later, the need analysis company will have a very clear picture of four things:

> 1. the parents' available income
>
> 2. the parents' available assets
>
> 3. the student's available income
>
> 4. the student's available assets

The processor of the FAFSA form uses a federal formula (called the *federal methodology* or FM) to decide what portion of your income and assets you get to keep and what portion you can afford to put toward college tuition this year. This amount is called the Expected Family Contribution (EFC), and will most likely be more than you think you can afford.

However, some schools do not feel that the EFC generated by the FAFSA gives an accurate enough picture of what the family can contribute to college costs. Using the supplemental information on the PROFILE (which is analyzed using a formula called the *institutional methodology* or IM, that is developed by the College Board) and/or using their own individual forms, these institutions perform a separate need analysis to determine eligibility for aid that those schools control directly.

# A Family's "Need"

Meanwhile, the admissions offices of the different colleges have been deciding which students to admit and which to reject. Once they've made their decision, the financial aid officers (known as FAOs) get to work. Their job is to put together a package of grants, work-study, and loans that will make up the difference between what they feel you can afford to pay and what the school actually costs. The total cost of a year at college includes:

> *tuition and fees*
> *room and board*
> *personal expenses*
> *books and supplies*
> *travel*

The difference between what you can afford to pay and the total cost of college is called your "need."

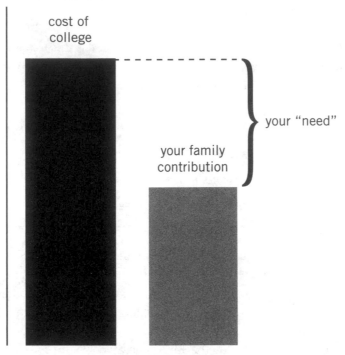

In theory, your Expected Family Contribution will be approximately the same no matter what schools your child applies to. If your EFC is calculated to be $20,300 and your child is accepted at a state school that costs $25,300, you will pay about $20,300, and the school will make up the difference—in this case $5,000—with an aid package. If you apply to a prestigious Ivy League school that costs $75,000, you will still pay about $20,300 and the school will make up the difference with an aid package of approximately $54,700.

In theory, the only difference between an expensive school and a cheaper school (putting aside subjective matters like the quality of education) is the amount of your need. In some cases, depending on how badly the college wants the student, parents won't pay a penny more for an exclusive private college than they would for a state school.

This is why families should not initially rule out any school as being too expensive. The "sticker price" doesn't necessarily matter; it's the portion of the sticker price that you have to pay that counts. Parents are often under the impression that no matter what type of school their child attends—be it a very expensive private college, an expensive out-of-state public institution, or their local state university—they will receive the same amount of aid. In fact, as you saw from the previous example, the amount of aid you get is in part determined by the cost of the school you choose.

# Theory vs. Reality

Of course, the reality is slightly more complicated. Because some schools are using supplemental data (such as home equity) to determine eligibility for their private aid, your expected contribution at a more selective university will most likely be different, and in some cases higher. In later chapters we'll be talking about what factors can cause the schools to adjust the EFC calculated under the federal methodology, and more important, we'll be showing you how to minimize the impact of these adjustments.

# The Aid Package

About the time your child receives an offer of admission from a particular college, you will receive an award letter. This letter will tell you what combination of aid the FAO has put together for you in order to meet your need. The package will consist of three different types of aid:

**Grants and Scholarships**—These are the best kinds of aid, because they don't have to be paid back. Essentially, a grant is free money. Some grant money comes from the federal government, some comes from the state, and some comes from the coffers of the college itself. Best of all, grant money is almost always tax-free. If you are in the 35% combined tax bracket, a $5,000 grant is the equivalent of receiving a raise of $7,692.

Scholarships are also free money, although there may be some conditions attached (academic excellence, for example). Contrary to popular wisdom, scholarships are usually awarded by the schools themselves. The amount of money available from outside scholarships is actually quite small.

**Federal Work-Study (FWS)**—The federal government subsidizes this program, which provides part-time jobs to students. The money earned is put toward either tuition or living expenses.

**Student Loans**—These loans, usually taken out by the student rather than the parents, are often subsidized (and guaranteed) by state or federal governments. The rates are usually much lower than regular unsecured loans. In most cases, no interest is charged while the student is in school, and no repayment is required until the student has graduated or left college.

# Preferential Packaging

The FAOs at the individual colleges have a lot of latitude to make decisions. After looking at your financial information, for example, they might decide your EFC should be lower or higher than the need analysis processor computed it originally.

More important, the package the FAOs put together for a student will often reflect how badly the admissions office wants that student.

If a school is anxious to have your child in its freshman class, the package you will be offered will have a larger percentage of grant money, with a much smaller percentage coming from student loans and work study. If a college is less interested, the award will not be as attractive.

Your award will also reflect the general financial health of the college you are applying to. Some schools have large endowments and can afford to be generous. Other schools are financially strapped, and may be able to offer only the bare minimum.

If the school is truly anxious to get a particular student, it may also sweeten the deal by giving a grant or scholarship that isn't based on need. A non-need scholarship may actually reduce your family contribution.

## Unmet Need

In some cases, you may find that the college tells you that you have "unmet need." In other words, they were unable to supply the full difference between the cost of their school and the amount they feel you can afford to pay. This is bad news. What the college is telling you is that if your child really wants to attend this college, you will have to come up with even more money than the college's need analysis decided that you could pay.

Usually what this means is that you will have to take on additional debt. Sometimes the colleges themselves will be willing to lend you the money. Sometimes you will be able to take advantage of other loan programs such as the Federal Parent Loans for Undergraduate Students (PLUS), which is a partially-subsidized loan to parents of college students. The terms are less attractive than the subsidized student loans but still better than unsecured loans you would get from banks if you walked in off the street.

## Sifting the Offers

The week acceptance and award letters arrive can be very tough, as you are confronted with the economic realities of the different schools' offers. The school your child really wants to attend may have given you an aid package you cannot accept. The week will be immeasurably easier if you have taken the financial aid process into account when you were selecting schools to apply to in the first place.

Just as it is important to select a safety school where your child is likely to be accepted, it is also important to select what we call a "*financial* safety school" that is cheap enough to afford out of your own pocket in the event that the more expensive schools you applied to do not meet your full need. In some cases, the admissions safety school and financial safety school may be the same. If a student is a desirable candidate from an academic standpoint, she is likely to get a good financial aid package as well. However, you should also consider the economic health of the schools you are applying to as well as the past history of financial aid at those schools. This information can be gleaned from many of the college guides (including The Princeton Review's *The Best 385 Colleges*, 2020 edition) available at bookstores and online booksellers.

It is also vital to make sure that there is a reasonable expectation that the package will be available for the next three years as well. How high do the student's grades have to be in order to keep the package intact? Are any of the grants or scholarships they gave you one-time-only grants? Once you've received an offer, these are questions to ask the FAO.

# Negotiating with the FAOs

Even if a school's award letter has left you with a package you cannot accept—perhaps the percentage of student loan money in your package is too high; or perhaps your need was not fully met—you may still be able to negotiate a better deal.

Over the past few years we have noticed that the initial offer of aid, especially at some of the more selective schools, seems to have become subject to adjustment. In many cases, if you just accept the first offer, you will have accepted an offer that was not as high as the FAO was willing to go.

Many parents feel understandably hesitant to go back to the table. However, if the aid package is actually too low for you to be able to send your child to that school, you have little to lose by asking for more. And most FAOs will appreciate learning that they are about to risk losing a qualified applicant solely because of money.

The key in these negotiations is to be friendly, firm, and in control. Know what you want when you talk to the FAO and be able to provide documentation. In some cases, the FAO will alter the aid package enough to make it possible for you to afford to send your child to the school.

There is an entire section of this book devoted to the award letter—how to compare award letters, how to negotiate with FAOs, and how to apply for next year.

# Same Time Next Year

The financial aid package you accept will last only one year. You will have to go through the financial aid process four separate times, filling out a new need analysis form each year until your child reaches the senior year of college. If your financial situation were to stay *exactly* the same, then next year's aid package would probably be very similar to this year's. We find, however, that most parents' situations do change from year to year. In fact, after you finish reading this book, there may be some specific changes you'll *want* to make.

# How the Aid Process Really Works

Parents and students who understand how to apply for financial aid get more. It's that simple. We aren't talking about lying, cheating, or beating the system. We're talking about understanding the system and taking advantage of the rules to get the best deal.

In Part Two, you will learn how to take control of the process. For those parents who are starting early, Chapter Two covers long-term investment strategies that minimize taxes and maximize aid eligibility. For those parents who have children in high school, Chapter Three through Chapter Six will show you how to use the financial aid formulas to save money. We'll explain in detail how the different parts of your finances and family situation affect your EFC—and what adjustments you can make to boost your aid eligibility. In addition, we discuss how to pick colleges that will give the best aid packages, how to apply for state aid, and—very important—what the *student* can do.

In Part Three, we provide step-by-step guidelines for handling the financial aid application process, along with detailed strategies for completing the two most commonly used standardized financial aid forms for the 2020–2021 award year.

In Part Four, we discuss the offer. What does an award letter look like? What are the different types of aid you may receive, in detail? How do you compare award letters? How do you negotiate with the FAOs to get an improved package?

In Chapter Seven, we talk about innovative payment options and in Chapter Eight, we discuss managing student loans during and after school. In Chapter Nine, we cover in more detail some special topics such as divorced and separated parents, graduate students, minority students, independent students, and other topics that may be of interest to some of our readers. In Chapter Ten, we'll discuss some important information involving educational tax benefits. For those who feel they need individualized guidance, Chapter Eleven provides tips on how to find a good financial aid consultant. In Chapter Twelve, future trends regarding financial aid and educational financing are covered, as well as some helpful tips for paying for college in these tough economic times.

In Part Five, you will find worksheets that will enable you to compute your expected family contribution for the federal methodology, a version of the 2020–2021 FAFSA, sample copies of promissory notes for the Direct Loan and PLUS loans, and copies of the 2018 U.S. personal income tax forms.

# Part Two

## How to Take Control of the Process

If you have read Part One of this book, then you now know the basics about how the financial aid process works. Now, it's time to start figuring out how to take control of that process—and prevent the process from taking control of you.

# Understanding What's Going On

The college FAOs don't really want you to understand all the intricacies of the financial aid process. If parents don't know what's going on, they can't ask embarrassing questions, and they will accept whatever the FAOs tell them.

We know of one case in which a financial aid officer from a private college told a parent who had called asking for an increase in aid, that "our hands are tied. Federal regulations prevent us from giving you any more money." The parent, not knowing any better, accepted this as the truth. In fact, it was a bald-faced lie. Almost all colleges (and this one was no exception) hand out their own grants, funded by private funds, which are not regulated by federal law at all.

Another thing parents are often too willing to accept at face value is the initial financial aid offer by the college. In a recent trend, many schools (particularly the most competitive) have begun to build some bargaining room into their initial offers. They expect you to ask for more. In many cases, accepting that first offer means taking a lower number than the FAO was willing to give. These are just two examples of the facts you will learn in the next few chapters—facts that will enable you to understand and begin to take control of the financial aid process.

Parents whose children are several years away from college will find the next chapter on long-term planning particularly useful. In it, we will show you how to begin building a fund for college that will take advantage of both tax law and financial aid law. Families who are getting ready to apply to college should skip long-term planning and go directly to Chapter Three on short-term strategies. There we will begin to show you how linking your income tax strategies and your financial aid strategies can save you big bucks. We will show you how the colleges assess your income, expenses, assets, and liabilities, and how to influence these assessments to your advantage.

# Don't Let the Terminology Intimidate You

A word of caution, before we begin. In the course of counseling thousands of families, we've seen how confusing financial aid jargon can be to the nonprofessional. Just remember, the FAOs don't mind if you are a little confused. In fact, they would prefer it. And since they have a large influence on the instructions that come with the aid forms you will have to fill out, it shouldn't surprise you to learn that the instructions to the forms are confusing and full of unfamiliar terminology as well. The introduction to one particularly confusing financial aid form states that some questions are "self-explanatory, and therefore no instructions are given."

Don't worry. By the time you finish reading this book, the jargon will be second nature. At the back of this book is a comprehensive glossary; feel free to refer to it at any time.

To avoid confusion, we have taken care to use the same terminology used by the need analysis companies and the IRS. Even though it seems a little ridiculous to refer to certain deductions as "unreimbursed employee expenses," we did so anyway, just so that you will know what the terms mean once you start completing the forms and negotiating with the FAOs.

# Chapter Two

## Long-Term Strategies for Paying for College

Congratulations! If you are reading this section you've had the foresight to begin planning early for the expense of paying for college. What do we mean by early? We will be presenting strategies for parents with children who are three years away, five years away, ten years away, and 15 years away from their first year of college.

The point of this chapter is not to make specific investment recommendations or tout individual stocks or investment instruments, but rather to show you the ways and means to begin a long-term college fund for your children. Our purpose is not to be your financial planner, for no financial planner could responsibly set up a 10-year plan without being around to administer it (and obviously, we can't do that). Things change. Investment opportunities come up suddenly. Interest rates go up or they go down. Tax laws are amended; financial aid laws are revised. We are going to outline some general strategies, but we advise you to invest cautiously, perhaps with the aid of a financial planner whom you can consult day to day.

If your child is applying for college next month, we recommend that you skip this section. It will only depress you. Instead, skip to the next chapter, where we begin talking about short-term strategies. We think you will be pleased.

# How Much Should We Save Every Month?

Any realistic long-term plan is more of an educated guess than an exact prediction. There are so many unknown factors—how much will college cost in ten years? Or 15 years? What will the inflation rate average over the next decade? Will stocks continue to be the best long-term investment as they have for the past 40 years, or will some unforeseen trend make real estate or bonds a better investment?

Any financial planner who says you have to save exactly $937 per month to reach your goal is being unrealistic—in part because you don't even know with certainty what that goal will be. We think the main thing such pronouncements do is scare parents into paralysis. "We don't *have* that kind of money," clients wail to us on the phone after they hear these figures. "What are we supposed to do?"

# The Important Thing Is to Start

It is easy to get so paralyzed by the projection of the total cost of a four-year college education that you do nothing. The important thing is to begin saving *something* as early as possible as regularly as possible. It doesn't matter if you can't contribute large amounts. The earlier you start, the longer you give your investments to work for you.

If you have not saved the total cost of four years' tuition at a private college (and very few parents ever have), all is not lost. That is why there is financial aid.

## So Why Bother to Save at All? If We Don't Have Any Money, We'll Just Get More Financial Aid

This is partly true, but only partly. A poor family without the means to pay for college will find concerned FAOs ready to look in every corner of their coffers to come up with the aid necessary to send that family's child to college. An affluent family that has lived beyond their means for years and is now looking for the college to support this lifestyle with financial aid will find the FAOs to be very unsympathetic and tightfisted.

An honest attempt to save money, and a willingness to make sacrifices can make a large impression on the FAOs. These men and women have broad powers to increase or decrease your family contribution; to allocate grants; to meet your family's *entire* need—or just part of it.

Trust us, you will be much happier if you have saved for college. Who can say whether in five years there will be many colleges left that can afford to continue "need-blind" admissions policies? Perhaps by the year 2030 virtually *no* colleges will be able to meet a family's full remaining need—meaning that if you are without resources, your child will simply not be able to attend college at all. If you still aren't convinced, think about this: A significant proportion of financial aid packages comes in the form of loans. You have the choice of saving now and *earning* interest, or borrowing later and *paying* interest. Earning interest is more fun.

Finally, under the aid formulas, colleges will assess parents' assets at a top rate of only 5.65%. In other words, if you have managed to build up a college fund of say, $40,000, as long as it is in the parents' name, the colleges will assess up to approximately five and a half cents of each dollar of that fund each year. We'll be discussing the pros and cons of putting money in your child's name later. You can certainly spend more if you like, but it is important to understand that having money in the bank does not mean the colleges get to take it all.

## Money in the Bank Gives You Options

A college fund, even a small one, gives you control over your own destiny. What if the college your child really wants to attend doesn't fully meet your need? What if you lose your job just as the college years are approaching? By planning a little for the future now, you can ensure that you'll have options when the college years are upon you.

# How Much Will a College Education Cost in *X* Years?

Every year, the price of a college education goes up. In the past couple of years the rate of increase at private colleges has actually slowed, the result in part of market forces: Families have been turning to state schools in greater numbers, forcing the private colleges to cut their prices, or at least to slow the increase of their prices. Partly in response to increased demand and partly because state budgets have been slashed, the rate of tuition increase at state schools has risen dramatically—especially for out-of-state students who must pay extra. Will these trends continue? The best we can do is make broad predictions based on current trends. Let's look at some numbers.

## The Cost of a Private College

The average cost of a year's tuition, room and board, and fees at a private college last year was $48,510 (according to the College Board). Many experts predict that the cost of private college will increase at a rate of about 3.5% per year. Here is a chart of what the average cost of a year of private college would be over the next 15 years, based on 3.5% yearly growth:

| Average Annual Cost of a Private College in | | | |
|---|---|---|---|
| 2019 | $50,208 (today) | 2027 | $66,114 |
| 2020 | $51,965 | 2028 | $68,428 |
| 2021 | $53,784 (2 years) | 2029 | $70,823 (10 years) |
| 2022 | $55,666 | 2030 | $73,302 |
| 2023 | $57,615 | 2031 | $75,868 |
| 2024 | $59,631 (5 years) | 2032 | $78,523 |
| 2025 | $61,718 | 2033 | $81,271 |
| 2026 | $63,878 | 2034 | $84,115 (15 years) |

Of course, if your child decides on one of the most prestigious private schools, the cost will be even more. This year, most of the top colleges have crossed the $70,000-a-year barrier. In five years, at 3.5% growth per year, that will be approximately $83,138.

## The Cost of a Public University

The average cost of a year's tuition, room and board, and fees at a public university last year was $21,370 (according to the College Board). Many experts predict that the cost of public university will also increase at a rate of about 3% per year over the next decade. Here is a chart of what the average cost of a year of public university could cost over the next 15 years, if the experts are right:

| Average Annual Cost of a Public University in | | | |
|---|---|---|---|
| 2019 | $22,011 (today) | 2027 | $27,883 |
| 2020 | $22,671 | 2028 | $28,719 |
| 2021 | $23,352 (2 years) | 2029 | $29,581 (10 years) |
| 2022 | $24,052 | 2030 | $30,469 |
| 2023 | $24,774 | 2031 | $31,383 |
| 2024 | $25,517 (5 years) | 2032 | $32,324 |
| 2025 | $26,282 | 2033 | $33,294 |
| 2026 | $27,071 | 2034 | $34,293 (15 years) |

Of course, if you are attending one of the "public Ivies" such as the University of Michigan as an out-of-state resident, the cost right now is already close to $63,000. In five years, at a 3% growth rate per year, that would be close to $73,000.

## How Much Money Will You Need?

If your child is 15, 10, or even five years away from college, she has probably not even begun to think about what kind of school she would like to attend. Since you can't ask your child, ask yourself: What kind of college could you picture your son or daughter attending?

If you have picked a private college of average cost, and your child is ten years away from college, look up the price on the first chart we gave you above. Rather than concentrating on the cost of freshman year, look at the cost of junior year, two years further on. Whatever this number is, multiply it by four. This is a rough approximation of an average college education at that time.

If you picked an average public university, and your child is five years away from college, look up the price on the second chart above. Count two years more and multiply that number by four. This is a rough approximation of a college education at an average public university at that time. Of course, if costs increase faster than the experts are projecting, the figure could be more.

If you wish to be even more precise, find a guide to colleges and look up the current price of a particular school you are interested in. Let's choose Spelman College, an Historically Black College for women, which has a current price of about $46,456, and let's say your daughter is going to be ready to go to college in five years. Multiply the current price by our assumed rate of increase:

$$\$46,456 \times 1.035 = \$48,082$$

The new number is the price of that school next year. To find out the projected price of Spelman in five years, just repeat this operation four more times ($48,082 × 1.035 = $49,765; $49,765 × 1.035 = $51,057; etc.). For 10 years, repeat the operation nine more times.

Of course, these will only be rough estimates since no one has a crystal ball. If your daughter were to start Spelman five years from now, the first year would cost roughly $55,176. By the time she is a junior, the projected cost would be $59,106. To figure out the grand total, multiply the cost of junior year by four. This is a rough projection of the cost of a four-year education. At Spelman five years from now, a college education will cost about $236,424. At Stanford or Yale, the bill will most likely exceed $350,000.

Now don't faint just yet. This is a great deal of money, but first of all, there's a lot of financial aid out there—and the majority of this book will be devoted to showing you how to get that financial aid. Second of all, you still have time to plan, save, and invest—and because of the joys of compounding, your investments can grow much faster than you might believe possible. Third, your earning power will most likely increase over time.

In the rest of this chapter you will find investment strategies for saving money for college. Try not to obsess about the total projected cost. The important thing is to begin.

# When Do You Begin Saving?

Right now. The more time you give your investments to multiply, the better. Even if you can manage only a small amount each month, you will be surprised at how much you have put away by the end of the year, and even more surprised at how quickly that money multiplies.

### The Joys of Compound Interest

Let's say that you had a pretty good year this year and were able to save $5,000. Sound like too much? Okay, let's say $4,000. You invest this money in a high-yield mutual fund. Some of these funds have been averaging a return of over 8% a year, but let's be more conservative and say you get a 7% rate of return, which you plow back into the fund. Don't like mutual funds? That's fine. If you are uncomfortable with this level of risk, we'll be discussing other investment vehicles a little later. This is just an example to show you how investments grow.

The calculation is actually the same one we used to figure out what college would cost in the future. To find out how much $4,000 would earn in one year at 7%, multiply $4,000 times 1.07.

$$\$4,000 \times 1.07 = \$4,280$$

To find the value of the investment over five years, repeat this calculation four more times ($4,280 × 1.07 = 4,580; $4,580 × 1.07 = $4,900; etc.) In five years, your original $4,000 will be worth $5,610. In 10 years, it will have grown to $7,869. Not bad, especially when you consider that this comes from only one year of saving.

Of course, this example is a little simplified. One or two of those years might be bad years and the fund might not pay 7%. Other years might be extremely good years and the yield could be much higher. There are tax implications to consider as well. However, $7,869 is a reasonable forecast of what one $4,000 investment could be worth in ten years.

And if you continued to invest another $4,000 each year for the next ten years, with the same rate of return—well, now we're talking real money. At the end of ten years, you would have a college fund in excess of $59,134.

## A Young Couple Just Starting Out

Let's take the fictional couple David and Carmen, who have a daughter who is now seven years old. David and Carmen are pretty young, and they can't afford to save much, but they decide they can manage $1,000 a year. They invest the $1,000 in a mutual fund with an average return of 8%, which they reinvest in the fund. By the time their daughter is ready to go to college in ten years, that first $1,000 has become $2,159. Each year, they invest another $1,000. The money they invest the second year has only nine years to grow, but it is still worth $1,999 by the time their child is ready for college. The money they invest the third year has only eight years to grow, but is still worth $1,850.

If Carmen and David invest $1,000 a year in this manner for ten years, they will have built a college fund of $15,645. Of course this is not enough to pay the entire cost of college, but there are several factors we haven't taken into account yet:

- No one is asking them to pay the entire amount. If David and Carmen aren't earning big money by the time the college years arrive, they may qualify for significant amounts of financial aid.

- David and Carmen might begin earning more money over the next ten years. Promotions and/or raises could allow them to save more than $1,000 per year as time goes on.

- The couple may have been able to make other investments as well (such as buying a house), against which they can borrow when their daughter is in college.

- During the college years, David and Carmen may be able (in fact are expected) to pay some of the cost of college from their current income.

## Timing

Because of the way compounding works it would be better, in theory, to make your largest contributions to a college investment fund in the early years when the investment has the most time to grow. Unfortunately the reality of the situation is that a couple just getting started often doesn't have that kind of money.

If you get a windfall—an inheritance, a large bonus, a year with a lot of overtime—by all means put that money to work for you. However, for most parents, it will be a matter of finding the money to invest here and there.

Many financial advisors recommend an automatic deduction plan, in which a certain amount of money is automatically deducted from your paycheck or your bank account each month. Parents often find that if the money simply disappears before they have time to spend it, the process of saving is less painful.

## Should Money Be Put in the Child's Name?

One of the most important decisions you will have to make is whether to put the college fund in your own name or in your child's name.

There are some tax advantages to putting the money in your child's name, but there can also be some terrible financial aid disadvantages. Let's look at the tax advantages first.

Each year a parent is allowed to make a gift of up to $15,000 per parent per child. Depending upon the state in which you live, funds in such "custodial accounts" will be governed by the Uniform Gift to Minors Act (UGMA) or the Uniform Transfer to Minors Act (UTMA). Thus if you live in a two-parent household, you can give up to $30,000 per year to your child, without gift-tax consequences. This is not a $30,000 tax deduction for you, but neither is it $30,000 in taxable income to the child. You have merely shifted money from you to your child. From now on, some of the interest that money earns will be taxed not at the parents' rate, but at the child's rate, which is almost always much lower.

The child is not allowed to have control over the account until the age of 21 (or 18 in some states). By the same token you are not allowed to take that money back either. The money can be spent only on behalf of the child. You could use the money to pay for an SAT prep course, or braces, say, but not on the rent or a vacation to Hawaii—even if you took the child along.

Of course, if this gift is being made as part of a fund for college, this should be no problem. You don't plan to touch it until your son or daughter is ready to enroll anyway. You can shift the money between different investments, or even give it to a financial planner to invest.

Years ago, many parents and other relatives—especially those in the higher tax brackets—found it beneficial to shift their funds into a child's name so that the unearned income (i.e. interest, dividends, and capital gains) would be taxed at the child's presumably lower tax rate. To thwart this income-shifting strategy, Congress passed legislation which would tax some of this unearned income of younger children at a parent's rate, once such unearned income in a given tax year passed a certain threshold amount (which is $2,100 for the 2017 tax year.) In the tax years 2006 and 2007, this tax on the unearned income of a minor child at the parent's tax rate—often referred to as the "Kiddie Tax"—applied to children under the age of 18 at the end of the tax year. For a child 18 and older, none of the money in the custodial account was taxed at the parent's rate. (Prior to 2006, age 14 was the magic number. But Congress tinkered with the rules to prevent more families from shifting unearned income into a lower tax bracket.) To avoid the kiddie tax rules, many parents invested custodial account money in growth stocks, which would presumably appreciate in value but pay small dividends. Then, after the child reached the age when the rules no longer applied, they would sell the stock and generate a capital gain which would then be taxed solely at the child's rate. In years past, this was a very effective strategy especially since capital gains have been taxed recently at a lower rate than most other types of income. However when Congress realized that the tax rate on capital gains (and qualified dividends) would drop to zero in 2008 for those in the lowest tax bracket, they passed a new (and far more complicated) kiddie tax in May 2007 that became effective January 1, 2008 in order to close this loophole. So that's the back story. Here are the latest rules:

For a child under the age of 18 at the end of the year: As long as the custodial account generates less than $1,050 per year in interest or dividend income and there is no other income, there will be no income tax due at all. As long as the custodial account generates less than $2,100 in income and there is no other income, the excess over $1,050 will be taxed at the child's rate (0% to 10% federal depending on the type of unearned income). Once the child's unearned taxable income exceeds the $2,100 cap, the excess will be taxed at the parents' higher rate, which can go up as high as 37% federal. State and local taxes will push this even higher.

For a child who is age 18 at the end of the year: The same rules apply as with younger children, though it is possible to avoid the kiddie tax if the child has earned income (e.g. wages, salary, income from self-employment) that exceeds half of her support.

For a child who is age 19 to 23 at the end of the year: If the child is unable to meet the "more than half support" rule, the kiddie tax will still apply if the child is a full time student for at least five months during the year. (While there may still be some clarification before the end of the year about what constitutes a "month", other provisions of the tax code related to months of attendance in school have viewed enrollment for even one day in a particular month to be considered the same as if the student is enrolled for the entire month.) Given this increased age limit, it is possible that some students—including younger graduate students—who escaped the kiddie tax for a few years due to their age may again be subject to it post-2007. And if the child has not yet reached age 24 by the end of the year, it makes no difference whether the child is claimed as a dependent or not on a parent's tax return.

So if you wish to avoid the kiddie tax, you would want to have some investments generate a little less than $2,100 in income per year, and the remaining funds allocated to investment instruments that generated little or no income. For example: if your child's college fund was paying 4% interest, the fund could contain $52,500, and the interest the money earned would still be taxed at the child's rate. As the fund gets larger than $52,500, some of the interest would begin to be taxed at your rate. It is important to note that there are other rules that apply if the child has both earned and unearned income.

Even with these new more restrictive rules, it is still possible to achieve some tax savings from putting money in the child's name. Unfortunately, because of the regulations under which financial aid is dispensed, putting any money in the kid's name can be a very expensive mistake.

## If You Have Any Hope of Financial Aid, *Never* Put Money in the Child's Name

When you apply for financial aid, you will complete a need analysis form, which tells the colleges your current income, your child's income, your assets, and your child's assets. The colleges will assess these amounts to decide how much you can afford to pay for college. Under the federal formula, your income will be assessed up to 47%. Your assets will be assessed up to 5.65%.

However, your *child's* income will be assessed at up to 50% and your *child's* assets will be assessed at a whopping 20%. A college fund of $40,000 under *your* name would be assessed (as an asset) for up to $2,260 the first year of college. That is to say, the college would expect you to put as much as $2,260 of that money toward the first year of school.

The same fund under your child's name would be assessed for $8,000.

That's a big difference. You might say, "Well that money was supposed to be for college anyway," and you would be right—but remember, the colleges aren't just assessing *that* money. They will assess 20% of *all* of the child's assets, up to 5.65% of the parents' assets, up to 50% of the child's income, and up to 47% of the parents' income. By putting that money in the child's name, you just gave them a lot more money than you had to.

We've already noted the similarities between a college financial aid office and the IRS. Both see it as their duty to use the rules to get as much money as possible from you. It is up to you to use those same rules to keep as much money as possible away from them. It is an adversarial relationship, but as long as both sides stick to the rules, a fair one.

If you are going to qualify for financial aid, you should never, ever put money in the child's name. It is like throwing the money away. You've worked too hard to save that money to watch it get swallowed up in four giant gulps. By putting the money in the parents' name, you keep control over it. If you choose to, you can use it all, or not use it all, on your timetable.

*The College Board made a number of significant changes to the Institutional Methodology (IM) starting with the 2000–2001 academic year. The maximum assessment rates under the IM for the 2019–2020 award year are as follows: 25% of the child's assets, up to 5% of the parents' assets, up to 46% of the child's income, and up to 46% of the parents' income. When we went to press, the rates for 2020–2021 were not available.*

## What If You're Pretty Sure You Won't Qualify for Aid?

If you are certain you won't qualify for aid, then you're free to employ every tax-reducing strategy your accountant can devise, including putting assets in the kid's name. But be very certain. People are often amazed at how much money you have to make in order NOT to qualify for aid.

In the introduction we told you about a family who received financial aid despite huge assets. Parents always want to know exactly what the cutoff is. Unfortunately, it is not as simple as that. Each family is a separate case. Don't assume that just because your friend didn't qualify for aid that you won't either. There are so many variables it is impossible to say the cutoff is precisely *X* dollars. It just doesn't work that way.

If you are close to the beginning of the college years and you want to figure out if you qualify for aid, read the rest of this book and then use the worksheets in the back to compute your Expected Family Contribution. There is really no shortcut. We have seen books that give you a simple chart on which you can look up your EFC. These charts are much too simplistic to be of any real use. We've also seen a number of websites with outdated formulas.

And as you'll soon discover, there are strategies you can employ to increase your chances of receiving aid.

## What If You Aren't Sure Whether You'll Qualify for Aid?

If your child is a number of years away from the freshman year of college, your dilemma is much more difficult. How can you predict how much you'll have in five years or 15 years? For safety, it would be better to avoid putting large sums of money in the child's name until you are sure you won't be eligible for aid.

Once the money is put into the child's name it is extremely difficult to put it back in the parents' name. If you set up a custodial account sometime in the past and have come to regret it, consult a very good financial consultant or tax lawyer who is also knowledgeable about financial aid.

Now that you've decided whose name to put the money under, let's talk about what kind of investments you can make.

# What Types of Investments to Choose for a College Fund

The key to any investment portfolio is diversity. You will want to spread your assets among several different types of investments, with varying degrees of risk. When your child is young, you will probably want to keep a large percentage of your money in higher-risk investments in order to build the value of the portfolio. As you get closer to the college years, it is a good idea to shift gradually into less volatile and more liquid investments. By the time the first year of college arrives, you should have a high percentage of cash invested in short-term treasuries, CDs, or money market funds.

To stay ahead of inflation over the long term, there is no choice but to choose more aggressive investments. Despite the recent declines, most experts still agree that the stock market is your best bet for long-term high yields. However, as we saw in late 2008 and early 2009, there can be significant volitility with stock prices. Yet it is worth noting that over the past 40 years, in spite of various bear markets, recessions, crashes, and acts of God, stocks have on average outperformed every other type of investment.

## Stock Mutual Funds

Rather than buying individual stocks, you can spread your risk by buying shares in a mutual fund that manages a portfolio of many different stocks. Most newspapers and financial magazines give periodic rundowns of the performance of different mutual funds. In general, we recommend no-load or low-load funds that charge a sales commission of 4.5% or less. The minimum investment in mutual funds varies widely, but often you can start with as little as $1,000. Many of the large mutual fund companies control a few different funds and allow you to switch from one type of fund to another or even to a regular money market fund without charge. In this way, you can move in and out of investments as events change, just by making a phone call.

You can spread your risk even further by purchasing stock mutual funds that specialize in several different areas. By putting some of your money into a blue-chip fund and some into whatever you think will soon be hot, you can hedge your bets.

It should be noted that over the past several years, individuals who never invested in the stock market before have been putting money into mutual funds in an effort to earn a higher return than the current rates offered on CDs and savings accounts. We would just like to add our cautionary voice to the chorus of experts who have been warning the public that investing in mutual funds is not the same thing as having money in the bank.

## High-Yield Bonds

Another aggressive investment to consider is high-yield bonds. For high yield, read "junk." Junk bonds, which pay a high rate of interest because they carry a high level of risk, helped to bring the boom-boom decade of the 1980s to its knees. However, if purchased with care, these bonds can get you a very high rate of return for moderate risk. The best way to participate in this market is to buy shares in a high-yield bond fund. The bonds are bought by professionals who presumably know what they are doing, and again, because the fund owns many different types of bonds, the risk is spread around.

## Normal-Yield Bonds

If you want less risk, you might think about buying investment-grade bonds (rated at least AA) which can be bought so that they mature just as your child is ready to begin college. If you sell bonds before they mature, the price may vary quite a bit, but at maturity, bonds pay their full face value and provide the expected yield, thus guaranteeing you a fixed return. At present, the total annual return on this type of bond if interest is reinvested can top 4.0%.

One way of avoiding having to reinvest interest income is to buy zero-coupon bonds. You purchase a zero-coupon at far below its face value. On maturity, it pays you the full face value of the bond. You receive no interest income from the bond along the way; instead the interest you would have received is effectively reinvested at a guaranteed rate of return. You still have to pay tax every year on the "imputed interest," but the rate of return on zero-coupons can be substantial.

## EE Savings Bonds

If you don't earn too much money, Series EE Savings Bonds offer an interesting option for college funds as well. The government a few years ago decided that if an individual over 24 years of age with low to moderate income purchases EE Savings Bonds after 1989 with the intention of using them to pay for college, the interest received at the time of redemption of the bonds will be tax-free. The interest earned is completely tax-free for a single parent with income up to $81,000 or a married couple filing jointly with income up to $121,600. Once you hit those income levels, the benefits are slowly phased out. A single parent with income above $96,100 or a married couple with income above $151,600 is not eligible for any tax break. All of these numbers are based on 2019 tax rates and are subject to an annual adjustment for inflation. EE Savings Bonds are issued by the federal government, and are as safe as any investment can be. They can also be purchased in small denominations without paying any sales commission.

However, EE Savings Bonds have several drawbacks. One is their low rate of return. You might do better with a taxable investment that pays a higher rate, even after taxes. It is also hard to predict in advance what your income level will be when you cash in the bonds. If your income has risen past the cutoff level for the tax break, your effective rate of return on the bonds just plunged into the low single digits. To make it worse, the IRS adds the interest from the bonds to your income *before* they determine whether you qualify for the tax break. Finally, whether the interest from these bonds is taxed or untaxed, it will still be considered income by the colleges and will be assessed just like your other income.

## Tax-Free Municipal Bonds

Those families that are in the 22% income tax bracket (or higher) may be tempted to invest in tax-free municipal bonds. If you factor in the tax savings, the rate of return can approach 6%. As usual, you can reduce your risk by buying what is called a tax-free muni fund. These come in different varieties, with different degrees of risk.

One thing to be aware of is that while the IRS does not tax the income from these investments, the colleges effectively do. Colleges call tax-exempt interest income "untaxable income" and assess it just the way they assess taxable income. If you're eligible for aid, the real effective yield of munis will be pushed down by these assessments.

## Trusts

Establishing a trust for your child's education is another way to shift assets and income to the child. Trusts have all the tax advantages of putting assets in the child's name—and then some; they allow more aggressive investment than do custodial accounts; they also give you much more control over when and how your child gets the money.

The drawbacks of trusts are that they are initially expensive to set up, costly to maintain, and very difficult to change—more important, they also jeopardize your chances of qualifying for financial aid.

If you have no chance of receiving aid, a trust fund can be an excellent way to provide money for college. There are many different kinds of trusts, but all involve you (called the grantor) transferring assets to another party (called the trustee) to manage and invest on behalf of your child (called the beneficiary). Typically, the trustee is a bank, financial advisor, or a professional organization chosen by you. You can design the trust so that your child will receive the money in a lump sum just as she enters college, or so that it is paid out in installments during college, or so that the child receives only the interest income from the trust until she reaches an age selected by you. Trusts must be set up with care to envision all eventualities because once they are in place, they are almost impossible to change. When you create the trust, you essentially give up the right to control it.

The tax advantage of a trust over a simple custodial account is that the trust pays its own separate income tax, at its own tax bracket. Not the child's bracket. Not yours. This is especially useful when the child is under the age of 24: A regular custodial account of any significant size would most likely be taxed at the parents' higher rate due to the "kiddie tax".

The investment advantage of a trust is that there is no limit on the type of investment instrument that may be used. Unlike custodial accounts, which are not allowed to invest in certain types of instruments, a trust can dabble in real estate, junk bonds, or any new-fangled scheme the investment bankers can invent.

Obviously, trusts must be set up with care, and you have to find a suitable trustee; someone you can, well, trust. Parents should never try to set up a trust on their own. If you are considering this strategy, consult a good tax attorney.

# Financial Aid and Trusts

For various reasons, financial aid and trusts do not mix. It is partly the "rich kid" image that trust funds engender in the FAOs, and partly certain intricacies of the financial aid formulas, which we will describe in more detail in Chapter Three of this book. A trust of any size may very well nix any chance your family has of receiving aid.

## Qualified State Tuition Programs (529 Plans)

Forty-nine states—all except Wyoming—and the District of Columbia now offer special programs that are designed to help families plan ahead for college costs. These Qualified State Tuition Programs, which are more commonly called Section 529 plans (after the relevant section of the Internal Revenue Code), come in two basic forms: tuition prepayment plans and tuition savings accounts. Most states offer one type or the other, but a number of states offer or will soon offer both. Some plans have residency requirements for the donor and/or beneficiary. Others (like California) will allow anyone to participate. While some states limit who can contribute funds to the plan (usually the parents and grandparents), other states have no such restrictions. And with some plans, it is possible for the contributor to name herself as the beneficiary as well.

With some states, the buildup in value is partially or entirely free of state income taxes (provided the beneficiary is a resident of that state.) Most plans allow you to make payments in a lump sum, or on an installment basis. In some states these payments can be automatically deducted from your bank account—or even your paycheck provided your employer agrees to participate.

With some plans, contributions are partially tax-deductible for the donor as well. For example, New York gives its residents up to a $5,000 deduction (up to $10,000 for joint filers) on the state income tax return for amounts contributed during a particular tax year. Many states have added some unique features to their plans.

Years ago, the prepaid tuition plans used to be a rotten deal as the funds could only be used in-state and normally only for public colleges and universities. Otherwise, you got your money back with little or no interest. But now, many of these state-sponsored plans have become more flexible, letting you take money out-of-state or to a private university in your own state. A major benefit of these prepayment plans is the peace of mind that comes from knowing that no matter how much tuition inflation there is, you've already paid for a certain number of course credits at the time of purchase. This peace of mind was rather costly during the Wall Street boom when returns on stocks far exceeded the rate of tuition inflation. However, given the recent volatility in the stock market and the reduced rates of return on CDs and bonds, the prepaid plans have regained some of their luster. So while many investment advisors still tell families they are better off avoiding these prepaid plans and funding the college nest egg using other investment vehicles which are likely to earn a higher rate of return, the prepaid plans are something to consider if the student will start college in the next few years.

Under the old tax laws, you had to pay federal income taxes on the difference between the initial investment and the value of the course credits when they were re-deemed, but such investment income was taxed at the beneficiary's presumably lower tax rate. Starting in 2002, there are no longer any federal income taxes involved pro-vided the funds are used to cover qualified higher education expenses (i.e. tuition, and fees as well as allowances for room and board) at a federally accredited school, which includes most U.S.-based four-year colleges and universities, many two-year programs and vocational schools, and even some foreign schools.

*Note: Given the high rate of tuition inflation at public universities, some prepaid plans have temporarily stopped accepting contributions or have added a premium onto the current price for each credit purchased.*

Unlike the prepaid plans, the state-sponsored tuition savings accounts do not guarantee to meet tuition inflation. A major benefit over traditional investment options is that earnings in these accounts grow tax-deferred from a federal standpoint. Just as with the prepaid plans, withdrawals from these accounts for qualified educational expenses are now also completely free of federal income taxes. (Under the old law, the pro-rated share of the withdrawal that represented investment income—and not the original investment—was subject to tax at the beneficiary's rate.) The funds in these plans are invested by professional managers. But if you choose to put some or all of the funds into any equity-based investment option that is offered, you could lose part of your initial investment. Just as with the prepaid plans, a number of states do not consider part or all of the earnings as income on a resident beneficiary's state tax return.

Most of these tuition savings plans offer the choice of an age-based asset alloca-tion model to determine how your funds will be invested. This means that the younger the child, the greater the percentage of the principal is invested in equities. As the child grows older, the percentage of equities falls, and the percentage of assets in bonds, money markets, and other fixed-income investments increases. The allocation models can vary tremendously from plan to plan. Besides the age-based models, most plans have other investment options that vary in the degrees of risk.

Most prepaid plans and tuition savings accounts allow you to change beneficiaries—which just means you can switch money you might have earmarked for one child to another child—or even to another family member. You'll need to read the fine print if you envision actually trying this, because there are tax consequences if the new beneficiary is of a different generation. With the savings plans, you'll also want to find out whether or not the asset allocation model will change to reflect the age of the new beneficiary. For example, if your oldest child decides not to go to college and you decide to transfer the funds to her kid brother, you would want to be sure that the mix of investments will be changed to reflect the age of the younger beneficiary. Otherwise, your nest egg may be invested mostly in money market funds for a number of years.

Another benefit of these Section 529 plans, from an estate-planning standpoint, is that a person can contribute up to $75,000 in one lump sum to any one beneficiary's plan, provided you do not make any further gifts to that person for the next five years (and provided the state's plan permits contributions of this size). So, in effect, you are being allowed to use the $15,000 annual gift allowance for the next five years and accelerate it into one lump sum. This allows a contributor to remove up to five years' worth of income and growth on the contributed funds from her estate. Of course, if the contributor dies before the five-year period has elapsed, there could be estate tax consequences.

## Coverdell ESAs

These special educational savings accounts were originally called Education IRAs even though they were never really retirement accounts. While contributions to these accounts (currently up to $2,000 per year per child under age 18) are not tax deductible, any withdrawals used for post-secondary education will be totally tax-free. While there are income limits that affect your ability to contribute to such an account—for 2018, this benefit phases out between $190,000 and $220,000 for married couples filing jointly, and between $95,000 and $110,000 for others—the law does not specify that contributions must be made by the beneficiary's parents. Other relatives or even friends who fall below the income cutoffs could presumably contribute. However for 2019, no child can receive more than $2,000 in deposits to a Coverdell ESA in a given tax year from all contributors combined. But before you rush to fund one of these accounts, you should realize that the U.S. Department of Education currently views such accounts to be the asset of the student if the student is the owner of the account and also an independent student. In most cases, the parent will be the owner as long as the beneficiary is a minor, so this will not be a big problem. However, the situation gets tricky once the student reaches majority. Unless an election was made to keep the parent as owner after that point, the fund would then become student-owned, and could be assessed at the 20% federal financial aid assessment rate if the student is independent. Under the institutional methodology, any Coverdell owned by the student is considered a student asset.

*Note: The current tax law permits tax-free withdrawals to cover certain qualified expenses from kindergarten through the senior year of high school including private school tuition, certain computer equipment and software, as well as internet access. So if you are otherwise eligible for financial aid for college, you should consider withdrawing funds from Coverdells to cover these expenses as well as any qualified higher education expenses if **a)** the ownership will soon revert to the student and **b)** the student is either applying for financial aid at a school that requires completion of the CSS PROFILE or is an independent student. (Check with the financial institution where you have the account if you are not sure who owns the account and when, if ever, the ownership changed or will change to the student in the future.). In this way, student assets in the aid formulas will be minimized.*

## Sunrise . . . But No Sunset

Coverdell ESAs and Section 529s are wonderful ways to save money for college, but for years there had been a couple of important question marks about these programs. This was because some key provisions of the federal tax law pertaining to these programs had been scheduled to expire—or "sunset"—on Dec. 31, 2012. The good news is that these uncertainties have gone away as the American Taxpayer Relief Act, which became law in January 2013, made permanent some of the enhancements to Coverdells that were made in 2001. So for the time being, these enhancements will continue to be available:

- The annual contribution limits for Coverdells will continue to be $2000 per beneficiary per year.

- Withdrawals from Coverdells for certain expenses other than college tuition and fees (i.e. elementary and secondary school tuition, certain computer-related expenses, internet access) will continue to be tax-free.

- In a given tax year, a child can continue to receive contributions to both a Coverdell and a 529 plan.

- Any tax-free distribution from a child's Coverdell will not automatically eliminate one's ability to claim certain Federal educational tax credits (i.e. the American Opportunity Credit, the Hope Credit, or the Lifetime Learning Credit) for that child in the same tax year. However, in order to be able to claim the full credit and have all the distributions from a Coverdell and/or 529 plan be tax-free, any funds paid for that child's tuition for purposes of claiming the credit cannot be coming from a Coverdell, a 529 plan, or other tax-advantaged funds used to pay for college. This is because federal tax law does not currently permit one to claim two or more educational tax benefits with the same funds used to pay for tuition. So to be able to claim the tax credit AND have the distributions from a Coverdell and/or a 529 plan be completely tax-free, some funds to pay for the student's tuition will have to come from your cash and/or your checking, savings, and/or money market account(s) and/or be paid with the proceeds of a loan.

It's anyone's guess what will happen in the future—which makes decisions down the road difficult. For example, if you think the law will change, and you're likely to qualify for the American Opportunity Credit (which allows you to reduce your taxes based on money you've spent on college tuition for your child), then it would not be a good idea to make any more contributions to a Coverdell. In addition, if you believe the laws will change and you want to plan ahead to reduce any existing funds in a Coverdell, you should then consider paying for other qualified educational expenses—such as private elementary or secondary school tuition, computer equipment, etc.—which are currently permitted.

Because of all the fine print in these plans, and the possibility that the tax law may change, we suggest you consult with a competent advisor before contributing any funds to these plans or making any withdrawals.

# Look Before You Leap

Even though the tax law did NOT sunset, there are still a number of potential pitfalls that you should be aware of before you sign up for these plans—or have any well-intentioned relatives do the same. And unfortunately, while the brochures for these plans might make you think they are the best things to come along since white bread, the promotional materials are often light on specifics—especially the drawbacks.

**The Financial Aid Impact of These Plans**  The Higher Education Reconciliation Act of 2005 (HERA) made a number of important changes to Federal student aid programs—including the way Coverdell Education Savings Accounts (ESAs) and Qualified State Tuition programs (prepaid and savings plans) will be treated in the federal aid formula. Previously, Coverdells and 529 savings accounts were considered to be the asset of the owner of the plan. This was not a big problem if the parents were the owners of the plan; however, if funds were moved from a custodial account into a 529 savings plan, those funds instead became a "custodial" 529 account, and were then still considered in the federal methodology to be an asset of the child. In addition, some Coverdell accounts were set up so that ownership would revert to the student upon reaching the age of majority. This created the odd situation where these accounts were considered a parental asset on one year's version of the FAFSA, only to become a student asset on subsequent federal aid forms once the student became a legal adult.

Also, some years ago under the federal aid formula, funds in a state-sponsored prepaid tuition plan were not considered an asset that needed to be reported on the FAFSA. That's because the dollar value of the tuition credits redeemed was considered a "resource" that reduced your aid eligibility dollar-for-dollar. So if you weren't able to save enough to prepay your entire tuition, the prepaid credits you used each year would reduce your aid eligibility (except for the Pell Grant) by the dollar amount of the credits redeemed. However, under HERA, prepaid 529 plans will now be treated the same way as 529 savings plans and Coverdells.

Unfortunately, in Congress's haste to enact this law, they created a terrible ambiguity: they specified that 529 plans and/or Coverdells owned by a dependent student would no longer need to be reported on the federal aid form as a student asset. Yet, they failed to define how these accounts would be assessed. Would they be parental assets, would they not be required to be reported at all—or would they be treated in some other way?

For the 2008–2009 FAFSA, the Department of Education took the position that any of these accounts owned by a student who was required to report parental information on the FAFSA would not be required to report the value of the student-owned account as an asset on the FAFSA. However, the College Cost Reduction and Access Act of 2007 resolved this ambiguity. As such for the 2009–2010 FAFSA and beyond, such student-owned 529 plans or Coverdell ESAs will be reported as part of the parental investments on the FAFSA. (However, if the student is not required to report parental information on the FAFSA, such student-owned funds will need to be reported as a student asset on the form.) Again, that's the back story.

With this clarification, the federal and the institutional methodologies now differ in their treatment of *student-owned* 529 plans and Coverdells. For a number of years, the College Board had considered student-owned 529s and Coverdells to be the assets of the parent if parental information needed to be reported on the PROFILE. However, such student-owned 529s and Coverdells are now considered to be student assets in all cases. In terms of income, any qualified tax-free distributions from a 529 or Coverdell owned by the student or the student's parent are not considered as untaxed income in both the IM and FM. Of course, the colleges themselves may decide to assess the value and/or the distributions of these plans differently than the Department of Education or the College Board when awarding their own funds.

Accounts owned by individuals other than the student or a parent who must report their information on the aid form—for example, a grandparent or an aunt—are a different story. On the FAFSA, the value of such accounts need not be reported as an asset. While these funds are not considered to be assets in the IM either, some colleges that require the PROFILE may choose to ask questions about these plans in the customized, institution-specific question section that can appear at the end of the form. Even if you need not list their value there, you are not out of the woods yet with such plans. There is still the question of how distributions from these accounts owned by others will be treated. Since this issue has not yet been specifically addressed in the financial aid regulations, there are many in the financial aid community who consider the dollar value of such distributions to be considered untaxed income for the student due to wording on the FAFSA regarding "money received, or paid on your behalf...not reported elsewhere on this form" which appears in the student income section. It is also important to note that each year more and more schools are asking questions about the value of and/or distributions from 529s and Coverdells owned by other individuals.

Under the Institutional Methodology, the College Board currently considers prepaid plans or tuition savings accounts originally funded and owned by parents to be parental assets. Of course, the colleges themselves may decide to assess these plans differently than the Department of Education or the College Board when awarding their own funds.

The promotional literature for most of these state-sponsored plans glosses over or puts the best spin possible on the financial aid consequences of these investments. So you need to take everything they say about this with a bucket full of salt.

**Tax Implications**   If the funds are not used for the child's education or are withdrawn prematurely, the portion of the distribution that represents investment earnings will be taxed at the contributor's (presumably higher) rate, plus a 10% penalty. So if junior decides not to go to school, you'd better hope you can find some other qualified family member who can use the funds for school and take the necessary steps to change the beneficiary on the account. Otherwise your Uncle Sam is going to get a nice windfall. (There are exceptions if the beneficiary dies or receives a scholarship for college.)

You should also realize that both types of 529 plans (as well as Coverdells) can impact your ability to take advantage of other higher education benefits (under both the old and new tax laws) that can sometimes be more advantageous to claim.

Even though Congress a number of years ago voted to permanently extend the ability to withdraw funds from 529s free of federal income taxes, there are still some thorny issues regarding state income taxes—especially if you invest in a 529 plan sponsored by a state other than the state in which you (or the student) live.

*Note: A handful of states will now grant a state tax deduction for contributions made to out-of-state 529 plans. So if you're choosing between an in-state and an out-of-state plan, you should see what benefits, if any, you're giving up by choosing an out-of-state program over your home state program.*

*The new federal tax law enacted at the end of 2017 now will permit one to withdraw up to $10,000 annually for qualified K-12 expenses from a 529 plan. However, there are still some unanswered issues that could cause such distributions to reduce college aid eligibility beginning with the 2020–2021 award year and beyond. Depending on where you live and which state's plan you have, there may be some state tax issues as well.*

**Limited Control Over the Funds**   As we have just mentioned, once you contribute funds to these state-sponsored plans there can be sizable penalties if the funds are withdrawn prematurely. With the state savings plan, after you make your initial contribution you can only move those funds to another state's plan or change your investment allocation plan once every 12 months to avoid any penalties.

If the plan uses an age-based asset allocation model, you may also find your assets being automatically transferred to fixed-income investments just after a significant short-term market correction. Any sane money manager would postpone such a transfer for a few months—but with many of these plans, the manager may not have that option: the transfer is automatically triggered on a certain date.

And because you're tying up your money for a number of years and giving up control, there are a number of questions you should be asking yourself before you contribute one penny to one of these plans.

1. Which type of plan are you investing in? Some states offer only the pre-paid option. Some offer only a tuition savings account. Others offer both.

2. Is the plan offered in your own state superior to plans available in other states? Many tuition savings plans will accept contributions from out-of-state residents and you may prefer another state's asset-allocation model to the one in your home state.

3. If you invest in an out-of-state plan, what additional benefits are you giving up? Funds invested in your home state's plan may not impact state-funded financial aid programs and the earnings may be free of state taxes. A state income tax deduction may be limited to contributions to your own state's plan. So, if you invest out-of-state, you won't necessarily get a state income tax deduction. The student may also owe some state income taxes to his home state when the funds are withdrawn. (He may even owe some state income taxes to the state whose program was used.) Funds invested in an out-of-state plan may also hurt your eligibility for state-based student aid.

4. If you invest in a plan sold to you by a financial advisor or offered by your employer, is it the best deal around? Your financial advisor may not even mention the benefits of your own state's plan or other more attractive out-of-state plans simply because she doesn't sell those plans. In addition, similar 529 plans sold by advisors may carry higher fees than if you contacted the plan administrators directly. A plan offered through your job may not be your home state's plan so be sure to read the fine print.

5. If you decide to transfer the funds to another state's plan, are there any penalties involved? While you may be okay from a federal tax standpoint, you should understand that many states have begun to implement their own penalties in response to the rather liberal federal transfer rules currently in effect. For example, New York residents who

claimed a tax deduction on their state tax return by contributing to the New York Saves 529 plan will have to recapture (add back) the amount of that deduction to their state taxable income in the year they transfer those funds out of the Empire State.

6.  Is the plan an approved Section 529 plan? Some states begin accepting contributions on newly announced plans before the IRS rules on the matter. You want to be sure that you qualify for the federal tax-deferred status before you lock up your funds.

7.  What asset allocation model are you comfortable with? For example, in New Hampshire, the age-based plan calls for 95% in equities for a newborn, versus the New York State plan which permits you to allocate 50%, 75%, or even 100% in equities for a similarly aged child depending on your risk tolerance level. Some states, such as California, let you choose among a number of investment options, including a social choice equity option.

8.  What fees are charged by the investment managers? While you won't be sent a bill, such charges can significantly reduce the return on your investment. Although traditional mutual funds are required by law to disclose such charges, tuition savings plans are not—and often bury this information in a thick prospectus (which you may not even see unless you specifically ask for it). Fees can vary tremendously from state to state, and are often much higher than ordinary mutual funds.

9.  What happens if you are on the installment plan and can no longer contribute? For example, if you lost your job and can't keep up with the payments, some programs might automatically cancel the contract and/or impose other penalties as well.

10. What is the likelihood you will move out of the state before college begins? If you are in a state prepaid program and then move to another state, most programs will only provide for tuition credits at the resident rates. You'll have to come up with the additional funds to cover the extra tuition charged to out-of-state students.

11. If you are investing in a prepaid plan, how will the state determine the amount of funds you'll receive if the student attends a college out of state? Some plans will use the dollar value of the credits at the public university based on the tuition charges for each academic year. Others simply use the total dollar value of all the credits at the start of the first academic year and then allocate one quarter of the value for each of the four years. In the latter case, your funds for the sophomore, junior, and senior year will stop increasing in value once the student begins freshman year, no matter how much tuition inflation subsequently occurs.

# Do You Have a Crystal Ball?

Unless you can predict the future, you should carefully think and rethink any decision that completely locks yourself and your loved ones into an investment that will mature so many years into the future. Obviously, these plans make sense for many people, especially since the new "kiddie tax" rules make custodial accounts less attractive. But because of all the fine print in each state's plan, you should know exactly what you're getting into and carefully review the prospectus to make sure it is right for you. Because of the various tax consequences involved, it would also be a good idea to discuss the plan with your accountant or financial planner before you make your first contribution as well.

The following is a listing of states that offer prepaid programs and/or tuition savings accounts along with telephone numbers. The type of program offered is indicated by a "P" for prepaid plans and an "S" for savings plans.

| State | Program Type | Telephone |
|---|---|---|
| Alabama | P* | 1-800-252-7228 |
| | S | 1-334-242-7500 |
| Alaska | S | 1-866-277-1005 |
| Arizona | S | 1-602-258-2435 |
| Arkansas | S | 1-800-587-7301; 1-888-529-9552 |
| California | S | 1-800-343-3548; 1-800-544-5248 |
| Colorado | S | 1-800-997-4295; 1-800-448-2424 |
| Connecticut | S | 1-888-799-2438 |
| Delaware | S | 1-800-544-1655 |
| Florida | P | 1-800-552-4723 |
| | S | 1-800-552-4723 |
| Georgia | S | 1-877-424-4377 |
| Hawaii | S | 1-866-529-3343 |
| Idaho | S | 1-866-433-2533 |
| Illinois | P | 1-877-877-3724 |
| | S | 1-877-432-7444 |
| Indiana | S | 1-866-485-9415 |
| Iowa | S | 1-888-672-9116 |
| Kansas | S | 1-800-579-2203; 1-888-903-3863 |
| Kentucky | S | 1-877-598-7878 |
| | P* | 1-888-919-5278 |
| Louisiana | S | 1-800-259-5626 |
| Maine | S | 1-877-463-9843 |

| State | Program Type | Telephone |
|---|---|---|
| Maryland | P | 1-888-463-4723 |
| | S | 1-888-463-4723 |
| Massachusetts | P (U. Plan) | 1-800-449-6332 |
| | S (U. Fund) | 1-800-544-2776 |
| Michigan | P | 1-800-638-4543 |
| | S | 1-877-861-6377 |
| Minnesota | S | 1-877-338-4646 |
| Mississippi | P | 1-800-987-4450 |
| | S | 1-800-987-4450 |
| Missouri | S | 1-888-414-6678 |
| Montana | S | 1-800-888-2723 |
| Nebraska | S | 1-888-993-3746 |
| Nevada | P | 1-888-477-2667 |
| | S | 1-800-587-7305; 1-800-235-5829; 1-866-734-4530 |
| New Hampshire | S | 1-800-544-1914; 1-800-544-1722 |
| New Jersey | S | 1-877-465-2378 |
| New Mexico | S | 1-877-337-5268 |
| New York | S | 1-877-697-2837 |
| N. Carolina | S | 1-800-600-3453 |
| N. Dakota | S | 1-866-728-3529 |
| Ohio | S | 1-800-233-6734 |
| Oklahoma | S | 1-877-654-7284 |
| Oregon | S | 1-503-373-1903; 1-866-772-8464 |
| Pennsylvania | S (guaranteed savings) | 1-800-440-4000 |
| | S | 1-800-294-6195; 1-800-440-4000 |
| Rhode Island | S | 1-888-324-5057 |
| S. Carolina | S | 1-888-244-5674 |
| | P* | 1-888-772-4723 |
| S. Dakota | S | 1-866-529-7462 |
| Tennessee | S | 1-855-386-7827 |
| Texas | P (Tuition Promise) | 1-800-445-4723 |
| | S | 1-800-445-4723 |
| Utah | S | 1-800-418-2551 |
| Vermont | S | 1-800-637-5860 |
| Virginia | P | 1-888-567-0540 |
| | S | 1-888-567-0540 |
| Washington | P | 1-800-955-2318 |

| State | Program Type | Telephone |
|---|---|---|
| West Virginia | P* | 1-866-574-3542 |
| | S | 1-866-574-3542 |
| Wisconsin | S | 1-888-338-3789 |
| | S | 1-866-677-6933 |
| Wyoming | | No plan available |
| District of Columbia | S | 1-800-987-4859; 1-800-368-2745 |
| * Closed to new enrollment | | |

# A Supplementary Form of College Fund

## Owning Your Own Home

If you can swing it, owning your own home is a top priority in any plan for paying for college. Equally important, building equity in your home provides you with collateral you can use to help pay for college.

In addition, owning your home provides you with an investment for your own future, which you should never lose sight of. When the kids rush off to embark on their own lives, clutching their diplomas, will there be something left for you? What good is a college education for the child if it puts the parents in the poorhouse?

## The Home as a Credit Line?

No matter how well prepared, many families end up at some point having to borrow money to pay part of the family contribution. Unfortunately, the financial aid formula doesn't recognize most types of debt; that is to say they do not subtract these liabilities from your assets before they decide how much in assets you have available to pay for college.

We will be explaining this in great detail in the chapters on financial aid strategies, but here's a quick example. Suppose you had $25,000 in assets, but you also owed $6,000 on a consumer loan. If you asked any accountant in the world, she would say your total net assets were only $19,000; but as far as the colleges are concerned, you still have $25,000 available for them to assess. Many kinds of debt (such as consumer loans and outstanding credit card bills) don't make sense during the college years.

However, the more selective colleges that elect to use the institutional methodology (which looks at home equity) rather than the federal methodology (which does not) do recognize one kind of debt—mortgages, first and second, on your home. This means that your home can be a particularly valuable kind of college fund. Generally, the more equity you have in your home, the more you can borrow against it. And the best part is that if your child attends a school that assesses home equity, and you borrow against your home, you reduce your total assets in the eyes of the FAOs, which can reduce how much you have to pay for college.

# Remember to Invest in Other Things Besides Your Child's College Education

Providing a college education for your child is probably not the only ambition you have in life. During the years you are saving for college you should not neglect your other goals, particularly in two important areas: owning your own home (which we have just spoken about) and planning for your retirement.

While the colleges assess your assets and income, they generally don't assess retirement provisions such as Individual Retirement Accounts (IRAs), 401(k) plans, Keoghs, tax-deferred annuities, etc. Any money you have managed to contribute to a retirement provision will be off-limits to the FAOs at most schools.

These contributions to retirement plans not only help provide for your future but also will shelter assets (and the income from those assets) from the FAOs. In addition, many employers will match contributions to 401(k) plans, in effect doubling your stake. And let's not forget that, depending on your income level, part or all of these contributions may be tax-deferred.

Now that you have an overview of some long-term investment strategies, let's talk about some specific plans for investing based on how many years away your child is from college.

## If You Have 15 Years . . .

Because there is so much time, you can afford to choose aggressive investments of the types we've outlined above. We recommend that you invest about 75% of your fund in these higher-risk investments, and the remaining 25% in investments that lock in a reliable rate of return. There is little point in keeping this money in a bank account because the rate of return will probably not even keep up with inflation. However, as college years get closer, start transferring out of stock funds into something less subject to temporary setbacks.

If possible, try to invest large amounts in the early years to take advantage of compounding. When you get closer to the first year of college, take a hard look at your college fund. You may find that you have already accumulated enough money to pay for school, in which case you can start investing your money in other directions. On the other hand, you may find that you need to increase the amounts you are saving in order to get closer to your goal.

In spite of what you may have heard, as long as you qualify for financial aid it is better to have two kids in school at the same time. If you are planning on having another child, but were putting it off to avoid staggering college bills, reconsider. Whether you have only one child in college, or two or three children in college at the same time, the parents' contribution (the amount colleges think you can afford to pay for college) stays almost the same. Having two kids in school at the same time is like a two-for-one sale.

With this much time to plan, you should consider long-term ways to increase your earning power. Perhaps you might go back to school to pick up an advanced degree. Perhaps if one parent is not working at present you could begin thinking about a long-term plan for setting up a career for that parent to increase your family's earning power.

As you get closer to the college years, you will need to consider other points. In order not to repeat ourselves too much, we will cover these points below. Please keep on reading.

## If You Have 10 Years . . .

With 10 years to go, you still have plenty of time to build a sizable college fund. To build your capital quickly, try to save as much as you can in the first several years when compounding will help you the most. Aggressive investments will also help to build your fund quickly. We recommend that with 10 years to go, you keep 70% of your money in aggressive investments of the type outlined above. The other 30% can be put into fixed-return investments with limited risk. As you get closer to the first year of college, you should gradually shift your fund into investments with more liquidity and no risk.

Because your child's academic ability will have an important effect not only on which colleges he can apply to but also on what kind of aid package the college will offer you, it is vital that you find a good elementary school that challenges his abilities.

In spite of taxes, braces, and saving for college, do not neglect your own future. If you have not already bought a home, consider buying one (in a good school district) if at all possible. Contributions to retirement provisions should also be made regularly.

Now is also the first time you can realistically speculate about how much money you might be earning by the time your child is in college. If you believe you will be earning too much to qualify for aid, it becomes even more important to build your college fund. If you are not going to qualify for aid, you might want to put assets into the child's name.

As you get closer to the college years, you will need to consider other points. In order not to repeat ourselves too much, we will cover these points below. Please keep on reading.

## If You Have Five Years . . .

There is still plenty of time to build up a large college fund. Even if it entails a sacrifice, a large contribution in the first year will help build your investment faster through the miracle of compounding. In the first year or so, you can still afford to invest aggressively, although we recommend that you keep only about 50% of your money in aggressive investments, with 30% in limited-risk fixed rate of return financial instruments, and 20% in liquid accounts that are completely insured.

With about four years to go, reconsider whether you are going to qualify for financial aid. You may have received promotions, raises, inheritances, or made investments that take you out of range of financial aid. In this case, consider moving assets into the child's name. On the other hand, you may discover that you are doing less well than you anticipated, in which case you will want to start thinking about the strategies that are outlined in the rest of this book.

Find a great high school for your child and try to encourage good study habits. Good grades will increase your child's options tremendously. It's probably too early to tell, but try to get a sense of what type of school your child will be applying to, and how much that school will cost.

As you get to the last three years before college, you will need to consider other points. In order not to repeat ourselves too much, we will cover these points below. Please keep on reading.

## If You Have Three Years . . .

Parents find that with the specter of college tuition looming imminently, they are able to save substantial amounts in only two years. After all, many parents are at the height of their earning power at this time. However, because you will need the money relatively soon, it is probably better to stay away from high-risk investments that may suffer a temporary (or permanent) setback just as you need to write a check.

These next academic years are the most important for your child. Sit down with him and explain (in as unpressured and nonjudgmental a tone as you can manage) that because colleges give preferential packaging to good students, every tenth of a point he adds to his grade point average may save him thousands of dollars in loans he won't have to pay back later.

If your child did not score well on the PSAT, consider finding a good test preparation course for the SAT. Several recent studies have shown that coaching can raise a student's score by over 100 points. Again, every ten points your child raises her score may save your family thousands of dollars—and of course allow her to apply to more selective colleges. We, of course, are partial to The Princeton Review SAT course.

If you have any interest in running a business on the side, this may be the ideal moment to start setting it up. Most businesses show losses during their first few years of operation. What better time to have losses than during the tax years that affect your aid eligibility? There are also many tax benefits to this strategy, but the business cannot exist  just on paper. For tax purposes it must be run with the intention of showing a profit in order not to run afoul of the "hobby loss" provisions of the tax code. If this seems like it might be for you, please read our financial aid strategies section, and the section on running your own business in the chapter "Special Topics."

# Maneuvering

The most important thing to realize is that at this point, you are one year away from the all-important base income year. Colleges now use the tax year two years *before* college begins (from January 1 of the student's sophomore year of high school to December 31 of the student's junior year in high school) as their basis for deciding what you can afford to pay during freshman year.

Thus you have one year to maneuver before the base income year begins. Read the financial aid strategies that we outline in the rest of this book extremely carefully. After you have read these chapters and consulted your accountant or financial aid consultant, you may want to move some assets around, take capital gains, take bonuses before the base income year begins, and so on. During the base income year itself, you may want to make some major expenditures, pay down your credit card balances, establish a line of credit on your home, and make the maximum contributions possible to retirement provisions.

Many times, parents come to consult us when their child is just about to fill out the need analysis forms in the senior year of high school. There is still a lot we can do to help them qualify for more aid, but we always feel bad for the family because if only they had come to us before the base income year started, there would have been so much more that we could have done.

You are in the fortunate position of having that extra year to maneuver. Read the rest of this book, and enjoy.

# Chapter Three

## Short-Term Strategies for Receiving More Financial Aid

# A "Snapshot" of Your Financial Picture

Each year your son or daughter is in college, the school will ask you to fill out a form reporting income and assets—in effect a snapshot of your overall financial picture. You've probably noticed that snapshots can be very misleading. In one picture, you may appear youthful and vibrant. In another, you may look terrible, with a double chin and 20 extra pounds. Perhaps neither photograph is exactly correct. Of course, when you are deciding which picture to put in the scrapbook, the choice is easy: throw away the one you don't like and keep the one you do.

In choosing which financial snapshot to send to the colleges, the object is a little bit different: send them the worst-looking picture you can find.

To be very blunt, the single most effective way to reduce the family contribution is to make your income and your assets look as small as possible.

# Well, This Is Not Revolutionary Advice

After all, you've been trying to do this for years.

We're sure you and your accountant are generally doing a fine job of keeping your taxes to a minimum. However, certain long-term tax strategies that normally make all kinds of sense, can explode in your face during college years. Neither you nor your accountant may fully grasp how important it is to understand the ins and outs of the financial aid formulas.

# How College Planning Affects Tax Planning

There are two reasons why tax planning has to change during college years.

First, the FAOs (unlike the IRS) are concerned about only *four years* of your financial life. Using strategies we will be showing you in the next few chapters, you may be able to shift income out of those four years, thus increasing your financial aid.

Second, financial aid formulas *differ* from the IRS formulas in several key ways. Certain long-term tax reduction strategies (shifting income to other family members, for example) can actually *increase* the amount of college tuition you will pay. However, astute parents who understand these differences will find that there are some wonderful, legal, logical alternatives they can explore to change the four snapshots the college will take of their income and assets.

Tax accountants who do not understand the financial aid process (and in our experience, this includes most of them) can actually hurt your chances for financial aid.

## The First Base Year Income

Colleges base your ability to pay *this* year's tuition *not* on what you made this year; not even on what you made *last* year; they base it on what you made the year before *that*. This may seem like ancient history, but the colleges have their complicated reasons (which we'll go into later). Thus the first financial aid scrutiny you will undergo will not be directed at the calendar year during which your child will start her freshman year of college, *but two years before*. That year is called the first base income year and is the crucial one.

The base income year (shaded in the diagram that follows) extends from January 1 of your child's sophomore year in high school to December 31 of your child's junior year in high school. This is when first impressions are formed. The college will get an idea of how much you are likely to be able to afford, not just for the first year of school, but for the remaining years as well. First impressions are likely to endure and are often very difficult to change. Thus it would be helpful to remove as much income as possible from this calendar year.

| Aug. | Sept. | Oct. | Nov. | Dec. | Jan. | Feb. | Mar. | Apr. | May | June | July |
|---|---|---|---|---|---|---|---|---|---|---|---|
| High School Sophomore Year Begins | | | | | | | | | | | |
| Aug. | Sept. | Oct. | Nov. | Dec. | Jan. | Feb. | Mar. | Apr. | May | June | July |
| High School Junior Year Begins | | | | | | | | | | | |
| Aug. | Sept. | Oct. | Nov. | Dec. | Jan. | Feb. | Mar. | Apr. | May | June | July |
| High School Senior Year Begins | | | | | | | | | | | |
| Aug. | Sept. | Oct. | Nov. | Dec. | Jan. | Feb. | Mar. | Apr. | May | June | July |
| College Begins | | | | | | | | | | | |

## What If I'm Already Past the Base Income Year?

If you are reading this book and your son or daughter is already in the spring term of junior year in high school, then you have probably missed the chance to make adjustments to your income for the base income year—but don't despair. First of all, there are three other years still to go; the strategies we outline below can be used to lower the appearance of income in the years to come. And second, you haven't missed the chance to make adjustments to your assets. *That* snapshot gets taken on the day you fill out the forms. We'll talk about assets a little later in this chapter.

# What If I'm In the Middle of the Base Income Year?

If you are reading this book and you are still in the base income year, there are a bunch of very specific things you can do to minimize the appearance of income.

# What If My Income Radically Changes Between the Base Income Year and When My Daughter Starts College?

If your income has gone *up* since the base income year, that's great. No need to report the change, unless you are asked to by an individual college. However, if your income has gone markedly *down* since the base income year, you can always write to the colleges and explain. We'll describe this process, called an "appeal", later in this book.

# I'm About to Get a Raise. Should I Say No?

It's easy to get carried away with the concept of reducing income, and it may appear at first that you would be better off turning down a raise. However, the short answer to this question is, "Are you crazy?"

More money is always good. Our discussion here is limited to minimizing the *appearance* of more money. Let's say you get a raise of $3,000 per year. This will certainly reduce your eligibility for college aid, but will it negate the entire effect of the raise? Not likely. Let's say you're in the 22% federal tax bracket, your raise is still subject to social security taxes of 7.65%, and your income is being assessed at the maximum rate possible under the aid formulas. Looking at the chart that follows, you'll see that even after taxes and reduced aid eligibility are taken into account, you will still be $1,119 ahead, though state and local taxes might reduce this somewhat.

| raise of: | $3,000 |
|---|---|
| minus:  federal tax | $660 |
| FICA taxes | $230 |
| reduced aid | $991 |
| what you keep: | $1,119 |

## My Spouse Works. Should He or She Quit?

The same principle applies here. More money is good. Not only are you getting the advantage of extra income but also under the federal financial aid formula, for a two-parent family with both parents working, 35% of the first $11,429 the spouse with the lower income earns is deducted as an "employment allowance". (The same deduction is granted for a single parent household if that parent works.) Even if this increased income decreases your aid eligibility, you will still be ahead on the income. In addition, you will be creating the impression of a family with a work ethic, which can be very helpful in negotiating with FAOs later. FAOs work for their living, and probably earn less than you do. They are more likely to give additional aid to families who have demonstrated their willingness to make sacrifices.

# Income vs. Assets

Some parents get confused by the differences between what is considered income and what are considered assets. Assets are the money, property, and other financial instruments you've been able to accumulate over time. Income, on the other hand, is the money you actually earned or otherwise received during the past year, including interest and dividends from your assets.

The IRS never asks you to report your assets on your 1040—only the income you received from these assets. Colleges, on the other hand, are very interested in your income and your assets. Later in this chapter, there will be an entire section devoted to strategies for reducing *the appearance* of your assets. For now, let's focus on income.

The colleges decided long ago that income should be assessed much more heavily than assets. The intention is that when a family is finished paying for college, there should be something left in the bank. (Don't start feeling grateful just yet. This works only as long as the colleges meet a family's need in full.)

# Income

When considering their chances for financial aid, many families believe that the colleges are interested only in how much income you make from work. If this were the case, the colleges would just be able to look at your W-2 form to see if you qualified for aid. Unfortunately, life is not so simple. The college's complicated formulas make the IRS tax code look like child's play.

For financial aid purposes, the colleges will be looking at the same income the IRS does. For most of us, that boils down to Line 7 of the 1040 IRS form: the Adjusted Gross Income or AGI. (As you may already know, beginning with the 2018 tax year, everyone who files a personal income tax return with the IRS must use the IRS 1040 form. The IRS Form 1040A and Form 1040EZ that both existed for decades are no longer a filing option.)

For those who file a tax return, the colleges also look at certain other types of income that are not subject to tax, for example, child support, tax-exempt interest, and voluntary contributions to a 401(k) or other tax-deferred retirement plan.

And for those who don't file any tax return, the colleges will still look at income earned from work plus other untaxed income.

## The Simplified Needs Test

Before we begin discussing the components of taxable and untaxed income, it is important to understand that by meeting certain requirements, you may be able to have parent and student assets excluded from the federal financial aid formulas. This could qualify you for increased federal aid via a financial aid loophole known as the "Simplified Needs Test" (SNT). Here's the way it works: you initially remain under consideration for the SNT if the (step)parents who are required to report their information on the FAFSA have an Adjusted Gross Income below $50,000. For non-tax filers, the applicable (step)parents need to have income from work totaling below $50,000, which for most means wages reported on a W-2 form.

In addition to the requirement that income be less than $50,000, the applicable (step)parents must also meet *at least one* of the following five criteria.

- During any time in the base income year and/or at any time during the year *after* the base income year: the student, the (step)parents who were required to report their information on the student's FAFSA, or anyone else in that parents' household must receive benefits under a means-tested U.S. federal government program (other than federal student aid). Such benefit programs normally include food stamps [SNAP], Medicaid *(which is not the same program as Medicare),* Supplemental Security Income [SSI] *(which is not the same as Social Security),* temporary assistance for needy families [TANF], certain means-tested school lunch programs, or certain supplemental nutrition programs for women, infants, and children [WIC].

- A (step)parent who reports his or her financial information on the FAFSA is considered a "dislocated worker" on the date the FAFSA form is filed. A parent can normally qualify for this dislocated worker status by being laid-off or receiving a lay-off notice from a job; receiving unemployment benefits (due to being laid off or losing a job, provided the person is unlikely to return to their prior occupation); was self-employed but is now unemployed due to economic conditions or a natural disaster; or by being a "displaced homemaker" (i.e., a stay-at-home mother or father who is no longer supported by their spouse, is unemployed or underemployed, and is having trouble finding or upgrading employment). The financial aid officer at the school will probably require additional documentation to prove such dislocated worker status.

- For the base income year, the applicable (step)parent(s) of a dependent filed the IRS 1040 but were not *required* to file any tax return because their income was below the tax filing threshold. (IMPORTANT: See italicized text on pages 179–180 about this.)

- For the base income year, the applicable (step)parent(s) of a dependent filed the IRS 1040, but did NOT have to file Schedule 1 as part of the return.

- For the base income year, the applicable (step)parent(s) of a dependent filed the IRS 1040 with Schedule 1, but only needed to file Schedule 1 to report one or more of the six additions or adjustments to income that we will shortly explain.

## The Simplified Needs Test Got Less Simple

In the old days (i.e., prior to the 2018 tax year) tax-filers with the IRS who did not have certain types of income and who did not claim certain adjustments to income could have filed IRS Form 1040EZ or Form 1040A (known as the "short forms"), instead of the IRS 1040 (often called the "long form"). And if the applicable (step)parent(s) who must report their income on the FAFSA were able to file the 1040EZ or 1040A, the student automatically qualified for the Simplified Needs Test if the parental AGI was below $50,000. Now that those short forms are gone, determining if you meet the SNT criteria based on tax filing status is likely going to relate to Schedule 1 of the IRS 1040. (An example of this form can be found near the back of this book, in the Sample Forms chapter.)

Schedule 1 is a new creation by the IRS. It is an additional document that follows page 1 and page 2 of the main 1040 return. Schedule 1 was developed to report additional types of income (such as business income, unemployment benefits, alimony) that do not have their own lines numbers on page 2 of the IRS 1040 as well as to report various adjustments to income being claimed (such as IRA deductions, student loan interest deductions, self-employment deductions and educator expenses). Some of these line items on Schedule 1 previously appeared on page 1 of the pre-2018 1040 as well as on page 1 of the 1040A. However, a number of the line item categories on Schedule 1 only appeared on page 1 of the pre-2018 1040, but did not appear on the 1040A or 1040EZ—in which case the 1040 long form had to be completed to properly account for them.

Because this is the first year the 1040EZ and the 1040A are no longer with us, the U.S. Department of Education (DOE) that develops the FAFSA had to come up with a new way to determine who could meet the Simplified Needs Test for the 2020–2021 award year (and beyond) based on how one completed their personal IRS return for the base income year being used. The DOE's initial workaround for this situation was to simply use Schedule 1 of the IRS 1040 as the litmus test. Specifically, those who did not file Schedule 1 as part of the IRS 1040 would be eligible for the SNT, provided their applicable income was also low enough. But for those who filed the Schedule 1, they would need to qualify for the SNT via one of the other four criteria (and also meet the income requirement.)

The DOE's initial proposal would have seemed (at least for the average person) to be a simple fix that would be easy for students and their parents to understand. But if there is one thing to remember about aid, it is that nothing is simple. That is because the new proposal would have meant that thousands of students who previously qualified for the SNT (under the "filed" or "could have filed" the 1040A or 1040EZ criteria), would now be at risk of having their aid significantly cut if Schedule 1 was only filed to report certain items that previously could be have been reported on the IRS 1040A.

Not surprisingly when the first draft of the 2020–2021 FAFSA, which reflected the DOE's initial proposal, was made available in the spring of 2019 for public comment, a plethora of financial aid professionals voiced their concerns. Many of those who submitted comments to the DOE—including the author of this book—suggested an alternate workaround. Namely, that those who only filed Schedule 1 to report items which previously could have been reported on a 1040A return should still be permitted to qualify for the SNT. As we send this book to print, the DOE has currently published a second draft of the 2020–2021 FAFSA that adopts these suggested alternative criteria. And so, as it stands now: if one filed Schedule 1 of the IRS 1040 only to report one or more of the six following additions or adjustment to income on Schedule 1, then one would be eligible for the SNT, provided, of course, that the applicable AGI is low enough to meet the income requirement. Here are the six key items on Schedule 1, which the DOE refers to as "exceptions": capital gains (Line 13 – but may not be a loss), unemployment compensation (Line 19), educator expenses (Line 23), IRA deduction (Line 32), student loan interest deduction (Line 33) and finally, other income (Line 21, provided the other income only represents an Alaska Permanent Fund dividend that is not less than zero).

But if one files Schedule 1 and reports anything on any other lines of the schedule and/or reports any additional income or adjustments to income other than these six exceptions, then one would have to meet at least one of first four criteria we mentioned earlier (and have low enough income) in order to qualify for the SNT.

It is important to remember that the above exceptions are only a proposal and the final policy guidelines adopted may have new or different fine print. If there are any changes or new developments, you can find out the latest details by registering your book online and accessing your free student tools (see page vi).

If adopted, the new DOE proposal has created certain financial aid opportunities for those who plan ahead. Obviously, if you have certain other types of income beyond the exceptions, then you must report them on Schedule 1 if required by the IRS to do so. But in some limited cases, it might make sense to arrange NOT to have them. For example, if you are otherwise eligible for the SNT, which therefore would result in significantly more aid, then starting a side business that would only generate a tiny amount of income (or even result in a loss) on Line 12 may not be the best idea.

There are similar strategies related to adjustments to income. Unlike income, there is no law requiring you to claim any adjustments to income. So if you incurred a small penalty on an early withdrawal from savings that would be claimed on Line 30 of Schedule 1, and you otherwise meet all the criteria for the SNT and are likely to get more grant aid as a result of meeting the SNT, you may be better off in the long run electing not to claim that adjustment to income, as it is not an exception. There are additional strategies involving the SNT as well, which work best for those families with low income but significant assets. Since you will be balancing your tax planning with your aid planning, we recommend you consult with a financial professional knowledgeable about student aid before considering any courses of action or inaction that involve more than a minimal amount of money.

## The Automatic Zero-EFC

The federal government has a great break for parent(s) in the household who 1) have a 2018 combined adjusted gross income of $26,000 or less (or if non-tax filers, have combined income from work of $26,000 or less), and 2) can meet at least one of the other five criteria .

Even if your child has substantial income, and/or you and your child have substantial assets, and/or you or your child have significant untaxed income, the student's EFC will be judged to be zero if you meet both of the above two requirements.

So if your income in a base income year will be below the Automatic Zero-EFC threshold, it is even more important that you understand the other five criteria, especially as to how your tax return is completed. Do not assume that your tax preparer will know the SNT or Automatic Zero-EFC criteria.

**TIP 1:**
There may be some financial aid advantages to completing your tax return in a certain manner if you do not otherwise qualify for the SNT or the Automatic Zero-EFC, provided the IRS permits you to do so. And if you were not required to file a personal tax return but still filed a 1040 form, you may still be eligible for the SNT or Automatic Zero-EFC.

# A Parents' Step-by-Step Guide to the Federal Income Tax Form

By reducing your total income reported on your tax return, you can increase your financial aid, which, you should remember, is largely funded by your tax dollars anyway. Let's examine how various items on your tax return can be adjusted to influence your aid eligibility. The IRS line numbers below refer to the line items on Page 2 of IRS 1040, while the Schedule 1 line items involve the different items that appear on that schedule. For your benefit, sample copies of Pages 1 and 2 of the IRS 1040 as well as Schedule 1 appear toward the end of this book in the Sample Forms section.

## Line 1—Wages, Salaries, Tips, etc.

For most parents, there is not much to be done about Line 1. Your employers will send you W-2 forms, and you simply report this income. However, there are a few points to be made.

## Defer Your Bonus

If you are one of the thousands of Americans in the workplace who receive a bonus, you might discuss with your boss the possibility of moving your bonus into a non-base income year. For example:

If your child is in the beginning of her sophomore year of high school (in other words, if the first base income year has not yet begun) and you are due a year-end bonus, make sure that you collect and deposit the bonus *before* January 1 of the new year (when the base income year begins). As long as the bonus is included on your W-2 for the previous year, it will not be considered income on your aid application.

The money will still appear as part of your *assets* (provided you haven't already spent it). But by shifting the bonus into a non-base income year, you will avoid having the colleges count your bonus twice—as both asset and income.

If you are due a year-end bonus and your child is starting his junior year of high school, see if you can arrange to get the bonus held off until *after* January 1. Yes, it will show up on next year's financial aid form, but in the meantime you've had the benefit of financial aid for this year.

Just as important, FAOs make four-year projections based on your first base income year. Your FAO will have set aside money for you for the next three years based on the aid your child receives as a freshman in college. Who knows what might happen next year? You might need that money. If the FAO hasn't already set it aside for you, it might not be there when you need it.

**TIP 2:**
Move your bonus into a non-base income year.

# If You've Had an Unusually Good Year

Maybe you won a retroactive pay increase during the base income year. Or perhaps you just worked a lot of overtime. If you can arrange to receive payment during a non-base income year that would, of course, be better, but there are sometimes compelling reasons for taking the money when it is offered (for example, you are afraid you might not get it later).

However, unless you explain the details of this windfall to the colleges, they will be under the impression that this sort of thing happens to you all the time.

If the base income year's income is really not representative, write to the financial aid office of each of the colleges your child is applying to, and explain that this was a once-in-a-lifetime payment, never to be repeated. Include a copy of your tax return from the year *before* the base income year, or from the year *after*, which more closely reflects your true average income. If helpful to your cause, you may wish to include a projection of your income for the "current year"—the calendar year that will end on December 31 in the middle of the academic year for which you are seeking aid.

Don't bother sending documentation like this to the companies that process the standardized analysis forms. They are only interested in crunching the numbers on the form, and anyway have no power to make decisions about your aid at specific schools. Documentation regarding a change in circumstances should never be sent to the processing companies. Send it directly to the schools.

**TIP 3:**
If you've had an unusually good year, explain to the colleges that your average salary is much lower.

# Become an Independent Contractor

If you are a full-time employee receiving a W-2 form at the end of the year, you have significant unreimbursed business expenses, and you are otherwise ineligible for the SNT or the Automatic Zero-EFC, you might discuss with your employer the viability of becoming an independent contractor. The advantage to this is that you can file your income under Schedule C of the tax form ("profit or loss from business"), enabling you to deduct huge amounts of business-related expenses *before* Line 7, where it will do you some good. Note: if you are otherwise eligible for the SNT or Automatic Zero-EFC, filing Schedule C will disqualify you from receiving such favorable aid treatment, unless you are not required to file a tax return or are eligible by meeting at least one of the other alternate criteria mentioned on pages 60–61.

An independent contractor can deduct telephone bills, business use of the home, dues, business travel, and entertainment—basically anything that falls under the cost of doing business—and thus lower the adjusted gross income.

You would have to consult with your accountant to see if the disadvantages (increased likelihood of an IRS audit, difficulties in rearranging health insurance and pension plans, possible loss of unemployment benefits, increased social security tax, etc.) outweigh the advantages. In addition, the IRS has been known to crack down on employers who classify their workers as independent contractors when they are really salaried employees. Like all fuzzy areas of the tax law, this represents an opportunity to be exploited, but requires careful planning.

**TIP 4a:**
If you have significant unreimbursed employee expenses, consider becoming an independent contractor so that you can deduct expenses on Schedule C of the 1040. However, be careful if you are otherwise eligible for the SNT or Automatic Zero-EFC.

Even better, you might suggest to your boss that she cut your pay. No, we haven't gone insane. By convincing your employer to reduce your pay by the amount of your business expenses, and then having her reimburse you directly for those expenses, you should end up with the same amount of money in your pocket, but you'll show a lower AGI and therefore increase your aid eligibility.

**TIP 4b:**
If you have significant unreimbursed employee expenses, try to get your employer to reimburse these business expenses directly to you—even if it means taking a corresponding cut in pay.

If your employer won't let you pursue either of these options, you should be sure to explain your unreimbursed employee expenses in a separate letter to the FAOs.

# Lines 2b and 3b—Taxable Interest and Dividend Income

If you have interest or dividend income, you have assets. Nothing prompts a "validation" (financial aid jargon for an audit) faster than listing interest and dividend income without listing the assets it came from.

For the most part, there is little you can do, or would want to do, to reduce this income, though we will have a lot to say in later chapters about reducing *the appearance* of your assets.

Some parents have suggested taking all their assets and hiding them in a mattress or dumping them into a checking account that doesn't earn interest. The first option is illegal and dumb. The second is just dumb. In both cases, this would be a bit like turning down a raise. More interest is *good*. The FAOs won't take all of it, and you will need it if you want to have any chance of staying even with inflation.

The one type of interest income you might want to control comes from Series E and EE U.S. Savings Bonds. When you buy a U.S. Savings Bond, you don't pay the face value of the bond; you buy it for much less. When the bond matures (in five years, 10 years, or whatever) it is then worth the face value of the bond. The money you receive from the bond in excess of what you paid for it is called interest. With Series E and EE Savings Bonds, you have two tax options: you can report the interest on the bond as it is earned each year on that year's tax return, or you can report all the interest in one lump sum the year you cash in the bond.

By taking the second option, you can in effect hold savings bonds for years without paying any tax on the interest, because you haven't cashed them in yet. However, when you finally do cash them in, you suddenly have to report all the interest earned over the years to the IRS. If the year that you report that interest happens to be a base income year, all of the interest will have to be reported on the aid forms as well. This will almost certainly raise your EFC.

The only exception to this might be Series EE bonds bought after 1989. The U.S. government decided to give parents who pay for their children's college education a tax break: low- or middle-income parents who bought Series EE bonds after 1989 with the intention of using the bonds to help pay for college may not have to pay any tax on the interest income at all. The interest earned is completely tax-free for a single parent making up to $81,100 or a married couple earning up to $121,600. Once you hit these income levels, the benefits are slowly phased out. A single parent earning above $96,100 or a married couple earning above $151,600 becomes ineligible for any tax break. All of these numbers are based on 2018 tax rates and are subject to an annual adjustment for inflation.

However, we still recommend that parents who bought these bonds with the intention of paying for college cash them in *after* the end of the last base income year (after January 1 of the student's sophomore year in college). Whether the interest from these bonds is taxed or untaxed, the FAOs still consider it income and assess it just as harshly as your wages.

Thus if at all possible, try to avoid cashing in any and all U.S. Savings Bonds during any base income year. With Series E or EE bonds, you may be able to roll over your money into Series H or HH bonds and defer reporting interest until the college years are over. There is also no law that says you have to cash in a savings bond when it matures. You can continue to hold the bond, and in some instances it will continue to earn interest above its face value.

**TIP 5:**
If possible, avoid cashing in U.S. Savings Bonds during a base income year, unless you've been paying taxes on the interest each year, as it accrued.

## If You Have Put Assets in Your Other Children's Names

Parents are often told by accountants to transfer their assets into their children's name so that the assets will be taxed at the children's lower rate. While this is a good tax reduction strategy, it stinks as a financial aid strategy, as you will find out later in this chapter. However, if this is your situation and you have *already* put assets under the student's *younger siblings'* names, there is one small silver lining in this cloud: The tax laws give most parents with children under age 18 (or under age 24 if the child is a full time student for at least 5 months during the tax year) the option of reporting their child's investment income on a separate tax return or on the parents' own tax return.

Either way, the family enjoys the benefit of reduced taxes due to the child's lower bracket. The principal advantage of reporting the child's income on the parents' return is to save the expense of paying an accountant to do a separate return.

However, if you are completing your tax returns for a base income year, we recommend that you do not report any of the student's or student's siblings' investment income (i.e. interest, dividends, and capital gains) on your tax return. By filing a separate return for those children, you remove that income from your AGI, and lower your Expected Family Contribution. (We'll discuss reporting of the student's income later in this chapter.)

**TIP 6:**
During base income years, do not report children's investment income on the parents' tax return. File a separate return for each child.

# Leveraged Investments

An important way in which the financial aid formulas differ from the tax code is in the handling of the income from leveraged investments. You leverage your investments by borrowing against them. The most common example of leverage is margin debt. Margin is a loan against the value of your investment portfolio usually made by a brokerage house so that you can buy more of whatever it is selling—for example, stock.

Let's say you had $5,000 in interest and dividend income, but you also had to pay $2,000 in tax-deductible investment interest on a margin loan. The IRS may allow you to deduct your investment interest expenses from your investment income on Schedule A. For *tax* purposes, you may have only $3,000 in net investment income.

Unfortunately, for *financial aid* purposes, interest expenses from Schedule A are not taken into account. As far as the colleges are concerned, you had $5,000 in income.

Of course you will be able to subtract the value of your margin debt from the value of your *total assets*. However, under the aid formulas, you cannot deduct the *interest* on your margin debt from your investment *income*.

During base income years, you should avoid—or at least minimize—margin debt because it will inflate your income in the eyes of the FAOs. If there is no way to avoid leveraging your investments during the college years, you should at least call the FAO's attention to the tax-deductible investment interest you are paying. Be prepared to be surprised at how financially unsavvy your FAO may turn out to be. He may not understand the concept of margin debt at all, in which case you will have to educate him. In our experience, we have found that if the situation is explained, many FAOs will make some allowance for a tax-deductible investment interest expense.

**TIP 7:**
During base income years, avoid large amounts of margin debt.

## Schedule 1, Line 10—Taxable Refund of State and Local Income Taxes

Many people see their tax refunds as a kind of Christmas club—a way to save some money that they would otherwise spend—so they arrange to have far too much deducted from their paychecks. Any accountant knows that this is actually incredibly dumb. In effect, you are giving the government the use of your money, interest-free. If you were to put this money aside during the year in an account that earned interest, you could make yourself a substantial piece of change.

## So Why Does Your Accountant Encourage a Refund?

Even so, many accountants go along with the practice for a couple of reasons. First, they know that their clients are unlikely to go to the bother of setting up an automatic payroll savings plan at work. Second, they know that clients feel infinitely better when they walk out of their accountant's office with money in their pockets. It tends to offset the large fee the accountant has just charged for his or her services. Third, a large refund doesn't affect how much tax you ultimately pay. Whether you have your company withhold just the right amount, or way too much, over the years you still end up paying exactly the same amount in taxes.

So accountants have gotten used to the practice, and yours probably won't tell you (or maybe doesn't know) that a large refund is the very last thing you want during base income years. Unfortunately, a large refund can seriously undermine your efforts to get financial aid. Here's why:

If you itemize deductions and get a refund from state and local taxes, the following year you'll have to report the refund as part of your federal adjusted gross income. Over the years, of course, this will have little or no effect on how much you pay in taxes, but for aid purposes, you've just raised your Line 7. This might not seem like it could make a big difference, but if you collect an average state and local refund of $1,600 each year over the four college years, you may have cost yourself as much as $3,000 in grant money.

During college years, it is very important to keep your withholding as close as possible to the amount you will actually owe in taxes at the end of the year.

**TIP 8:**
If you itemize your deductions, avoid large state and local tax refunds.

## Schedule 1, Line 11—Alimony Received

Even though this may seem like an obvious point, we have found it important to remind people that the amount you enter on this line is not what you were *supposed* to receive in alimony, but the amount you actually got. Please don't list alimony payments your ex never made.

In fact, if your ex fell behind in alimony payments, it's important that you notify the college financial aid offices that you have received less income this year than a court of law thought you needed in order to make ends meet.

By the same token, if you received retroactive alimony payments, you would also want to contact the colleges to let them know that the amount you listed on this line is larger this year than the amount you normally receive. In a situation like this, you might be tempted to put down on the financial aid form only the amount of alimony you were supposed to receive. Please don't even think about it. Your need analysis information will be checked against your tax return. By the time they've finished their audit, and you've finished explaining that this was a retroactive payment, all the college's aid money might be gone.

## Schedule 1, Line 12—Business Income

As we mentioned earlier, it can be to your advantage to become an independent contractor if you have large unreimbursed business expenses. A self-employed person is allowed to deduct business expenses from gross receipts on schedule C. This now much smaller number (called net profit or loss) is written down on Line 12 of Schedule 1 of the 1040 form, thus reducing both taxable income and the family contribution to college tuition.

We will discuss running your own business in greater detail in the "Special Topics" chapter of this book; however, a few general points should be made now.

Many salaried people run their own businesses on the side, which enables them to earn extra money while deducting a good part of this income as business expenses. However, before you run out and decide that your stamp collecting hobby has suddenly become a business, you should be aware that the IRS auditors are old hands at spotting "dummy" businesses, and the colleges' FAOs aren't far behind.

On the other hand, if you have been planning to start a legitimate business, then by all means, the time to do it is NOW (provided this entity will not result in a great loss of aid due to you no longer being eligible for the SNT or Automatic Zero-EFC).

---

 **TIP 9:**
Setting up a legitimate business on the side will enable you to deduct legitimate business expenses, and may reduce your AGI.

---

Just bear in mind that a business must be run with the intention of showing a profit to avoid running afoul of the IRS "hobby loss" provision. The institutional methodology now adds back business losses to your AGI.

## Schedule 1, Lines 13a and 14—Capital Gains or Losses, Other Gains or Losses

When you buy a stock, bond, or any other financial instrument at one price and then sell it for more than you paid in the first place, the difference between the two prices is considered a capital gain. If you sold it for less than you paid in the first place, the difference may be considered a capital loss. We say "may be" because while you are required to report gains on all transactions, the IRS does not necessarily recognize *losses* on all types of investments.

When you sell an asset, your net worth really stays the same; you are merely converting the asset into the cash it's worth at that particular instant. However, for tax and financial aid purposes, a capital gain on the asset is considered additional *income* in the year that you sold your asset.

During base income years, you want to avoid capital gains if you can because they inflate your income. When you sell a stock, not only does the FAO assess the cash value from the sale of the stock (which is considered an asset) but she also assesses the capital gain (which is considered income).

If you need cash it is usually better to borrow against your assets rather than to sell them. Using your stock, or the equity in your house as collateral, you can take out a loan. This helps you in three ways: you don't have to report any capital gains on the financial aid form; your net assets are reduced in the eyes of the FAO since you now have a debt against that asset; and in some cases, you get a tax deduction for part of the interest on the loan.

**TIP 10:**
If possible, avoid large capital gains during base income years.

However, there may be times when it is necessary to take capital gains. Below you will find some strategies to avoid losing aid because of capital gains. The following are somewhat aggressive strategies, and each would require you to consult your accountant and/or stockbroker:

- If you have to take capital gains, at least try to offset them with losses. Examine your portfolio. If you have been carrying a stock that's been a loser for several years, it might be time to admit that it is never going to be worth what you paid for it, and take the loss. This will help to cancel your gain.

- You can elect to spread your stock losses and gains over several years. One example: The IRS allows you to deduct capital losses directly from capital gains. If your losses exceed your gains, you can deduct up to $3,000 of the excess from other income—in the year the loss occurred. However, net losses over $3,000 *are carried over to future years*. It might be possible to show net losses during several of the base income years, and hold off on taking net gains until after your kids are done with college.

- The institutional methodology does not recognize capital losses that exceed gains. However, certain kinds of government aid are awarded without reference to the schools— for example, the Pell Grant and some state-funded aid programs. Because this aid is awarded strictly by the numbers, a capital loss can make a big difference. (Consult your state aid authorities and the individual schools to see how capital losses will be treated.)

- If you are worried about falling stock prices but don't want to report a capital gain, you should consult your stockbroker. There may be ways to lock in a particular price *without* selling the stock.

- If you have any atypically large capital gain in a base income year that you must report on an aid form, you should write to the colleges explaining that your income is not normally so high.

# The Sale of Your Home

The Taxpayer Relief Act of 1997 changed the way capital gains from the sale of a primary residence are treated. For any sale after May 6, 1997 you are permitted to exclude up to $250,000 in capital gains every two years on the sale of your home (up to $500,000 for a married couple filing jointly). To qualify, the home must have been your primary residence that you owned and occupied for at least two of the last five years prior to the sale. Any gains in excess of the exclusion limits would, of course, be subject to income taxes.

Representatives at the Department of Education and the College Board have stated that only gains above the excludable amounts need to be reported on the aid forms, since they are then part of your Adjusted Gross Income. If you sold your home and must complete the aid forms before you purchase another property, you'll need to report the money you have from the sale as part of your assets on the aid forms. However, you should be sure to write a letter to the FAOs explaining that you will no longer have those assets once you purchase another property, if that is the case.

# Line 4b—IRAs, Pensions, and Annuities

This line on the 1040 form covers any withdrawals (called "distributions" by the IRS) made during the year from Individual Retirement Accounts (IRAs). Most financial planning experts advise against early withdrawals before retirement since one of the biggest benefits of an IRA is the tax-deferred compounding of investment income while the funds are in the account. In many cases, early withdrawals will trigger a 10% penalty (if you took out the funds before age 59 1/2) and you'll have to pay income taxes on part or all of the money withdrawn. (Which part of the withdrawal will be subject to income taxes will depend on whether your prior contributions were deductible or not.)

If that is not enough bad news to discourage you, consider the financial aid implications. Any IRA withdrawal during a base income year will raise your income in the financial aid formulas thereby reducing aid eligibility. The part of the withdrawal that is taxable will raise that all-important Line 7 on your tax return; the portion that is tax-free will also affect your EFC, since the aid formulas assess untaxed income as well.

To demonstrate the negative impact of an early IRA withdrawal, let's look at an example of a parent, age 55, who took funds out of an IRA during the first base income year. The family is in the 22% federal tax bracket and since all prior IRA contributions were tax deductible, the withdrawal will be fully taxable. After subtracting the early withdrawal penalties, income taxes, and reduced aid eligibility, there will be only about 32 cents on the dollar left. Get the point? Early withdrawals from IRAs should be avoided at all costs.

A legitimate rollover of an IRA (when you move your money from one type of IRA investment into another within 60 days) is not considered a withdrawal. You do have to report a rollover to the IRS on the 1040 form, but it is not subject to penalties (so long as you stick to the IRS guidelines) nor is it considered income for financial aid purposes.

---

**TIP 11:**
Try to avoid IRA distributions during base income years.

---

Parents sometimes ask whether it is possible to borrow against the money in their IRAs. You are not allowed to borrow against the assets you have in an IRA. The IRS calls this a "prohibited transaction."

*Note: The Taxpayer Relief Act enacted in August 1997 provides for penalty-free distributions from IRAs after December 31, 1997 if the funds are used to pay for qualified educational expenses (tuition, fees, books, supplies, room and board for the undergraduate or graduate studies of the taxpayer, taxpayer's spouse, or taxpayer's child or grandchild). The words "penalty-free" only apply to the 10% early withdrawal penalty. As such, you should not assume that you will not be penalized in the financial aid process or that you will not owe any income taxes if you withdraw funds for qualified education expenses.*

*The Act also provides taxpayers the opportunity to convert an existing IRA into a Roth IRA, provided certain criteria are met. The major benefit of this type of IRA is the fact that almost all withdrawals from a Roth IRA after age 59 1/2 will be totally tax-free. While the 10 % early withdrawal penalty will not apply to this conversion, income taxes must be paid on the entire amount converted unless part of the account represents prior contributions to a non-deductible IRA. If you converted your IRA into a Roth IRA in 2018 you must report this conversion as part of Line 4b on the IRS 1040, thereby raising your income and your EFC in the aid formulas. However, it is important to notify the financial aid offices about any such conversion since the U.S. Department of Education has granted colleges the ability to adjust the family contribution for this unusual transaction. (We'll discuss the IRAs and Roth IRAs in more detail in Chapter Ten.)*

## If You've Just Retired

As people wait until later in life to have children, it is becoming more commonplace to see retirees with children still in college. If you have recently retired and are being forced to take distributions from traditional IRAs, we suggest that you pull out the minimum amount possible. The government computes what this minimum amount should be based on your life expectancy (the longer you're expected to live, the longer they are willing to spread out the payments). Because it turns out that the average American's life expectancy is higher at 66 than it is at 65, it pays to get them to recalculate your minimum distribution for each year your child is in college. Obviously, if you need the money now, then you should take it. But try to withdraw as little as possible, since IRA distributions increase your income and thus reduce financial aid.

*Note: You are not required to take distributions from Roth IRAs regardless of your age.*

Regarding aid, the same is true of pension distributions, as well as any distributions from annuities, which are now combined with IRA distributions on the same line of the IRS 1040. Sometimes it is possible to postpone retirement pensions or roll them over into an IRA. If you can afford to wait until your child is through college, you will increase your aid eligibility. The money isn't going anywhere, and it's earning interest.

*Note: Any unusually large or early distributions from IRAs or pensions should be explained to the college financial aid offices. Any "rollovers" should also be explained when you submit a copy of your taxes to the school. Since you must include "rollovers" as part of the amount you list on Line 4a of the IRS 1040, some FAOs have been known to incorrectly assume that the family received the funds, but failed to report this untaxed income on the aid forms. If they make this error, the EFC they determine will be much higher than it should be.*

## Schedule 1, Line 17—Rents, Royalties, Estates, Partnerships, Trusts, and Schedule 1, Line 18—Farm Income

Like Schedule C income, items coming under these categories are computed by adding up your gross receipts and then subtracting expenses, repairs, and depreciation. Be especially thorough about listing all expenses during base income years.

If you have a summer house or other property, you may have been frustrated in the past, because costly as it is to operate a second home, you haven't been able to deduct any of these expenses. You could consider renting it out while your son or daughter is in college. The extra income might be offset (perhaps significantly) by the expenses that you'll now be legitimately able to subtract from it. By changing how interest expense and real estate taxes are reflected on your tax return (from an itemized deduction on Schedule A to a reduction of rental income on Line 17 on Schedule 1) you reduce the magical AGI. There are special tax considerations for "passive loss" activities and recapture of depreciation, so be sure to consult your advisor before proceeding with this strategy, and remember that many private colleges and a few state schools will not recognize losses of this type when awarding institutional funds since the institutional methodology adds back losses to income.

## Schedule 1, Line 19—Unemployment Compensation

If you are unemployed, benefits received during the base income year are considered income under the aid formula. However, some special consideration may be granted to you. We will discuss this in more detail under the "Recently Unemployed Worker" heading in Chapter Nine.

## Lines 5a and 5b—Social Security Benefits

Total social security benefits are listed on Line 5a. The taxable portion of those benefits is listed on Line 5b. Whether you have to pay tax on social security benefits depends on your circumstances. Consult the instructions that come with your tax return. For some parents who have other income, part of the social security benefits received may be taxable.

## Schedule 1, Line 21—Other Income

Any miscellaneous income that did not fit into any of the other lines goes here. Some examples: money received from jury duty or from proctoring SAT exams, extra insurance premiums paid by your employer, gambling winnings.

Gambling winnings present their own problem. The IRS allows you to deduct gambling losses against winnings. However the deduction can, once again, only be taken as part of your itemized deductions on schedule A. Since this happens *after* Line 7, it is not a deduction as far as the need analysis computer is concerned.

Since gambling losses are not likely to provoke much sympathy in the FAOs, we don't think there would be any point to writing them a letter about this one. During the college years, you might just want to curtail gambling.

This is the last type of taxable income on the 1040, but don't start jumping for joy yet. The colleges are interested in more than just your taxable income.

## Untaxed Income

We've just looked at all the types of income that the IRS taxes, and discussed how the financial aid process impacts on it. There are several other types of income that the IRS doesn't bother to tax. Unfortunately, the colleges do not feel so benevolent. While the IRS allows you to shelter certain types of income, the colleges will assess this income as well in deciding whether and how much financial aid you receive.

Here are the other types of income the need analysis forms will ask you to report, and some strategies.

## Untaxed Social Security Benefits

Any social security benefits that are not taxable are defined as "untaxed social security benefits" in the financial aid regulations. Untaxed social security benefits (as well as certain other untaxed income items that years ago were previously assessed as income in the Federal Methodology) do not need to reported as untaxed income on the FAFSA. Such excluded untaxed social security benefits could include any untaxed benefits paid for the student (whether such benefits are paid to the student directly or paid to the parent for the benefit of the student), untaxed benefits paid to a parent for other children, or the untaxed portion of any social security benefits paid for the benefit of the parent(s) themselves. Depending on other income received by the parents during the year, a parent's own social security benefits may be fully tax-free or partially tax-free. Since any taxable social security benefits are part of the Adjusted Gross Income, they will continue to be assessed in the federal formula and the institutional formula.

Since the social security benefits for most students normally end before the student starts college (and are normally tax-free), the Institutional Methodology has excluded any untaxed social security benefits received for the student from untaxed income for a number of years. However, untaxed benefits paid to a parent for children other than the student and/or the untaxed portion of any social security benefits received by the parent(s) themselves will continue to be assessed in the IM.

We'll discuss social security benefits in greater detail in Part Three, "Filling Out the Standardized Forms."

## Payments Made into IRAs, Keoghs, 401(k)s, 403(b)s, and TDAs

IRAs (Individual Retirement Accounts), Keoghs, 401(k)s, 403(b)s, and TDAs (short for Tax Deferred Annuities) are all retirement provisions designed to supplement or take the place of pensions and social security benefits. The tax benefit of these plans is that in most cases they allow you to defer paying income tax on contributions until you retire, when presumably your tax bracket will be lower. The investment income on the funds is also allowed to accumulate tax-deferred until the time you start to withdraw the funds.

The 401(k) and 403(b) plans are supplemental retirement provisions set up by your employer in which part of your salary is deducted (at your request) from your paycheck and placed in a trust account for your benefit when you retire. Some companies choose to match part of your contributions to the plans. Keoghs are designed to take the place of an ordinary pension for self-employed individuals. TDAs fulfill much the same purpose for employees of tax-exempt religious, charitable, or educational organizations.

IRAs are supplemental retirement provisions for everyone. Contributions to these plans are tax-deductible in many cases. For example, if an unmarried individual is not covered by a retirement plan at work or a self-employed retirement plan, she can make tax-deductible contributions to an IRA of up to $6,000 (up to $7,000 if age 50 or older) regardless of her income level. If a person is covered by a retirement plan, his contribution to an IRA may or may not be tax-deductible, depending on his income level.

*Note: The tax bills enacted in August 1997 and June 2001 involve many changes to the IRA rules. Before making any new contributions, withdrawals, or changes to an IRA, you should be sure to consult IRS Publication 590 for the corresponding tax year (it covers the IRA regulations and is free from Uncle Sam), or seek the advice of a qualified professional who is familiar with the tax laws as well as the financial aid regulations.*

## Financial Aid Ramifications of Retirement Provisions

Retirement provisions are wonderful ways to reduce your current tax burden while building a large nest egg for your old age—but how do they affect financial aid?

The intent of current financial aid laws is to protect the money that you have built up in a retirement provision. Assets that have *already* been contributed to IRAs, Keoghs, 401(k)s, and so on by the date you fill out the standardized aid form do not have to appear on that form. In most cases, the FAOs will never know that this money exists. Thus loading up on contributions to retirement provisions before the college years begin makes enormous sense.

However, any tax-deductible contribution that you make into these plans voluntarily during the base income years is treated just like regular income. The IRS may be willing to give you a tax break on this income, but the FAOs assess it just like all the rest of your income, up to a maximum rate of 47%. Deductible contributions made to retirement provisions during base income years will not reduce your income under the aid formula. If you can still afford to make them, fine. Most parents find they need all their available cash just to pay their family contribution. Contributions to Roth IRAs or non-deductible Traditional IRAs are not considered untaxed income since they do not reduce your AGI.

These plans remain an excellent way of protecting assets. Try to contribute as much as you can before the first base income year. Parents sometimes ask us how colleges will know about their contributions to 401(k) or 403(b) plans, or to tax-deferred annuities. These contributions usually show up in boxes 12a-d of your W-2 form, codes D, E, F, G, H, and S. Don't even think about not listing them.

A possible exception to this scenario would come up if contributions to these plans would reduce your income below the $50,000 AGI cut-off for the Simplified Needs Test. For example, let's say your total salary from work is $45,000, and your only other income is $7,000 in interest income (from $500,000 in assets you have parked in Certificates of Deposit). By deferring $2,500 for the year into a 401(k) plan, your adjusted gross income will now be $49,500, and your untaxed income will be $2,500—making you potentially eligible for the simplified needs test which will exclude your assets from the federal formula. Had you not made the contribution to the 401(k) plan, your AGI would be $52,000 and your assets would be assessed (at up to 5.65% per year for parental assets, and 20% per year for student assets).

## Tax-Exempt Interest Income

Even though the government is not interested in a piece of your tax-free investments, the colleges are. Some parents question whether there is any need to tell the colleges about tax-free income if it does not appear on their federal income tax return.

In fact, tax-free interest income is supposed to be entered on Line 2a of the 1040. This is not an item the IRS tends to flag, but there are excellent reasons why you should never hide these items. For one thing, tax law changes constantly. If your particular tax-free investment becomes taxable or reportable next year, how will you explain the sudden appearance of substantial taxable interest income? Or what if you need to sell your tax-free investment? You will then have to report a capital gain, and the FAO will want to know where all the money came from.

## More Untaxed Income

Other untaxed income that is included in the federal financial aid formula includes but is not limited to the tax-free portion of any pensions or annuities received (excluding rollovers), the tax-free portion of IRA distributions (excluding rollovers), child support received, workers' compensation, veterans noneducation benefits, the Health Savings Account (HSA) deduction (Schedule 1, IRS 1040 Line 25), and living allowances paid to members of the military and clergy. Some other categories of untaxed income (for example, untaxed disability benefits) will need to be reported on the FAFSA form as well. There is little to do about this kind of income except write it down. As with alimony, child support reported should include only the amount you actually received, not what you were supposed to receive.

*Note: The federal methodology excludes contributions to, or payments from, flexible spending arrangements. The institutional methodology will consider pre-tax contributions withheld from wages for dependent care, medical spending, and HSA accounts as part of untaxed income for the 2020–2021 award year. But along with the HSA deduction, schools will have the opportunity to exclude them. In addition, the following types of untaxed income (which previously were assessed in the federal formula, but are now not considered in the FM) will continue to be considered part of untaxed income in the IM: the earned income credit, the additional child credit, welfare benefits, the credit for federal tax on special fuels, and the foreign income exclusion.*

# Expenses

After adding up all your income, the need analysis formulas provide a deduction for some types of expenses. A few of these expenses mirror the adjustments to income section of the 1040 income tax form. Many parents assume that all the adjustments to income from the IRS form can be counted on the standardized financial aid forms. Unfortunately this is not the case. Likewise, many parents assume that all of the itemized tax deductions they take on schedule A will count on the financial aid forms as well. Almost none of these are included in the financial aid formula. Let's look at adjustments to income first.

## Expenses According to the IRS: Adjustments to Income

### Schedule 1, Line 23—Educator expenses

This adjustment to income involves educators in both public and private elementary and secondary schools who work at least 900 hours during a school year as a teacher, instructor, counselor, principal, or aide and who have certain qualifying out-of-pocket expenses. The maximum deduction for this item is $250 per taxpayer, and there are other criteria you need to meet. If allowable, it is to your advantage to take the deduction as an adjustment to income.

### Schedule 1, Line 26—Moving Expenses

Job-related moving expenses are deductible as an adjustment to income. Years ago, these expenses could be taken only as part of your itemized deductions, and did not affect your aid eligibility. Since this item will both reduce your tax liability and potentially increase your aid eligibility, you should be sure to include all allowable moving expenses. There is a great deal of fine print in the tax law regarding what constitutes a moving expense, so be sure to read the IRS instructions or consult a competent advisor.

### Schedule 1, Line 27—Deductible Part of Self-Employment Tax

Self-employed individuals can deduct one half of the self-employment taxes they pay. The federal and institutional formulas take this deduction into account.

### Schedule 1, Lines 28 and 32—IRA Deductions and Self-Employed SEP, SIMPLE, and Qualified Plans Deductions

As we explained above, while these constitute legitimate tax deductions, contributions to deductible IRAs, SEPs, KEOGHs, and other plans that can be deducted on Line 28 or Line 32 of Schedule 1 will not reduce your income under the FM or IM aid formulas.

However, some forms of state aid (which do not use the federal methodology employed by the colleges themselves) may be boosted by contributions to retirement plans that reduce your AGI as some state programs are based solely on taxable income. We'll discuss this in detail in Chapter Six, "State Aid." As we mentioned earlier, contributions to an IRA could lower your AGI below the $50,000 cap for the Simplified Needs Test. Individuals who make contributions to plans that are deducted on Line 28 of Schedule 1 are either self-employed or a partner and therefore cannot meet the Simplified Needs Test.

### Schedule 1, Line 29—Self-Employed Health Insurance Deduction

This is another adjustment to income recognized by the FAO. If you are self-employed or own more than 2% of the shares of an S corporation, there are two places on the 2018 IRS 1040 form where you may be able to take medical deductions. On Line 29 of Schedule 1, you can now deduct 100% of your qualifying health insurance premiums. It is to your advantage to take the deduction here, rather than lump it with all your other medical expenses on Schedule A. First, because it will reduce your AGI, and second, because it is a sure deduction here. If your total medical expenses do not add up to a certain percentage of your total income, you won't get a deduction for medical expenses at all on your taxes. In addition, high medical expenses (other than those included here on Line 29) are no longer an automatic deduction in the federal aid formula as they were prior to the 1993–94 school year. We'll describe this in detail, under "Medical Deduction" on pages 88–89.

### Schedule 1, Line 30—Penalty on Early Withdrawal of Savings, and Line 31a—Alimony paid

If you took an early withdrawal of savings before maturity, which incurred a penalty and/or you paid out alimony, these amounts will be claimed here. The FM and IM aid formulas grant you a deduction for these two adjustments to income as well.

### Schedule 1, Line 33—Student Loan Interest Deduction

The Taxpayer Relief Act of 1997 created this adjustment to income. This can involve loans used to cover your own post-secondary educational expenses as well as those of your spouse or any other dependent at the time the loan was taken out. We'll discuss more of the fine print in Chapter Ten. You should realize that any deduction claimed here will reduce your income under both the federal and the institutional formulas.

### Schedule 1, Line 24—Certain Business Expenses of Reservists, Performing Artists, and Fee-Basis Government Officials; Other Write-In Adjustments not Reported on Schedule 1, Lines 23–35, but included as Part of Schedule 1, Line 36

While each of these adjustments to income will lower your AGI—and therefore your EFC—they are not applicable for the vast majority of tax filers.

# Other Expenses According to the Financial Aid Formula

You've just seen all the adjustments to income that the IRS allows. The colleges allow you a deduction for several other types of expenses for financial aid purposes as well:

## Federal Income Tax Paid

The advice we are about to offer may give your accountant a heart attack. Obviously, you want to pay the lowest taxes possible, but timing can come into play during the college years. The higher the taxes you pay during a base income year, the lower your family contribution will be. This is because the federal income taxes you pay count as an expense item in the aid formula. There are certain sets of circumstances when it is possible to save money by paying higher taxes.

The principle here is to end up having paid the same amount of taxes over the long run, but to concentrate the taxes into the years the colleges are scrutinizing, thus increasing your aid eligibility.

Let's look at a hypothetical example. Suppose that you make exactly the same amount of money in two separate years. You are in the 22% income tax bracket, and the tax tables don't change over these two years. Your federal tax turns out to be $6,000 the first year and $6,000 the second year, for a total tax bill of $12,000 for the two years.

Let's also suppose that you decide to make an IRA contribution during only one of the two years, but you aren't sure in which year to make the contribution. You're married, 52 years old, and neither of you is covered by a pension plan at work, so you are able to make a tax-deductible IRA contribution of $6,500. This turns out to reduce your federal taxes by $1,430 for the year in which you make the contribution. Since, in this case, your tax situation is precisely the same for both years, it doesn't make much difference in which year you take the deduction.

| | |
|---|---|
| $12,000 | total taxes over 2 years (if no IRA contribution made) |
| − $ 1,430 | tax savings for IRA contribution |
| $10,570 | total taxes for the 2 years |

Over the two years, either way, you end up paying a total of about $10,570 in federal taxes.

# It's All a Matter of Timing

Here's where timing comes in. What if the second of the two years also happens to be your first base income year? In this case, you're much better off making the contribution during the previous year. By doing so, as we've already explained, you shelter the $6,500 asset from the need analysis formula, and get a $1,430 tax break in the first year.

But much more important, by making the contribution during the first year, you choose to pay the higher tax bill in the second year—the base income year—which in turn lowers your Expected Family Contribution. Over the two years, you're still paying close to the same amount in taxes, but you've concentrated the taxes into the base income year where it will do you some good.

**TIP 12:**
Concentrate your federal income taxes into base income years to lower your Expected Family Contribution.

Obviously, if you can afford to make IRA contributions every year, you should do so; building a retirement fund is a vital part of any family's long-term planning. However, if like many families, you find that you can't afford to contribute every year during college years, you can at least use timing to increase your expenses in the eyes of the FAOs. By loading up on retirement provision contributions during non-base income years, and avoiding tax-deductible retirement contributions and other tax-saving measures during base income years, you can substantially increase your aid eligibility.

*The above example assumed that tax rates would be the same from year to year. Should tax rates change from one year to the next, you will need to balance your tax planning with your financial aid planning to determine the best course of action.*

## Charitable Contributions

Large donations to charity are a wonderful thing, both from a moral standpoint and a tax standpoint—but not during a base income year. When you lower your taxes, you raise your family contribution significantly. We aren't saying you should stop giving to charity, but we do recommend holding off on large gifts until after the base income years.

# Extra Credits

When you are asked questions about U.S. income taxes paid on the FAFSA, the government and the colleges are not interested in how much taxes you had withheld during the year, or whether or not you are entitled to a refund. Instead, they are interested in your federal income tax liability after certain tax credits are deducted, which happens to be the amount of Line 13 on the 1040 minus Line 46 on Schedule 2 of the 2018 1040. While most tax credits that you claim will eventually reduce your aid eligibility (since lower taxes mean lower expenses against income in the formulas), the tax benefits from these credits will be much greater than the amount of aid that is lost. As such, you should be sure to deduct any and all tax credits that you are entitled to claim on your tax return.

Be aware that under the federal formula, any education tax credits claimed (such as the American Opportunity Credit and the Lifetime Learning Credit) will not reduce aid eligibility. While any nonrefundable education credits claimed—for 2018, these would be claimed on Line 50 of Schedule 3 of the IRS Form 1040—will reduce the amount of U.S. income taxes paid, they will also be considered an "exclusion from income," which in aid speak means a deduction against income. So in effect, any education credits claimed will reduce expenses and income by an equal amount, thereby allowing families and students the full benefit of the American Opportunity Credit or the Lifetime Learning Credit. (Later in Chapter Ten, we'll discuss some strategies to insure you get the maximum credits allowed by law; for now, we just want to focus on their aid impact.)

Unfortunately, the institutional formula has not been as benevolent. Since the nonrefundable education credits are not considered an exclusion against income, any nonrefundable credits claimed will partially reduce aid eligibility. However, the College Board will give colleges the option of having any refundable education credits added back to the amount of U.S. income taxes paid, so that any impact on aid will be negligible.

*Currently, the Federal Methodology reduces the amount of U.S taxes paid (reported on Line 13 of the 2018 1040) by the amount of any excess advance premium tax credit reported on Line 46 of Schedule 2 of the 1040. As we went to press, the College Board had not yet decided for the IM if they would use the amount on Line 13 of the 1040 for this item—or if they would mirror the FM and deduct any amount on Line 46 on Schedule 2.*

*Both the FM and IM do not consider any refundable portion of the American Opportunity Credit to be untaxed income. This would be claimed on Line 17c of the 2018 IRS 1040, using Form 8863 to calculate the amount of the refundable amount as well as the nonrefundable amount, if any, for the AOC or LLC. A nonrefundable credit can only be claimed if a taxpayer has income tax liability, while a refundable credit can be claimed even if the taxable income is so low that there is no resulting income tax liability.*

# The Alternative Minimum Tax

Until recently, those families who were subject to the Alternative Minimum Tax were actually penalized in the aid formulas—for while they had to pay the tax, the formulas did not take this additional tax into account. The Alternative Minimum Tax (AMT) is an additional tax that is incurred if certain deductions or tax credits reduce the amount of U.S. income taxes paid below a certain level. Many of our readers don't have to worry about the AMT since it usually impacts more individuals in the top income tax brackets.

But we have good news for those few readers who must pay the AMT. Federal income taxes paid in the financial aid formulas currently includes any Alternative Minimum Tax liability. This will generally reduce the EFC in both the federal and institutional methodologies for those subject to the AMT, since the amount of federal income taxes paid is a deduction against income in the formulas.

# Deduction for Social Security and Medicare Taxes

The financial aid formulas give you a deduction for the Medicare and social security taxes (otherwise known as FICA) that you pay. Parents often ask how the colleges do this since there doesn't seem to be a question about social security taxes on the financial aid forms. The deduction is actually made automatically by computer, but it is based on two questions on the financial aid form. These questions are in disguise.

On the FAFSA and the PROFILE, the two questions are "father's income earned from work," and "mother's income earned from work." At first glance these questions appear to be about income. In fact, for tax filers these are expense questions. If you minimize the amounts you put down here, you may cost yourself aid.

Therefore, you should be sure to include all sources of income from work on which you've paid FICA or Medicare taxes: wages (box 1 of your W-2), income from self-employment (Line 12 on Schedule 1 of the 1040), income from partnerships subject to self-employment taxes (not including income from limited partnerships), deferred compensation (tax-filers only), and combat pay (for servicemen and servicewomen).

# A Financial Aid Catch-22

Wages that you defer into a 401(k), 403(b), or other retirement plan are not subject to income tax by the IRS, but you still pay social security taxes and/or Medicare taxes on them. (For 2018, income above $128,400 was exempt from FICA. However, there is no income ceiling on Medicare taxes.)

The strange thing is that, while the purpose of the questions regarding income earned from work on the financial aid forms is to allow the need analysis companies to calculate the social security and Medicare taxes you paid, the instructions for the forms don't tell you to include deferred income. For example, if your income was $40,000 last year and you deferred $5,000 of it into a 401(k), the instructions tell you to put down $35,000 as your income from work.

## Welcome to the Wacky World of Financial Aid

The instructions are wrong. It's just that simple. Other aid professionals agree with us. So please ignore the instructions. If you contributed any pre-tax wage income (subject to Social Security and/or Medicare taxes) into tax-deferred retirement accounts, include it as part of the question on income earned from work on the FAFSA.

Will this make a real difference to your aid package? It depends on how much you defer. Say you and your spouse defer $5,000 each, and you are in the 47th percentile in aid assessment. By including this money as part of income earned from work, you could increase your aid eligibility by about $380 per year.

This might seem petty, but these small amounts—$380 here, $200 there—can add up. Put another way, this is $380 a year ($1,520 over four years) that you may not have to borrow and pay interest on.

*Note: There are two situations when you should not include your tax-deferred contributions to retirement plans as part of income earned from work. If you do not file a tax return, your income earned from work will be treated as an income item when the data is processed. Since you must also include such contributions as untaxed income on the forms, your income will be overstated in this situation. You should also avoid adding such contributions to your income earned from work if this would disqualify you from otherwise meeting the criteria for the Simplified Needs Test or the Automatic Zero-EFC (see pages 58–61).*

## State and Local Tax Allowance

This is another calculation that is done automatically by the need assessment computer. The computer takes the sum of your taxable and untaxable income and multiplies it by a certain percentage based on the state you live in to determine your deduction. The formula for each state is slightly different. (See Table 8 in the Worksheets and Forms section of this book.)

This works very well for people who live and work in the same state, but presents real problems for everyone else. If you live in one state but work in another where the taxes are higher, you may be paying more in taxes than the formula indicates. The financial need computer isn't programmed to deal with situations like this, and people who don't fit the program get penalized.

The only way to deal with this is to write to the individual colleges' aid offices to let them know about your special situation.

# Employment Allowance

Under the federal and institutional methodologies, if you are a single parent who works, or if you are part of a two-parent, two-income family, then you qualify for the employment allowance. In the 2018 base income year, under the federal formula married couples will get a deduction of 35% of the lower wage earner's income earned from work up to a maximum deduction of $4,000. Single parents (i.e., separated, divorced, widowed, or never married) will get a deduction of 35% of their income earned from work up to a maximum deduction of $4,000. The employment allowance is figured out for you automatically by the need analysis computer based on three questions you answered on the FAFSA—namely father's income earned from work, mother's income earned from work, and of course, the question about the parent's marital status.

As we've said before, while these questions look like income questions, they are actually expense questions for tax filers. It is in your interest to make these figures as big as possible if you will file a tax return. Remember to include all your sources of income from work. While the College Board will not be publishing the institutional methodology for 2020–2021, it is expected a similar deduction will be granted.

# The Income Protection Allowance

Most parents find the income protection allowance (formerly known as the standard maintenance allowance) to be a bad joke. This is the federal financial aid formula's idea of how much money your family needs to house, feed, and clothe itself during one year. According to the formula:

- a family of 6 (one in college) can live on $40,490

- a family of 5 (one in college) can live on $34,620

- a family of 4 (one in college) can live on $29,340

- a family of 3 (one in college) can live on $23,760

- a family of 2 (one in college) can live on $19,080

The income protection allowance is based solely on the number of family members currently living in the household and the number of dependent children in college. It is determined by the U.S. government figures for the poverty line and does not take into account the cost of living in your part of the country. (See Table 10 in the Worksheets and Forms section.)

Many parents assume that a portion of their monthly mortgage payments will be deducted from their income on the aid formulas in much the same way as it is on their taxes. Unfortunately, this is not the case. The income protection allowance is supposed to include all housing expenses.

We strongly recommend that you sit down and write out a budget of how much it actually takes to keep your family going, and send it to the individual colleges. Include everything. In many parts of the country, the income protection allowance is fairly ludicrous, but it is up to you to show the FAO just how ludicrous it is in your case.

The institutional methodology uses current consumer expense survey data to determine this allowance in the formula. While the formula is not available, in the past the numbers have been somewhat higher than in the federal formula.

# Annual Education Savings Allowance

Recognizing the fact that parents should be saving for any younger siblings' college expenses while simultaneously financing the older child's college expenses, the College Board's IM includes a deduction against income called the Annual Education Savings Allowance. The PROFILE processor will automatically calculate the amount of this allowance, which was 1.52% of the parents' total income (up to a maximum of $2,770 for the 2010–2011 formula, which was the last year the IM was published) multiplied by the number of pre-college children, excluding the student applicant.

# Optional Expenses

Under the federal methodology, high unreimbursed medical and dental expenses as well as elementary/secondary school tuition for the student's siblings are no longer automatically deducted from income. However, you may well have to answer questions about these categories anyway on both the PROFILE form and the school's own aid forms—the reason being that under the institutional methodology or the schools' own aid policies, these items may be considered as deductions against income.

Even if you are only completing the FAFSA (which does not ask about these items) it still makes sense to let the FAOs know about any high expenses they would not otherwise find out about. As we have already mentioned, information like this should be sent directly to the schools under separate cover.

Here are some tips on how to answer questions about medical and tuition expenses.

## Medical Deduction

To be able to deduct medical expenses on your federal tax return, you must have expenses in excess of 10% of your AGI. (In 2017 and 2018, the threshold was temporarily lowered to 7.5%.) However, college financial aid guidelines are not necessarily as strict. Some families who don't qualify under federal tax law just assume they won't qualify under the financial aid rules either, so they enter "0" for their medical expenses on the aid forms. This can be a costly mistake.

Here's a quick example. Let's say your family's adjusted gross income is $50,000, and you had medical expenses of $3,000. As far as the IRS is concerned, you won't get a medical deduction this year. Your $3,000 medical bills fall well short of 10% of $50,000 ($5,000). However, under the financial aid formulas, you may indeed receive a deduction against income. Under the federal methodology, the FAOs can use their discretion for this item. Under the institutional methodology, the rules for this expense category are more defined.

Therefore even if you don't have enough medical and dental expenses to qualify under the federal tax law, don't assume that it would be a waste of time to disclose these figures. Many colleges are using the institutional methodology which in the past has granted an allowance for unreimbursed medical expenses in excess of 3.5% of your income. If you are filling out the PROFILE form, there is a place on the form to report this information. Many of the schools' separate financial aid forms ask for this information as well.

## What Constitutes a Medical Expense?

There are more than 100 legitimate medical deductions. Here are just a few: doctors, dentists, prescription eyeglasses, therapists, after-tax health insurance premiums that were deducted from your paycheck or that you paid personally, medical transportation and lodging.

*Note: Self-employed individuals and owners of more than 2% of the shares of a subchapter S corporation are better off deducting their health insurance premiums on Line 29 of Schedule 1 of the IRS 1040 form.*

## Whose Medical Expenses Can Be Included?

You should include medical expenses for every single member of your household, not just the student who is going to college. When families come in to see us, they inevitably start out by saying that they do not have much in the way of unreimbursed medical expenses.

However, when we get them to write it all down, it often turns out to be a hefty sum. Keep careful records and include EVERYTHING. Did you take a cab to and from the doctor's office? Did anyone get braces? Did anyone get contact lenses?

## And If We Have Very Low Medical Expenses?

Congratulations, but keep records anyway. The PROFILE form now will advise you to list 0 (zero) for an applicable year when the total is less than 3% of your income. But you may have to answer questions about these items on the schools' own aid forms. You might as well give the FAOs a realistic sense of what your monthly bills look like.

## Last Medical Point

We recommend that if you don't have medical expenses in excess of 3.0% of your total taxable and untaxable income each year, you might consider postponing some discretionary medical procedures and advancing others, in order to bunch your deductions together and pass the 3.0% mark during one particular year. This might seem at first to fly in the face of conventional wisdom. Facing the burden of college, many parents' first thought would be to put off braces for a younger child, for example. In fact, if you are in a base income year, it makes much more sense to get them now. Once you reach the 3.0% threshold, each dollar in excess may increase your aid eligibility by 47 cents.

Finally, if you anticipate large medical bills in the near future, you should certainly let the colleges know what's coming up.

# Elementary and Secondary School Tuition

If the child going to college will have a younger brother or sister concurrently attending a private elementary or secondary school, you may be able to get a deduction for part of the tuition you pay for the private school during the academicyear. Neither the federal nor the institutional methodologies provide an automatic deduction, but the PROFILE form and many of the individual college aid forms do ask questions about this category. The FAOs are supposed to use their judgment in deciding whether to make any deduction for younger children's tuition.

Obviously, you can't include the private high school tuition of the child who is now applying to college, because next year the student won't be there anymore. You are also not allowed to include the cost of pre-school (unless specified on the school's aid form). Nor can you include college tuition of other siblings. (Don't worry. If you have more than one child in college at the same time, this will be taken into account elsewhere.) When you write down the amount you pay in elementary and secondary school tuition, remember to subtract any scholarship money you receive.

*Years ago, the College Board's IM was interested in payments for siblings during the calendar year. Beginning with the 2017-2018 version of the PROFILE, the questions will now pertain to payments made during a particular academic year.*

## Keeping Track of Information

What makes all this complicated is that some of the schools you will be applying to will require just the FAFSA (which does not ask about medical expenses and siblings' tuition), others will also require the PROFILE form (which asks about medical expenses and siblings' tuition), and others will have their own forms as well. It's easy to forget which schools know what information.

If you apply to a school that requires only the FAFSA, they will not see any of the information you filled out on your PROFILE form. If that school does not ask questions about items such as unreimbursed medical expenses on their own aid form, and you consider this information important, you should send it to the school under separate cover.

In addition, some state grant aid programs will increase award amounts if you send them proof of high medical expenses.

## Good News for a Few Parents

The IRS will not allow you to deduct child support payments from your taxable income (although they may allow you to deduct alimony payments). However, the colleges do allow a deduction for the payment of child support, under both the FM and IM (excluding support paid for children in the household). The same is true for any part of your taxable income that consists of financial aid received by a parent in school.

## So Far So Good

Now that you've given the need analysis people all this information, they will add up all your taxable and untaxable income and then subtract all the expenses and adjustments they have decided to allow. What's left is your available income.

Available income will be assessed on a sliding scale. If your available income is zero (or less), the parents' contribution from income will be zero. If your available income is greater, the contribution will be greater. The parents' contribution from income can go only as high as 47% of available income under the federal formula and as high as 46% under the institutional methodology.

If you are applying to colleges that require the PROFILE form (and thus use the institutional methodology) the parents' contribution from income may be higher or lower than it would be under the federal methodology.

# Income and Expenses: How the Methodologies Differ

## Federal Methodology

- Excludes medical/dental expenses

- Income protection allowance based on poverty line figures from the 1960s, adjusted for inflation

- Excludes all untaxed social security benefits, the earned income credit, the additional child credit, welfare benefits, the foreign income exclusion, and the credit for federal tax on special fuels

## Institutional Methodology

- Provides an allowance for unreimbursed medical and dental expenses in excess of a percentage of income. (Based on historical data—as the formula is no longer published—which has been 3.5% for the past few years' versions of the IM)

- Excludes any untaxed social security benefits received for the student

- Income protection allowance based on current consumer expenditure survey data

- Provides a set-aside for younger siblings' educational costs

- Adds back losses that appear on Lines 12, 13, 14, 17, 18, and 21 of Schedule 1 of the IRS 1040

- Considers pre-tax flex-plan contributions for medical spending accounts and dependent care to be untaxed income. However, individual schools will have to option to exclude both from income—as well as deductible contributions to Health Savings Accounts (Line 25 on Schedule 1 of the IRS 1040)

- Gives colleges the option of making an allowance for elementary/secondary tuition paid for the student's siblings

- No Automatic Zero-EFC or Simplified Needs Test

- Nonrefundable education tax credits reduce aid eligibility, unless the school chooses to have them added back to U.S. income taxes paid

# Assets and Liabilities

Now that the need analysis companies know about your available income, they want to know about your assets and liabilities. On the standardized financial aid forms, these two items are joined at the hip. Liabilities are subtracted from assets to determine your net assets. In a nutshell, the strategies you will find in this section are designed to make the value of your assets look as small as possible, and the debts against your assets as large as possible.

## What Counts as an Asset?

Cash, checking and savings accounts, money market accounts, CDs, U.S. Savings Bonds, Educational IRAs, stocks, other bonds, mutual funds, trusts, ownership interests in businesses, and the current market value of real estate holdings other than your home.

None of these items appear directly on your tax return. However, your tax return will still provide the colleges with an excellent way to verify these assets. How? Most assets create income and/or tax deductions, both of which do appear on your tax return in the form of capital gains, capital losses, interest, dividends, and/or itemized deductions on Schedule A.

Assets in insurance policies and retirement provisions such as IRAs, Keoghs, annuities, and 401(k)s are generally not assessed in the aid formulas (though as we have already said, voluntary tax-deductible contributions to retirement provisions made during base income years must be listed as part of untaxed income). Cars are also excluded from the formula and don't have to be listed on the form. Coverdell ESAs (formerly known as Education IRAs) and Section 529 plans have some interesting quirks which we'll explain shortly.

### What About My Home?

Under the federal methodology, the value of your home is not considered part of your assets. This is great news and will help many families who own their own home to qualify for a Pell Grant and other federal aid programs. However, many colleges are using the more stringent institutional methodology to award their own funds. Under this formula, the value of your home will not be excluded from your assets.

Which schools will exclude the value of your home? It's safe to say that most state schools will do so. If a school asks you to complete the PROFILE form and/or asks you for the value of your home on their own aid form, then most likely the value of the home is going to be treated like other assets. You can bet that the highly selective private colleges that meet a high percentage of their financial aid students' need, will be looking closely at home equity. Other private colleges may or may not.

However, even if you're considering colleges that have decided to look at home value, the news is not all bad. Starting with the 2003–2004 award year, 28 highly selective private colleges and universities agreed to cap home value at 2.4 times the parents' total yearly income. In other words, if you earn $50,000 for the year, at these schools the value of your home (for assessment purposes) will be considered to be no more than $120,000 ($50,000 × 2.4)—even if you own a home worth $200,000.

It appears that the actions by these schools has had a "trickle down" effect as more and more schools that used to look at the full value of the home have ceased taking the total home equity into account when awarding their own aid funds. Some schools, including a number of those 28 schools, have more recently decided to cap the amount of home equity at two times income, while others will no longer assess home equity at all or will not assess it if the family's income is below a certain level.

One of the questions you may want to ask the FAO at any school you are considering is the way(s) they will treat home value—not at all, only if the income exceeds a certain amount, with the value capped at a certain percentage of income, with the equity capped at a particular percentage of income, or at full value.

Under the federal methodology, the definition of "home" is the primary residence. If you own a vacation home in addition to your primary residence, the vacation home will not be excluded from your assets. If you own a vacation home, and you rent your primary residence, the value of the vacation home will still not be excluded under the federal formula—as it is considered "other real estate."

## What About My Farm?

The value of your farm is not included as an asset under the federal methodology provided that the family lives on the farm and you can claim on Schedule F of the IRS 1040 that you "materially participated in the farm's operation." The Feds call this type of farm a "family farm." We'll discuss how to handle this situation in Part Three, "Filling Out the Standardized Forms." Under the institutional methodology, the value of any farm property is considered an asset.

## How Much Are My Assets Worth?

To repeat, the need analysis form is a snapshot of your financial situation. The value of most assets (with the exception of money in the bank) changes constantly, as financial markets rise and fall. The colleges want to know the value of your assets *on the day* you fill out the form.

### Remember, This is One Snapshot for Which You Don't Want to Look Your Best

When people sit down to fill out financial statements they have a tendency to want to put their best foot forward. After all, most of the time when you fill out one of these forms it is because you are applying for a credit card, or a bank loan, or hoping to be accepted by a country club or an exclusive condominium. Trying to look as fiscally healthy as possible has become almost automatic. However, you have to remember that in this case you are applying for financial aid. They aren't going to give it to you if you don't let them see the whole picture, warts and all. On the financial aid form, you don't want to gloss over your debts.

## What Counts as a Debt?

The only debts that are considered under the financial aid formulas are debts against the specific assets listed on the aid forms.

For example, you do NOT get credit for: unsecured loans, personal loans, educational loans like Stafford or PLUS loans for college, consumer debt such as outstanding credit card balances, or auto loans. If you have any debt of these types, you should realize that it will NOT be subtracted from your assets under the financial aid formulas.

It will be to your advantage to minimize these types of debt during the college years. In fact, you may want to convert these loans into debts that do get credit under the financial aid formulas.

You DO get credit for: margin loans, passbook loans, as well as home equity loans, first mortgages, and second mortgages on "other real estate." Of course, you will only get credit for debts on your *primary* residence if the college has decided to look at your home value.

**TIP 13:**
Convert debts that are not counted by the aid formulas into types of debt that do count.

Let's go through the different types of assets you have to report and discuss strategies for minimizing the appearance of those assets.

### Cash, Checking Accounts, Savings Accounts

The need analysis forms ask you to list any money in your accounts on the day you fill out the forms. However, you can't list this money if it isn't there.

We are not counseling you to go on a spending spree, but if you were planning to make a major purchase in the near future, you might as well make it now. If roof repairs are looming, if you can prepay your summer vacation, if you were going to buy a new car sometime in the next year, do it now, and pay cash. You were going to make these purchases anyway. By speeding up the purchase, you reduce the appearance of your cash assets.

---

**TIP 14:**
If you were going to buy soon, buy now and use cash.

---

Another way to reduce assets in the bank is to use the cash to pay off a liability that the colleges refuse to look at.

## Plastic Debt

If you have credit card debt, your need analysis form won't give a realistic picture of your net worth, because as far as the colleges are concerned, plastic debt doesn't exist. You could owe thousands of dollars on your VISA card, but the aid formula does not allow you to subtract this debt from your assets, or to subtract the interest on the debt from your income.

Any financial advisor will tell you that if you have any money in the bank at all, it is crazy not to pay off your credit card debt. Recently we had one parent say to us, "But it makes me feel secure to have $7,000 in the bank. I know I could pay my $2,000 MasterCard bill, but then I would have only $5,000 left."

There are three reasons why this is wrong-headed thinking.

First, any way you look at it, that parent really did have only $5,000. It is a complete illusion to think that you have more money just because you can see it in your bank account at the moment.

Second, this guy's $2,000 credit card debt was costing him a lot of money—12% each year. This was 12% that could not be deducted from income on his taxes or on his financial aid form. Meanwhile, the $2,000 he was keeping in the bank because it made him feel better, was earning all of 1% after taxes. He was being taken to the cleaners.

Third, and most important, by paying off his credit card debt he could reduce his net assets on the need analysis form, and pick up some more aid.

**TIP 15:**
Use cash in the bank to pay off credit card balances. This will reduce your assets and thus increase your eligibility for aid.

### Your Tax Bill

If you did not have enough tax withheld from your wages this year, and you will end up owing the IRS money, consider speeding up the completion of your taxes so that you can send in your return—with a check—before you complete the need analysis form.

If you are self-employed, you might consider prepaying your next quarterly estimate. The IRS is always pleased to receive the money early. You will lose out on the interest the money would have earned if it had stayed in your account a little longer, but this will probably be more than offset by your increased aid eligibility.

**TIP 16:**
Use cash in the bank to pay off tax bills to reduce your assets and increase your eligibility for aid.

You will notice on the FAFSA that next to the item "cash, savings, and checking accounts," there is no mention of debts as there is for the other asset categories on the form. For the most part, you can't have debts on these kinds of assets. There is one exception.

## Passbook Loans

With a passbook loan, you use your savings account as collateral for a loan. This is a legitimate debt against your asset. To get credit for the debt, you should include your savings account and the debt against it under "investments" (on the FAFSA) and under "investments" (on the PROFILE form).

# IRAs, Keoghs, 401(k)s, 403(b)s

In most cases, money that you contribute to a retirement provision—such as an IRA, Keogh, 401(k), or 403(b)—*before* the base income years begin is completely sheltered from the FAOs. That money isn't part of the snapshot; they can't touch it.

However, as we stated in our section on income, contributions that reduce your Adjusted Gross Income (AGI) made *during* base income years are a different story. While the IRS may allow you to deduct retirement provisions from your income, the financial aid formula does not. During base income years, voluntary tax-deductible contributions to these plans will be assessed just like regular income; they will be considered as part of your untaxed income that will be added to your AGI to help determine your total income in the aid formulas. (Note: non-deductible contributions have no impact on aid)

This does not mean that retirement provisions are a complete waste of time during the college years. To see the big picture, it helps to remember that the aid formula assesses both your income and your assets. Let's say a family had $30,000 in income last year. The FAOs will assess the $30,000 as income. Then, if any of that $30,000 is left in the bank on the day the family fills out the need analysis form, it will also be assessed a second time as an asset. However, if that family had made a contribution to a deductible IRA before filling out the need analysis form, the contribution would have been assessed at most, only once—as untaxed income (assuming the contribution reduced your AGI for a base income year. It would not be required to be listed as part of your assets on the FAFSA because the funds in retirement accounts are not a reportable asset category for purposes of that form. And while the CSS does include questions about the value of tax-deferred retirement accounts, funds in such accounts are not assessed as an asset in the IM; and the overwhelming majority of schools that require the PROFILE do not consider such accounts when awarding aid.

A tax deductible contribution to a retirement provision that reduces your AGI for a base income year will always be assessed as income, but it will never be assessed as an asset—so long as you make the contribution before you fill out the need analysis form.

Thus retirement provisions are still a good way to shelter assets while building your retirement fund and possibly getting a tax deduction all at the same time. If you can afford to keep contributing during college years, it will be to your benefit. But when during the year should you make the contribution?

## Timing on IRA Contributions

The IRS allows you to make contributions to an IRA from January 1 of one year through April 15 of the following year. Many people wait until after they've done their taxes in March or April to make a contribution to an IRA for the preceding year. Unfortunately, if you make the contribution *after* you fill out the financial aid form, the money won't be shielded from the FAOs.

In fact it makes sense to make retirement provisions as soon as possible in a calendar year. Not only will you shelter the money itself from assessment as an asset but you will also shelter the *interest* earned by that money: If you leave that money in a regular bank account for most of the year, the interest will have to be reported on the need analysis form as regular income. Your AGI will be larger, and your financial aid package will be correspondingly smaller. By making the contribution early in the year, the interest earned by that contribution will be out-of-bounds to the FAOs. How much money are we talking about? A married couple that makes an allowable IRA contribution of $6,405 on January 1 of a base income year instead of April 15 of the next year can increase its aid eligibility by as much as $400 each year.

**TIP 17:**
Make your contributions to retirement provisions as early in the year as possible.

## Other Retirement Provision Strategies

Let's say it's January of a new year. You go to see your accountant and she says, "You've got some extra money. Let's make an IRA contribution. Which year do you want to take the contribution in?" Remember, the IRS allows you to make contributions to an IRA from January 1 (well, realistically January 2; the banks and brokerage houses are all closed on January 1) all the way through April 15 of the next year. That means there are three and a half months during which you can contribute to either the preceding year or the year you are in now. In which year do you make the contribution?

## If Possible, Contribute to Both Years

*The following section assumes that you have not yet completed the FAFSA form. Contrary to conventional wisdom, financial aid is not awarded by most schools and state agencies on a first-come first-serve basis. Later in Part Three of this book we will explain the optimal time for completing and submitting the forms—and those particular situations in which you should be filing the FAFSA as soon as possible once the FAFSA for the next school year becomes available on October 1st. If any of those specific situations is applicable for the student, then you should not delay filing the aid forms to be able to implement the strategy that follows in the next paragraph.*

Let's say this is your child's senior year in high school. You are just about to fill out a FAFSA. From January 2 through April 15, you can contribute to the year that has just ended (in this case, the base income year) and the year that is just beginning. If you are married, you and your spouse can make an IRA contribution of up to $12,000 ($14,000 if you and your spouse are both 50 years of age or older) toward last year, and up to $12,000 ($14,000 if you and your spouse are both 50 years of age or older) toward the year that has just begun. By making these contributions before you sign the need analysis form, you can completely shelter up to $24,000 ($28,000 if you and your spouse are both 50 years of age or older) in assets from the scrutiny of the FAOs. This is such a good deal that you might even want to consider making an IRA contribution even if it isn't tax deductible.

# We Don't Have $24,000. We Might Not Even Have Enough to Make IRA Contributions Every Year.

Many people don't contribute the maximum allowed amount into their retirement accounts every year. Many people don't contribute anything in a given year. Sometimes, of course, you just haven't got it. Other times, it is a matter of which year it makes the most sense tax-wise to make the contribution:

# During College Years, Some Tax Strategies Have to Change

Why shouldn't you make retirement contributions based solely on tax considerations? It's all in the numbers. Remember our IRA example from the "Expenses" section of this chapter? Given a choice of making a tax-deductible contribution to an IRA in a base income year or a non–base income year, you were better off making the contribution in the non–base income year. Tax-wise, there was no real difference, but by *concentrating* your taxes into the base income year, you effectively raised your expenses during the year the colleges were looking at it, and thus lowered your expected family contribution.

Parents and accountants find this hard to believe. "How could an IRA contribution possibly hurt a family's chances for aid?" they demand.

Federal income tax is an expense that is deducted from your total income under the aid formula. A tax-deductible retirement provision contribution *reduces* your tax. Reduced taxes increase your available income, and thus increase the amount of money the colleges think you can afford to fork over for tuition next year.

# You're Saying Parents Should Try to Pay More Taxes?

Never. But by *concentrating* your taxes into the base income years, you can end up paying the same amount in taxes over the course of time while *lowering* the amount you have to pay for college.

# The Big Picture

Extrapolating from this, if you were to load up on tax-deductible contributions to retirement provisions over the course of several years prior to the first base income year, and then avoided contributions to retirement provisions completely during the base income years, you could end up paying about the same amount in taxes over the years, but you would have made yourself eligible for far more financial aid.

**TIP 18a:**
If you can, try to load up your contributions to retirement provisions in the years prior to base income years.

Let's take the hypothetical case of Mr. Jones. Mr. Jones is doing pretty well: He has a substantial regular savings account, and every year he contributes $1,500 to his 401(k) plan at work. Over the next seven years, he figures he will be able to contribute $10,500 to the retirement provision. His daughter is entering college in five years. Before the start of the first base income year, Mr. Jones will have sheltered only $4,500 in his retirement plan. The FAOs will assess his entire regular savings account at the maximum asset rate. His pre-tax $1,500 401(k) contribution that effectively reduces his AGI for that base income year will lower his taxes a bit (thereby reducing his expenses against income in the FM and IM, but not his total income for aid purposes since the contribution is added back to one's AGI as untaxed income.) This would mean that his available income (after expenses and allowances) in those aid formulas will be just a bit higher, which will raise the EFC.

Consider what would have happened if Mr. Jones had contributed the same $10,500 to his 401(k) but had arranged to lump it all into the three years *before* the first base income year. Over the seven years his total tax bill would turn out to be about the same as before, but everything else would be very different. Now he would have $10,500 sheltered in his retirement plan. In order to make the contributions over only three years, he would probably have to take some money out of his savings account—but that's actually good news because it would reduce his assets in the eyes of the FAOs. During the four base income years, Mr. Jones wouldn't have to contribute to his retirement fund at all—this means that amount of federal income taxes paid (which are an expense item in the FM and IM aid formulas) would be concentrated into these years that would lower his EFC.

Mr. Jones had only $10,500 to contribute over seven years. However, by changing the timing of his contributions, he made them much more valuable. This strategy will work only if your voluntary contributions to retirement provisions are tax deductible. If you won't qualify for the tax break (because you contribute after-tax funds), you won't be able to concentrate your taxes into the base income years. However, the expense item for the amount of federal income taxes paid won't be reduced either.

## The Big, Big Picture

Mr. Jones (like most of us) could not afford to contribute the maximum amounts allowed by the law to retirement provisions; therefore it made sense to plan the timing of the contributions to get the most aid. However, if you can afford to make maximum contributions to IRAs, Keoghs, 401(k)s, or 401(b)s in every single year, it is in your interest to do so. This will enable you to shelter the largest amount of assets, and also build a sizable retirement fund.

## However, Before You Frame the Picture

The only reason not to follow the advice we've just given you is you Adjusted Gross Income for a base income year will be just over $50,000 and you are otherwise eligible to qualify for the Simplified Needs Test (SNT). In this case, by making tax-deductible and/or pre-tax contributions to retirement provisions *during* the base income years, you could lower your AGI to below the $50,000 magic number for the Simplified Needs Test. As we said earlier, anyone who meets the SNT will have all assets excluded for federal aid purposes. The same situation applies if such a contribution will lower your AGI below the $26,000 threshold for the Automatic-Zero EFC.

You would have to work out the numbers very closely on this to see if it really makes sense. Factors to consider: how much you have in the way of assets; does the school look at your assets anyway in awarding their own aid funds; the difference in your EFC with the SNT or Automatic-Zero EFC or not qualifying for those items. Since these factors are all pretty complicated, consider discussing this with a financial aid consultant.

**TIP 18b:**
If a contribution to a retirement provision will lower your AGI for a base income to below the income threshold for the SNT or the Automatic-Zero EFC and you otherwise qualify for the SNT or the Automatic Zero EFC (see pages 58–61), you should load up your contributions to retirement provisions during that base income year.

## Prying Colleges

Although the FAFSA doesn't ask questions about the money in parents' retirement provisions or insurance policies, a few private colleges ask for this information on their own forms. Short of refusing to apply to these colleges, there is nothing you can do but supply the information gracefully. Unless you have several hundreds of thousands of dollars of these assets, however, there should be little effect on your family contribution. (While the PROFILE now asks questions regarding retirement accounts, such assets are not assessed in the IM.)

## They Won't Give Aid to *Us*—We Own Our Own Home

One of the biggest myths about financial aid is that parents who own their own home will not qualify for aid. This is not the case at all. As we have already mentioned, the federal methodology (used to award Pell Grants and other federal aid programs) does not look at home equity anymore. While many private colleges and some state universities continue to use home equity in determining eligibility for their own aid programs, it has been our experience that most homeowners—even in this situation—do get aid. In some cases, this will be true even if they have several properties, if they apply for it in the right way.

## Real Estate Strategies

Because we know that many of our readers will be applying to schools that assess home equity in awarding the funds under their own control, the next few sections of this chapter will suggest strategies that focus on both your primary residence and any other real estate you may own.

If none of the schools you are considering assess home equity, then the following strategies will apply only to your other real estate holdings.

## Valuing the Property—Be Realistic

Figuring out the value of your home can be difficult. Is it worth what your neighbors down the street sold their's for last week? Is it worth what someone offered you three years ago? Is it worth the appraised value on your insurance policy? Figuring out the value of other properties can be even more difficult, especially if you rarely see them.

You want to try to be as accurate as possible. The temptation to over-represent the value of your real estate should be firmly controlled. The forms are asking for the value of the property if you had to sell it right this minute, today—not what you would get for it if you had a leisurely six months to find a buyer. If you had to sell it in a hurry—at firesale prices—how much is it worth? Remember also that there are always attendant costs when you sell a property: painting and remodeling, possible early payment penalties for liquidating your mortgage, real estate agent's commission. If the colleges want to know what your real estate is worth, these costs should be taken into account. Be realistic. Inflating the price of your property beyond what it is really worth will reduce your aid eligibility.

At the same time, you don't want to under-represent the value either. The colleges have verification procedures to prevent parents from lowballing. One of the procedures: the PROFILE form asks when you purchased your home and how much you paid for it. The analysis computer will then feed these numbers into the Federal Housing Index Multiplier to see whether your current valuation is within reasonable norms. Some schools have also started to use zillow.com to value properties.

## Equity

Ultimately, what your real estate is worth is much less important than how much equity you've built up in it. Your equity is the current market value of your real estate minus what you owe on it (mortgages, home equity loan balances, debts secured by the home). Let's assume for a moment that two families are looking at a private college that considers home equity as an asset. All other things being equal, the family with a $100,000 house fully paid up would probably pay a higher family contribution to that college than the family with a $300,000 house with a $250,000 mortgage. Sounds crazy? Not really. The first family has built up equity of $100,000; the second family has equity of only $50,000.

Parents often don't remember when they are filling out the need analysis forms that their first mortgage need not be their only debt against their property. Did you, for example, borrow money from your parents to make a down payment? Have you taken out a home improvement loan? Have you borrowed against a home equity loan line of credit? Is there a sewer assessment? All of these are also legitimate debts against the value of your real estate.

If you are a part-owner in any property, obviously you should list only your share of the equity in that property.

# The Home Equity Loan: A Possible Triple Play

One of the smarter ways to pay for college is the home equity loan. A home equity loan is a line of credit, secured, most likely, by the equity in your home. Of course, it is also possible to get a home equity loan using one of your other properties as collateral. You draw checks against this line of credit, up to the full value of the loan, but you pay no interest until you write a check, and you pay interest only on the amount that you actually borrow.

There are two possible benefits to a home equity loan. First, you temporarily reduce the equity in your property, which, in turn, lowers your net assets, which lowers your family contribution—provided, of course, that the loan is taken against a property that is being considered an asset by the college. Second, because it is a secured loan, the interest rates are fairly low. As always, you should consult with your accountant or financial planner on this.

If you have any outstanding loans that cannot be used as a deduction under the financial aid formulas (personal loans, car loans, large credit card balances, etc.), it might make sense to use a home equity line of credit to pay off these other obligations. The interest rate will probably be lower and the value of one of your prime assets may look smaller to the FAOs.

# Which Property Should I Borrow Against?

If you have only one property, the decision is easy. Borrow against your one property. You'll almost certainly get a low interest rate. Whether you will reduce your equity in the eyes of the FAOs depends on whether they have decided to assess the value of the primary residence—and if so whether they are choosing to assess it at full market value or at a lower rate.

If your college is actually going to follow the federal methodology, a home equity loan on a primary residence would no longer help you to qualify for more aid (although it still may be a good idea). If you own two homes, take out the loan on the second residence instead.

If your prospective colleges are using the institutional methodology *and* electing to cap home value at 2.4 times income (and a number of private colleges will be), the effectiveness of our strategy will depend on how much equity you have in your home. Let's take a family with income of $60,000 and a home valued at $200,000, with a $100,000 mortgage. At schools that choose to cap the home value at 2.4 times income, the maximum value of this family's home would be 2.4 times $60,000 or $144,000. The colleges will subtract the $100,000 debt from the $144,000 asset and decree that the family has equity of $44,000—which the colleges feel is available to help pay for college, and will assess at a rate of up to 5% per year. In this case, it would still make sense to take out a home equity loan of up to $44,000 to reduce the appearance of equity in the house.

However, let's take a family with a combined income of $60,000, a home valued at $300,000 and a mortgage of $200,000. If the schools choose to cap home value at 2.4 times income, the maximum value for the house (for assessment purposes) is $144,000. The colleges then subtract the mortgage of $200,000. In this case, there is, in fact, no equity at all in the home as far as those colleges are concerned. Thus, if this family took out a home equity loan on their primary residence, their assets would not be reduced in the eyes of the colleges (since as far as the colleges are concerned, the family has no equity in the house in the first place). To reduce the appearance of their assets, this family could borrow instead against a second home, other real estate, or their stock portfolio.

If the schools you are considering either use a cap on home value or a cap on home equity, our tips #2 through #11 (which describe ways to lower the appearance of your Adjusted Gross Income) become even more important. Lowering your AGI will keep your capped home value or capped home equity down, and may thus protect more of the value of your home from the FAOs.

**TIP 19a:**
Take out a home equity loan to pay for college and/or to consolidate debt not taken into account in the aid formulas.

A home equity loan is not something to be done lightly. Unlike unsecured loans and credit card balances, a home equity loan uses your real estate as collateral. If you default, the bank can foreclose. Nonetheless, if you have a low mortgage to begin with and your income seems stable, this is an excellent alternative.

# A Home Equity Loan vs. a Second Mortgage

When you take out a second mortgage, the bank writes you a check for a fixed amount, and you begin paying it back immediately with interest. Parents sometimes ask, "Isn't a second mortgage just as good as a home equity loan?" It depends on what you're going to do with the money you get from the loan. If you put it in the bank to pay for college bills as they come due, then a second mortgage is not as good at all. Consider: You are paying interest on the entire amount of the loan, but you aren't really using it yet. The money will earn interest, but it will not earn nearly as much interest as you are paying out. For financial aid purposes, the interest you earn will be considered income, yet the interest you are paying on the second mortgage will not be taken into account as an expense.

Even worse, if the money you received from your second mortgage is just sitting in the bank, the debt does not reduce your net assets either. The reduced equity in your house will be offset by the increased money in your bank account. Under these circumstances, a home equity line of credit loan is a much better deal. You pay interest only when you withdraw money, and you withdraw only what you need.

But if the school you select has opted not to look at home equity, then a second mortgage becomes the worst deal in the world. You will have taken an asset that the college could not touch and converted it into an asset with no protection at all. This could actually raise your EFC by several thousand dollars.

## Should We Buy a House Now?

We're all for it if you want to buy a house, but don't think of it as an automatic strategy for reducing your assets in the eyes of the FAOs. If the school assesses home equity, then exchanging the money in your bank account for a down payment on a house just shifts your assets around, rather than making them disappear. Your net assets will be exactly the same with or without the house (at least until the house starts appreciating in value). On top of that, your monthly housing costs will probably increase. As you may remember from the "Expenses" section of this chapter, you don't get credit in the aid formulas for mortgage payments.

However, if the school uses only the federal methodology or excludes home equity, then a first-time home purchase could make a lot of sense. You would be exchanging an unprotected asset for an asset that could not be touched.

By the same token, it might also make sense to prepay or pay down the mortgage on your primary residence since this will reduce your net assets in the federal formula. You will need to consider any prepayment penalties you may incur before you pursue this course of action.

**TIP 19b:**
If the college your child will attend does not look at home equity, consider buying a primary residence if you currently rent. If you already own your primary residence, consider liquidating unprotected assets to prepay your home mortgage.

# The Perils of Inheritance and Gifts from Grandparents

Many accountants suggest that elderly parents put assets in their children's name. In this way, the elderly parents more readily qualify for government benefits such as Medicaid; they avoid having their investments eaten up by catastrophic illness; and, if they are wealthy, their heirs avoid having their inheritance eaten up by estate taxes.

If a grandparent is contemplating putting assets in the parents' name, the parents should at least consider the possible financial aid consequences before accepting. Obviously, such a transfer will inflate your assets and possibly your income as well (the interest on monetary assets could be considerable). In many cases, while the grandparents may have transferred their assets to the parents, the parents do not feel that this money really belongs to them yet. When grandparents decide to move to a nursing home, or need health care not provided by insurance, the parents often pay the expenses. Since the money is not really yours to spend, you may feel dismayed when the colleges ask you to pony it up for tuition.

If it is possible to delay the transfer of assets until you no longer have to complete aid forms, you might wish to do so. Or perhaps the assets could be put in the name of another relative who does not have college-age children. If that is impossible, you should explain to the FAOs that this money really does not yet belong to you.

An even worse situation arises when grandparents transfer assets to the grandchild's name. These assets will be assessed at a much higher rate than those of the parents (20% versus a maximum of 5.65%). If the only possible choice left to you is to put the grandparents' gift in the name of the parent or the child, it is better to put it in the parents' name.

# Trusts

While trusts have much to recommend them, their effect on the financial aid formulas can be disastrous. We are not speaking of the general feeling among FAOs that "trust fund babies don't need aid" (although this is a pervasive feeling).

The real problem is that the FAOs assume the entire amount in the trust is available to be tapped even if the trust has been set up so that the principal can't be touched. Let's see how this works:

Suppose your child Johnny has a $10,000 trust, which has been prudently set up so that he can't touch the principal, a common practice. He gets a payment from the trust every year until he reaches age 25, at which time he gets the remaining balance in the trust. Parents often set up trusts this way under the mistaken impression that the colleges will thus never be able to get at the principal.

However, because the money is in his name, it is assessed for his freshman year at 20% in the federal formula, or $2,000. Never mind that Johnny can't get $2,000 out of the trust. He, or more likely you, will have to come up with the money from somewhere else.

Next year, the need analysis company looks at the trust again, and sees that it still contains $10,000. So it gets assessed at 20% again, and again Johnny gets up to $2,000 less in aid.

If this continues for the four years of college, and it will, Johnny's $10,000 asset may have cost you $8,000 in aid. The trust may have prevented you from getting aid entirely, but couldn't actually be used to pay for college.

## Don't Put Your Trust in Trusts

If you are counting on any kind of financial aid and you have any control over a trust that is being set up for your child, prevent it from happening. If a grandparent wants to help pay for schooling, the best way to do this is to wait until the child has finished college. Then the grandparent can help pay back the student loans when they become due.

If a trust has to be set up, make sure at least that it is set up so that the principal money can be withdrawn if necessary. You might also consider setting the trust up in *your own* name. Parents' assets are assessed at the much lower rate of 5.65% each year.

Setting up a trust that matures just as your child is entering college would at least ensure that the money could be used to pay for tuition. However, if the trust is sizable, you may be jeopardizing any chance to receive financial aid.

If Grandmother wants to provide for Johnny's *entire* education, but doesn't want to wait until after graduation, perhaps a better idea would be for her to take advantage of one of the prepayment plans being offered by a growing number of colleges. We generally don't think a prepayment plan makes economic sense (see Chapter Seven), but in this one case, it would be infinitely better than a restrictive trust.

## Direct Payments to the School

If you are in the happy position of having a rich uncle who wants to pay for part of your child's college education, he can avoid paying gift tax on the money (even if it is above the $15,000 annual limit) by writing the check directly to the school. However, he and you should realize that if your uncle is paying less than the entire amount of the tuition, this won't necessarily save you any money.

If you are eligible for aid and you receive any money from a third party toward college, the FAOs will treat this money like a scholarship. They will simply reduce the amount of aid they were going to give you by the size of your uncle's payment. Your family contribution will probably remain exactly the same.

If your uncle wants to be of maximum help, he could wait until your child is finished with college and then give you the money. If you were going to qualify for aid, this would ensure that you actually got it. You can then use your uncle's money to pay off any loans you've taken out along the way.

# Stocks, Bonds, Money Market Accounts, and CDs

The need analysis forms ask for the value of your assets on the day you fill out the forms. For stocks and bonds, you can find the prices online or by consulting your broker. Remember that bonds are not worth their face value until they mature. Until that time, they are worth only what someone is willing to pay for them at a given moment.

In the aid formulas, debts against these assets reduce your net assets. However, the only real debt you can have against these types of assets is a margin debt.

Many parents shudder when they hear the word *margin*. "Oh, that's just for people who really play the market," they say. In fact, this is not true at all, and margin debt may be one of the more sensible approaches to paying for college if you run out of liquid assets. Here's how it works:

In most cases, you set up a margin account with a brokerage firm. Using stock that you own as collateral, they will lend you a certain amount of money. Traditionally, you would then use this money to buy more stock. However, there are no rules that say you have to buy stock—these days, the brokerage firms are just as happy to cut you a check for the full amount of the loan.

Because this is a secured loan based on the value of your stock portfolio, the interest rates are far superior to unsecured personal loans. You still own the stock, and it continues to do whatever it was going to do. (Out of all the long-term investment possibilities, the stock market has been the single best way to build principal over the past 50 years.) In most cases, you get to deduct the interest expense against your income on your tax return. And—here's the beauty part—you get to deduct the entire loan from your assets on the need analysis forms.

# Margin Can Pay for College

If you own stocks or bonds and you need the money to pay for college, it may make sense to borrow against these assets rather than to sell them. If you sell the investment and write the college a check, the money is gone forever. By borrowing on margin, you can avoid capital gains (which will raise your AGI) and still retain your assets.

A margin loan is a bet that the value of your stock will increase faster than the interest you are paying on the loan (and based on long-term past performance, this is a reasonable bet). Even if you don't make money on the deal, it will cost far less than an unsecured personal loan, and your assets will still be there when your child walks back from the podium with his diploma and tells you he wants to go to graduate school.

Margin allows you to avoid paying taxes on capital gains, keep your investment working for you, and reduce your assets in the eyes of the FAOs.

**TIP 20:**
Use a margin loan to pay for college and reduce the appearance of your assets.

A major drawback to this type of loan is that if the stock market declines drastically, you may be asked to put up additional stock as collateral, or even (it would have to be a very drastic decline) pay back part of the money you borrowed. If you were unable to put up additional stock or money—or if you couldn't make the loan payments—you could lose the stock you put up as collateral. This is the kind of calculated risk you should discuss with your broker or accountant before you jump in.

# Doesn't This Margin Strategy Conflict with What You Said Earlier?

In the "Income" section of this chapter we suggested that you avoid margin debt as an investment strategy. How then can we turn around now and say it's a good strategy for paying for college? Whether margin makes sense for you depends on what you're using it for. If you are using it to purchase more stock, this should be avoided as it will overstate your investment income and therefore your AGI.

On the other hand, if you do not have sufficient income or liquid assets (such as savings, checking, or money market accounts) to pay the college bills, margin debt is infinitely preferable to:

a.  borrowing at high rates from loan sources that are not considered debts under the aid formulas and/or

b.  selling off assets that will generate capital gains during a base income year.

# Mortgages Held

This category has nothing to do with the mortgage you have on your house. It refers to a situation in which you are acting as a bank and someone else is making monthly payments to you. This situation might have come up if you sold your house to a person who could not get a mortgage from a bank. If you were anxious to make the sale, you might agree to act as the banker. You receive an initial down payment, and then monthly installments until the buyer has paid off the agreed price of the house plus interest. The exact terminology for this is an installment or land sale contract.

If you are the holder of a mortgage, the amount owed to you is considered a part of your assets. However, you should not write down the entire amount that is owed to you. A mortgage, installment contract, or land sale contract is worth only what the market will pay for it at any particular moment. If you had to sell that mortgage right now, it might not be worth its face value. You should consult a real estate professional or a banker who is familiar with second mortgage markets (yes, there actually is a market in second mortgages) to find out the current market value of your investment.

# 529 Plans (Prepaid Tuition Programs & Tuition Savings Accounts) and Coverdell ESAs

Since these are generally long-term planning options, see pages 37–40 for more details on how these plans are treated under the federal and institutional methodologies.

As with the prepaid plans, the tax-free earnings portion of any withdrawal from a 529 savings plan or a Coverdell ESA for the student will not be considered income to the student for the purposes of the 2020–2021 aid forms.

# What About Contributions from Grandma or Uncle Joe?

If someone other than a custodial parent or student is the owner of a 529 plan or Coverdell, then it appears that the account would be completely sheltered as an asset from the federal formula for the 2020–2021 academic year. However, don't jump for joy just yet. For while the assets may be sheltered, the dollar value of the funds withdrawn or tuition credits redeemed may well be considered untaxed income that will eventually need to be reported on a subsequent year's aid form—thereby raising the base year income for the year when that transaction occurred. If the student is beneficiary of such an account, there may be strategies you can follow to minimize the impact of such transactions. Yet, because this situation is too complicated for us to give general advice, we recommend you consult with a competent financial advisor who is thoroughly familiar with financial aid regulations as well as such accounts. For the institutional methodology, these accounts owned by others will be treated the same way as they are in the federal formula. However, colleges will have the option of asking additional questions regarding 529 plans or Coverdells that were funded by individuals other than the student or the parents. These optional questions will appear in the Supplemental Questions section of the PROFILE. As we went to press, it was impossible to determine how many colleges would be exercising this option.

Warning: with each successive year, more and more colleges are asking questions about these plans. Who set them up? Who owns them? How much will be withdrawn or redeemed in a given year? What's the total value? Because of this increased scrutiny… because the colleges know these funds are specifically set up for the student beneficiary's education… and because the FAOs can choose to ignore the federal and institutional formulas when awarding the school's own money, placing funds in these accounts is increasingly risky if the student is otherwise eligible for aid—especially for grants awarded by the colleges themselves. Well-intentioned relatives should be alerted to the possible problems with these programs as well. We will cover any late-breaking developments regarding these plans, should they occur before the 2021 edition of this book is published in the fall of 2020.

# Ownership of a Business

If you own and control a business with fewer than 101 full-time (or full-time equivalent) employees, prepare yourself for one of the most amazing new loopholes we have ever seen—courtesy of the HERA legislation.

Previously, any business equity—that is, the value of the business assets minus the liabilities—needed to be reported on the FAFSA. However, starting with the 2006–2007 academic year, the net worth of these small businesses (which the US Department of Education classifies as "family businesses") need no longer be reported as part of business/farm assets on the FAFSA.

However, if your business falls outside this definition (for example if you have more than 100 full-time employees) you will still need to include the net worth of the business as part of your assets on the FAFSA, which may very well increase your federal EFC.

And either way, you will still be required to list ALL of your business assets and business debts on the PROFILE form—whether yours is a "family business" or not. This could have a chilling effect on your eligibility for aid from the schools themselves.

Remember, though, if you need to report the equity of your business on any aid form, net worth is NOT the same thing as what you would get if you sold the business. It does not include good-will; it has nothing to do with gross receipts.

The net worth of a business consists of the cash on hand, receivables, machinery and equipment, property, and inventory held, minus accounts payable, debts, and mortgages. In most cases you can find the figures you will need from the company's year-end balance sheet, or a partnership or corporate income tax return (IRS forms 1065, 1120, or 1120S).

The main thing to realize here is that just like when you are assessing the value of your real estate, there is no point getting carried away with your valuation of your company. Business owners are rightfully proud of what they have accomplished, but this is not the time to brag.

The higher your net assets, the worse your chances of receiving aid. The FAOs are interested in only selected portions of your balance sheet. Don't look any further than they do.

For example, if your company is part of the service industry, it may have a very small net worth, even if it is extremely successful. Let's assume for a moment that you own a small advertising agency. Like most service industry companies, you would have no real inventory to speak of, little in the way of property, and, because you're putting your profits back into the company, not much money in the bank. The net worth of this company—even if you were required to report its equity on an aid form—would be almost nil. This would be true even if it were one of the most well-respected agencies on Madison Avenue.

## Business Footnotes

The government has further clarified the definition of a family business. Specifically, more than 50 percent of the value of the business must be owned by the family, which can include relatives by blood (including cousins, nieces, nephews) or by marriage.

Obviously these rules may well be changed if and when Congress determines that this new law is being exploited. For example, if too many people start placing their investments into family partnerships or corporations established solely to qualify as "family businesses" for aid purposes, Congress may quickly close this loophole.

## Business Assets Are Much Better Than Personal Assets

Because the FAOs acknowledge that a parent's business needs working capital to operate, the net worth of the entity reported on the FAFSA or PROFILE is assessed much less harshly than the parent's personal assets. For example, of the first $135,000 in net worth, the colleges count only 40 cents on the dollar.

So even if you do not "own and control" a business and must report the value of the business on the FAFSA, all is not lost. As long as you own at least 5% of the stock in a small corporation, it may be possible to call yourself a part-owner and list the value of your stock as a business asset on the aid form instead of as a personal investment. How much difference would this make? If you had $40,000 in stock in a small, privately held corporation, you could find yourself eligible for up to $1,300 per year in increased aid simply by listing this stock as a business asset rather than as a personal asset.

## Real Estate as Business

Can you turn your various real estate properties into a business? It depends. If you own several properties, receive a significant portion of your income from your properties, and spend a significant proportion of your time managing the real estate, then you probably can.

If you own your own business and the building in which you conduct business, then you certainly can. If you rent out one or more properties and file business tax returns, then you perhaps can. Some schools will want to see extensive documentation before they will buy this strategy. The benefits, of course, are enormous. Business assets are assessed much less severely by the formula. Listing your real estate holdings as a business could reduce your expected family contribution by thousands of dollars—if the FAOs buy it.

## Ownership of a Farm

If you live on your farm and can claim on schedule F of your IRS 1040 that you "materially participated in the farm's operation," the equity in the farm will be protected under the federal methodology. While the federal FAFSA form still includes a question regarding the net worth of farms, the instructions to the form tell you not to include "a family farm that you live on and operate."

Unfortunately, the institutional methodology used by many private colleges and some state schools will assess your farm equity, regardless of where you live.

If you are filling out the PROFILE form, be sure not to count the value of your farmhouse twice. If you list it under "home," then there is no need to count it again as part of your farm property.

All of our other strategies for ownership of a business apply to ownership of a farm as well. And similar to a parent-owned business, a parent's farm equity report on the FAFSA or PROFILE will be assesed much less heavily than the parent's personal assets.

## Limited Partnerships

Under the aid formulas, limited partnerships are also considered assets. Determining a value for limited partnerships can be difficult. If you can't sell your interest in the partnership, and the other general partners are unable to buy back your shares, then it isn't worth anything at the moment, and you should list this worth as "zero." Again, the FAOs may not buy this strategy, but let them tell you that you can't do it.

## The Business/Farm Supplement

Some schools ask the owners of businesses and farms to fill out a standardized form that asks about your business or farm net worth and income in greater detail. We will discuss this, as well as some more complicated strategies in the "Special Topics" chapter of this book.

## Asset Protection Allowance

After the FAFSA processor has determined your net assets, there is one final subtraction, called the Asset Protection Allowance.

This number, based on the age of the older custodial parent (or custodial stepparent), is how much of your net assets can be exempted from the federal financial aid assessment. The older you are, the more assets are sheltered. Below is a chart that will give you a rough idea of the asset protection allowance permitted at various ages under the federal methodology. According to the Department of Education, this allowance is calculated to yield the same amount of money as "the present cost of an annuity which, when combined with social security benefits, would provide at age 65 a moderate level of living for a retired couple or single person." Of course, their idea of "a moderate level of living" probably means a more spartan existence than you had in mind.

| Asset Protection Allowance (Approximate) | | |
|---|---|---|
| Age | Two-Parent Family | One-Parent Family |
| 34 or less | $2,900 | $1,000 |
| 35–39 | $3,900 | $1,400 |
| 40–44 | $5,200 | $1,700 |
| 45–49 | $5,800 | $1,900 |
| 50–54 | $6,600 | $2,200 |
| 55–59 | $7,500 | $2,500 |
| 60–64 | $8,600 | $2,800 |
| 65 or more | $9,400 | $3,000 |

After subtracting the asset protection allowance, the remaining assets are assessed on a sliding scale (depending on income). The maximum assessment on parents' assets is 5.65%. In other words, the most you will have to contribute is slightly more than five and a half cents for each additional dollar of assets.

Parents with few assets worry that the colleges will take what little they have. In fact, a family with low income and, say, $5,000 in assets would almost certainly not have to make any contribution from assets at all. If your total net assets are less than your protection allowance, then your assets will not be touched by the FAOs. In the federal methodology, the assessment of assets is related to the parents' available income. After the asset protection allowance is subtracted, any remaining assets are then assessed at 12%. The result is then added to the available income to come up with what is called the adjusted available income (AAI). Since the maximum assessment rate on the AAI is 47%, the maximum contribution from assets is therefore approximately 5.65%

$$(.12 \times .47 \approx .0565 \text{ or } 5.65\%).$$

## College Board Asset Allowances

Starting with the 2000–2001 academic year, the institutional methodology will no longer contain an asset protection allowance similar to the federal formula. Since the aid formulas do not assess assets in retirement accounts, the College Board feels that it is redundant to also protect some non-sheltered assets for retirement. Instead, the institutional formula has contained three other asset allowances: The Emergency Reserve Allowance, The Cumulative Education Savings Allowance, and The Low Income Asset Allowance.

The first allowance recognizes the fact that every family should have some assets available to handle emergencies, such as illness or unemployment. The emergency reserve allowance for the 2010–2011 award year was as follows: $20,330 for a family of two; $24,560 for three; $28,230 for four; $31,620 for five; $34,450 for six. Above six family members, $2,830 will be granted for each additional person. (Data for 2020–2021 will not be published by the College Board. However given low inflation, we expect the numbers will not be significantly higher.)

The cumulative education savings allowance is granted to shelter those assets that the family has presumably set aside each year to meet their annual goal for the educational savings allowance (see page 87). For the student applicant and any other siblings also enrolled in college during the same academic year, the institutional formula assumes that the savings goal was met for each child for 18 years and that the accumulated savings are then used up during the student's college career. For younger siblings, the allowance will be based on the number of children and their ages. All families received a minimum allowance of $23,130 in the 2010–2011 version of the institutional formula. Because this allowance protects assets for each dependent child in the household, any parental assets held in the names of the student's siblings will be considered as part of the parents' assets.

Lower income families who have negative available income in the institutional formula will be given a third asset allowance equal to the amount of the negative available income. This low income asset allowance is granted because such families generally need to use up some of their assets to cover those basic expenses in excess of their income.

The emergency reserve allowance, the cumulative education savings allowance, and the low income asset allowance (if applicable) will automatically be calculated by the PROFILE processor. These allowances are then subtracted from the parents' net assets (the value of the assets less any debts secured by those assets) to determine the parents' discretionary net worth. This net worth is then assessed to calculate the parents' contribution from assets. Previously the asset assessment rate was based in part upon the family's available income, with higher income families having their assets assessed at a higher rate. Under the new institutional formula, there is no longer any linkage between income and the rate of asset assessment. For the 2010–2011 academic year, the first $34,450 of the parents' discretionary net assets was assessed at 3%. The next $34,450 was assessed at 4%. Any assets in excess of $68,900 were assessed at the rate of 5%. We expect these brackets to widen only marginally in future years. In addition, families with negative discretionary net worth will not have their available income reduced in the institutional methodology.

# Multiple College Students

After the parents contribution is calculated, it is then adjusted based on the number of family members in college on at least a half-time basis. Beginning with the 2000–2001 academic year, the federal formula will no longer recognize a parent as a family member in college for the purposes of this adjustment—even if mom is pursuing a Ph.D. The institutional methodology will continue to only view dependent children as household members in college, so the two formulas are now alike in this respect. If a parent plans to attend graduate school during the same academic year as the student seeking aid, it would be a good idea to explain this situation to the FAO directly, since some may take the parent's educational expenses into account on a case-by-case basis.

While the federal formula simply divides the parents' contribution by the number in college to arrive at the parents' contribution per student, the College Board has used a different formula for multiple students. If there are two in college, the parents' contribution for each student has been 60% of the total parents' contribution. If there are three in college, 45% will likely be the applicable rate. If there are four or more in college, 35% of the total parents' contribution will likely apply to each student in the institutional formula.

# Assets and Liabilities: How the Methodologies Differ

## The Federal Methodology

- Does not assess home value

- Does not assess farm value provided the family lives on the farm and can claim on Schedule F of the IRS 1040 that they "materially participated in the farm's operation"

- Does not assess business net worth for a "family business" provided your "family" owns and controls more than 50% of the business and it has 100 or fewer full-time (or full-time equivalent) employees

- Asset protection table based on present cost of an annuity

- Provides for exclusion of all assets if you meet the Simplified Needs Test

- Asset assessment on a sliding scale based in part on income

## The Institutional Methodology

- Assesses home value, but some colleges will choose to ignore home equity (though sometimes only if family income is below a certain threshold) or cap home value at 2.4 times income or cap home equity at 2 times income

- Assesses all farm equity and all business equity

- All assets are assessed, regardless of whether or not you meet the Simplified Needs Test

- Asset assessment is unrelated to income, except for those with negative available income

- Assets held in names of siblings considered as parental assets

- Asset allowances based on emergency reserves, educational savings, and low-income supplements

# Student Resources

Need analysis companies ask precisely the same questions about students' income and assets that they do about the parents' income and assets, but there is one major difference in the way students' money is treated.

Colleges take a much larger cut of students' money. In the federal formula (FM), a student's assets are assessed at a whopping rate of 20% each year (versus a ceiling of 5.65% on parents' assets). In the institutional formula (IM) for the past few years, the assessment rate has been 25%. A student's income under the FM is assessed at up to 50% (versus a ceiling of 47% on parents' income). For the IM we'll soon discuss how student income is assessed.

## Student Income

Under the federal formula, there is no minimum contribution from student income, and the first $6,840 (after tax) dollars earned by a dependent student are excluded.

Thus an incoming freshman can earn about $7,400 before he will be assessed one penny. Once he crosses the $7,400 threshold, his additional income will most likely be assessed at a rate of 50%. If he then saves his money, it will also be assessed as an asset at a rate of 20%. Thus, if he banks his 7,401st dollar, 50 cents of it will be assessed as income and 20 cents of it will be assessed as an asset. The extra dollar he earned could cost him 70 cents in reduced aid. While this is much better than the old ridiculous rule under which the same child would have been assessed $1.05 for each dollar earned over a certain amount, most students will still be better off devoting their extra time to their studies once they have hit the $7,400 mark.

And that's only if the college is using the federal formula. If your child attends a private college that uses the institutional methodology, she may be responsible for a minimum freshman year contribution as high as $2,200 ($2,950 as an upperclassman) and there is no $6,840 income protection allowance. A student at a private college will owe no more than the minimum contribution as long as she keeps her income below $5,175 as a freshman and $6,945 as an upperclassman. Over $5,175, she may be losing 71 cents in aid eligibility on each additional dollar she earns and saves. Recognizing that a student from a lower income family may be using their earnings to supplement the parent's income, the institutional methodology now uses a complicated formula for calculating a student's contribution from income.

**TIP 21a:**
For a student who hopes to receive aid from a school using only the federal methodology, it doesn't make sense to have income higher than $7,400.

**TIP 21b:**
For a student who hopes to receive aid from a school using the institutional methodology, it doesn't make sense to have income higher than $5,178 as an incoming freshman, or $6,945 as an upperclassman.

The current assessment rates have set up a bizarre situation, in which the best way a student receiving financial aid can help his parents pay for college is by not working very much. If your family has no chance of receiving aid, then by all means encourage your child to make as much money as possible. However, any student who might qualify for aid will find that most of the money he earns will just be canceled out by the money he loses from his aid package.

Under current rules, it makes more sense for students receiving financial aid to earn the minimum amount of money the college will allow, and concentrate on doing as well as possible in school. Most aid is dependent at least in part on the student's grades. A high GPA ensures that the same or better aid package will be available next year; a good GPA also helps students to find better-paying jobs when they graduate so they can pay back their student loans.

There is only one type of job that really benefits a student who receives financial aid:

## The Federal Work-Study Program (FWS)/Co-op Programs

The Federal Work-Study program, funded by Uncle Sam, pays students to work, perhaps in the college library, the dining hall, even sometimes in nearby off-campus businesses. Work-study earnings, while subject to income tax, are excluded from the financial aid formulas and will not decrease your aid. The money a student earns through work-study goes either toward tuition or toward the student's living and travel expenses. It does not count as part of the minimum contribution from income in the institutional formula that each student is expected to earn during the summer.

Because they are excluded from the financial aid formula, work-study wages are in effect worth much more than wages from a regular job. For an upperclassman receiving aid who has already earned $7,400 from non-FWS jobs, a work-study job paying minimum wage makes more sense than a $10.00 per hour regular job off-campus. Note: as of the 2010–2011 FAFSA, earnings from a co-op program will also be excluded.

## It's Too Late. My Daughter Already Earned $9,500 Last Year!

Earning extra money is not the end of the world. Just remind her that as much as $965 of that $9,500 will have to go to the college. If she buys a car with it, she—or you—will have to come up with the money from some other source. You might also want to remind the colleges that while your daughter managed to earn $9,500 as a senior in high school, she is unlikely to earn that much again now that she is in college and has a tough work load. They might bear this in mind when they are allocating aid for the coming year. Some schools (Cornell is one) specifically ask you if your child will be earning less money in future years.

## Student Income and Taxes: Not Necessarily Joined at the Hip

When does a student have to file a tax return? Generally, an individual who is being claimed as an exemption on his parents' tax return has to file if he has gross income of over $1,100 and at least $350 of that income is unearned income (i.e., interest or dividends). If the student has NO unearned income at all, he can earn up to $12,000 in wages reported on a W-2 form before he is required to file a federal return. If the student is working as an independent contractor (with earnings reported to the IRS on a 1099), there are special rules to follow. Ask your accountant if the student has to file.

The rules used to be more lenient. The IRS is cracking down on parents who are sheltering assets by putting them in the child's name. If your child has any investment income at all, his standard deduction can drop from $12,000 to as low as $1,050.

A student who cannot be claimed as a dependent on her parents' taxes can have income up to $12,000 without needing to file a federal tax return, provided that she gets no more than $400 net earnings from self-employment.

As long as your children are under 24 years old, and are full-time students, they can be claimed as dependents on the parents' tax return, whether they filed income taxes or not, and regardless of how much money they earned.

You should also realize that the colleges' criteria for who can be considered an independent student are much tougher than the IRS's. A student could have been filing a separate return for years, not been claimed as a dependent by someone else, while paying taxes, but that does not necessarily mean that she will qualify as an independent under the financial aid formula.

## Can My Child Go the Independent Route?

If the colleges decide that a student is no longer a dependent of his parents, then the colleges won't assess the parents' income and assets at all. Since independent students are often young and don't earn much money, they get large amounts of financial aid. The key point to grasp here is that it is the federal government and the colleges themselves who get to decide who is dependent and who is independent, and it is obviously in their best interest to decide that the student is still dependent.

We will discuss the criteria for becoming an independent student in Part Three, "Filling Out the Standardized Forms," and in Chapter Nine, "Special Topics," but don't get your hopes up. The rules are tough, and getting tougher all the time.

## Student Assets

Accountants and other financial counselors love to advise parents to "put some of their assets in the kid's name."

As a tax reduction strategy, this may be pretty good advice, since some of the income generated by the money in your child's name will almost certainly be taxed in a lower bracket than yours. Unfortunately, as many parents learn the hard way, following this advice during college years is virtually economic suicide.

Parental assets are assessed by the colleges at a top rate of 5.65% each year, after subtracting your protection allowance. Your child's assets, on the other hand, will be hit up for 20% in the federal formula (25% in the institutional formula) each year, *and your child has no protection allowance at all*. Any potential tax benefits of putting assets in the child's name can be completely wiped out by the huge reduction you will see in your aid package.

---

**TIP 22:**
If you think you will qualify for financial aid, do not put assets in the child's name.

---

Even worse, some of the assets in the child's name can be hit twice each year: first, colleges take 20% off the top of the entire amount of the asset; second, the colleges take up to 50 cents out of every dollar in income generated by the asset.

Let's say a parent puts $10,000 in the child's name and invests it in a bond fund that pays 6%. When he fills out the FAFSA form, he enters the $600 interest the fund earned that year as part of the student's income; because the $600 was reinvested in the bond fund, the fund now has $10,600 in it, so he enters $10,600 under the student's assets. The need analysis company assesses the $10,600 asset at 20% (in this case $2,120). The need analysis company also assesses the $600 income at a rate of up to 50% (in this case, $300). Note that the $600 income got assessed twice—20% as an asset, and 50% as income, for a total of 70%. That $600 in income may have cost the family $420 in lost aid.

## It's Too Late. I Put Assets in My Son's Name!

If you have already transferred assets to your child in the form of a custodial account (such as an UGMA or UTMA) or a trust, you should pause and consider three things before you strangle your accountant.

1. You may not have been eligible for need-based aid in the first place. If you weren't going to qualify for aid anyway, those assets may be in just the right place, and your accountant is a genius. However, you should probably contact her to discuss the "kiddie tax" provisions (See pages 31–32).

2. You may have been offered only a subsidized Direct loan. If you were going to qualify only for minimal need-based aid in the form of student loans, the tax benefits of keeping assets in the child's name may well exceed the aid benefits, and you did just the right thing.

3.  Even if it turns out that putting assets in your child's name was a bad mistake, you can't simply undo the error by pulling the money out of your child's account now. When you liquidate a custodial account, the IRS can disallow the gift, come after you for back taxes and back interest, and tax the money at the *parents'* tax rate from the time the funds were first transferred to the child.

## Is There Anything We Can Do to Get Assets Back in Our Name?

There may be, but this situation is much too complicated for us to give general advice. You should consult with a competent financial advisor who has a sound understanding of both the tax code and the ins and outs of financial aid.

## Student Income and Assets: How the Methodologies Differ

### The Federal Methodology

- First $6,840 in student's after-tax income is sheltered for a dependent student

- No minimum contribution from income

- Asset assessment rate of 20%

### The Institutional Methodology

- No income protection allowance

- Minimum contribution from income as high as: $2,200 for incoming freshmen, $2,950 for upperclassmen

- Asset assessment rate of 25%

# Putting It All Together

## Making an Estimate of How Much You Will Be Expected to Pay

After receiving all your financial data, the need analysis service crunches the numbers to arrive at your family contribution:

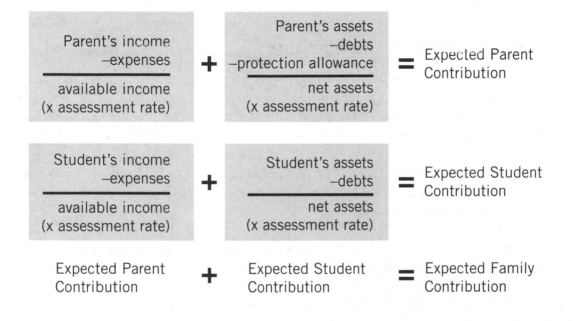

If you have read this book carefully up to now, you know that behind the apparent simplicity of the chart above lies a wealth of hidden options that can save—or cost—you money.

By using the worksheet at the back of this book, you can get a rough approximation of what your Expected Family Contribution will be under both the federal methodology. Bear in mind that it will be just that—an approximation. Our worksheet uses basically the same formula(s) used by the need analysis companies, but because you will be estimating many of the numbers there is little likelihood that it will be exact.

Parents always want the bottom line. "How much will I have to pay?" they ask, as if there were one number fixed in stone for their family. In fact, you will see as you begin to play with your numbers that there are numerous ways to present yourselves to the colleges. By using the strategies we have outlined in Part Two of this book, you can radically change the financial snapshot that will determine your Expected Family Contribution.

Your bottom line will also be determined in part by whether you choose schools that use the federal or the institutional methodology to award institutional aid. We'll discuss this in more detail in our chapters on "How to Pick Colleges" and "The Offer."

Filling out our worksheet will be a quite different experience from filling out the need analysis form. The need analysis form asks you for your raw data, but does not allow you to do the calculations to determine your family contribution.

## The FAOs Tinker with the Numbers

You should also bear in mind that the college financial aid officers have a wide latitude to change the figures the need analysis companies send to them. If a school wants a particular student badly, the FAO can sweeten the pot. If a school has a strict policy on business losses, your Expected Family Contribution at that school may be higher than the Feds said it would be.

It's as if you submitted your tax return to five different countries. Each of them will look at you a little differently. One country may allow you to have capital losses that exceed capital gains. Another country may disallow your losses.

We know of one parent with unusual circumstances whose need analysis form generated an Expected Family Contribution of $46,000 but who still ended up getting $7,000 in financial aid for his son's freshman year at a $22,000-per-year school. We know of another couple whose family contribution was calculated to be $10,000, but who ended up having to pay $15,000 because there was not much aid money left.

Even if your numbers look high, you should not assume that you won't qualify for aid.

# Chapter Four

## How to Pick Colleges

# How to Pick Colleges—with Financial Aid in Mind

Richard Freedman, a former guidance counselor at prestigious Hunter College High School in New York City, used to keep a copy of *Who's Who* handy in his office. When parents came in with visions of Ivy dancing in their eyes, he invited them to look up famous people they admired in *Who's Who*. It turned out that their heroes almost never attended Ivy League schools.

We aren't suggesting that Ivy League schools are no good, or that your child should not apply to one of them, but it is worth noting (even as you look at the $65,000 price tag) that many important, interesting people managed, and are still managing, to get good educations else-where—and for less money.

There are many factors that go into a decision to apply to a particular college, and one factor that cannot be ignored is money. You and your child are about to make a business decision, and it's vital that you keep a clear head. How much are you willing to pay for what level of quality of education under what circumstances? It is possible to pay $48,000 per year for a worth-less education, and possible to pay $5,000 per year for an outstanding education. Price is not always synonymous with quality. The real determining factor in the kind of education a student comes away with is how seriously the student took the experience.

## This Is a Joint Decision . . .

Many parents feel that it is somehow their duty to shield their children from the harsh economic realities of higher education. It is a form of need-blind application, in which parents do their level best to remain blind to their own needs. They allow their children to apply to any school they like, without thinking through the consequences of what an acceptance at that school would mean. Taking on large amounts of debt should be a rational rather than an emotional decision, and any important decision like this should involve the student as well. Especially if money is a concern, your child should be included in every step of the decision making, from computing a rough estimate of the expected family contribution to picking colleges with a view toward financial aid.

## . . . That You Must Make in the Dark

One of the frustrating parts about applying to college is that you have to apply without really knowing what it is going to cost. Well, of course you do know the sticker price, but as we've already said, the vast majority of families don't actually pay the sticker price. The $64,000 question is what kind of aid package the different schools will give you to reduce that sticker price.

The process has been made even more difficult by a Justice Department investigation years ago into possible violations of anti-trust law by many of the highly selective colleges, including the Ivies. Prior to the investigation, the FAOs from these schools would get together at an annual "overlap" meeting to compare notes on students who were going to be accepted by more than one of these colleges. After these meetings, there was usually an amazing similarity between the financial aid packages offered to an individual student by the competing colleges. While the Justice Department eventually worked out an agreement with the colleges on this matter, it remains to be seen to what extent colleges will be sharing information with each other after this experience.

Therefore, financial aid offers are still likely to differ by many thousands of dollars. Any counselor who says he can predict the precise amount and type of aid you will receive at one of these selective schools is lying. Thus applying for college is something of a financial crapshoot.

# Applying to More Schools

Many counselors feel that it is now necessary to apply to more schools than before, to ensure that one of them will give you a good deal.

One good offer can frequently lead to others. If you have received a nice package from school A, you can go to a comparable school B that your child is more interested in, and negotiate an improved package. For the same reason, even if your child has been accepted "early action" or "early notification" by her first-choice school, you might want to apply to several other schools as well.

An early action or early notification acceptance (unlike a "restrictive early decision" acceptance) does not bind the student to go to that school. The college is just letting you know early on that you have a spot if you want it. Your child has just been accepted by her first-choice school, which is great news, but you won't receive an aid package for several months. If the college knows that you applied only to one school, they will be under no pressure to come up with a good aid package. However, if you have received several offers, you may find that the first choice will be willing to match a rival school's package.

Students who need financial aid should always apply to a variety of colleges. Perhaps one or two of these should be "reach" schools at which the student is less certain of admission; the student should also apply to several schools that not only fit his academic profile but also have good reputations for meeting students' "remaining need"; finally, the student should apply to what we call a "financial safety school."

# The Financial Safety School

Now it may well be that your child will ultimately get into his or her first choice. (According to a survey conducted by the Higher Education Research Institute at UCLA, 77.8% of applicants to colleges in the United States *were* accepted by their first-choice school). Just as important, your child's first choice may even give you a financial aid package that is acceptable to you. However, part of picking colleges entails selecting second, third, fourth, and fifth choices as well.

This is an opportunity for your child to get to know several schools better. Students sometimes seem to pick their first-choice schools out of thin air. We have often seen students change their minds as they actually go to visit the schools and read the literature. If money is a consideration, discuss this openly with your child. Look at the relative merits of the schools as compared to their price tags, and discuss what sacrifices both the parent and the student would have to make in order to send the student to one of the more expensive schools if the aid package you get is low.

At least one of the schools you apply to should be a "financial safety school." There are three factors to take into account when picking a financial safety school. You want to pick a school that . . .

**(A) . . . the student is pretty much guaranteed to get into.**    What is an admissions safety school for one student may be a reach for another. Force yourself to be dispassionate. A good way to figure out a student's chances for admission is to look up the median SAT scores and class ranking of last year's freshman class (available in most college guides). A particular college qualifies as a safety school if the student who is applying is in the top 25% of the students who were admitted to the college last year.

**(B) . . . you can afford even if you received no aid at all.**    For most families, of course, this means some sort of state or community college. There are some extremely fine public colleges, whose educational opportunities rival those of many of the best private colleges.

**(C) . . . the student is willing to attend.**    We've met some students who freely admit they wouldn't be caught dead going to their safety school. As far as we are concerned, these students either haven't looked hard enough to find a safety school they would enjoy, or they have unreasonable expectations about what the experience of college is supposed to be.

Let's examine what you might be looking for in a financial safety school based on a rough approximation of your Expected Family Contribution.

# Federal vs. Institutional

In the previous chapters we have constantly referred to the differences between the federal and the institutional methodologies. By now you have probably figured out that in many cases the federal methodology is kinder on a parent's pocketbook than the institutional methodology. However, before you start looking only at schools that use the federal methodology, there are a number of points to be made:

First, a college that uses the institutional methodology must still award federal money such as the Pell Grant and the subsidized Direct loan using the federal criteria. Thus, the institutional methodology will only affect funds under the institution's direct control—principally, the school's private grant money.

Second, families may find that the difference in aid packages from two schools using the different methodologies is actually not very significant. Families who don't have a lot of equity built up in their primary residence, who don't show business or capital losses, or losses on property rental may not notice much difference at all.

Third, most of the competitive schools will be using the institutional methodology this year to award the funds under their control. It would severely limit your choice of colleges to apply only to schools that use the federal methodology.

The best way to find out which methodology is being used at a particular school is to ask an FAO at that school. However, as a rough guide, if the school wants you to fill out the CSS PROFILE form, then it will most likely be using the institutional methodology.

## Should We Apply Only to Schools that Use the Federal Methodology?

No. There are so many other factors that determine an aid package—demographics, special talents, academic performance, just to name a few. Any of these factors could make an FAO decide to award merit-based aid or to be more generous in awarding need-based funds. However, if money is a concern, then it makes sense to apply to a financial safety school.

## If You Have Extremely High Need

If your Expected Family Contribution is in the $700 to $5,000 range, a good safety school would be a public university or community college located in your own state. This type of school has two advantages. First, the likelihood that you will be eligible for state aid is extremely good. Second, your child may be able to live at home and commute, thus saving many of the expenses of room and board.

However, a student with high need should not neglect to apply to private colleges as well, preferably colleges where that student will be in demand. If the student has good grades, or some other desirable attribute, the student may receive an aid package that makes an expensive private school cheaper to attend than the local community college. Remember, by good grades we are not necessarily talking straight As. At many colleges, there are scholarships available for students with a B average and combined SAT scores of over 1,000 (or the equivalent on the ACT). We've sometimes even seen students with C averages and high need get generous aid packages at some private colleges.

## If You Have High Need

We are frequently amazed at how often families with high need choose an out-of-state public university as their safety school. For most families with an EFC of between $5,000 and $20,000, an out-of-state public university is the most expensive option they could possibly choose. Why? First, students from out-of-state are charged a lot more. Second, much of the financial aid at these schools is earmarked for in-state students. Third, you will most likely not be able to take aid from your own state across state lines. Fourth, if the student is likely to fit into the top half of the entering class, he will probably get a better deal from a private college.

Families with limited means have difficulty imagining that they could get an aid package of $40,000 per year or more, but in fact this is not out of the bounds of reality at all. Choose schools with high endowments where the child will be in the top quarter of the entering class.

Naturally, you can't depend on a huge package from a private college, so again, a financial safety school is a must. For families with high need, the best financial safety school is probably still an in-state public university or community college.

## If You Have Moderate Need

A family with an expected family contribution of from $20,000 to $35,000 is in a tough position. This is a lot of money to have to come up with every year, perhaps more than you feel you can afford. As Jayme Stewart, a counselor at York Preparatory in New York City, says, "A four-year private school education is not an inalienable right guaranteed by the Constitution."

A family with moderate need might want to choose two financial safety schools consisting of either in-state or out-of-state public universities. Depending on your circumstances, either choice may actually cost you *less* than your EFC.

Financial planning is particularly vital to moderate-need families. The strategies we have outlined in the previous chapters can make a much bigger difference in the size of your aid package than you probably think, and may make it possible for your child to attend a private college. For private colleges, you should again be looking at several schools where the student will be considered desirable and stands a good chance of getting institutional grants and scholarships.

Preferential packaging is particularly important to moderate-need families, as is the practice of applying to a wide variety of schools. By applying to more schools, you increase the likelihood that one of the schools will give you a particularly good package. You can then either accept the offer or use it to try to get a better deal at another college.

## If You Have Low Need

A family with an EFC of between $35,000 and $55,000 (or more) must decide how much it is willing to pay for what kind of education, and how much debt it is willing to take on. If you are willing to go into debt, then your financial safety school becomes merely a regular safety school.

If you are unlikely to get aid, some of the advice we have given in this book to people who want aid does not apply to you; for example, you might be well advised to put some assets into the child's name, you might want to set up a trust for the child, and the child should be earning as much money as possible in the years before and during college.

However, even families with low need should apply for aid. For one thing, with the cost of college being what it is, you may still qualify for some. You also have to look ahead four years. Perhaps your situation will change; for example, you might have only one child in college now, but next year you might have two.

Finally, with their high sticker prices, some private colleges are having trouble filling their classrooms. The FAOs at many of these schools seem to be more and more willing to play "let's make a deal." As a result, a family's final family contribution may end up being several thousand dollars less than was calculated by the need analysis company. If you have used our worksheets in the back of the book to determine your Expected Family Contribution, you should bear this in mind before you decide that your EFC is too high to bother applying for aid.

## The Public Ivies

Over the past few years, the cost of some of the best public universities has skyrocketed, to the point at which an out-of-state resident can pay more to attend a public university than a private college. At the University of Michigan and the University of California—Berkeley, for example, the cost to an out-of-state student is over $57,500 per year—hardly a bargain, even if the quality of education is high. However these and other "public ivies" remain good deals to in-state residents.

In the past, it was relatively easy to change your state of residence and qualify for lower tuition and state aid. However, in recent years, it has become almost impossible for an undergraduate student to pull this off, unless the entire family moves to that state.

Nevertheless, some of the "public ivies" remain bargains for everyone—for example, Georgia Tech, University of Wisconsin (Madison) and SUNY Binghamton are all first-class schools with undervalued price tags.

# What to Look for in a Private College

If you are selecting a private college with financial aid in mind, there are some criteria you should bear in mind as you look at the colleges:

- What is the average percentage of need met? You can find this statistic in most college guides. A high percentage is a sign that the school is committed to meeting as much of a student's "need" as possible. This statistic should not be misunderstood, however, for it is based on an average. A school that normally meets only a low percentage of need may come through with a spectacular offer for a student the school really wants. Another school that normally meets a very high percentage of need may make a very poor offer to a student the school considers marginal.

- Does the student have something this particular school wants? Is the student a legacy? Is he a track star applying to a school known for its track stars? Is she a physics genius applying to a school known for its physics department?

- How does the student compare academically to last year's incoming class? If this is a reach school for the student, the aid package may not be outstanding.

- Some colleges are very open about their academic wants; they mention right up front in their promotional literature that a student with SAT scores above $x$ and a GPA of above $y$ will receive a full scholarship.

- What percentage of gift aid is NOT based on need? If a student has an excellent academic record, this statistic might give some indication of whether she will be eligible to receive non-need scholarships. Of course, this statistic might be misleading for the same reasons we mentioned above.

- What is the school's endowment per student? If the school is on its last legs financially, then it may not be able to offer a great aid package—to say nothing of whether it will remain open long enough for the student to graduate. Don't necessarily be scared if a small school has a small endowment—take a closer look at what that actually means. Earlham College in Indiana has a small endowment compared to, say, Harvard, but it has a very high endowment *per student*.

- Will the school use the institutional methodology in awarding aid under the school's direct control?

# A General Note of Caution

Take the statistics in the college guides with a grain of salt. These statistics may show general trends, but (like all statistics) they are subject to interpretation. First of all, the information presented in these books usually comes from the colleges themselves, and as far as we know, is never checked.

Second, a particularly affluent (or poor) pool of applicants could skew the statistics. It would be easier for a school to meet a high percentage of need if the applicants to that school tend to be well off.

# Chapter Five

## What the Student Can Do

# What the *Student* Can Do

Until now, most of our discussion has concerned what the *parent* can do to pay for college. Income and asset strategies, tax strategies, home equity loans—these are subjects that have little relevance for high school students. After all, in many cases, they have no income or assets, pay no taxes, and almost certainly don't own their own home. Is there anything *the student* can do to help pay for college?

The most obvious idea would seem to be for the student to get a job. However, under "Student Income and Assets" in Chapter Three we explained that earning more than a certain dollar amount will decrease a student's aid faster than the earnings can be deposited in the student's bank account. After $7,000, every dollar a college freshman earns and saves can decrease his aid eligibility by 70 cents in the federal formula. Of course, if his family is not eligible for aid, the student should be out there earning as much as possible; but if his family stands a chance of qualifying for aid, the student's time would be better spent (at least under the current ridiculous law) by making the most of his educational opportunities.

There are, however, some very tangible ways a student can help pay for college. The first of these may make it sound like we've been paid off by high school teachers, but here goes anyway:

## Study Like Crazy

It's the gospel truth. Good grades make a student desirable to the colleges. Yes, this will help you get in, but in these budget-tight times, good grades also translate directly into dollars and cents. As we said in Chapter Two, every tenth of a point a student raises her high school GPA can save her thousands of dollars in student loans she won't have to pay back later.

Even at the prestigious Ivy League schools, where students are supposedly awarded aid based only on their "need," applicants with high academic achievement do get preferential packaging—award packages with a higher percentage of grants and a lower percentage of loans.

If a student's dream is to attend an expensive private college, it isn't going too far to expect the student to contribute to help make that dream a reality. Parents are about to invest a sizable portion of all the money they have ever been able to save. It seems only fair that the student should be prepared to invest in his own future as well. And the single most productive way a student can invest in his future is by doing as well as possible during high school.

There are some colleges out there who state up front, "If you have a GPA of more than 3.5 and SATs of 1900 or above, we will offer you a full scholarship." There are other schools (more and more in recent years) that give out large merit-based grants, irrespective of need. These grants are not necessarily just for geniuses. We know of several colleges that award merit-based grants for students with B averages.

## Take an SAT Review Course

Nothing can change a student's fortune *faster* than a big increase on the SAT. Look at it this way: it takes four years to accumulate your grades from high school. It takes six weeks to take a prep course. A study by FAIRTEST, published in *The New York Times,* showed that students who took these prep courses had an average improvement of over 100 points.

Every ten points a student can raise his score on the SAT can save his family thousands of dollars by increasing his desirability in the eyes of the FAOs, and hence, increasing the size of the aid packages they offer him. This is too important to leave to chance.

There are many companies that offer test preparation, some affordable and some quite expensive. We, of course, are partial to The Princeton Review course. If there are no preparation courses offered in your area, we suggest you at least buy a book such as The Princeton Review's *9 Practice Tests for the SAT*. Books such as these will provide the student with actual SAT practice sections. If money is a consideration, don't lose heart: The books are available at libraries, and test prep companies often offer financial aid.

## Take AP Courses

Many high schools offer advanced placement (AP) courses. By passing an advanced placement test at the end of the year, a student can earn college credits without paying college tuition. Not all schools accept AP credits, but many do, again enabling a student to save his family literally thousands of dollars. Some students are able to skip the entire freshman year in this way, thus cutting the entire cost of their college education by one quarter. Consult with the colleges you are interested in to see if they accept AP credits, and with your high school to see which AP courses are offered, and how to sign up.

## Saving Money by Earning Credits on the CLEP Exams

The College Board has developed exams that—like AP tests—allow students who score high enough to earn college credits. These are offered under the College-Level Examination Program, more commonly known by its acronym: CLEP. There are currently 33 different CLEP exams, with at least one of them currently accepted by 2900 colleges and universities. You earn the same number of credits you would earn by taking a course—simply by taking a test. This could potentially save you thousands of dollars in tuition.

Needless to say, this is a great option to explore, but you need to do your homework first. Some colleges don't award credits for CLEP exams at all, while others have fine print. It is up to the individual college to determine which exams can be taken, the minimum score you need in order to get credit, and the total number of credits the school is willing to give students for CLEP exams. Bear in mind that the minimum score needed on one test might be different than the minimum score on another test. And some colleges might not give you credit, but will use the test results to allow you to place out of entry-level courses or to fulfill core distribution requirements. Each test costs $80, and there are prep books and interactive tutoring websites available. For more information, visit clep.collegeboard.org

## Condense Your College Education

You have to be a little crazy to try this, but for motivated students it is sometimes possible to complete a four-year education in three years. The family may not realize big savings on the tuition itself (since some schools charge by the credit) but there will be savings on room and board, and the student will be able to get out into the workforce that much sooner.

A more reasonable goal might be to reduce time in college by half a year. By attending summer school (which is often less expensive than the regular terms) a student can reduce her time on campus by one full semester.

Even at half a year, this strategy may take its toll on the student. Academics are only one part of the college experience, and by accelerating the process, a student may lose out on some of the opportunities and friendships that make the college years meaningful.

## Defer Admission

Many schools allow students to defer admission for a year. If the family is financially strapped, a student could use this year to earn money. You should always remember that at least under current law, student earnings above a certain dollar amount will reduce aid eligibility—thus for many students, this strategy could backfire. However, if the college the student really wishes to attend decides the family is not eligible for aid, and the family cannot shoulder the entire cost of college, this might be the only way the student could make up the difference. Be extremely careful in making a decision like this. If there is no reasonable plan for how you can meet the entire *four years'* worth of college bills, it may not make sense to begin the first year.

# Go to School Part-Time

Some schools allow students to attend college part-time so that they can earn money while they are in school. Points to be aware of:

- Student loans become due as early as six months after the student stops taking classes or goes below half-time status. If the student takes too much time off between classes, she may have to start paying off the loans, even though she's still in school.

- The financial aid available for part-time students is much reduced. Particularly if the student is attending less than half-time, there will be little chance of substantial aid.

- Any money the student earns is going to be assessed by the colleges at a very high rate, thus reducing aid eligibility. You should consider carefully whether a job will actually help pay for college. It will depend on whether your family was judged eligible for aid, and what kind of package you have been offered. If you were not eligible, or if the aid package left you with a substantial piece of "unmet need," then part-time study may make sense. However, before you take that course of action, ask the FAO what would happen if the student earned, say, $15,000 after taxes this year. Would the student's aid package remain the same, or would the extra income simply reduce the aid package by $4,000 or more?

# Transfer in Later: Option 1

If a family is on a very tight budget, a good way to finance a four-year college education is to start with a two-year college education. Two-year public community colleges or junior colleges, where the average in-state tuition for 2016–2017 according to the College Board was just $3,520, represent an outstanding way to save money. A student with a good academic record at a community college (perhaps earned while still living at home) can then transfer to a slightly more expensive state college for two more years to earn a BA. The total cost would be only a fraction of the cost of a private college, and still thousands of dollars less than that of a four-year program at the state college.

# Transfer in Later: Option 2

If a student really has her heart set on a particular private college but the family cannot afford the costs of four years' tuition, there is another option: The student could go to a public college for the first two years and then transfer into the private school. The student will get the private college degree at a much more affordable price. Obviously, the student would have to get accepted by the private school as a transfer student, and this can be quite difficult. Outstanding grades are a given. We will go into this strategy in more detail in Chapter Seven, "Innovative Payment Options."

# Transfer in Later: Option 3
# Inexpensive College, Pricy Graduate School

Extending the previous strategy, a student could attend an in-state public university during all four of the undergraduate years, and then go to a top-of-the-line private graduate school. The undergraduate savings would be huge, but again, whether the student attends a private or a public undergraduate college, a compelling academic record is always very important to ensure acceptance.

## The Senior Year

The family will complete its last standardized need analysis form in the spring of the student's junior year of college. Once that form has been filed, there are no longer any financial aid considerations to worry about. During the summer between junior and senior year, students who want to help out with the last year's tuition can earn unlimited amounts of money without hurting their eligibility for financial aid.

Of course, if the student goes straight on to graduate school, then the senior year of college becomes the first base income year for graduate school, and the process begins again.

# Chapter Six

## State Aid

States sometimes don't get the credit they deserve for their most pervasive and sweeping form of financial aid: an affordable college education for in-state residents through public state university programs. These programs are still terrific values (as we explored in Chapter Four, "How to Pick Colleges") and in some cases, the quality of education is at least as good as it is at the best private colleges.

However, it is the other kind of state aid that we are going to discuss here. It comes in the form of need-based and merit-based grants and loans to qualifying students who attend public *or* private colleges and universities within their own state. All 50 states have need-based financial aid programs for their residents, and more than 25 states now have merit-based awards as well. While some states are richer than others, the amount of money available for state aid is substantial; in some states students can qualify for more than $4,000 each year in grant money alone.

To qualify for this aid a student must generally attend a public university or private college within the student's state of legal residence. A few states have reciprocal agreements with specific other states that allow you to take aid with you to another state.

*Note: In recent years, some states have eliminated or reduced their state grant programs as a result of budget deficits in the recent economic downturn. For the latest information regarding the availability of state aid you should contact the appropriate state agency (See pages 146–152). Be aware that some states (i.e., Alaska, Illinois, Indiana, Kentucky, Nevada, North Carolina, North Dakota, Oklahoma, Oregon, South Carolina, Tennessee, Texas, Utah, Vermont, and Washington) award funds on a first-come first-served basis.*

## Even If You Don't Qualify for Federal Aid, You May Qualify for State Aid

Because of the differences between the state aid formulas and the federal formula, it is sometimes easier to qualify for state aid. Federal aid is based on your adjusted gross income (along with information about your assets). In some states, however, aid is based solely on your taxable income (the AGI minus deductions) *without reference to your assets*.

Thus if you miss out on federal aid because you have been industrious and managed to save enough to make investments, you may be able to qualify for state money anyway. In some states, it is possible to own a mansion, a business, and sizable investments, and—as long as your *taxable* income is within state parameters—still qualify for thousands of dollars in aid.

There are too many states with too many different types of programs and formulas for us to go into each one separately. Suffice it to say that state aid is one of the more overlooked ways for middle- and upper-middle-class families to help pay for college. We estimate that thousands of these parents, under the impression they make too much money, never even apply.

## How to Apply for State Aid

Some states use the data you supply on the federal FAFSA form to award their aid. Other states require you to complete a supplemental aid form that is processed directly by that state's higher education agency.

Confused? Your high school guidance counselor should have the correct forms for your situation. If, for some reason, forms are not available at your high school, or your guidance counselor doesn't seem to know what is what, contact your state agency (a list of all the state agencies with their addresses and phone numbers is at the end of this chapter).

The only time the forms you find at your high school might not be the right forms for you is when the student goes to school in one state but lives in another. If this is the case, again contact your state agency.

If your family is eligible for state financial aid, your state grant will appear as part of the aid packages you receive from the colleges sometime before April 15. Obviously, unless your state has reciprocal agreements, the state money will appear only in the aid packages from colleges in your own state. Families that are pondering several offers from schools within their own state, sometimes notice that the amount of state money they were offered at each of the schools differs. This might be because aid is based not just on need, but also on the size of tuition at different schools. A more expensive school will often trigger a larger grant. However, if you applied to two comparably priced schools within your own state, and one school gives you significantly less state aid than another, then something is amiss because you should be getting approximately the same amount of state aid at similarly priced schools.

## Alternative State Loans

Some states make guaranteed student loans much like the Stafford loans provided by the federal government. These are sometimes called "special loans." Again, if your state offers these loans and if you qualify, they will appear as part of your aid package.

# Establishing Residency in a State

In-state rates are much cheaper than out-of-state rates at public universities; at the University of Vermont, for example, an out-of-state student pays over $23,000 more than an in-state resident. So it should come as no surprise that students have tried over the years to establish residency in the state of the public university they were attending. Until recently, it was much easier for a student to establish residency in a state if he wished to take advantage of the in-state rates. It has since become much more difficult, with the exception of one or two states. We will discuss establishing residency in greater detail in the "Special Topics" chapter.

# The State Agencies

### Alabama

Alabama Commission on
Higher Education
P.O. Box 302000
Montgomery, AL 36130-2000
(334) 242-1998
www.ache.state.al.us

### Alaska

Alaska Commission on Postsecondary
Education
P.O. Box 110505
Juneau, AK 99811
(907) 465-2962 or (800) 441-2962
acpe.alaska.gov

### Arizona

Commission on Postsecondary Education
2020 N. Central Ave.
Phoenix, AZ 85004
(602) 258-2435
https://azgrants.az.gov

### Arkansas

Arkansas Department of
Higher Education
423 Main Street, Suite 400
Little Rock, AR 72201
(501) 371-2000
www.adhe.edu

### California

California Student Aid Commission
Grant Programs–Customer Service
P.O. Box 419026
Rancho Cordova, CA 95741-9026
(888) 224-7268
www.csac.ca.gov

### Colorado

Colorado Commission on Higher Education
1600 Broadway, Suite 2200
Denver, CO 80202
(303) 862-3001
http://highered.colorado.gov

## Connecticut

Connecticut Department
of Higher Education
450 Columbus Blvd.
Hartford, CT 06103
(860) 947-1800
www.ctohe.org

## Delaware

Delaware Higher Education Office
The Townsend Building
401 Federal Street, Suite 2
Dover, DE 19901
(302) 735-4000
www.doe.k12.de.us

## District of Columbia

Office of the State Supt. of Education
Division of Higher Education &
Financial Services
810 First Street NE
Washington, DC 20002
(202) 727-6436
www.osse.dc.gov

## Florida

Florida Department of Education
Office of Student Financial Assistance
325 West Gaines St.
Tallahassee, FL 32399
(850) 245-0505 or (888) 827-2004
www.floridastudentfinancialaid.org
or www.fldoe.org

## Georgia

Georgia Student Finance Commission
State Loans & Grants Division
2082 East Exchange Place
Tucker, GA 30084
(800) 505-4732
www.gsfc.org

## Hawaii

Hawaii State Postsecondary Education
Commission
2444 Dole Street, Room 209
Honolulu, HI 96822
(808) 956-8213
www.hawaii.edu

## Idaho

Office of the State Board of Education
P.O. Box 83720
Boise, ID 83720-0037
(208) 334-2270
www.boardofed.idaho.gov

## Illinois

Illinois Student Assistance Commission
1755 Lake Cook Road
Deerfield, IL 60015-5209
(800) 899-4722
www.isac.org

## Indiana

Indiana Commission for Higher Education
101 West Ohio Street, Suite 300
Indianapolis, IN 46204
(888) 528-4719
www.in.gov/che

## Iowa

Iowa College Student Aid Commission
430 East Grand Ave.
3rd Floor
Des Moines, IA 50309
(877) 272-4456 or (515) 725-3400
www.iowacollegeaid.gov

## Kansas

Kansas Association of Student
Financial Aid Administrators
Kansas Board of Regents
1000 S.W. Jackson Street
Suite 520
Topeka, KS 66612-1368
(785) 430-4240
www.kansasregents.org

## Kentucky

Kentucky Higher Education
Assistance Authority
100 Airport Road
Frankfort, KY 40602
(800) 928-8926
www.kheaa.com

## Louisiana

Louisiana Office of Student Financial
Assistance
602 North 5th Street
Baton Rouge, LA 70802
(800) 259-5626
www.osfa.la.gov

## Maine

Finance Authority of Maine
Maine Education Assistance Division
5 Community Drive, P.O. Box 949
Augusta, ME 04332-0949
(800) 228-3734
www.famemaine.com

## Maryland

Maryland Higher Education Commission
Office of Student Financial Assistance
6 North Liberty Street
Ground Suite
Baltimore, MD 21201
(410) 767-3300 or (800) 974-0203
www.mhec.state.md.us

## Massachusetts

The Massachusetts Office of Student
Financial Assistance
75 Pleasant Street
Malden, MA 02148
(617) 391-6070
www.osfa.mass.edu

## Michigan

Michigan Higher Education
Assistance Authority
Office of Scholarships and Grants
P.O. Box 30462
Lansing, MI 48909-7962
(888) 447-2687
www.michigan.gov/mistudentaid

## Minnesota

Minnesota Higher Education
Services Office
1450 Energy Park Drive
Suite 350
St. Paul, MN 55108-5227
(800) 657-3866 or (651) 642-0567
www.ohe.state.mn.us

## Mississippi

Mississippi Office of State
Student Financial Aid
3825 Ridgewood Road
Jackson, MS 39211
(800) 327-2980 or (601) 432-6997
www.ihl.state.ms.us

## Missouri

Missouri Department of
Higher Education
205 Jefferson Street
P.O. Box 1469
Jefferson City, MO 65102-1469
(800) 473-6757 or (573) 751-2361
https://dhe.mo.gov

## Montana

Montana University System
Office of the Commisioner of Higher
Education
560 N. Park Avenue, P.O. Box 203201
Helena, MT 59620
(406) 449-9124
https://mus.edu/che

## Nebraska

Coordinating Commission for
Postsecondary Education
P.O. Box 95005
Lincoln, NE 68509-5005
(402) 471-2847
https://ccpe.nebraska.gov

## Nevada

State Department of Education
700 E. Fifth Street
Carson City, NV 89701
(775) 687-9200
www.doe.nv.gov

## New Hampshire

New Hampshire Department of
Education
101 Pleasant Street
Concord, NH 03301
(603) 271-3494
www.state.nh.us/postsecondary

## New Jersey

HESAA
P.O. Box 545
Trenton, NJ 08625-0545
(800) 792-8670
www.hesaa.org

## New Mexico

State of New Mexico
Higher Education Department
2048 Galisteo St.
Santa Fe, NM 87505
(800) 279-9777 or (505) 476-8400
www.hed.state.nm.us

## New York

New York State Higher Education Services
Corporation
99 Washington Avenue
Albany, NY 12255
(518) 473-1574 or (888) 697-4372
www.hesc.ny.gov

## North Carolina

College Foundation of North Carolina
P.O. Box 41966
Raleigh, NC 27629-1966
(888) 234-6400
www.cfnc.org

## North Dakota

North Dakota University System
Tenth Floor, State Capitol
600 E. Boulevard Avenue-Dept. 215
Bismarck, ND 58505-0230
(701) 328-2960
www.ndus.edu

## Ohio

Ohio Dept. of Higher Education
State Grants and Scholarship Dept.
25 South Front Street
Columbus, OH 43215
(614) 466-6000
www.ohiohighered.org

## Oklahoma

State Regents for Higher Education
655 Research Parkway
Suite 200
Oklahoma City, OK 73104
(800) 858-1840 or (405) 225-9100
www.okhighered.org/student-center

## Oregon

Oregon Student Access Commission
1500 Valley River Drive
Suite 100
Eugene, OR 97401
(541) 687-7400 or (800) 452-8807
www.osac.state.or.us

## Pennsylvania

Pennsylvania Higher Education Assistance
Agency
P.O. Box 8157
Harrisburg, PA 17105-8157
(800) 692-7392
www.pheaa.org

## Rhode Island

Rhode Island Higher Education
Assistance Authority
560 Jefferson Boulevard, Suite 100
Warwick, RI 02886
(800) 922-9855 or (401) 736-1100
www.riopc.edu

## South Carolina

South Carolina Higher Education
Tuition Grants Commission
115 Atrium Way, Suite 102
Columbia, SC 29223
(803) 896-1120
www.sctuitiongrants.com

## South Dakota

Dept. of Ed. and Cultural Affairs
Office of the Secretary
800 Governors Drive
Pierre, SD 57501
(605) 773-3134
www.doe.sd.gov

## Tennessee

Tennessee Student
Assistance Corporation (TSAC)
Parkway Towers, Suite 1510
404 James Robertson Parkway
Nashville, TN 37243-0820
(800) 342-1663
(615) 741-1346
www.tn.gov/collegepays

## Texas

Texas Higher Education Coordinating Board
P.O. Box 12788
Austin, TX 78711-2788
(512) 427-6101
(800) 242-3062
www.thecb.state.tx.us

## Utah

Utah State Board of Regents
Board of Regents Building
The Gateway
60 South 400 West
Salt Lake City, UT 84101-1284
(877) 336-7378
or (801) 321-7294
www.uheaa.org

## Vermont

Vermont Student
Assistance Corporation
Champlain Mill
P.O. Box 2000
Winooski, VT 05404
(802) 654-3750
(800) 882-4166
www.vsac.org

## Virginia

State Council of Higher
Education for Virginia
James Monroe Building
101 North Fourteenth Street
Richmond, VA 23219
(804) 225-2600
www.schev.edu

## Washington

Washington State Higher
Education Coordinating Board
917 Lakeridge Way SW
Olympia, WA 98502
(360) 753-7800
www.wsac.wa.gov

## West Virginia

West Virginia Higher Education Policy
Commission
1018 Kanawha Blvd. East
Charleston, WV 25301
(304) 558-2101
http://wvhepc.edu

## Wisconsin

Higher Education Aids Board
PO Box 7885
Madison, WI 53707-7885
(608) 267-2206
www.heab.state.wi.us

## Wyoming

University of Wyoming
Student Financial Aid
1000 East University Avenue
Laramie, WY 82071
(307) 766-2116
www.uwyo.edu

## American Samoa

American Samoa Community
College Board of Higher Education
P.O. Box 2609
Pago Pago, AS 96799-2609
(684) 699-9155
www.amsamoa.edu

## Guam

University of Guam
Financial Aid Office
University Drive
UOG Station
Mangilao, GU 96913
(671) 735-2288
www.uog.edu

## Northern Mariana Islands

Northern Marianas College
P.O. Box 501250
Saipan, MP 96950
(670) 234-5498
www.marianas.edu

## Puerto Rico

Council on Higher Education
Box 19900
San Juan, PR 00910-1900
(787) 641-7100
www.ce.pr.gov

## Trust Territory of Pacific Islands

Palau Community College
P.O. Box 9
Koror, Republic of Palau, 96940
(680) 488-2470
www.pcc.palau.edu

## Virgin Islands

Board of Education
Box 11900
60B, 61 & 62 Dronningens Gade
St. Thomas, VI 00801
(340) 774-4546
http://myviboe.com

# Part Three

## Filling Out the Standardized Forms

# Filling Out the Forms

Any prospective college student who wants to be considered for financial aid must complete the Free Application for Federal Student Aid (FAFSA). If you are applying to private colleges (as well as a few state schools and certain private scholarship programs) you will probably also have to complete the College Board's CSS/Financial Aid PROFILE Application.

After you finish completing your form or forms (usually online), you'll send the data to the processor, which then analyzes your information and sends a detailed report to the colleges you designate. The FAFSA processor also generates a report you can access online called the Student Aid Report or SAR. After you submit the PROFILE form, you will be able to view a private online "dashboard" with a list of schools your information has been submitted to and, in some cases, additional steps you need to take. There will also be an option to view and print your submitted PROFILE data.

In this part of the book, we will give you line-by-line instructions for filling out the 2020–2021 version of the FAFSA as well as tips for the key questions on the 2020–2021 PROFILE form.

## First Step: Decide Which Form(s) to Fill Out

As your child narrows down his choice of colleges, you should find out which financial aid forms are required by each of the schools. Don't rely on the popular college guides sold in stores for this information. These books sometimes get their facts wrong, and can contain incorrect or outdated information. You also shouldn't rely on information you receive over the telephone from the schools themselves. We are amazed at how often schools have given us misleading or wrong information over the telephone. If you must rely on information given over the telephone, get the name and title of the person you're talking to. In the financial aid process, Murphy's Law is in full effect, and when things do go wrong, remember it will always be your fault. The best filing requirement and deadline information comes from each school's own financial aid office website.

When applying to several schools, you should keep in mind that you are only allowed to file one FAFSA form per student per year. You don't have to fill out a separate FAFSA for each college being considered. The form (whether you use the popular online version or the paper version) will allow you to list the schools to which the student is applying. However if you will have more than one child in college in the same academic year, a separate FAFSA form for each child will need to be submitted. The same holds true with the PROFILE form. If there is more than one child attending a school that requires the PROFILE, then separate PROFILES need to be completed. This Is because with the college aid process, an individual student and not their family is the aid applicant.

## Sometimes the Schools Have Their Own Aid Applications as Well

To make things even more confusing, some of the schools have supplemental financial aid forms for you to fill out in addition to the forms we've just mentioned. For example, any undergraduate freshman applying for financial aid at the University of Pennsylvania must complete the Penn Financial Aid Supplement in addition to the FAFSA and the PROFILE forms. Carefully check through the financial aid requirements of all the schools under consideration to see if there are any supplemental aid forms that you need to complete. For now, we are going to talk only about the FAFSA and the PROFILE form.

## Filling Out the Right Form

Make sure you are using the right version of the form. Don't laugh. It's actually quite easy to fill out the wrong form. That's because the filing period of the next academic year's FAFSA form overlaps for nine months with the filing period of the current academic year's FAFSA form. Similarly, the different years' filing periods for the PROFILE overlap for four months. The FAFSA form you want to file needs to correspond to the academic year for which you want to receive aid. If you submit the wrong version during these overlap periods, your forms will be processed, but you will be up the proverbial creek.

## Take Your Pick: Three Ways to File the FAFSA

Before you start in on the forms, you have an important choice to make as to what method you'll use to file the FAFSA. The Department of Education offers three options:

1. **The FAFSA on the Web (also known as the FOTW)**

2. **A new APP version of the FAFSA**—This is relatively new, and still has some gliches, so we still do not recommend using the app version. Why risk being a guinea-pig with so much on the line?

3. **A downloadable PDF FAFSA**—Instead of using the two electronic options, you can also download and print a PDF version, which you then fill out by hand and send by mail to the FAFSA processor.

While this choice will not affect how the processor calculates your EFC under the federal formula, there are a number of advantages to using the FOTW option:

• You can list up to 10 schools to receive your data (compared to only 4 with the PDF version).

• You don't need to worry if the post office lost your form or delivered it late.

- The online FAFSA form has an interactive data retrieval tool that takes you to an IRS website that allows you to transfer some information from your tax return (provided you've already filed for that year) directly onto the FAFSA. (We'll explain this in more detail later in the book.)

- Your FAFSA data will be processed faster

- The skip logic built into the online form helps you to avoid submitting inconsistent data.

- You don't have to worry that some responses on the PDF version of the FAFSA will be incorrectly inputted by the processor.

- As soon as you hit the final "SUBMIT MY FAFSA NOW" icon on the FOTW, you will instantaneously receive that vital number we've referenced so often in the pages of this book: your EFC under the  federal methodology.

Details on how to complete the FAFSA on the Web, or how to download the PDF version, are available on the U.S. Department of Education's (DOE) comprehensive federal aid web page (https://studentaid.ed.gov). Veterans of the aid process in prior years may discover that their former "favorite" webpage for the FAFSA  (www.fafsa.ed.gov) may have been eliminated by the DOE by the time the filing period begins for the new 2020–2021 FAFSA on October 1, 2019).

*Note:  The FOTW utilizes "skip logic"—which means certain questions may not be asked based on your answers to previous questions. For example, if the student says he won't file a tax return, further questions about his tax return will be omitted. Because of this "skip logic", the questions on the online FOTW are not asked in the same (numerical) order as they are on the PDF version. However in the interest of clarity, and since some of our readers may still be using the PDF version, our line-by-line tips for completing the FAFSA questions that follow will be done in numerical order. Regardless of the version you file, the same questions will have the same question numbers. On the FOTW version, the question number will appear in the "Help and Hints" area on the top or side of your monitor. By placing the cursor into the response area, the question number will appear for the corresponding question. (Key point: for some questions, you may need to answer the question to see the appropriate "Help and Hints" text and then change or delete your response due to a quirk with the online FAFSA application.)*

*The strategies in this chapter for answering each question on the FAFSA to the best advantage will apply for any version of the 2020–2021 FAFSA that you choose to file. A number of the tips in this chapter relating to the completion and filing of the FAFSA may apply only to the PDF version. If you prefer to file the FOTW, you should be sure to read our line-by-line instructions below, since the online "Help and Hints" text for the FOTW are not as complete as the instructions on the PDF version. The PDF version of the form follows the letter of the law and goes through a formal comment period and review process by the feds. After the FAFSA is processed, the Student Aid Report (SAR) that is generated will list your data in the same numerical order, regardless of the method you chose to fill out the form.*

| COLLEGE | Admissions deadline | Which standardized need analysis forms (FAFSA, PROFILE) are required? When are they due at the processor? | Is there an institutional aid form required? If so, when? | Are income tax returns required? When? What year(s)? | Ary other forms required? (Noncustodial form, business/farm supplement, etc.) When are they due? | Name of contact FAO at college & phone number |
|---|---|---|---|---|---|---|
| | | | | | | |
| | | | | | | |
| | | | | | | |
| | | | | | | |
| | | | | | | |
| | | | | | | |
| | | | | | | |

# Second Step: Know Your Deadlines

Missing a financial aid deadline is worse than missing a mortgage payment. Your bank will probably give you another chance; the colleges probably will not. Schools process their financial aid candidates in batches. At most schools, student aid applications are collected in a pile up until the "priority filing deadline" (set by the school) and then assessed in one batch. If you send in your application three weeks early, you will not necessarily be better off than someone who just makes the deadline. However, if your application arrives a day late, it could sit unopened in a small pile of late applications until the entire first batch has been given aid. Then, if there is anything left in their coffers, the FAOs look at the second batch on a rolling basis.

## Meeting Deadlines

There are so many different deadlines to remember during the process of applying for college admission and financial aid that the only way to keep everything straight is to write it all down in one place. We suggest that you use the chart that appears on the preceding page.

You should realize that if a school requires both the FAFSA and the PROFILE, the school's deadlines for filing these two forms may be different. However, as they become available at the same time (October 1) and have a lot of identical questions, it's usually a good idea to complete both at the same time. And if possible, it would be best to hold off submitting either form until both are completed so as to provide an opportunity to review all the data and resolve any inconsistencies before the two forms are submitted. Keep in mind that while the information relating to the prior-prior year income will involve a time period that has long since ended, the asset information and other demographic details of your situation will be as of the date you submit the form.

Since the majority of students apply only to schools that require the FAFSA but do not also require the PROFILE form, the strategies for completing both forms that follow will start with the tips for the FAFSA (so that those readers who do not need to complete the PROFILE can skip the PROFILE section that follows). However, for those students who must complete the PROFILE: it would be best if possible to complete the PROFILE before the FAFSA (as long as you do not risk missing any FAFSA deadline for any other non-PROFILE schools or state aid programs that may require earlier submission than your earliest PROFILE school's aid deadlines). This is because the FAFSA is child's play compared to the PROFILE—which requires significantly more detailed information than the federal form. Or as one senior administrator at the College Board once said in using an analogy to a student's academic record to compare the two forms: "FAFSA is to grade point average, as PROFILE is to an academic transcript". To help insure that your responses to similar questions on the two forms are consistent: in the tips for completing the PROFILE that follow, we provide guidelines to assist you in identifying and matching up your responses to those similar questions on both forms.

*Note: In addition to the schools' deadlines, some state aid programs or private scholarship programs may have earlier deadlines than the priority deadlines set by the particular schools for the FAFSA, PROFILE and/or their own aid form. And some state agencies awards funds on a first-come, first-serve basis until their coffers are empty. (See pages 146–152.)*

## There Are Three Types of Financial Aid Deadlines

1.  The school, private scholarship program, or state agency says your application must be mailed (and postmarked) by a particular date.

    If filing a paper version: Send the form by Priority Mail at the post office and make sure the postal worker and/or your payment receipt shows you the postmark on the envelope before you leave the post office. Priority Mail with 2–3 day delivery also provides a tracking number, provided you go to window clerk or use an automated postal machine at the post office when you pay the postage.

2.  Your application must be received and "date stamped" by the need analysis company by a particular date.

    In this case, you must factor in delivery time if mailing a paper form. Again, send the application by regular Priority Mail at the post office (provided you can track the delivery). If you are mailing the standardized form within two weeks of this type of deadline, use the U.S. Postal Service's more- expensive "Express Priority" service (which assigns a tracking number and also guarantees delivery by a specified date). You cannot use Federal Express or any of the other private carriers because standard-ized forms must be sent to a post office box. Since the FAFSA processor is located in a somewhat remote location, it may take two business days for your form to be delivered via Express Priority Mail.

3.  Your standardized application must be processed and the results made available to the school, private scholarship program, or state agency by a certain date.

    To be on the safe side allow four weeks processing time. If the deadline is March 1, for example, then you should submit the form (via some method that provides tracking or submission confirmation) to the need analysis company by February 1.

If you are filing a form online, then the first two types of deadlines will be the same; namely the date you must transmit the completed form to the processor (since it will be considered received on the date you transmit it). Last minute filers should be aware that the processors may be located in an earlier time zone which could affect the official receipt/transmission "date" for your form. So for example, a filer in Oregon would have to file a form online by 9 P.M. Pacific Time if the data is sent to a processor that uses Eastern Time for date-stamping the form. If the form were filed at, say, 9:04 P.M. Pacific Time it would be considered as received the next day. If your form must be processed by a certain date, you should allow 2 to 3 weeks processing time.

**TIP 23:**
Determine early on which forms you must file,
and when they are due.

## So When is the Optimal Time to Submit the Aid Forms?

One of the most difficult things about financial aid is that the answers to most questions are: "It depends on your situation and other factors". While conventional wisdom holds that one should always file "as soon as possible after a certain date", the reality is that you should file at the appropriate time when you will demonstrate the greatest need for aid. So.....

1.   If you are applying for aid at one of the few schools (Florida State is one such school that comes to mind) that still awards financial aid on a first-come, first-served (FCFS) basis instead of setting a priority filing date, then you should file the 2020–2021 aid forms as soon as possible after September 30, 2019. Be aware that the overwhelming majority of colleges no longer award funds this way, as they learned a long time ago it is better for their enrollment goals to leverage their aid by rationing their funds instead. If a school's aid requirements advise you to complete the forms "as soon as possible after X date but before Y date", then the Y date is the priority filing deadline and they do not award funds on a first come-first served basis.

2.   If you reside in one of the states that awards state aid on an FCFS basis until funds run out, then you would want to file the FAFSA and other required forms ASAP after September 30, 2019. Based on state aid information for the 2020–2021 school year, the applicable states were: Alaska, Illinois, Indiana, Kentucky, Nevada, North Carolina, North Dakota, Oklahoma, Oregon, South Carolina, Tennessee, Texas, Utah, Vermont, and Washington. The other 35 states and the District of Columbia do not appear to have such policies (providing a fixed cut-off deadline to apply), though the situation may change, so it's best to contact your state agency for full details. (See pages 146–152 for your state's contact info.)

3.   If none of the colleges or your state agency award funds on an FCFS basis, the earliest school's deadline by which a standardized need analysis form must will be sent to or received by the need analysis company becomes your overall deadline. In this case, you should file the form after October 1 but before your earliest deadline, during the time period when your family contribution is likely to be the lowest number. Let's say your earliest deadline is January 31, 2020 for the 2020–2021 award year, but you will be getting a large bonus check from your employer right after New Year's Day for the prior

year. You would be better off filing the form before that the bonus money inflates your assets. Do you make estimated tax payments? You would be better off making that next payment and have the payment clear your account before you file so that your reportable assets are lower at the time you file.

And even though the FAFSA filing period now begins three months earlier, from what we have heard so far from our contacts in the financial aid trenches it does not appear that many schools will be moving up their admission or aid deadlines—at least for applications involving the 2020–2021 school year. So if you don't fit into category 1 or 2 above, your aid forms may not be due until sometime in early 2020, unless the student is applying for admission as an "early decision" or "early action" candidate.

Once the need analysis company has your numbers, it sends them to all the schools you designated on that form. If the student subsequently decides to apply to some additional school(s) after you filed the standardized form(s), you will need to remember to send the data to the additional school(s). (We'll advise how to do this later.)

Regardless of your situation, keep in mind that the instructions for the FAFSA say that you have until late June 30, 2021 (that is, at end of the academic year for which you want aid) to fill out the FAFSA. What they mean is that the need analysis company is willing to accept and process the form until this date, but by then there will be virtually no money left at almost any college in the land.

## The Standardized Form Deadlines May Be Different from the Individual Aid Form Deadlines

If you are applying to a school that asks you to fill out their own separate supplemental financial aid form in addition to a standardized form, make sure you know the deadlines for each form. Unfortunately, these deadlines are usually different. Even if they are the same, the standardized form may have a postmark deadline while the college form has a receipt deadline, or vice versa. The only way to keep all this straight is to read each college's bulletin carefully and then use a deadline chart like the one we provide on page 157.

## Supplemental Forms at the Highly Selective Colleges

Some Ivy League schools, the "little Ivies," and many other selective schools have rather extensive financial aid forms of their own. The quantity of paperwork may seem daunting at first, but when you start answering the questions you will begin to notice that many of the questions on the forms are identical—designed to get more detailed responses to the questions already asked on the FAFSA and/or the PROFILE form and to discover inconsistencies in your responses. Individual schools may also ask a few questions that may strike you as bizarre. This is less Big Brotherish than it sounds. The FAOs are just trying to find recipients for restricted awards donated by alumni that the aid office would prefer to award before they tap their unrestricted funds.

*Be aware that some schools (Boston University is one that comes to mind) may establish earlier filing deadlines than their normal deadlines for prospective students who wish to be considered for special scholarships. So if your child is an above average candidate for admission at the college, it is best to review the information on the school's admission office's website regarding institutional scholarships based on merit or a combination of merit and need to determine if there are earlier deadlines than the stated deadlines listed on the college's aid office website.*

## Third Step: Determine if Any of the Colleges You are Applying to Require the College Board's PROFILE Application

Many private colleges and a handful of state schools will require completion of the CSS/Financial Aid PROFILE form in addition to the FAFSA if one wishes to be considered for institutional aid as well as federal aid. While a PDF version of the FAFSA can be printed and submitted through the mail, the PROFILE form can only be filed electronically via the Collegeboard.org website. While it's possible for parents to use the student's College Board account to complete the PROFILE, we do not recommend that for a variety of reasons. For example, if the two biological or adoptive parents are no longer living together, the noncustodial parent could view all the intimate financial details of the custodial parent if the student's College Board account was used for the PROFILE and the noncustodial parent knew the valid log-in information for that student account. And so, it is best for another College Board "student account" to be created for the PROFILE process.

For dependent students, parental information is required on the PROFILE just as it is on the FAFSA. Yet some students who can be classified as independent students for federal aid purposes via the FAFSA may still find that parental information will be required on the PROFILE; we'll get into this later.

But perhaps the most confusing part for children of divorced, separated, or never-married parents who are living apart, is that many colleges requiring the PROFILE will also require information from a "noncustodial parent". Don't worry—we'll get into this later too.

There is a $9 PROFILE application fee, as well as a $16 processing fee per school—for a PROFILE application submitted by the student and/or the custodial parent(s). A noncustodial parent will pay a $25 one-time processing fee for their "Noncustodial parent PROFILE", regardless of the number of colleges who need it. Since you will have to pay this fee using a credit card or an electronic debit when you submit your completed PROFILE data, you should carefully review each college's financial aid requirements in order to determine which ones (if any) need the PROFILE information. Certain users may be eligible for a fee waiver for an unlimited number of PROFILE schools. There are also some private scholarship programs that require the PROFILE, which will set their own application filing deadlines.

## Not Too Early

While counseling thousands of individual clients over the past 35 years, we've noticed that many families fit into two distinct categories: those who like to do things right away and those who like to wait until the last minute. When handling the PROFILE application either course of action could get you into trouble.

While you can register for, complete, and submit the 2020–2021 PROFILE anytime on or after October 1, 2020, keep in mind that you will be paying a $16 processing fee for any school or program that you designate to receive your PROFILE information. So it would make sense to wait a while to submit your completed PROFILE to the processor until the student has a better idea of their list of schools. (You might also want to wait until you make any appropriate changes to your financials that could lower your EFC!) While you can change the list of schools/programs that you have provided before you submit the form, you will be charged for any school that you have selected to receive your PROFILE data at the time you submit your completed application to the processor. So unless the college requests the completion of the PROFILE form in the early fall for an Early Decision or Early Action application (see pages 274–275), it is a good idea to wait to submit the PROFILE until you are closer to your earliest school's or program's PROFILE deadline. Otherwise, if you apply too soon you may be paying a fee for schools to which the child never decides to apply. Note: once you submit your PROFILE for processing, you cannot electronically correct any information. So unless a PROFILE deadline is imminent, you should take your time, carefully read the online instructions, review our strategies, and double-check all your responses before you submit the original PROFILE to the processor.

Once you submit the form, you can always add additional schools or programs to the PROFILE at a later data (at an additional cost of $16 per school or program added unless you received a fee waiver before). You will be asked any additional supplemental questions that are required by the school(s)/programs you wish to add that have not been previously asked. However except for any comments you wish to add or change in the Special Circumstances section of the PROFILE, you will not be able to electronically revise any of the other PROFILE responses originally submitted online to the processor.

And if you discover any errors after the PROFILE is submitted for a given award year, you will need to print out the submitted application data, write in the applicable corrections, and then send a copy of your handwritten corrections to the financial aid offices at each school that requires the PROFILE. (If you plan to add any school to the PROFILE in the future, you should wait to send such school(s) any handwritten corrections until after you have electronically added the school and they have received your PROFILE data.)

### Not Too Late

While you can now set up a free account on the College Board's website  and then complete and submit the PROFILE in one online session, it is still not a good idea to wait until right before your earliest school's PROFILE deadline to get started. During peak processing periods, the College Board website may run slowly or be difficult to access. If additional supplements are required, you will also need some time to complete them and work out the logistics of getting the data to the appropriate schools by their deadlines.

And if a noncustodial parent is required to complete the Noncustodial parent PROFILE form, it would make sense for the student and the custodial parent to at least begin the PROFILE process and complete the first few sections of their PROFILE, sooner rather than later so that the noncustodial parent has sufficient time to work on their own form. We will also provide more details later in this part of the book.

## Fourth Step: Decide Whether You Can Get Your Taxes Done in Time to Fill Out the FAFSA and/or the PROFILE Form

Prior to the 2017–2018 FAFSA and PROFILE, most families had to estimate their base year income on the forms because they needed to file the aid forms before they could complete their tax returns for the "prior-year".

However, with the switch to the use of prior-prior year (PPY) data on the standardized aid forms, most individuals who were required to file a tax return for the PPY will have done so before they need to file the forms. However, it would still be much better if you were not reading this chapter on the day of the deadline, because this is going to take more time than you think—if you want to maximize your aid. A ten-year-old child can fill out the form, but HOW you fill it out will determine your aid package. As you will soon find out, the questions involving PPY income only encompass a fraction of the data required to submit the forms. As such, you should begin gathering together all this information weeks before you plan to submit the aid forms.

Here are the records you will need:

1.  Completed 2018 federal tax return (including all schedules), if filed. (If 2019 return not filed, see below)

2.  2018 W-2 forms

3.  Records of 2018 untaxed income (social security payments received, welfare payments, tax-exempt interest income, etc.)

4.  Bank statements

5. Brokerage statements

6. Mortgage statements (for all properties other than the primary residence)

7. Student's social security number and driver's license (if available)

8. If you are an owner of a business, the business's financial statements or corporate tax return

9. Other investment statements and records (including any farm you own, but don't live on and operate)

10. Records of 2018 child support paid to or received by former spouse and if you will be filing the PROFILE in addition to the FAFSA, you will also need:

11. Records of 2018 medical and dental expenses (must have been actually paid or charged on your credit card during 2018)

12. Records of any post–secondary tuition paid or that will be paid during the 2019–2020 school year

13. Records of any educational loan payments made (or to be made in 2018 and 2019)

14. Mortgage statement(s) for your primary residence

15. The amount of any financial aid awarded for the 2019–2020 school year (for any household member)

**If you have NOT completed your 2018 tax return by the time you need to complete the aid forms:**

Obviously, it will be easier to complete the 2020–2021 standardized aid form(s) if you first complete your 2018 tax returns and then file the aid form(s). However, if you are applying for aid at the relatively rare school that actually awards aid funds on a first-come, first-served basis and/or you are a resident of a state that awards state aid funds on a rolling basis until such funds are depleted, then you should not delay filing the aid forms. You should simply use your best estimates for your PPY information and submit the aid forms. (In this case, it would be helpful to have a copy of your 2017 return as well as a blank copy of the 2018 tax return as the line items on the tax returns changed.) However, you will want to file your tax return(s) as soon as possible (if required to do so), and then revised your estimated information reported on the aid forms as soon as you are able to do so.

If you are not required to file a U.S. tax return: you should not feel that it is necessary to do so in order to apply for aid. The financial aid application process and forms are designed to also accommodate those who do not file a U.S. tax return (or those who are only required to file a foreign tax return).

## A Word About Confidentiality

The information you supply will go directly to the financial aid office and will stay there. You can trust them to keep information confidential. No one else at the school will see your personal data. And no one else at the school—not professors, students, or administrators—will know who is getting financial aid and who isn't.

Some parents are reluctant to share intimate details with a stranger. No matter how spectacular the details of your private life are, the FAOs have seen worse. And frankly, the FAOs are too busy coping with the needs of thousands of students to have time to make value judgments.

Currently the only way the IRS can see a copy of your need analysis form is by getting a subpoena, although the laws could always change. However, the Secretary of Education now has the authority to verify the information on the FAFSA with the IRS.

## Practice, Practice, Practice

If you're completing a paper form: It would be a good idea to make an extra copy for use as a draft version. Once you are satisfied with all of your entries, you can transfer the information carefully onto a new blank version. The PDF version of the FAFSA sent to the processor should be free of any corrections, comments in margins, or other stray marks. Otherwise, it may be rejected by the FAFSA processor. When you've finished, make a photocopy of the completed form and put it in a safe place before you mail the original to the processor.

If you're filing a form online: you should exercise care when inputting any responses. And before to review your responses before you hit the submit button. If you are in the habit of just dumping all of your financial records at your accountant's office, change your habits for the next four years. Photocopy every conceivably relevant document, and then dump them at your accountant's office.

## Read ALL the Instructions

You should read all the instructions on the form while working on them. In many cases, these instructions will be sketchy or misleading. Hopefully this book will clarify what the forms do not.

If you're completing a PDF version of a form: Make sure you use the proper writing implement. Also, be sure you complete the response areas the proper way. If they want a ●, don't give them a ✔ instead. Writing in the margins is forbidden. You are also not allowed to give a range of numbers for a particular item. For example, you cannot write down $700–$800. It must be $750.

And regardless of the way you file a form: Use whole dollar amounts only. Do not include cents or decimals. When writing down the numeric equivalent of a single-digit date, the MMDDYYYY format is usually requested. Thus, January 9, 2001 would look like this: 01 09 2001.

# Which Parent(s) Must Report Information on the FAFSA and PROFILE

Beginning with the 2014–2015 FAFSA, new guidelines for dependent students were established involving which of the student's parents' information will be required to be reported on the FAFSA. The PROFILE form mirrors these guidelines as well. Here is the gist of them:

- If the biological and/or adoptive parents of the student are living together, then information from both parents is required to be reported on the FAFSA and PROFILE, regardless of their marital status and regardless of their genders.

- If the biological and/or adoptive parents of the student are living apart (that is, they are divorced, separated or were never married and are living in separate residences): then only the parent with whom the student spent the most time in the 12-month period prior to completing the FAFSA should report their data in the parent sections of the FAFSA and PROFILE. That parent will be known in financial aid circles as the "custodial parent". If that amount of time is exactly equal, then the parent who provided the greater amount of support during the past 12 months (or if no support, the greater support during the last year when support was provided) will be the criteria used. So under the current rules, it does not matter which parent claims the student on their taxes, which parent was awarded custody and/or which parent is legally responsible to pay for college.

- If a divorced custodial parent or widowed parent is remarried (or the student's parents were never married, but now the biological or adoptive custodial parent is married to someone other than the student's other parent), then the information of the custodial parent and custodial stepparent is required to be reported. If this is the case, then when completing both the FAFSA and PROFILE all references to "parent(s)" on the form will be applicable to the custodial parent and the custodial stepparent.

- If one of the student's biological or adopted parents is deceased and the surviving parent is not married, then only the surviving parent's information is reported.

Be aware that this determination is made based on the situation on the date the aid form is completed, not the situation during the prior-prior year. Given all the fine print, it makes sense to carefully review the applicable parts of the FAFSA and PROFILE instructions.

**KEY POINTS:** If the parents are living apart, one cannot randomly choose who to use as the custodial parent. Be aware that it is illegal to report the parental financial and other information of a parent on the FAFSA, if such parent does not meet the federal government's criteria for being a "parent" for purposes of completing that student's FAFSA. However if you plan ahead, it is possible to arrange the time spent with each parent so that during the 12-month period prior to the filing of the FAFSA, that student will have spent the majority of time with the parent who will have the lower parent contribution in the federal aid formula. For schools that require noncustodial parent information for their own aid funds, this planning approach may or may not save you any money since any increased federal grant aid may or may not reduce the amount of institutional need-based gift aid awarded dollar-for-dollar.

If the PROFILE is required, it is critical that the same parent who is required to report their information on a student's FAFSA be the custodial parent for that student's PROFILE form. And if that custodial parent is currently married to the student's stepparent, then that stepparent's information must be reported on both forms as well. More on this later, as well.

## Don't Skip

Finally, don't skip any question unless the instructions specifically tell you that you can. If you do not own a business, for example, put down "0" for any values related to a business. If you leave certain items blank on the PDF version of the FAFSA, the processor will just send the paper form back to you to correct. You can't afford to lose the time that takes.

## Getting Started If You Are Filling Out the Online FAFSA (FOTW)

To find the FAFSA online, go to studentaid.gov and click on the "Start a New FAFSA" tab. If the student has an FSA ID, you'll be invited to enter it. If you don't, you can start by entering the student information instead—but it actually makes sense to get an FSA ID before you start filling out the FAFSA.

The FSA ID came into being in May 2015—and has been causing mass confusion ever since among parents, students, guidance counselors, and even financial aid officers. The FSA ID has several important functions: first, it can serve as a signature when you submit your FAFSA data. Second, it permits you to access your processed FAFSA data online at a later date, and if necessary revise or correct it. Third, it permits you to apply for federal education loans online. Fourth, it allows you to access your federal education loan history via the National Student Loan Data System (NSLDS). And fifth, it allows you to complete the Agreement to Serve (ATS) for the federal TEACH grant program.

What it does NOT do, is serve as a "password" for your FOTW application prior to submission. When you start filling out the FAFSA form, one of the first things you'll be asked to do is create a 4 to 8 character, case-sensitive "Save Key". If you don't create and submit the FAFSA in one session (and who does?), you'll need this "Save Key" to go back online and access your previously-saved FOTW data. (Forgot your Save Key? You can enter the zip code that was listed as part of the student's address on your saved FAFSA, and you'll be able to create a new Save Key.)

To get an FSA ID, go to fsaid.ed.gov. On this site, you'll be asked to create a user name/password combination. Because the FAFSA of a dependent student must be signed by both the student and one custodial parent/step-parent whose information is reported on the FAFSA, both the student and the parent/step-parent must create their own FSA ID user name and password combination. (The passwords can be the same for multiple individuals, but each user name created must be unique.) The user name doesn't have to be your own name—if fact, it is probably not a good idea to do that. The 6 to 30 character user name can be any combination of numbers and/or (non-case sensitive) letters so long as no one has already taken that exact same user name for their FSA ID. For the 8 to 30 character case-sensitive password, one can use any combination of: uppercase letters, lowercase letters, and numbers. When creating an FSA ID, an email address will be requested. This is an optional response, but if supplied the email must be unique to the individual. You'll be asked some personal identification information, including your social security number, and then you will create four challenge questions and then supply your answer to the four questions. It is critical that you know the exact way you entered your answers to all of the questions when you create the FSA ID. The validity of the answers does not matter. So if you create a question such as "What is the capital of France" and then supply "London" as your created answer you will be fine as long as you remember if asked in the future that your answer to that question is London—or even london, as your answers are not case-sensitive. (The case of the letters in the FSA password is the only case-sensitive item applicable to the FSA ID system). So all that matters with the answer to a security question is the character-by-character way you initially typed your answer when the FSA ID was initially created. This is because the security built into the FSA ID system uses character recognition for the user name, case-sensitive password, and the answers to every security question. So take your time when you create the FSA ID. Pick answers to the security questions that are easy for you to remember, but difficult for someone else to figure out. And we do not recommend that you select a question that involves a two-word answer. If you use multiple word answers to any question, you will then need to be able to recall—perhaps years later—if you used a space between words or not since the system considers a space between letters as a separate character. You will also be asked at some point if you wish to supply a mobile phone number.

If you forget your user name and/or password, you can retrieve the user name using the method involving responses to the security questions. If you listed an optional unique email address and/or mobile phone as well, then those applicable options can be used as well, provided those options were verified via the FSA ID system when provided. You will need to choose whether to provide an email address and/or a mobile phone number. On the plus side, this will make it easier to retrieve a forgotten user name or password. On the other hand, linking one or both of those optional items to one's FSA ID will increase the chances that one's identity can be stolen. Keep in mind that the FSA ID can provide anyone access to an individual's verified Social Security Number, Date of Birth and other personal information if that individual's correct user name and password is known. So you need to carefully guard the user name and password created. You should also never provide the password in response to any unsolicited email, phone call, or text message. The Department of Education may use an email address or cell phone number to contact you. But it will never ask you to provide your FSA ID user name and password in response to their contacting you. If you are asked to access a web site and enter your FSA ID log in information, be careful. The website may be run by phishers hoping to fool you into providing the FSA ID user's name and password via a bogus website (that looks official) so that the ID thieves can steal your identity. You should only access the Department of Education web sites by your typing the URL or using a known URL you saved on your device.

So if you do not want to assume this added risk by providing an email address or mobile phone number when you create the FAFSA, then it is critical that you are able to recall in the future each and every character, including spaces, for the answers you created to each of the four challenge questions. If you cannot supply the correct user name and password combination when inputting the FSA ID, and the challenge question method is the only available way to help you if you forgot your user name and or password, then you will need to correctly answer two of the challenge questions selected by the FSA ID system (out of the pool of the four questions you initially created). If you incorrectly answer at least one of the asked questions, the system will not tell you which questions you got right (if any). At some point, the FSA ID site will change the combination of the particular questions you are asked to answer. This will help if you are able to eventually provide the correct combination of characters for the selected questions as the mix of the questions asked changes. But if you do not know your correct FSA ID user name and case-sensitive password combination and you cannot enter the correct combination of characters for the answers, you will need to contact the U.S. Department of Education (DOE) to fix the problem. It can take several weeks to resolve this issue. So again, make sure you securely keep a record of the unique user name, case-sensitive password, and the specific characters (including spaces if applicable) for the respective answer for each of the four security questions you chose. As you can tell by now, the FSA ID system has enhanced security measures to protect your sensitive information. It is not like a typical web site where it is a simpler process to retrieve a forgotten user name or create a new password.

After you provide all the required data when you are creating an FSA, you'll hit the Submit tab. It will take up to 3 business days for your submitted information to be verified with various government agencies. Once verified, the FSA ID you created can be used to access all the U.S. DOE websites that you are likely to need in the course of obtaining federal aid. However if your FSA ID information has not yet been verified, a recently-created FSA ID can still be used immediately after it is created to electronically sign a new FOTW. Be aware that no ID number will be generated for the FSA ID; the unique user name and case-sensitive password combination created is the actual FSA ID! There is no assigned ID number. Keep in mind that the password you created may expire. At that point, you can simply add another character, delete a character (provided you still have the required minimum number, or change the case to one or two letters, so long as the new password meets the password criteria. Of course, you will want to revise your securely stored record of your FSA ID to reflect the change as well. And if the email account you originally decided to link to your FSA ID is not longer able to be used (for example, the student used their high school email address and have now graduated and so that email address expired) and/or for some reason you no longer have the mobile phone number you linked to the FSA ID, you will want to be sure to log in and update those items associated with your FSA ID!

## Moving Right Along

When we went to press, only a draft version of the 2020–2021 FAFSA had been released by the feds. So the best we can do is provide a copy of the most recent draft in the Sample Forms section at the back this book to help you familiarize yourself with the layout of the PDF form. We don't anticipate any major changes to the questions asked with the actual 2020–2021 FAFSA, but you should review the actual PDF version when it becomes available. Finally, any reference to Individual Retirement Accounts (IRAs) in this part of the book does not include Education IRAs (which are not retirement accounts and are now more commonly called Coverdell Education Savings Accounts).

# Filling Out the 2020–2021 FAFSA

**1.–3.   Your name.** By this, they mean the student's name. On need analysis forms, "you" always refers to the student. This name must agree exactly (down to the middle initial) with the name listed on the student's social security card. It should also agree with the name of the student on the admissions application. If the first name is listed as Giovanni on the social security card, don't write down John on the need analysis form. Please be aware that if one is completing the FAFSA online via the FOTW and the student's FSA ID is provided to begin the FAFSA, the student's name and some other "identifiers" for that student will have some responses pre-filled using the "identifiers" provided when the student's FSA ID was created. However, you will need to input the student's middle initial even if the given name and surname are pre-filled.

If you have two children applying for aid, you must fill out two separate forms, even though the information will be largely identical. Do this even if the children are planning to attend the same college.

**4.–7. Address.** Do not use the student's address at boarding school or any other temporary address. Much of the mail you will receive from the colleges will be time sensitive. It's important that you get it quickly. When filling out question 6—your home state—be sure to use the proper abbreviation.

**8. Your social security number.** By this, they mean the student's social security number. These days, all students are required to have one. If your child does not have one, get one immediately; your form will be returned unprocessed if you do not complete this item. If you can't get a number in time for the deadlines, call the need analysis company. If your child does have one, be careful copying the social security number onto the form and make sure it agrees with the number on the admissions application. At some schools students are still called up on the computer by their social security number. The Department of Education will now check this number against the social security database. If the number doesn't match the name, there will be no aid until the problem is corrected and it does match. If you are applying to any college using the Common Application for admission and intend to apply for aid at any of your Common App schools, be sure that you list the student's correct SSN on the Common App. Otherwise, the college will likely not be able to "find" your processed FAFSA information until that glitch is resolved by editing the Common App. and providing the correct SSN.

**9. Your date of birth.** Again, this is the student's date of birth. For a student who was born March 5, 1999, the correct answer should be "03 05 1999" not "3 5 1999."

**10. Your permanent home phone.** Remember to include the area code.

**11.–12. Your driver's license number and state.** This question is presumably here so that there is some means of tracking the student down later for student loan payments. When you copy down the license number itself, do not include dashes or spaces even if you see them on your license. If the student has no license, leave these two questions blank. These questions are optional on the online FOTW.

**13. Your e-mail address.** If you provide an e-mail address, you will only be able to view your information at a later date via the internet. If you wish to get a paper version of your SAR (as well as being able to access it online), you should leave this question blank.

**14.–15. Are you a U.S. citizen?** To get federal aid the student must be either a U.S. citizen or an eligible noncitizen (in most cases, the holder of a green card, although there are some exceptions. Consult the instructions for the FAFSA). If the student will have a green card by the time she starts school, but doesn't have one on the day you fill out the form, you should contact the financial aid offices of the schools she is interested in for further instructions on how to proceed.

If the student is not a U.S. citizen or eligible noncitizen (or is a U.S. citizen/eligible noncitizen living overseas), you may also have to complete special "international student" aid forms. Ask the FAOs for details at the schools to which you are applying.

**16.–17.  As of today, what is your marital status?** This refers to the student's marital status, not the parents'. If the student is married, separated, widowed, or divorced, answer question 17 as well; otherwise, leave it blank. Note: If you indicate that the student is "married / remarried", then all required student income and asset questions for the FAFSA (as well as the PROFILE, if required) must include information regarding the student's spouse as well.

**18.  Your state of legal residence.** This can be quite important if you are applying to state schools. Be sure to use the proper abbreviation.

**19.–20.  Date you began living in your state of legal residence.** This is a double check to see if you really meet the residency requirements of the state you put down in question 18. If you answer "no" for question 19, then you must also answer question 20. For a student who became a legal resident in March, 2017, your answer should be, "03 2017", not "3 2017."

**21.–22.  Are you male or female?** Do you give Selective Service permission to register you? To receive federal aid, males 18 years old and older are required to register. If the student is male, then you may need to answer question 22 as well.

You can answer "Register me" for question 22 only if the student is already 18 (but not yet 26) and has not yet registered. Since few students are just turning 18 when the FAFSA is completed, it is probably best to put a reminder in your calendar for your son to go to the post office and register the week he turns 18. (Since there is no draft at present, this only involves filling out a form.)

A note for potential conscientious objectors: by registering for the Selective Service, you are not expressing a willingness to serve. The first step in the process of achieving conscientious objector status is to register.

**23.  Drug conviction information.** This is a very important question. If the student has never been convicted of any illegal drug offense, while receiving federal student aid, be sure that you enter "No" for the response. If you file the online version, this question will only be asked if the student has previously received federal student aid.

**24.–25.  Parents' education.** These questions do not affect federal aid. They may affect state aid or institutional aid in some cases. Note well that that these questions relate to the biological or adoptive parents of the student—not a stepparent who is married to the custodial parent. These questions refer to the highest level completed, not the highest grade. Thus, if the student's father attended only one year of college, use the response for "High school".

**26. High school diploma/GED/homeschooling/other information.** This question refers to the student's educational status before the first day of college. For most students, the answer will be "High school diploma".

**27. Your high school information.** Follow the instructions and answer accordingly. If you are filing the online FOTW, the name of the school you input will be matched with a database. If you encounter trouble, ask your high school counselor for the exact way to enter the name.

**28. Will you have your first bachelor's degree before you begin the 2020–2021 school year?** For most undergraduate students, of course, the answer will be no.

**29. Your grade level during the 2020–2021 school year?** If your child will be enrolling for the first time as a freshman, use the appropriate response for "never attended college & 1st year undergraduate" even if he took college courses while he was in high school. This question is used to determine annual borrowing limits for student loans and refers to the student's academic standing at school, not the number of years he's been attending college. Enter the appropriate response for the grade level the student has attained at the start of the academic year, rather than the level the student will attain during the year. For example, a student who in the fall term will be a second semester sophomore should use the response "2nd year under-graduate/sophomore" even though she will be a junior by mid-year.

**30. Your degree/certificate code.** You should choose the most appropriate response from the choices provided.

**31. Are you interested in being considered for work study?** You would like the colleges to come up with their best offer before you start to commit yourself. Because of this, we recommend that you indicate you are interested in work-study. This does not commit you; you can change your mind later. This question has no effect on grant or scholarship eligibility.

Now that you've completed some basic information regarding the student, it's time to move on to the more important questions on the FAFSA. You will notice that questions 32–44 for the student and questions 79–92 for the parent(s) are almost identical, though the numbering of the questions is different. Since most of our readers will be having to complete all of these questions, for simplicity's sake we will be pairing up these questions later in this chapter. To determine for sure whether or not you'll need to complete the questions in the "parent" areas of the FAFSA, you'll need to first determine the student's status. So let's skip questions 32–44 for now and go directly to Step Three, questions 45–57.

These questions are here to establish whether a student is independent or dependent. (A dependent student usually receives financial help from her family. An independent student does not.) The colleges would prefer that all their students were dependent. Independent students are much more expensive for a school since they usually require more financial aid.

Of course it would be wonderful if your child could establish that he is independent, but there are several tough criteria to meet and they get tougher all the time. If a student can answer "yes" to any of the questions 45–57, then he is undoubtedly independent for federal aid purposes for the 2020–2021 academic year.

**45.** Were you born before January 1, 1997?

**46.** As of today, are you married?

**47.** During the school year 2020–2021, will you be working on a masters or doctorate program?

**48.** Are you currently serving on active duty in the U.S. Armed Forces for purposes other than training?

**49.** Are you a veteran of the U.S. Armed Forces?

**50.** Do you have children who will receive more than half of their support from you between July 1, 2020 and June 30, 2021?

**51.** Do you have dependents (other than your children or spouse) who live with you and receive more than half of their support from you, now and through June 30, 2021?

**52.** When you were age 13 or older, were both of your parents deceased, were you in foster care, or were you a dependent/ward of the court?

**53.** As of today, are you an emancipated minor as determined by a court in your state of legal residence?

**54.** As of today, are you in legal guardianship as determined by a court in your state of legal residence?

**55.** At any time on or after July 1, 2019, did your high school or school district homeless liaison determine that you were an unaccompanied youth who was homeless?

**56.** At any time on or after July 1, 2019, did the director of an emergency shelter program funded by the U.S. Department of Housing and Urban Development determine that you were an unaccompanied youth who was homeless?

**57.** At any time on or after July 1, 2019, did the director of a runaway or homeless youth basic center or transitional living program determine that you were an unaccompanied youth who was homeless or were self-supporting and at risk of being homeless?

If you are able to answer "Yes" to any of these questions, according to federal guidelines, you are an independent student and you can usually skip any questions about the "parents" on the rest of the form.

Veterans of the financial aid process will notice that there are more ways for a student to be considered independent for the 2020–2021 academic year than there were a few years ago. But before you answer "yes" to any of these questions you should read them carefully. And for questions 48–49, and 52–57, you should be sure to read the notes regarding them in the FAFSA instructions—because there is a lot of fine print involved.

If you answer "No" to each of the questions from 45–57, then most likely the child will be considered a dependent student in which case you get to skip the independent student questions (93–100) in Step Five of the form.

One exception to these rules would be for certain graduate health profession students. Graduate students who apply for federal aid from programs under title VII of the Public Health Service Act may need to give information about their parents, even if they filled in "yes" to any of the questions in Step Three. In this instance, we suggest you contact the FAOs at the schools to which you are applying and inquire about this before you fill out the FAFSA.

A few years ago, claiming that the child was an independent student was a popular financial aid loophole that many parents took advantage of. The colleges and the government have since cracked down and every year the rules get more stringent. If you can go the independent route, be prepared to provide extensive documentation to the financial aid office—i.e., birth certificate (proving you will be at least 24 by January 1 of the academic year you are seeking aid), marriage license, court decisions, discharge papers, etc. You should also be aware that many schools have even tougher criteria for proving independence than the federal guidelines. Some colleges require independent students to fill out the parent information on the FAFSA form even if they do meet the federal guidelines, and a few will insist that parents are still responsible for some portion of their child's tuition.

In very rare circumstances, the FAOs can use their professional judgment to decide that a student is independent even if the student can't answer "Yes" to at least one of these diagnostic student status questions.

Now that you've completed Step Three on the form, let's move on to the financial questions on the form, which are the most important ones. As mentioned earlier, questions 32–44 for the student and questions 79–92 are very similar. To simplify matters, we'll be pairing them up. Thus, for example, we will address question 36—the adjusted gross income for the student—and question 84—the adjusted gross income for the parent—simultaneously. Before you begin writing your responses for these questions, we first recommend that you read the instructions that appear online if you are completing the FOTW—or that appear at the top of these steps for the PDF version of the FAFSA. We also suggest that you reread Chapter Three of this book.

If you are filing the online version of the FAFSA and the student and/or the student's parent(s) have already completed a final version of the 2018 U.S. tax return and filed it with the IRS: then you and/or the student may or may not be able to use the "IRS Data Retrieval Tool" (or DRT) to have a tax filers income tax data automatically transferred from the IRS database onto the form. By using this tool, you also reduce the chances your application will be subject to additional scrutiny through a financial aid process known as "Verification" (which we discuss later in this part of the book and is not nearly as onerous as it sounds).

Given that the 2020–2021 FAFSA will be using 2018 as the prior-prior year (PPY) and most individuals will have already completed their 2018 personal return when the FAFSA is completed, more students and their parents will be able to use the IRS DRT when they file the original 2020–2021 FAFSA compared to former versions of the FAFSA years ago—when prior year (PY) data was required on the FAFSA and estimated income and tax return information needed to supplied on the aid forms if the tax returns could not be done before the earliest aid deadline.

If you are not able to use the IRS DRT for whatever reason—for example, you have not yet filed the return or the tool is generating some error message—this is no reason for panic. While use of the IRS DRT is encouraged by the feds and the colleges, it is not mandatory. And you should not delay filing the FAFSA until you can get the tool to work, if such a delay could result in a possible reduction of aid. (See pages 160–161 for guidelines as to when to file for optimal aid.)

Be aware that through the skip logic built in the FOTW, some individuals may not even be given the opportunity to use the IRS DRT—for example, if you filed a joint return for the PPY even though you are considered separated.

But even if you are invited to use the IRS DRT (which is recommended), there are still a few possible glitches that may prevent you from doing so. Some examples: the IRS site may be temporarily shut down due to technical problems (in which case you should try again later unless a FAFSA deadline is looming) or you were a victim of Identity Theft (if which case the IRS tool will likely never work for you that year).

Whether or not you are able to use the IRS DRT, we will still provide line-by-line tips for each of the remaining questions on the FAFSA, which you should be sure to review even if the tool provided the answer. Given that the IRS tool does not provide pre-filled answers for all the financial questions, we will also note those that will transfer from the tool with the words "IRS transfer" for easier identification. Finally, you should be aware that if a particular response to a FAFSA question was transferred on the FAFSA via the IRS DRT, the dollar amount will not be visible to the FAFSA applicant. Only the words "Transferred from the IRS" will appear for each of the transferred responses. Be aware these words will appear even if the transferred response was a zero amount or even if the applicable IRS line item on your return did not apply and was correctly left blank. You should not manually override any of the responses transferred via the IRS; don't worry, such transferred data will exactly agree with your return data on file at the IRS. This is because any change to any transferred response (or going back and deciding not to use the tool after it was already used to transfer the responses) will raise red flags when your FAFSA data is received by any college and will no doubt lead to automatic verification. If you can't help yourself or accidently change at least one of the transferred DRT responses, you should go back before you submit the FAFSA and again use the IRS DRT to transfer all of responses that should be transferred if you used the IRS tool.

Before we go on with those FAFSA questions that may be transferred with the IRS DRT there is one important scenario that may be applicable to you. Namely, what to do if you filed an amended return with the IRS. For those of you not too familiar with the IRS lingo, an amended personal return (known as the 1040X) is filed if a correction needs to be made to a personal return already filed with the IRS (i.e., the IRS 1040, 1040A or 1040EZ forms). This could occur, for example, if you received a corrected W-2 or 1099 form after you submitted your original return to the IRS. If you merely were preparing your tax return, noticed a mistake or omission, and corrected the error before you submitted any return to the IRS for that tax year, you did not file an amended return.

Years ago, those who filed an amended return were unable to the IRS DRT. But beginning with the 2018–2019 FAFSA, the IRS DRT can be now be used if you are invited to do so. However, the IRS DRT will transfer the tax data from the original return, not the amended return. In this case, you will need to send a signed copy of the amended 1040X return to the individual aid offices of all colleges that are receiving your FAFSA and explain the situation. (Include all pages and schedules submitted to the IRS with the 1040X you send to any aid office and be sure to list the student's name and either her SSN or university-assigned ID somewhere with the document.) Be aware that the IRS DRT will automatically trigger a special code on the report sent to the college with your FAFSA data, provided the IRS has processed the amended return. If you were unable to use the IRS DRT or are completing the PDF FAFSA, you should still list the original tax return data on the FAFSA and not the amended figures. However, when you are completing the PROFILE you should list the amended return data on the CSS form—and explain that fact in the Special Circumstances of the PROFILE so that the college realizes the reason for the discrepancy between the tax return data on the different forms. And if you are required to submit tax returns when applying for aid (per a college's own aid policy), be sure to send both the original return as well as the 1040X return (with all pages, schedules, and attachments that were sent to the IRS with either form). If applicable, send any corrected W-2s or corrected 1099s as well as the original versions if those documents are required by a particular school.

**32.–35. and 79.–82. Basic tax return filing details.** (IRS transfer for some of these.) These preliminary questions regarding basic tax return items are being asked, in part, to determine if you meet some of the criteria for the Simplified Needs Test or the Automatic Zero-EFC. The responses are also used in conjunction with other responses on the FAFSA (such as one's marital status) to diagnose whether or not the tax filer will be invited to use the IRS Data Retrieval Tool. For dependent students, all the required parental financial information will be requested first on the online FAFSA (FOTW) before the student information beginning with question 32 needs to be inputted.

As stated earlier on pages 160–161: If you have not yet filed a 2018 tax return *AND* you are required to do so *AND* you are in a situation involving a school and/or your state government awarding funds on a first-come, first-served basis: then you should complete the FAFSA form and submit your data using estimated income tax return information. Be sure to select the response for **questions 32 and 79** indicating you will file but have not yet filed your return. And if you have not yet filed a return but know that there will soon be a change to your situation that will result in your family contribution increasing by a significant amount, then it would also make sense to file using estimated tax return data if you are required to file.

Of course if you are not required to file a return, it can be to your advantage not to do so. The beginning of the instructions for the 2018 IRS 1040 as well as the 2018 version of IRS Publication 17, both of which are freely available online at www.irs.gov, have a section at the outset that covers who is required to file a U.S. income tax return.

On the other hand, if you are required to file a tax return but have not yet done so *AND* you are not in one of the situations mentioned above where time is of the essence: It would be better to first complete that 2018 tax return and then complete the FAFSA with the actual tax return information. Be aware that it will take 2–3 weeks for the IRS DRT tool to work if the IRS 1040 was filed electronically and as much as 6–8 weeks if a paper return was filed the IRS. It would be best to wait to use the IRS tool for the FAFSA as long as you will not miss any school's priority filing deadline to reduce the likelihood of verification.

*KEY POINT FOR THE CUSTODIAL PARENT(S) OF A DEPENDENT STUDENT OR FOR AN INDEPENDENT STUDENT (AND IF MARRIED, THEIR SPOUSE)WHO HAVE NOT YET FILED THEIR 2018 TAX RETURN AND WHO ARE NOT REQUIRED TO FILE A TAX RETURN: As discussed on pages 58–61, the Department of Education needed to create new criteria to qualify for the Simplified Needs Test (SNT) and the Automatic Zero-EFC given changes to the IRS 1040 tax return and the elimination of the 1040A and 1040EZ. When we went to press, all the fine print involving these two alternate federal EFC formulas covering the 2020–2021 award year had not yet been published by the U.S. Department of Education (DOE). Only a revised draft version of the FAFSA has been made public. Additionally, the printed language used on the form and instructions does not necessarily follow the actual regulations and policy guidelines adopted.*

*We mention these points for those not required to file any tax return in 2018 because as the most recent draft of the FAFSA is currently written, the qualifying criteria involving one who was not required to file a tax return but who filed a 1040 return anyway may no longer be in effect.*

*Therefore if you are not required to file any tax return (including any foreign return) and you have not yet filed a return for 2018, it is crucial that you understand your filing of an unnecessary return could cost you thousands of dollars.*

*We of course will cover any late-breaking developments through our update service freely available to those who registered their purchase of this book. However, for now you should assume that the option to qualify for the SNT or Auto-Zero if you filed the IRS 1040 even if you were not obligated to do so may no longer be a criterion.*

For **Questions 33, 34, 80, and 81** (tax filer only): Select from the appropriate menu choices based on the anticipated or actual type of return filed as well as the filing status on the tax return. (If you used the IRS DRT on the FOTW, the initial responses you provided online will be replaced with the words, "Transferred from the IRS" after the DRT is issued. Additionally due to the skip logic of the FOTW, some additional questions that we'll soon cover may not be asked.)

If you filed, or will file, a foreign tax return, or a tax return for Puerto Rico, certain U.S. territories (such as Guam, American Samoa, the U.S. Virgin Islands, Swain's Island or the Marianas Islands) or one of the freely associated states (i.e., the Republic of Palau, the Republic of the Marshall Islands or the Federated States of Micronesia), be sure to read the corresponding Notes in the FAFSA instructions. Those who file a foreign tax return should also consult page 277 in the "Special Topics" chapter of this book. And if your country's tax year does not end on December 31st, you want to be sure you will supplying the proper prior-prior year tax information.

**Questions 35 and 82** regarding Schedule 1 of the IRS 1040 appear for the first time on the 2020-2021 version of the FAFSA. Even if you have filed a prior version of the FAFSA, it is crucial that you be especially careful with your response to this question if the adjusted gross income (which we will discuss shortly) is below $50,000—in which case you may qualify for the SNT or the Auto-Zero EFC based on your response. If Schedule 1 is required as part of  your 2018 IRS 1040, it is important that you read all the help comments or notes on the FAFSA that relate to these FAFSA questions, since there are certain "exceptions" that will allow you to select "No", even if you filed Schedule 1 as part of the IRS 1040.

**36. and 84.  Adjusted gross income.** (IRS transfer) If you've already filed your taxes with the IRS and there has been no change in the tax filers marital status since January 1, 2019: just copy the appropriate line requested from line 7 of your 2018 federal return if you are not able to use the IRS DRT. However, if you filed as "married filing jointly" for the 2018 tax return, but now at the time of FAFSA filing are subsequently separated or divorced from the other person with whom you filed jointly (or that other person with whom you filed jointly passed away after December 31, 2017 but before you file the FAFSA):

1.    You should not be given the option to use the IRS DRT. If you are, most likely you answered some prior question incorrectly.

2.    You will need to provide the proportionate share of your Adjusted Gross Income (as well as your proportionate share of U.S. Income Taxes Paid for FAFSA question 37 or 85). See Item 3 on pages 297–298 for more details on how to do this.

Conversely if you are now married (or remarried) but your current spouse did not file a joint tax return with you for 2018: you should not be able to use the IRS DRT. So you will need to add the adjusted gross income of your current spouse to your AGI to derive your answer to FAFSA 36 or 84. The same is true for the amount of U.S. Taxes Paid for FAFSA questions 37 or 85.

And finally if you filed jointly in 2018, are no longer married to that other person, but are now remarried (and/or your current spouse was married to someone else until at least December 31, 2018 and so filed a joint 2018 tax return with that person): you will need to determine your proportionate share of the AGI and the U.S Taxes paid on the return filed with that former spouse, and then combine the appropriate dollar amounts with your current (new) spouse's amounts to arrive at the correct responses to use. In this way, the combined number will exclude any former spouse(s)' share of the AGI and taxes paid.

If you have not yet filed your 2018 tax return: then use the worksheet we provide at the back of this book (See pages 303–304) to derive your best estimate. The 2017 returns can be very helpful in reminding you of all the different kinds of income and expenses you have had in the past. A blank copy of the 2018 return is important as the IRS line items have changed.

**37. and 85. U.S. income tax paid.** (IRS transfer) If you have already filed an income tax return and are not able to use the IRS DRT, you should write down the total federal income taxes that you paid. The FAFSA form will tell you where to find this on the 2018 tax forms. Do not include any self-employment taxes.

If you are estimating, remember that this number is not necessarily the same as the amount your employer withheld. You may have to pay more or less than your withholdings. Remember also that you paid taxes even if you got a refund. The amount of federal taxes you paid will be a deduction in the aid formula, so it is in your interest to report all of it. Use a draft of the 2018 return and the IRS instructions as well as Table 6 on page 307 to assist you.

Self-employed parents, who make quarterly estimated payments to the IRS, sometimes forget that a large part of the money they send to the IRS is self-employment tax, which should not be included here. Although this mistake would be in your favor, the FAOs would almost certainly catch it, causing delays and frustration.

**38.–39. and 86.–87.   Income earned from work.** (Possible IRS DRT transfer)  If only one parent's information is required on the FAFSA (or the student applicant is unmarried), then the IRS DRT (if used) will transfer the response for the applicable questions on the FAFSA. But if both parents (or the custodial parent and custodial stepparent are required to report their combined information on the aid form (and/or if the student applicant is married and the student's spouses information is also required), then you will need to answer these questions even if the IRS DRT was used. This is because the combined income from work must be broken out with dollar amounts manually reported separately—and the IRS DRT is not able to do that. So if the responses for these questions are not transferred from the IRS DRT for any reason, see pages 62–66 and 84–85 for suggested strategies. Parents always ask, "We already gave them our adjusted gross income. Why do they want to know our income earned from work?"

Although they don't look like it, for tax filers  these are expense questions, in which case the only purpose of these questions is to compute how much social security tax you paid (the computer will subtract this from your income) and to see whether you qualify for the employment allowance. Therefore, you want these numbers to be as high as possible.

This is about the time we hear screams of alarm from our clients. "Why are you including my 401(k) contributions? Whose side are you on?" We know these questions are in the "income" section of the form, but trust us, these are expense questions. For most families, the higher this number, the lower your contribution towards the college. Include everything: wages (Line 1 from the 1040 or the W-2), business and farm income from Schedules C and F (Lines 12 and 18 on Schedule 1 of the 1040), income from any business partnerships other than limited partnerships  (use the amounts listed on Box 14 of the K-1 for IRS Form 1065 for the partnership), and—for tax-filers only: contributions to tax-deferred pension and savings plans such as 401(k) plans, 403(b) plans, or tax-deferred annuities (which can usually be found in boxes 12a-d of your W-2 form with codes D, E, F, G, H, and S).

If applicable, include the total amount of combat pay received as a member of the U.S. Armed Forces.

If you had a loss from business income or from partnerships, don't subtract the loss from your total earned income. This will underreport the amount of social security tax you paid.

Be aware that questions 86 and 87 are not supposed to add up to question 84, your adjusted gross income. The same holds true for 38 and 39: these should not necessarily equal 36. The sum of your income earned from work and, if applicable, your spouse's income earned from work could be higher or lower than your AGI.

And if you are able to use the IRS DRT, you should do so but be aware that the tool will not include the amount of any contributions to tax-deferred retirement plans found in boxes

12-12d of your 2018 W-2 if the words "Transferred from the IRS" appear for any income for work FAFSA items. However, you should NOT override the transferred data to include the amount(s) in box 12 of any W-2s. This will insure verification, which is best to be avoided if it can be helped—even if the EFC will be higher. The college will likely follow the federal guidelines to the letter during verification and will exclude the box 12 amount from your response anyway—so you will be back to square one in the end.

**40.–42. and 88.–90.   The value of your assets.** If you meet the requirements of the Simplified Needs Test (SNT) or the Automatic Zero-EFC, you may be able to skip these questions if you file the FAFSA online. If you download, complete, and submit the PDF version of the FAFSA, the processor will not assess any assets you list here provided you meet all the SNT and/or all the Automatic Zero-EFC requirements (though some state agencies may).

We don't intend to repeat all the advice we gave under "Assets and Liabilities" in Chapter Three. Look through that chapter again—it could save you some serious money. Remember not to list retirement provisions such as IRA accounts. Under the federal financial aid formulas, assets in retirement provisions are protected from assessment.

Understand that real estate (other than your home) is considered an "investment" for purposes of the FAFSA. You should be sure to read the FAFSA instructions carefully for details about what types of assets to include and what types you should exclude. You should realize that for the questions relating to investments, businesses, and investment farms, you are to list their "Net Worth" which is defined as the current value minus the current debt. If the net worth for a particular question is a negative number, then list "0" in the far right box. Veterans of the aid process may recall that years ago you would list the value and the debt separately. The processor now wants you to do the math. You should also keep in mind that you are not allowed to deduct credit card debt from the value of your assets—only debts secured by those assets that are to be included for these questions.

Be careful not to double-count assets. While the instructions for the FAFSA may seem confusing, keep in mind that an asset belongs to you or to your child. Don't list the same asset twice. If you have set up a bank account "in trust for" your child, it is legally part of your assets as long as your social security number is listed as the taxpayer I.D. However, if the asset is under the child's name (or in your name "as custodian for" the child—most likely in a regular UTMA or UGMA account) it will be assessed severely. (Consider consulting a financial advisor who understands the aid process to discuss your options.) It is important to note that the reporting requirements for 529 plans, and Coverdell Education Savings Accounts are now as follows: For a student who does not report parental information on the FAFSA, such accounts owned by the student—and if applicable, the student's spouse—are reported as part of student investments in question 41. However, for a student who must report parental information on the form, these student-owned 529s (often referred to as custodial 529 accounts) or student-owned Coverdell accounts, should be reported as part of parental investments in question 89, and not as part of student assets.

If you have a passbook loan, remember to include the net worth of the account (value minus debt) as part of "investments," instead of as part of "cash, savings, and checking."

Do not include your home as long as it is your primary residence. If you own "other real estate", even if you do not own your primary residence, include this other real estate as part of your "investments" response but remember to subtract any mortgages or other debts secured by the property from the value of the real estate. In other words, only the equity of any other real estate (the value of any property minus the debt on it) becomes part of your "investments" response. If you own your primary residence, but rent out a part of it, the proportionate share of the total equity for that part of the home that is rented out is to be included as part of the response as well unless a) you rent out the part of the property to a relative OR b) there is no separate entrance to the rented portion OR c) there is no separate bathroom or kitchen.

Owners of businesses and farms should also read our advice on this subject (in Chapter Nine, Special Topics) before they answer these questions. Remember that if you are a part-owner, you should list only your share of the net worth. Also, if your farm is your primary residence and you can claim on Schedule F of your 1040 form that you "materially participated in the farm's operation," the net worth of the "family farm" should not be included on the FAFSA.

*Note: As we mentioned earlier, the value of any "family business" should not be included as an asset on the FAFSA. A family business is defined as one with 100 or fewer full time or full time equivalent employees in which the "family" owns more than 50 percent of the business. The "more than 50 percent" figure does not apply solely to individuals who must report their financial information on the FAFSA form. Other relatives by blood or by marriage (e.g. siblings, step-parents, relatives-in-law, cousins, etc.) with a stake in the business should also be considered when determining if more than 50 percent is owned by the "family".*

**43. and 91.   Additional Financial Information.** (IRS transfer for one item)  For students, the most common item they will report will be federal work-study income. For parents, the most common items will probably be the education credits (e.g., American Opportunity Credit and Lifetime Learning Credit) and child support paid (not received). These education credits will transfer from the IRS DRT, if used. Those who had to report a proportionate share of AGI and U.S. taxes paid on the FAFSA should use the same percentage of AGI used for those calculations AND then multiply that number by the total amount of the education credits reported on Schedule 3, Line 50 of the IRS 1040. Do not include any refundable portion claimed on Schedule 5. Do not include child support paid for other family members who are included on the FAFSA as being part of the household. (We will get to the household size questions shortly.) Members of the armed forces who received combat pay or special combat pay should only report the taxable portion of such pay received, and only if they included this pay as part of their adjusted gross income on their tax return. List zero for any category that does not apply.

**44. and 92.  Untaxed income.** (IRS transfer for some items. See below for warning about DRT issues) See page 76 for our suggested strategies. This is where you must report certain types of income and benefits that the IRS lets you shelter. Some types of untaxed income that a few years ago had to be reported on the FAFSA are no longer considered to be income in the federal methodology. These items include untaxed social security benefits, welfare benefits, the earned income credit, the additional child credit, the foreign income exclusion, and the credit for federal tax on special fuels. There are some additional points to keep in mind regarding certain untaxed income categories:

- **Child support received.** As we've said before, the amount you include here should include only the money you actually received during the year, not what was promised.

- **Deductible IRA contributions.** (IRS transfer) As we've mentioned before, IRA contributions are not necessarily deductible. If you (and your spouse, if married) are not already an active participant in an employer or self-employed retirement plan, then for 2018, IRA contributions are fully deductible up to the $5,500 per person maximum  (up to $6,500 if age 50 or older). If you (or your spouse, if married) are an active participant in a retirement plan, then your contribution may be fully or partly deductible, depending on your income. To determine whether you qualify for a deduction in 2018, consult your accountant or the IRS instructions for the 2018 forms.

Realize that nondeductible portions need not be listed. However, the tax-deductible portion of your retirement contributions is considered untaxed income. It is the tax-deductible portion of your IRA contribution that must be included on the FAFSA in either **44b** or **92b**. This response for an IRA should correspond to Line 32 on Schedule 1 of your 2018 IRS 1040 and will transfer if the IRS DRT is used. Any contributions to other plans reported on Line 28 of Schedule 1 need to be included for your response and will also be transferred if the DRT is used. Contributions to Roth IRAs should not be included as part of your answer, since they do not reduce your Adjusted Gross Income. But if you voluntarily contribute pre-tax dollars to any tax-deferred retirement plan such as 401(k), 403(b) or similar plan, these contributions are to be listed in FAFSA **44a** or **92a**. The applicable amount(s) are can be found inside one or more of the Boxes 12a-d that appear on the W-2 form. Include only those with the capital letter D, E, F, G, H or S next to the dollar amount in the Box 12 area. Do not include any amount with other letters such as C or DD. Be aware that the IRS DRT will never transfer these responses from your W-2s onto the FAFSA. Indeed, one of the complaints about the IRS DRT is that some of the items that are part of FAFSA **43, 44, 91, and 92** for which responses transfer are interspersed with other items that are never transferred and need to be manually entered, if applicable, even though 0s (zeros) are already pre-filled. So be careful and make sure you do not accidentally skip over any applicable parts of those four FAFSA questions that are not transferred.

For **FAFSA 44e and 92e (IRS DRT alert!!)** The rollover of any funds from an IRA or pension plan that are placed into another plan which meet the IRS definition of a **qualified rollover** are to be excluded in your response for these FAFSA questions. This is good news, as any qualified rollover is not considered untaxed income to be reported on the FAFSA (or the CSS PROFILE). If applicable and if the IRS tool is not used: for any of these two FAFSA responses be sure to subtract the amount of any qualified rollover before you enter your response on the FAFSA. But If the IRS DRT is used, there is an added wrinkle. If the tool detects any dollar amount reported on Line 4a of the IRS 1040, the IRS DRT should generate a special message asking you to input the dollar amount of any rollover(s) in an additional response area that will appear on your computer screen. It is critical that you report the correct amount before you proceed so that the correct amount will be automatically excluded for you. This exclusion may lead to Verification, but that is a small price to pay for insuring the rollover amount is not incorrectly added to your income for the EFC formula. If you need to provide the school with an official "IRS transcript" as part of the verification process—this transcript is requested from the IRS—be sure to write the word "Rollover" next to the appropriate line(s) items on the IRS transcript. If applicable, be sure to write out "Rollover" (if it is not already printed) on your IRS 1040 near line 4a if you need to submit a signed copy of your return to an aid office. Be prepared to provide third-party documentation of the rollover from your financial institution that now has your funds after the rollover. (If you are completing the CSS PROFILE you should also be sure to provide the same dollar amount of any qualified rollover as well when reporting your 2018 income information. A noncustodial parent or noncustodial stepparent should list the dollar amount of any qualified rollover on their Noncustodial parent PROFILE.)

- **Combat pay.** This item pertains only to servicemen and servicewomen. Any untaxed combat pay you receive should not be included as part of 44h (if received by the student or the student's spouse) or 92h (if received by parent).

It may be tempting to think about not listing untaxed income you are required to report, but do not give in to temptation. The schools are extremely good at reading between the lines and IRS reporting requirements change from year to year. What doesn't need to be reported this year on a tax return might very well be reportable next year. You should also bear in mind that the odds of being selected for "verification" by the colleges and/or the government are much greater than the odds of being audited by the IRS.

Now that you've finished the financial questions on the FAFSA, the hardest part of completing the form is over. There are still a few more questions that you will have to answer.

As previously mentioned, if the student is dependent you can skip questions 93–100. If the student is independent, you'll need to answer them. However, since the majority of our readers will be completing the FAFSA for dependent students, we are going to go back and cover the remaining parent questions first (questions 58–78 and 83). If you are independent, we'll cover questions 93–100 on page 189 since these are very similar to a number of the parent questions.

**58. What is your parents' current marital status?** Given the state of modern relationships in this country, this is often a complicated question and there is often erroneous advice dispensed by others. So as a reminder: For financial aid purposes, "parent" is defined as the person or persons the child lived with most during the past 12 months—known as the custodial parent(s). This is not necessarily the same parent who claims the child on a tax return or the person who was awarded custody by the courts. If you are divorced or separated or were never married and living apart, please read Chapter Nine of this book, "Special Topics." Also carefully review the FAFSA instructions as well as the text earlier in this part of the book regarding which parent(s) information is to be reported on the FAFSA and PROFILE.

And remember that one's "Marital status" refers to the custodial parents' current status on the day the FAFSA is submitted to the processor.

**59. Date married, separated, divorced, or widowed.** If you answered "Never married" for question 59, refer to the FAFSA instructions. Otherwise, you should answer accordingly using two digits for the month and four digits for the year.

**60.–67. Parents' social security numbers, last names, first initials, and dates of birth.** The FAFSA processor will verify this parental information. As such, the parents' correct social security numbers, surnames, and first initials will be needed. These questions refer to the custodial parents (or custodial parent and stepparent if applicable). The name for a parent should agree with the name reported on the 2018 tax return and the individual's social security card. If a parent has no SSN, enter 000-00-0000.

If your answer to question 58 was never married, divorced/separated, or widowed (and you are not living with the other biological or adoptive parent of the student), you should only be listing this information for one parent on the paper or PDF version of the FAFSA, leaving the information about the other parent blank. For the online version, these questions will only be asked of one parent.

If a custodial parent has remarried, you should be reporting information for the custodial parent and the stepparent. Since the IRS forms do not require that the husband be listed first on a joint return, you should be careful writing down the social security numbers on the FAFSA. Make sure you have the correct number for the correct parent or stepparent reporting data on the FAFSA.

For dates of birth, see pages 115–116 regarding the Asset Protection Allowance. This is one of the few times when you don't want to lie about your age. The purpose of questions 63 and/or 67 is to determine your asset protection allowance.

It is very important that you list the same last name as it appears on the social security card for questions 61 and 65. Otherwise, there can be processing problems if the surname reported doesn't agree exactly with the social security database.

**68.  Parents' e-mail address.** Unlike question 13, the listing of an email address for this question will not prevent the Department of Education from sending the student a paper version of the Student Aid Report (SAR).

**69.  Parents' state of legal residence.** Be sure to use the correct abbreviation.

**70.–71.  Date parents became legal residents.** Use the earliest date that either of the student's custodial parents (or the custodial stepparent) began living in the state when answering question 71. Answer question 71, only if your answer to question 70 is "No".

**72.  Number of family members.** This question is used to help determine the income protection allowance. You would like this number to be as high as possible. The more family members, the higher your allowance. Include the student whose name is on the FAFSA, custodial parents (this includes a stepparent as long as he or she is living in the household), other children (even if they don't live at home as long as they are receiving more than half of their support from the custodial parents or they are not "independent" for federal aid purposes for the 2020–2021 academic year), grandparents or other individuals (if they live in the household and get more than half support from the custodial parents and will continue to get this support from July 1, 2020 through June 30, 2021), and newborn babies (even if they are not yet born when you are filling out the form).

**73.  Number of college students in the household.** One of the myths about college is that it is better not to have two kids in school at the same time. In fact, if you qualify for aid, the more members of your household who can attend college at the same time, the better. In addition to being enrolled at least half-time during 2020–2021 (6 credits or more for at least one term or the equivalent), the other household member must be enrolled in a degree or certificate program. The student applying for aid should always be included even if he is attending college less than half-time.

In theory, the parents' expected contribution stays the same regardless of how many students are in school. If you have one daughter in school, you will be expected to pay the full amount of the parents' contribution toward her tuition. If you have two daughters in college at the same time, the two colleges will usually divide the parents' contribution between them and make up the difference with a larger aid package. For example, let's suppose that Mr. and Mrs. Jones have two sons, Frank and Tom. Last year, only Frank was attending college. The Joneses' expected contribution was judged to be $9,000, and they paid the full $9,000 to Frank's college. This year both Frank and Tom will be in college, but the Joneses' expected contribution is still just $9,000. Each school will receive $4,500 and will try to make up the difference with additional aid. In effect, the Joneses are getting two educations for the price of one.

In addition, some parents who might not have qualified for aid with only one child in college find that with two children in school at the same time, they do qualify for substantial amounts of aid. This is why it is worth applying for aid each year, even if you were refused the first time. If one of your children is trying to decide whether to take a year off from college, this might be a factor when it comes time to make that decision. You want as much overlap as possible.

Parents are not to be included as family members in college for the purposes of this FAFSA question. If a parent is attending college, graduate school, or some other post-secondary institution, you should be sure to notify the FAOs directly about this fact, as some schools may take these added family expenses into account when they are reviewing your application materials.

**74.–78. In 2018 and/or 2019, did any members of the household receive certain need-based benefits from the federal government?** These questions are being asked to determine if you meet some of the criteria for the Simplified Needs Test or the Automatic Zero-EFC. You need only receive the benefit at some point in 2018 and/or 2019—not necessarily for the entire 24 months. For the online FOTW, you may need to reply "None of the above" if you did not receive any of these benefits in 2018 or 2019.

**83. and 100. Can you qualify as a dislocated worker?** Be sure to carefully read the Notes in the FAFSA instructions. We'll discuss the dislocated worker in more detail on pages 270–271 as well.

You have to answer questions 93–100 only if you are an independent student. The strategy for questions 93 and 94 here is virtually the same as it will be for questions 72 and 73: the more family members the better; the more family members considered in college the better. Compared to question 72, question 93 has a slightly more rigid definition of which children can be considered to be members of the household. Therefore, if you are completing Step Five of the form, be sure to read the FAFSA instructions related to these questions carefully. Questions 95–99 are the corresponding questions to help determine if you meet the criteria for SNT or Automatic Zero-EFC eligibility for independent students. Question 100 is similar to question 83 in the parent's section. Review the corresponding Notes in the FAFSA instructions and see pages 58–61 for more details.

**101. What college(s) do you plan to attend in 2020–2021?** *If you're completing the PDF version of the FAFSA:* List all the schools (up to four) to which you want the data sent. List only one school per line and don't cross out or skip any lines. You have a choice of writing in the complete name and address of the school, or of listing the six-character code for the school. (The instructions printed above these questions on the FAFSA tell you how to find the codes.) The feds say that using the codes will speed up processing time. On the other hand, if you make a mistake when you write down the code, your information will not be sent to the school you wanted and you may not find out about the snafu until it is too late. Either way, we recommend that you take great care in writing down the information on the FAFSA. If you are applying to a particular branch or division of a university, be sure to specify that as well or use the correct code for that branch or division. If you are applying to more than four schools, you should first list those schools with the earliest FAFSA deadlines. After your FAFSA has been processed, there are ways you can have the data sent to the colleges you were not able to list on the FAFSA. At the far right of this section, you must list the correct housing code for each school. If you aren't sure, fill in the "on campus" response oval since the cost of attendance will be higher if you are living on campus.

*If you're filing the FAFSA online:* List the codes (or search for the schools by name) for all the schools (up to ten) to which you want the data sent. After you input the code for a particular school, make sure that the name of the correct school appears on your screen. You must also select the correct housing status for each school. If you aren't sure, use the "on campus" response since the cost of attendance will be higher if you are living on campus. If you are applying to more than ten schools, you should first list those schools with the earliest FAFSA deadlines. After your FAFSA has been processed, there are ways you can have the data sent to the colleges you were not able to list on the FAFSA.

*Regardless of how you file the FAFSA:* If you are applying to any schools in your home state, we recommend that you list at least one of them first on the FAFSA.

**102.–103. Certification.** The student's signature is always required on the form. If parental information was required, then one of the custodial (step)parent's signatures must appear on the form as well. Simply by signing the FAFSA, you are applying for all types of federal aid, including the Pell Grant. When you sign, you are affirming that to the best of your knowledge, the information you have supplied is true and complete. An unwitting mistake will not be grounds for electrocution. However, a deliberate lie is fraud—a federal crime.

You cannot sign, date, or mail in, the 2020–2021 FAFSA until October 1, 2019. Be sure to enter the date and fill in the correct year for question 102. If you're filing the FAFSA online, see comments below on how to "sign" the form.

As part of the FAFSA instructions, there is a comment concerning "unusual circumstances." With the exception of a family member who recently became unemployed (also sometimes referred to as a dislocated worker), we have already discussed these items. Recently unemployed workers will be covered in the "Special Topics" chapter, as well as in our instructions on how to fill out the PROFILE form (section PF) which follows.

**104.–106.** **FAFSA preparer information.** You can skip this section if you are filling out the FAFSA on your own. The only person who would have to fill out this section is someone other than the student, the student's spouse, or the student's parents or stepparents. For example, if the form were filled out by a financial aid consultant, a tax preparer, a high school guidance counselor, or a financial aid officer, then this person would have to complete this section and sign off on the form.

Some FAOs have already hinted to parents that the appearance of a preparer's name on the form will make the application subject to much closer scrutiny. Aside from the questionable legality of such a practice by the school, at the time of this writing the Department of Education had not yet determined if they would release this information to the schools. In addition, details as to what constitutes a "preparer" and at what point someone must sign on the form have not yet been completely clarified.

*Note: If you are filing the FAFSA online, you will need to provide the required signature(s). Dependent students must "sign" the form as must the parent (or stepparent) who provided information on the FAFSA. This can be done by either printing a signature page and mailing the signed page to the processor OR by submitting the required signatures electronically using a FSA ID for each person who is "signing" the form. (The latter method is best, if at all possible.)*

*It is generally easier to submit your FAFSA after you have the necessary FSA ID(s). However if you have a deadline looming and you are having difficulty obtaining the necessary FSA ID(s), you should submit the FAFSA without the FSA ID(s) and indicate you will sign the form using a signature page. Even though the FAFSA will not be processed until the form is signed electronically with the FSA ID(s) or a completed signature page is received by the processor, your form will still be considered "received" by the processor as of the date you submit your data. However, once you get the FSA ID, you should then log back in and "sign" the form. If you have "signed" the form with the required FSA ID(s) and submitted the data, you should click on the "Exit" icon on the Confirmation page to check your status. You should see a message that indicates Current Application Status: Processing.*

That does it for the FAFSA. Congratulations! If none of the schools to which you are applying require the PROFILE form, skip ahead to the section "Are You Done?" that follows our PROFILE tips. Otherwise, let's go to the PROFILE form.

# Filling Out the 2020–2021 PROFILE Form

It is critically important that the data on the FAFSA form be consistent with the PROFILE. Inconsistent data between the forms will likely cause delays with the review of your data by the aid office and will likely result in requests for additional documentation to resolve the discrepancies.

So as mentioned earlier: If you are a resident of state which has limited state aid funds that are awarded on a first-come, first-served basis and/or you're applying to at least one of the limited number of colleges that still awards aid on a first-come, first-served basis, then you should be filing the 2020–2021 FAFSA as soon as you can after September 30, 2019 (even if that means you will be filing the PROFILE at a later date). However if there is no urgency to file the 2020–2021 FAFSA right after the filing period begins on October 1, 2019, then you should ideally start working on the PROFILE first and then the FAFSA before you submit either form to its respective processor. However, we do suggest that you review our FAFSA strategies earlier in the part of the book before you work on the PROFILE in earnest, as our tips in the prior pages for completing the FAFSA cover many of the overlapping questions that appear on both forms.

The PROFILE is a much more detailed form than the FAFSA. And for those schools that require it, the responses you provide on the PROFILE are likely to be even more important that your FAFSA data, given the PROFILE application determines the eligibility for the large amounts of need-based gift aid awarded out of the school's own coffers. So you should allow plenty to time to complete both forms and be sure you are satisfied with your responses before you hit the submit button.

If a noncustodial parent must also complete a separate PROFILE form (which to avoid confusion we will refer to as the "Noncustodial parent PROFILE" in this book, even though the College Board does not use that term), the student and their custodial parent need to begin working on their PROFILE in order for the noncustodial parent to be able to complete and submit their own PROFILE form. We'll discuss this issue in more detail in the following pages. In the meantime, be aware that the noncustodial parent should never complete another FAFSA for same student, though they may need to report their information on a FAFSA for a different student for which they would be considered the custodial parent.

The PROFILE has much more sophisticated skip logic than the FAFSA. So it is critical that the early sections of the PROFILE be properly completed. Otherwise the wrong questions will be asked—and likely many questions that should be asked will not be generated by the skip logic. As you progress through the form, the initial questions at the start of each section will further refine the questions you will be asked to complete. Certain responses in one sub-part of a section may also immediately generate additional follow-up questions on the same screen.

Because the PROFILE is so personalized, it is impossible to provide you with line-by-line tips for every possible question you will be asked. However the information in Chapter 3, the line-by-line strategies for the FAFSA, and the recommendations and suggestions that follow should have you thinking the right way in order to answer the questions to your best advantage. Yet while many questions on the PROFILE are similar to those on the FAFSA, here are some important differences that you should realize before you begin work on the PROFILE.

1. On the PROFILE form, real estate (other than your primary residence) should not be included as an "Investment". It will be listed in a separate category as "Other real estate". Exception: if part of the primary residence is rented and is considered part of your "Investments" response for the FAFSA, on the PROFILE you will provide the total value and total debt for the primary residence In the Housing Section of the PROFILE. Then you will simply list the percentage rented out to others when asked. The PROFILE processor will do the calculations to segregate the percentage considered the home and the percentage that will be considered other real estate when the data is submitted. So you should not provide the value and debt of the rented share of the home on the PROFILE form as other real estate. If you do, that rented share will be assessed twice.

2. Regarding certain assets, the PROFILE requires you to list "What is it worth today" (value) and "What is owed on it" (debt) separately. The College Board will then do the subtraction for you to determine your net assets.

3. Even if you can skip the asset questions on the online FAFSA, you must answer all the asset questions on the PROFILE.

4. Unlike the FAFSA form which only asks for financial information of the custodial parent (and if applicable, the stepparent residing with the custodial parent), the PROFILE process provides schools the opportunity to request information from the noncustodial parent (and if applicable, the stepparent residing with the noncustodial parent) when the student's biological or adoptive parents are no longer living together. However, the noncustodial parent's information will go on a separate PROFILE application. Be aware that responses provided on the noncustodial parent's own "Noncustodial parent PROFILE" will not correspond to the FAFSA data, since the noncustodial parent should never complete a FAFSA for that particular student.

5. In most cases, students completing the FAFSA who are considered independent do not need to provide parental financial information on the FAFSA. However depending on the student's situation and the school's aid policies, an independent student may need to provide parental information on the PROFILE if the student wishes to be considered for institutional aid.

6.   List whole dollar amounts; do not list cents. Do not use the dollar sign—just list the dollar amount. Do not use commas to separate numbers. For example, $53,205 should be listed as 53205. Use the minus sign before any negative numbers; do not use parentheses.

7.   Since the overwhelming majority of our readers live in the United States, the PROFILE tips that follow do not cover the PROFILE questions that may be asked of international students. Most of these international questions do not correspond to items on the FAFSA, since only students classified as international who are U.S. citizens or eligible non-citizens living outside of the United States or its possessions are normally eligible for federal student aid programs funded by the U.S. federal government.

## Getting Started

As we suggested, it would be a good idea for a separate College Board student account to be created for the express use of completing the PROFILE. It would be best for the parent's email address and phone numbers to be listed as the "student's email address" and "student's phone number" when creating the College Board account and for the preliminary questions at the beginning of the PROFILE. However, the other identifiers—the actual student's name, the student's date of birth, the student's social security number, school, etc., need to be provided for the new College Board account. We simply recommend the parent's email address and phone number be used instead, as from our experience counseling families we know parents constantly have a problem with their child not being diligent in viewing their emails, answering their phone, and responding to voicemail messages.

And if the Noncustodial parent PROFILE is required by at least one college, the PROFILE instructions will mention at some point that the noncustodial parent needs to create their own College Board account. However, since only a "student" and not a parent can create a College Board account this means that noncustodial parent needs to create another College Board "student account" (so there may be three College Board accounts if the custodial parent followed our suggestion above. There's no need to worry if you have three accounts for the same student. There will be a separate user name and password to log into each account. As long as the respective parents do not share the log in details for the "student" account they created, their information will not be available to anyone else (unless another person have ready access to the email account they listed when they created the College Board account.

Once you get to the sign in page for the PROFILE application with your College Board account, you will want to select the correct application for the year you are seeking aid, as the PROFILE for two different school years will both be available until sometime in February 2020. Be sure to select the 2020–2021 version if the student will commence their studies in the fall 2020 and spring 2021 school year. Due to the skip-logic built into the PROFILE application, you should carefully follow the instructions and help comments so that the proper questions will be generated based on your individual situation. Since the PROFILE is a more detailed form than the FAFSA, it is best for the custodial parent of a dependent student to complete the PROFILE form instead of the student to better insure that the proper questions are generated.

In the **Getting Started** section of the PROFILE that appears shortly after you log onto the form with the College Board account you will be using to complete the form, you will first notice that some questions are required; these are denoted by an asterisk (*) in a red font appearing next to any questions on the form. However, we recommend that you answer all of the questions on the PROFILE form, even the optional ones such as the student's social security number, if applicable to your situation.

As you begin to fill out the PROFILE, you may experience déjà-vu—because many of the questions seem identical to the questions on the FAFSA—but be sure to carefully read the questions and any help comments that may appear on the screen—as you complete the PROFILE form. Be aware that many of the questions on the PROFILE will correspond exactly to the questions on the FAFSA. However, in some cases similarly worded questions may require a different response as we explain in the text that follows.

As we went to press, information regarding the exact questions and the ordering of the sections for the 2020–2021 PROFILE was not yet available. We are making an informed guess regarding the data that will required for the various sections of the form. We have used the same ordering of the sections in the text that follows that was used for the 2019–2020 version of the PROFILE. But because there may be changes to the required data, the ordering of the sections, and/or other items when the College Board makes the 2020–2021 PROFILE available online beginning on October 1, 2019, please be sure to check the free online student tools included with this book (see page vi) to see if there are any late-breaking updates. Please be aware that this update text will be available to you before any school's 2020–2021 PROFILE deadline. In that update, we will be providing more specifics about the 2020–2021 PROFILE application and process as well as the 2020–2021 FAFSA.

In our comments that follow, we have tried to anticipate the most common questions you are likely to be asked. But remember that because of the skip logic built into the form, you very well may not be asked all the questions that we cover below. For example, if the student's parents do NOT own their own home, they will not be asked questions regarding its value or purchase price.

For clarity, on the pages that follow, we may have boldfaced references to particular questions you may be asked for a particular section of the PROFILE. However, the exact wording of such questions may well differ on the actual PROFILE form you view online.

Once all the key identifiers are completed on the first few pages, you will be asked to confirm them. Keep in mind that it is still fine at this stage—and even preferable—for a parent of the student to supply their email address and phone number as if they are those of the student. However, the other information at the start of any PROFILE needs to be accurate information regarding the student so that the aid office at a school receiving your submitted PROFILE data will be able to match the processed PROFILE data with the student identifiers supplied to the aid office as a result of the admissions application or enrolled student database. Keep in mind that these PROFILE responses will also be asked of the noncustodial parent at the start of the Noncustodial parent PROFILE, if that is required. All the responses used to identify the student need to match so that the respective versions of the PROFILE applications will be linked up by the processor. In that way, the colleges will get the data from both processed forms and know which PROFILE form matches up with which Noncustodial parent PROFILE form. As with the regular PROFILE, the noncustodial parent can use their email address and phone number for those "student" questions.

On the next page of the PROFILE (and the Noncustodial parent PROFILE), there will be questions to determine if the student is an independent student for federal aid purposes. However as mentioned earlier, some students completing the PROFILE may still be asked for parental data even if they could skip the parent questions on the FAFSA. Carefully read those questions and select "Yes" or "No" for each one based on the how those questions apply to the student (and not the student's parent).

For students where both biological or adoptive parents are living together (whether or not they are married and regardless of their gender), the next section is straightforward, as you will provide information about both adults. However for students where the two parents are living apart, you will need to provide the names of both biological parents and any stepparents (provided the stepparent is alive and still married to the parent). So you may need to list as many as four significant adults in the student's life if both parents are remarried. If any parent is deceased, indicate that as well. Make sure all the required adults are listed.

You will then be asked some follow-up questions to ascertain who is the custodial parent and who is the noncustodial parent. As mentioned earlier, it is critical that the parent required to report their information on the FAFSA (i.e., the custodial parent) will be the same parent who will be considered the custodial parent for the PROFILE. If there is a discrepancy, this will soon cause major problems down the road, especially if the forms are submitted with this conflicting information. You may be asked to confirm this information. It is advisable to alert the noncustodial parent about this potential problem as well.

Be aware that if there was only one biological or adoptive parent of the student at the time the student was born or adopted respectively and that sole parent is not married and living with the student's stepparent, then the response areas for the name, date of birth etc. of the second parent should be deleted by clicking on the "X". This will trigger a follow-up question with menu options to determine why a 2nd parent is not listed. Select the best option for situation—but be prepared to provide appropriate supporting documentation to the college such as a birth certificate or the adoption papers. In this way, noncustodial parent information will be waived if it is otherwise required. And if that sole parent is married to a stepparent, then the stepparent's info needs to be listed.

Since the application's skip logic will now take over to determine if the rest of the form is going to be considered the student and custodial parent's PROFILE or if it will be "Noncustodial parent PROFILE" (if such a form is required), it cannot be stressed enough how important the responses in this **Parent Information** section are, especially for any family situation in which the student's two biological or adoptive parents are no longer living together. Some basic information about any noncustodial parent, if applicable, will be requested a bit later on the PROFILE. The data on this one webpage about the noncustodial parent that appears on the PROFILE with the student's and custodial parent's detailed information is NOT the Noncustodial parent PROFILE form. That requires a separate College Board account to access and will be completed by the noncustodial parent.

The **Academic Information** section that follows for the PROFILE will first ask questions about the student applicant's enrollment during the 2019–2020 school year and then will require you to list at least one school that requires the PROFILE for the 2020–2021 school year. Be sure to select the appropriate status for the student. If the student will be a first-year student, select the proper admissions application option. If the student is applying Early Decision 1 to a PROFILE school, it would be best to hold off on listing any other colleges here unless they have a PROFILE deadline before the ED school's admission decision is known. In this way, fees can be minimized if accepted. And if not, you can still select "Early Decision" in this section if the student is applying ED2 to that school. Once this section is completed and saved, the noncustodial parent can complete and submit their entire Noncustodial parent PROFILE, even if the regular PROFILE is not yet submitted (provided at least one of the saved schools requires a PROFILE from the noncustodial parent.) Noncustodial parents do not provide a list of schools to receive their data; the processor will automatically make sure that their data goes to those schools that require the online Noncustodial parent PROFILE, even if more schools are added at a later date by the student or custodial parent on their version. If a waiver is needed because the noncustodial parent will not complete the noncustodial parent form, the home page for the PROFILE form before one signs in has details on the procedures to follow.

For the remaining questions on either the PROFILE or the Noncustodial parent PROFILE, the word "parents" refers to the parent(s), and if applicable their spouse, who is to provide information on that particular form. So for example, if both parents are divorced and remarried: the "parents" for the PROFILE will be the custodial parent and custodial stepparent for most questions, similar to Parent 1 and Parent 2 on the FAFSA (though which one is Parent 1 and which is Parent 2 can differ between those two forms). And for the Noncustodial parent PROFILE, the word "parents" refers to the noncustodial parent (and if applicable, the noncustodial stepparent) who should not complete the FAFSA for that student.

The next section of the form, **Parent Details,** will show the name of the person whose information is being requested on that web page listed at the top. Be aware that as with any other webpage on the form requiring at least one response, all the required responses on that web page must be completed in order to save the information and proceed. If you leave a web page before all the required responses are provided, you will likely get a warning; but in any event, if you go to another page before the data can be saved, all the inputted data on that web page will not be saved.

Be honest, but humble, when listing occupations. If true, be sure to indicate if you are a veteran of the U.S. Armed Forces. You should then provide the appropriate responses for any applicable retirement programs if you will receive any funds from such programs at some point in the future, even if not doing so now. If you have previously contributed to IRAs, 401(k)s, 403(b)s, a TDA plan and/or other tax-deferred retirement plans, you should indicate that you have these retirement plans. Then list the current value of such plans in the appropriate response areas. If applicable, list zero if no funds have ever been contributed to such plans or there are no longer any funds in these plans. Be aware that most colleges do not factor such dollar amounts into account when determining your eligibility for aid.

After the preliminary sections are completed, the more detailed financial and other information will be requested. Unless the student is an independent student not required to provide parental information on the PROFILE, the next few sections of the PROFILE (as well as the Noncustodial PROFILE) will pertain to income, expenses, and assets of the parent(s) or parent/stepparent required to provide such information. Unlike the FAFSA, these questions go into much more detail. Care should be taken with each question due to the skip logic that generates follow-up questions for each section.

The **Parent Income** section begins with questions about the PPY 2018 tax return status. However, before you input any data, you should read the remaining text in this section about 2018 income. Tax filers should simply refer to individual IRS line references that appear on the PROFILE form for each question, and input the appropriate responses that appear on the return. While most of these questions are optional, you should answer all of them to avoid possible problems later on in the aid process. Most of these IRS line items will appear in the far right column of the IRS 1040 and its Schedule 1, but there are some others not in that far right column that should also be carefully inputted. (e.g., IRS 1040 Line 2a regarding tax exempt interest). If any line item is blank on the return, enter 0 (zero) for the corresponding PROFILE question. If you had any qualified rollovers with IRAs or other retirement plans, be sure to enter the correct amount you rolled over so that the processor will deduct the rollover when calculating your income. Some, but not all, individual adjustments to income are requested; though the total adjustments to income amount on Line 36 of Schedule 1 of the IRS 1040 is asked as well. Those individual adjustments to income above Line 36 with questions on the PROFILE will be considered untaxed income in the IM aid formula. The other adjustments are not, but do reduce your AGI.

Most likely, your earliest PROFILE deadline will not be until November 1, 2019. So if you are on extension and won't file your 2018 tax return until the extension deadline of October 15, 2019, if at all possible you should wait to complete the PPY income questions until your 2018 return(s) are completed. That way, you will be able to use completed tax return data. If you are not required to file a return, then use your best estimates about your other income items. If you used the IRS DRT on the FAFSA, it will not be possible to compare the answers to similar tax return questions between the two forms due to encryption on the FAFSA. Otherwise, make sure you provide similar responses for the 2018 adjusted gross income and U.S Taxes paid questions on both forms. Our same FAFSA tips on pages 180 and 181 (in the Adjusted gross income section) that apply to these PROFILE questions will normally also apply for the PROFILE if you needed to combine information from two returns and/or provide only one individual's proportionate share of information from a joint return. However, you will also need to make the same combinations or exclusions for any other additional PROFILE questions not asked on the FAFSA. If you filed an amended 2018 return (IRS 1040X): unlike the FAFSA in which the original return data is transferred via the IRS DRT or manually inputted if you could not use the DRT, you should provide the amended return data on the PROFILE—and be sure to note this when you get to the **Special Circumstances** section of the PROFILE. This is important since the colleges will most likely be getting different tax return data on the two forms.

Once you complete all the appropriate responses relating to the 2018 tax return, you should click on the tab to save your work and continue, since the PROFILE may time you out if you do not change screens in a certain time period. However, it would be a good idea once the 2018 tax data is saved to then navigate back to that screen and double and triple check your figures to be sure the proper answers from your return were entered in the correct spaces.

The next screen in the **Parent Income** section will ask questions about **income earned from work**. If you only were required to report information about one parent on the FAFSA (and no stepparent data is required on the FAFSA) **and** you were able use the IRS DRT, follow the instruction on the PROFILE to complete this item which is the sum of amounts on certain line items on your tax return and/or W-2s. Your response will then be consistent with the transferred FAFSA amount that only the school can see. (Per our comments on pages 182–183, remember that the DRT doesn't include contributions to tax-deferred plans here—so they should not be included for this PROFILE item either, if the income from work amount was automatically transferred. Otherwise, the same applicable amount(s) for the respective individual(s) named on the PROFILE should agree with either FAFSA 86 and/or 87.)

If applicable: When answering questions about Social Security benefits, exclude any benefits you received that were reported on the 2018 tax return and therefore are reported on the prior PROFILE web page. Also exclude any benefits the parent received for the student and exclude any benefits the parents received for any dependent that will be in college during the 2020–2021 school year. So if the parents filed a 2018 return, this question should only include the benefits *paid to the parent* for the benefit of a minor child or other dependent who will not be in college in the 2020–2021 school year.

Be careful when answering the question on this web page about pre-tax deductions from your salary and other untaxed income. The amount of voluntary pre-tax contributions to a 401(k), 403(b) or other tax deferred plans listed on any W-2 form should agree with the amount reported in FAFSA question 92a. Do not include contributions to IRAs and other plans deducted on the tax return that should have been reported on the prior web page. Unlike the FAFSA, the PROFILE asks questions about FSA and HSA contributions that do not appear on your tax return as they are deducted pre-tax from your salary (and oftentimes, but not always, are listed on your W-2 form.). Any HSA deduction claimed on Line 25 of Schedule 1 of the IRS 1040 that was required to be reported as part of "other untaxed income" for FAFSA 92h. should have been listed on the prior PROFILE web page. For the question about other 2018 untaxed income, do not include any child support received in 2018 as this will be reported in the **Child Support** section later in the PROFILE.

Unlike the FAFSA, the 2020–2021 PROFILE also requires information regarding the "recent year" 2019 aka the "prior year" or "PY" as well as the "anticipated year" (2020). Yet these questions are not as detailed as the 2018 PPY ones. Because similar data is required for these 2019 and 2020 income questions, our tips are the same for both years.

Since your 2019 income tax returns will likely not be completed until after your earliest PROFILE deadline—even for regular decision schools—there is no question of getting into trouble if your figures are off a bit. In most cases, the colleges will be awarding aid using your 2018 PPY income year data rather than your projections for the PY year and/or the year after the PY year. However, some schools have been known to reduce aid if income for either year is larger than income listed for the PPY base income year. Of course, if 2019 and/or 2020 income will be significantly less than 2018 income, you should explain the situation in the Explanation and Special Circumstances Section (ES) towards the end of the form. You should also contact the financial aid office directly as well. Using "professional judgment", the FAOs may ignore the PPY income and focus instead on the projections you have made for the years after the base income year. And be prepared to provide supporting documentation. Anyone who is out of work or even just feeling that her employment situation is unstable should read our section about "The Recently Unemployed Worker" in the "Special Topics" chapter.

When projecting the 2019 and 2020 income, be conservative. Don't talk about a raise you are supposed to get but haven't yet received. If you are out of work, give the FAOs the worst-case scenario. If you are self-employed, use your expected NET business income, not the gross receipts. If you just took a job at a lower salary or you know you will have less overtime or a smaller bonus in the coming year, make sure the figures reflect this. If you are already aware of any extreme changes in your situation compared to 2018, you should probably write to the individual FAOs directly rather than relying on them to take these projections on the PROFILE into account.

For **2019 and 2020 Income earned from work**: These questions are not quite the same as the 2018 questions on an earlier web page. For the 2018 PPY income from work questions, such amounts for tax filers are used to calculate expense allowances in the aid formulas. Here they count as income questions, *even for tax-filers*. Be careful not to double-count your income. If you project that you will be contributing to deferred compensation provisions next year [such as 401(k) or 403(d) plans], you should include the contributions as part of your regular income earned from work for that year—and exclude them from the 2019 and 2020 **untaxed income and benefits** responses.

For **2019 and 2020 other taxable income** questions: make a rough projection of your other taxable income for the respective years (see pages 65–75 for our suggested strategies)—include interest, dividend, real estate income, etc. and subtract any losses. Include the taxable portion, if any, of your social security benefits. Use a minus sign if the sum is a negative number.

For the **2019 and 2020 untaxed income** questions: The PROFILE instructions will advise you about the types of untaxed income to include. However despite what they say, do not include any adjustments to income that are considered untaxed income in the federal or institutional aid formulas, such as IRA contributions. Their inclusion would overstate your income for 2019 and/or 2020. Also, do not include 2019 and/or 2020 taxable combat pay which should be included in as part of your income from work. If applicable, include only the sum of the untaxed portion of your social security benefits plus any benefits you received or will receive for any person who will NOT be enrolled in college in 2020–2021. You should also be sure to include child support that will be received for all children, not just the student, in 2019 and/or 2020.

You will be asked to explain the types of untaxed income if your response is a number other than 0 (zero).

The last sub-section in Parents Income will ask about various need-tested benefits received, if any. The responses should be similar to FAFSA 74–78. As with the FAFSA, remember that Supplemental Security Income (SSI) is NOT the same program as social security death or disability benefits.

The next section on the PROFILE, **Child Support**, first asks two preliminary questions: the first about such payments paid in 2018 and 2019 and then the second regarding 2018 payments received. If you answer yes to either question, follow-up questions will be asked about annual (not monthly) support. Be sure to read them carefully, as some will ask about total support for all children while others will only apply to the student. Any 2018 responses you provide regarding total support for all children should be the same as the responses for the identical questions on the FAFSA, if any such response on the FAFSA is an amount great than zero.

The next section on the PROFILE, **Household Information**, refers to your living arrangements for your primary residence. Answer the preliminary question accordingly, and remember that in this section the word "home" only refers to your main domicile, which is likely your legal address. If you do not own your primary residence, the questions in the section are straightforward. But if you do indeed own your home, please refer to our strategies in Chapter Three regarding value and debts on the home (pages 92–93). Be sure to report the total value as well as total debt currently outstanding, even if part of this "home" is rented out to others. You will be asked to also give the year purchased and the purchase price. This is a check on the value of your home. Using the Federal Housing Index Multiplier and other tools, the colleges can see if you have low-balled the value of this property. If you inherited the house, the purchase price is "0." If you built the house yourself, the purchase price is the cost of the house plus the cost of the land. For the "Amount owed on home" question, include the amounts owed on any mortgage(s) plus the balance owned on any home equity line of credit (HELOC). You will then be asked to list the amount owed on the primary mortgage, which will be different if there's also a second mortgage and/or HELOC balance owed.

The next PROFILE section, **Parent Assets**, involves various sub-sections for different types of assets. When answering these questions, it is critically important that you don't double count assets by listing the same assets in different sub-sections or questions on the PROFILE. Qualified retirement accounts listed earlier on the PROFILE are not to be reported here. Just as with the FAFSA, it will be helpful to review to the asset section in Chapter Three before you answer these questions.

Regarding **"investments"**: Unlike the FAFSA (which considers other real estate as part of your investments), the PROFILE only considers financial assets such as stocks, bonds, mutual funds, CDs, etc. as investments. For the preliminary question regarding parental assets held in the names of their children: Be sure to read the PROFILE instructions for this section care-fully before you provide any dollar amounts in the **Parent Asset Details** sub-section. If you have any debt outstanding secured by these investments, such as margin debt, deduct the amount of such secured debt; however be sure to mention you reduced the value of your investments by the dollar amount of this debt in the **"Special Circumstances"** section at the end of the PROFILE. The **Cash, checking and savings** amount reported should agree with your answer for FAFSA 88. The next PROFILE sub-section pertains to other real estate. If any of the situa-tions mentioned apply, you will then be asked to provide additional information. If you rent out part of your home and the equity in that portion rented out is required to be reported as part of your investments on the FAFSA (see page 184), the ONLY applicable statement regarding this situation with your home to be selected is the last one about renting out a portion of the primary residence. You will then simply indicate the percentage rented out; the processor will then divide the total value of your home and total debt previously reported in the **"Housing Details"** section earlier in the PROFILE into the proper portion considered to be your home and the portion that will be considered other real estate. The top three statements should only be checked if you own real estate other than your primary residence that cannot be classified as business property. Answer the detailed follow-up questions accordingly.

The next final asset sub-section begins with the **"Parent Business/Farm Setup"**. If you do not own or have a partial interest in any corporation (other than shares in a publicly-traded company), or in any partnership, or in any farm, or if you are not self-employed: then most likely you will not be selecting any of the statements on this web page. Be aware that if you are only a "limited partner" in a partnership, the value of your stake in the limited partnership should be considered as part of your PROFILE and FAFSA investments, and not as a business entity for this set-up page—though you should also mention this fact in the **Special Circumstances** section of the PROFILE. If you have any activity reported on Schedule C of the 2018 IRS 1040 with such net income or loss from this activity also reported on Line 12 of Schedule 1 of the IRS 1040, this activity is considered a "business" on the PROFILE and you should select the appropriate statement. You will then be asked to provide the number of different entities in which you are involved.

If you do need to report information on any business or farm, including any "family business" or "family farm" excluded on the FAFSA (see page 184), it will be helpful to first refer to pages 266–269 of this book. If applicable, you will also need to have copies of any 2018 corporation or 2018 partnership returns available, as well as any financials about any farm ownership. With any questions involving dollar amounts such as assets, debts, revenue and expenses, be sure to list only the proportionate share of those items on the PROFILE and not the total figures for the entity—unless, of course, you own 100% of it either individually or jointly with the other "parent" on that PROFILE. The percentage owned by the "parents" should be reported as well as the separate percentage owned by other relatives (by blood or marriage). However the definition of other family members for other questions about the entity may be different, so be sure to read the fine print in the PROFILE instructions for these questions.

The **"Parent Expenses"** section that follows next on the PROFILE first asks about various types of expenses you may have incurred in 2018 and/or 2019. Follow-up questions involve annual figures (unless otherwise stated.) Regarding **medical and dental expenses not paid by insurance**: be sure to refer to pages 87–89 for our suggested strategies. These expenses are among the most underreported by parents. Use all the IRS allowable expenses. These include medical or dental expenses you've charged on a credit card during the year, even if you haven't paid for them yet. We find that many families forget about health insurance premiums deducted from their paycheck and medical-related transportation costs. However, do not include insurance premiums that are deducted on Line 29 of Schedule 1 of the 2018 1040. After you have figured out 2018 expenses, estimate 2019 as best you can if final numbers are not yet available. If either number is more than the threshold percentage of your total income for the corresponding year specified in the PROFILE instructions for these two questions, list that total number you calculated. Otherwise, enter 0 (zero) if instructed to do so. Regarding the **repayment of parents' educational debt**: Be sure to read the instructions carefully for this type of expense and only include payments on those types of loans specifically mentioned. If you are asked questions about alimony paid in this section or elsewhere, read the fine print. If the alimony is paid to an ex-spouse other than the student's parent and the question does not cover that situation, mention this fact and mention the alimony paid amount for 2018, 2019 and 2020 in the **"Special Circumstances"** section. Parents of international students may need to provide monthly or annual amounts for various household expenses.

For the next PROFILE section, **"Household Summary"**: be aware that unlike FAFSA 72 and 73 regarding household size and the number in the college, the PROFILE no longer asks these two similar questions (as it did prior to the 2018–2019 PROFILE.) The enhanced skip logic built into PROFILE now indirectly derives this data based on responses in this and other sections of the form. At the start of this section, the names of the student and the custodial parents (or the custodial parent and also, if applicable, the custodial stepparent) will appear. As you continue to the next web page, the **"Dependent Summary"** sub-section will appear. If you have determined there is no other family member who qualifies as a member of the household—but be sure to read all he fine print in the instructions for this section—you can then click on "Save and Continue" and you will advance to the PROFILE regarding the student's income. However if there is any other family member who can be considered a member of the household—enter their identifying information one-at-a-time until all the additional family members information is inputted and appears on this web page. After reviewing this data for accuracy (and editing any incorrect responses), you can click on the Save and Continue tab to advance to the more-detailed questions regarding each of the other family member's year in school in 2019–2020 and in 2020–2021. If a family member is in grades K-12 for a given year, follow-up questions will ask if the student attends or will attend a private school. If so, additional questions will appear asking about the amount of various costs paid by the parent and the amount of any gift aid awarded. The responses to these questions will be used to determine if you qualify for a deduction against income for these tuition payments (see pages 89–90). And if another family member is in college in 2019–2020 or will be in college in 2020–2021, then information will be asked about the enrollment. **NOTE WELL:** this is the only section on the PROFILE now used to determine if another family will be concurrently enrolled during the 2020–2021 academic year in a higher education institution for purposes of determining the parent contribution per student (see page 118). Because the size of the household, the ages of the other family members (see page 117), possibly their K-12 educational expenses paid, and *especially the number of family members in college (excluding the student's parents)* impact the parent contribution for the student in the IM aid formula, it is critical that your situation be properly represented in this section of the form before the PROFILE is submitted to the processor. Independent students on the PROFILE may be asked slightly different questions about other household members.

For the PROFILE's **Student Income** section: The 2020–2021 PROFILE will now ask questions in various subsections about **the student's (2018) tax return status** as well as questions about the student's 2018 income. Just as with the parents, if the student is on extension until October 15, 2019, it would be better to wait to complete the PROFILE until the 2018 tax return is prepared (though the FAFSA may need to be filed earlier with estimated figures if at least one college under consideration and/or the student's home state government awards funds on a first-come first served basis.) Unlike the parents, for tax-filers the specific questions regarding certain IRS line items to be listed on the PROFILE do not include any questions regarding wages or self-employment income. These items are to be reported in the **Student income earned from work** question, asked on the PROFILE of both tax filers and non-filers. For other 2018 income questions: Be sure you do not include benefits paid to the parent for the student in the untaxed social security benefits question in this section. And for a student who has attended college before 2020–2021: be sure to list any 2018 income earned in a college work-study program (that is part of the PROFILE income earned from work figure listed) as well as the amount of any taxable grants or scholarships reported on the student's 2018 tax return in the appropriate PROFILE question. (This PROFILE question's response will likely agree with the sum of FAFSA 43c, 43d and 43f.)

Unlike the **Parent Income** section on the PROFILE, students will not be asked any questions about their 2019 income. However, the **Student Expected Income and Benefits** sub-section asks questions about income for the summer of 2020 and during the 2020–2021 school year. Be conservative with your estimates here as your responses may trigger a higher student contribution from income in the IM (see pages 119–120)—and be sure to exclude work-study earnings!

The **Student Resources** sub-section in the **Student Income** section includes some very important, though tricky, questions about various contributions from others to assist with college costs. (On the Noncustodial Parent PROFILE, some of these questions are the only ones for that form's somewhat awkwardly-named **"Student Income"** section.) For the response to the question on either version of the PROFILE regarding **The student's parents:** For dependent students, the best way to answer this question is to use the worksheets at the back of this book to determine the parents' expected contribution per student in the FM (Line R on page 318) and then understate it by 30% for your response. Independent students should list only a minimal figure if any help is expected; otherwise list "0."

For the question about **"Other relatives ..."**: Before answering this question, you should review the section "Direct Payments to the School" on pages 108–109. And be sure to carefully read the PROFILE help comments before you answer this question.

For the question regarding **Scholarships and grants from (other) sources..."** (See pages 238–239 and 242–243): When answering this question, you should not include any outside awards unless you are 100% certain you will be receiving the money. For the **tuition benefits** question: If there will be no tuition benefits, enter "0." If there will be benefits, but the amount of the benefits will be based upon the school attended, list the least amount of the benefit that you would receive based on your list of colleges under consideration that require the PROFILE. Some questions apply only to international students. Answer appropriately if asked. Depending on responses in the Parent Details section, questions regarding **Veteran's benefits** may also be asked. Read these questions carefully before you enter your responses.

The **Student Assets** section is arranged in almost the same way as the **Parent Assets** section earlier on the PROFILE. However, the questions in the **Student Assets Types** sub-section are different. For the PROFILE, a student's trust is treated as a separate category from other investments, while a parent's trust is included as part of the parent's investments. If you answer "Yes" to the statement in the **Student Asset Types** sub-section about the existence of a trust, additional questions about the trust and its value will eventually be asked. You should realize that when the word trust is used for this **"Student Asset Types"** question, it is not referring to a regular type of bank account that is maintained by one person "in trust for" another person. In that case, such an asset held by a parent reporting information on any aid form "in trust for" the student (and/or anyone else) should be reported as a parent asset and not as a student asset. For the **"Has Retirement accounts"** question:  Most students don't have IRAs, Keoghs or other retirement accounts, so most likely your answer for this will be "No." Otherwise, answer accordingly.

Whether or not any statement in the **Student Assets Types** sub-section is answered in the affirmative, all students will be asked about the current amount of their **Cash, savings, checking account and deposit accounts**. Your response should be the same as FAFSA 40, unless you were eligible to skip the FAFSA asset questions (if you filed the FAFSA on the Web) because you met the Simplified Needs Test or the Automatic Zero-EFC. In which case, you should follow the instructions on the PROFILE to answer this questions as well as any other questions about the student's other assets including....

**Student investments:** Remember that for purposes on the FAFSA, investments in FAFSA 41 would include the equity in other real estate and the value of a student's trust(s). So if the student has any financial investments, the figure provided on the PROFILE for the investment value may or may not agree with FAFSA 41.

Regarding the **Student Real Estate** sub-section: If the *student* owns any real estate, then select the statement(s) that apply. Then answer the follow-up questions about each property. For any jointly-owned property, list only the student (and if applicable, the student's spouse's) share.

For the **Student Businesses and Farms**: The same tips for a parent's business and/or farms apply.

Be aware that most dependent students going to college immediately after high school will likely not select any statements in the **Student Real Estate** and the **Student Businesses and Farms** sub-sections because they do not yet own such types of assets.

**Student Home:** If you are asked any of these questions and the student does not own his or her primary residence, you should go back and check your prior responses in the earlier sections of the PROFILE as the student likely will not be asked these questions which apply to some independent students. Otherwise, answer accordingly. As we explained in more detail in our comments regarding a parent's home, the questions regarding current value, year of purchase and purchase price also serve an audit check to be sure you have not low-balled the value of real estate.

Most dependent students will not be asked questions in the **Student Expenses** section, which are primarily for independent students: **Child support paid in 2018** should be the same as FAFSA 43b. And for **Student's medical and dental expenses**: If the parents paid the medical and dental expenses for the student, don't include them here—do refer to the PROFILE instructions before answering this one.

# Explanations and Special Circumstances

We already mentioned a number of situations that should be explained here. You should also provide details regarding any other PROFILE items that you are required to explain. Otherwise, we suggest that you leave this section blank. It is far more effective to send a separate letter to each college explaining any unusual circumstances. Be aware that if you select any option other than "None" from the list of special circumstances listed in this section, you will then need to provide some written comments below that list and explain the applicable circumstances. You should of course select "Other" if any of your special circumstances is not applicable to any on the menu options on the list.

That about does it for the most common sections and questions on the PROFILE you are likely to be asked. Unfortunately, you may not be finished with the PROFILE form just yet. Depending on the colleges and the programs you designated to receive your PROFILE (which are listed in the **Academic Information** section), there may be one or more additional questions that you have to answer at the request of one or more of the listed schools. If you are asked any of these questions, they will appear in the **Supplemental Questions** section, which may be broken down into sub-sections depending on the questions being asked.

At the time we went to press, the pool of available questions for this section had not been finalized. Nor had many individual colleges decided which additional questions, if any, they would be requiring of PROFILE applicants. As such, it is impossible for us to give you any specific advice regarding questions that may appear in this section of your PROFILE form.

It seems a safe bet to assume, however, that the majority of questions in this part of the PROFILE will either be asking for further details regarding items previously listed on the PROFILE or about additional assets or resources not previously reported. After reading Chapter Three and this part of the book, by now you should have a very good idea of the strategy you should be applying in order to maximize your aid eligibility. If you also keep the following points in mind, any questions in this section should not pose too much of a problem for you:

- Read the questions carefully. Answer them honestly, but do not disclose more information than required. If a yearly amount is requested, be sure you provide data for the requested calendar or academic year.

- Avoid overstating or double-counting assets or income (especially if you are estimating).

- Remember to include all allowable expenses or debts.

- Keep your responses consistent with other data previously listed on any form.

Keep in mind that only those colleges that select a particular question for this section will receive your response to that question. However beginning with the 2018–2019 PROFILE, this section no longer provides information as to which college is requesting which supplemental questions from the pool of available questions. So if you are completing the PROFILE with more than one college listed, it is hard to know which schools are getting the various responses in this section, if any. And if you add any additional colleges or programs to a previously-submitted PROFILE for that student, only new questions not previously asked by another college that was already on the PROFILE will be asked. So if a school you are now adding to the PROFILE requests applicants to answer these questions, you will not know all the questions being asked by that school you are adding,  unless none of your colleges listed in any previous submission asked any questions in this section and you are only adding that one school at this time.

## Are You Done?

Congratulations! Save your data and/or put your work aside for a day (unless the form is due that day!) You've earned a rest. Tomorrow, look the forms over very carefully. Are you happy with the numbers? If you finished the PROFILE and saved your PROFILE data online, it would be best to make sure all the answers are consistent with the answers you gave on the FAFSA. In addition, do your answers on the PROFILE and the FAFSA agree with any supplemental aid forms required by the colleges? Check the newspaper today to see if your stock or bond investments have lost any value. If so, revise your figures downward.

When you are convinced that everything is ready, carefully review your data again before you submit any online form or mail/fax/upload any paper aid document. Date any paper form, sign it, and make photocopies for your records. When submitting your PROFILE information, be sure you have credit card or bank account information handy as you will likely be charged a processing fee. If you are filing the PDF FAFSA, send the original form via Priority Express Mail to the processor. Track delivery with your airbill number.

Your Student Aid Report (SAR) from the government should be available in three to four weeks (or sooner for online filers). Once you submit your PROFILE data, you will be able to save and print the submitted info.

# The SAR Report

If you filed the PDF version of the FAFSA and did not provide an e-mail address, you will receive a multi-page form sent by the government called the Student Aid Report (or SAR) a few weeks after you send in your 2020–2021 FAFSA to the processor. (You can also retrieve the SAR online at fafsa.ed.gov provided you have a verified FSA ID for the student.) If you filed the FAFSA and provided a student e-mail address on any version, you will need to retrieve your SAR electronically as no paper SAR will be mailed to the student. No matter which method you used, check the information on the SAR carefully to make sure it agrees with the information you entered on the FAFSA. (Note: If you filed the FAFSA online and listed five or more schools in Step Six of the form, only the first four schools listed in Step Six will appear on the paper version of the SAR. However depending on the number of schools you listed on the FAFSA, the 5th, 6th, 7th, 8th, 9th, and 10th school will be listed in the online SAR.) Be sure that the SAR includes the correct names of the colleges to which you are applying for aid. If you are applying for aid at more colleges than you could list on the original FAFSA and/or you have decided to add some additional schools and/or the processor did not list a correct school, you will need to get the FAFSA data to those additional schools. You should call the FAOs at each of the schools not listed, explain the situation, and ask them how to proceed. Be sure to keep a record of the person you spoke with at each college as well as a summary of what was discussed. They will probably tell you one of two ways to get the data to them:

1.  By sending them a copy of the 2020–2021 SAR. While a number of schools will accept your data this way, you should be sure to mention that the school is not listed in Step Six when you call the aid office. Since you should always have at least one original SAR for your records, you should call (800) 433-3243 to request a duplicate 2020–2021 SAR if you received an original orange SAR in the mail.

2.  By revising the SAR. Because the online version allows you to maintain a list of up to ten schools (and only four schools appear on the paper version of the SAR) it is probably better to revise the list online (at www.fafsa.ed.gov) since you can list more schools this way. If you're sending back the SAR to the processor, use Priority Express Mail and track delivery. Be sure to carefully follow the instructions so that the processor will make the necessary corrections. If you already listed the maximum number of schools on the FAFSA, you will be substituting the unlisted school(s) for one or more of the schools previously listed. Before you do this, however, you should make sure any school you are substituting out has received your FAFSA information before you remove them. If you are mailing the SAR back to the processor, make a photocopy for your records. Within a few weeks after mailing, you will receive a new SAR which you should again review for accuracy. If you still have not been able to get all the schools listed after this

first round of revising, keep repeating the process until every school gets the FAFSA data. Of course, if you have to do the process more than once, you should give preference on your first revision to those schools with the earliest deadlines.

*Note: If you substitute one school for another, the originally listed school will no longer receive any revised data that you send back to the processor. Therefore, if you have to correct or change any items other than those in Step Six, you may need to put the original school(s) no longer listed back on the new SAR that is generated and send it back to the processor.*

If you haven't received a SAR within three weeks of filing, call (800) 433-3243 during business hours for a status report. Be sure to have the student's social security number handy when you call.

## Two Moments of Truth

The SAR will tell you if you qualify for a Pell Grant. Don't panic if the SAR says you are ineligible. This is a federal grant for lower-income families and many people do not qualify. Just because you didn't get a Pell Grant does not mean you won't qualify for any aid at all. The Pell is often the toughest type of aid to get.

The SAR will also tell you your Expected Family Contribution. Below the date on the front page of Part One of the SAR in small type are three letters followed by some numbers.

Here's a sample of what it might look like:

March 1, 2020

EFC: 08920

The EFC is your Expected Family Contribution under the federal methodology. There is no dollar sign, no explanatory paragraph, nothing to let you know how significant this number will be to you. In this example, the Expected Family Contribution for one year of college for one child was judged by the need analysis company to be $8,920.

*Note: If you filed the FAFSA online, your EFC figure may be provided to you along with your confirmation number right after you submit your FAFSA for processing.*

# Counting Chickens

Unfortunately, the federal EFC is not necessarily the number the colleges will elect to use. Schools that asked you to fill out the PROFILE form will most likely be using the institutional methodology to determine the family contribution. This figure could be lower or higher than the federal number. The institutional EFC is never given to the parents by the PROFILE processor.

# The Verification Process

"Verification" is the financial aid version of an audit, although the process is generally much more benign. In prior years, either the Federal processor or the colleges themselves could select students for verification, and each college had to verify a minimum of 30% of their applicants. Only the Federal processor will determine who must be selected for verification, but schools can also select additional students.

There are certain rules of thumb:

If you estimated your tax information, you're more likely to be verified. The lower your EFC, the more likely you are to be verified. If you filled out the paper version of the FAFSA, you're more likely to be verified.

If you say you've already completed your taxes, but didn't use the IRS DRT: you more than likely will be selected for verification.

Essentially, a much higher percentage of students (and parents) will be verified than in years past. However, the process will be more streamlined for those who use the IRS data retrieval process (automatically pre-populating the FAFSA form) either when they fill out the form initially, or by later going back to correct/update the form after they've completed their taxes, as they will be considered to have verified their income.

If you are selected for verification, and you chose not to use (or are unable to use) the IRS tool on the online FAFSA form or you subsequently corrected any of the pre-populated responses that were generated by the IRS tool, you will likely be required to send the school either a signed copy of your complete 2018 income tax return (including all schedules and attachments) or an official transcript of your return(s). See pages 347–350.

The schools may also ask for documentation of social security benefits if you receive them or information about child support paid or received. You will likely also have to fill out a Verification Worksheet so that the colleges can double-check the number of members in your household as well as other income items.

While the IRS audits a minuscule percentage of taxpayers, financial aid verification is relatively commonplace. At some schools, 100% of the applicants are verified. Thus, if you receive a notice of verification, this does not mean that it is time to book plane tickets to a country that does not have an extradition treaty with the United States. It is all routine.

## Revising Your Information

If the numbers on the SAR are different from the numbers you sent in a PDF FAFSA, you will probably want to revise them immediately. The SAR gives you instructions on how to correct errors made either by the processor or by you. You will also want to revise immediately if you receive any notice stating that your FAFSA could not be processed, if there are comments on the SAR that there were problems with the processing, or if you need to change the list of schools.

## How to Update Your Estimated Figures

While the instructions to the SAR tell you how to handle revisions, these instructions may conflict with the procedures many colleges would prefer you to follow. To find out the correct way to revise your SAR you must call the FAOs at all of the colleges still under consideration. In general, the FAOs will tell you to do one of three things:

1.  Revise the SAR and send the revisions to the processor. (Most likely response.)

2.  Revise the SAR and send all pages of the SAR directly to the FAO.

3.  Send all pages of the unrevised SAR to the FAO; he or she will make the necessary revisions.

When you call the FAOs, ask when they expect you to send them the original SAR. See if you can hold off until you know for sure what college the student will be attending. If you received the SAR in the mail and a college requires a physical copy of the SAR before the student is sure of his educational plans, you should request a duplicate SAR for your records by calling (800) 433-3243. The duplicate SARs are free, so we suggest you call for a few duplicate copies just in case.

The question numbers on the SAR should correspond exactly to the question numbers on the FAFSA. To help you in your revisions, you can refer to your photocopy of the FAFSA and your worksheets, as well as to the detailed instructions we gave for completing each line of the FAFSA form. Most likely, you will be revising only your income, expense, and tax return information for the Base Income Year. The SAR processors prefer you to use a dark-ink ballpoint pen for any revisions on the paper SAR. The asset information should be the net asset figures at the time you completed the original FAFSA, not the net asset figures on the day you are revising. You should therefore revise your asset information only if a mistake was made when the FAFSA was originally filed. (If using the online IRS Data Retrieval Tool, see pages 347–350 and our tips for the FAFSA in Part Three of this book).

After you send your SAR revisions to the processor, a new version of the SAR with the revised data will be generated. Look over the new SAR data to make sure it's accurate.

## The PROFILE Acknowledgement

After you transmit your PROFILE data to the processor you will be able to view and print out an Acknowledgment that summarizes your responses to most of the PROFILE questions. Follow the directions regarding revisions, if necessary.

## Applying to More PROFILE Schools

If after transmitting the PROFILE data to the processor you decide to apply to additional schools that require the PROFILE form, you can have the data sent to the additional schools by accessing your PROFILE record with your College Board username and password. Details on how to add additional schools will then be provided. You will also have to get the FAFSA data to these schools by revising the SAR.

## What to Do If You Get a Notice Saying Your Form Could Not Be Processed

Your need analysis form may get rejected for any number of reasons, but the most common are forgetting to answer one of the questions or not signing the form.

If your paper FAFSA is returned to you unprocessed, the main thing is to get it back to the need analysis company as fast as possible. Even if the screw-up was your fault, you will minimize the odds of missing out on aid if you snap into action immediately. The need analysis company will probably send an incomplete version of their report to all the colleges, so you will still be in the running. To be on the safe side, contact the individual schools to let them know what is happening.

In some cases, the need analysis companies or the government will question specific items because they are unusually low or high for a "typical family" with your income level. Don't feel you must change a number if it is really correct. For example, if you have a negative AGI due to property rental losses, but have positive income earned from work, the computers will automatically "flag" the AGI item. If the item is correct, you may need to place a check mark next to it when revising your SAR.

As always, photocopy any new information you send to the need analysis company or to the government, and send it Priority Express Mail unless you are revising the FAFSA form online. And be sure that you follow all instructions to the letter.

## If Your EFC Is Much Higher than You Expected

Somehow, no matter how prepared you are, seeing the federal EFC in print is always a shock. Remember that the colleges do not expect you to be able to pay the entire amount out of current income. If they deem your resources sufficient, they expect you to liquidate assets each year that your child is in college and they expect you to have to borrow money on top of that. Your EFC is designed to include money that you have earned in the past (assets) and money that you will obtain in the future (loans) as well as the income you are currently earning.

Remember that your family contribution could be lower or higher than the EFC printed on the SAR. This will be especially true if the school uses the institutional methodology in awarding their own aid funds. Remember also that colleges have broad latitude to change the EFC in either direction. This is where negotiation can come into play. Consult Part Four, "The Offer." We know of one case in which the EFC was judged to be $24,000. The school brought the actual family contribution down to $13,000.

In addition, some state aid formulas differ from the federal formula. We know of another case in which the EFC was judged to be $99,999, but the family managed to receive $5,000 a year in state aid because of quirks in the state's formula.

If you have used our worksheets to compute your federal Expected Family Contribution, you should not be surprised by the number on the SAR. If there is a large discrepancy between what you thought your EFC would be and what the SAR says it is, then someone may have made a mistake. Go through your worksheets carefully, and double-check to see that the information on the FAFSA form you filed agrees with the numbers you used in the worksheets. Also, make sure that these numbers agree with the numbers on the SAR if you filed the PDF version of the FAFSA. If an error was made on the FAFSA, start revising.

# The Next Step: Supplying Completed Tax Returns

Some colleges will not give you a financial aid package until they've seen your taxes for the first base income year. Others will give you a "tentative" package, subject to change when they see the final numbers. And some may want to see 2019 returns too, especially if your income declined in 2019 and you are planning to appeal the aid package(s).

It is in your best interest to get your taxes done as fast as possible. Prod your accountant if he is dragging his heels. Better yet, if you are not reading this book at the eleventh hour, plan ahead. During the fall of senior year in high school, let your accountant know that you are going to need your taxes done as soon as possible this year.

Paying for College

Find out from the colleges that you are interested in whether they really do want to see your tax return. In many cases, the answer will be yes. In a few cases (such as New York University), they will not want your tax return unless you are randomly selected for verification. We recommend that you not send a return unless it is required. Why give them more information than they need?

The most effective time for negotiation with the FAOs is before May 1, the Universal Reply Date by which most colleges require you to commit to attend. Obviously, you will have more bargaining power if you can still decide to go to another school. The FAOs are much less likely to compromise once you are committed to their college.

## The School's Own Forms

The standardized need analysis forms are probably not the only financial aid forms you will have to complete. Many selective colleges have their own forms as well with deadlines that may differ from those of both the standardized forms and the admissions applications to the schools themselves. The purpose of these forms is sometimes difficult to comprehend, since in many cases they ask many of the same questions you have already answered on the FAFSA or the PROFILE form all over again. Some counselors suspect this is done for the same reason police interrogate suspects several times: to look for discrepancies.

## More Detailed Information

However, the individual forms do ask for some new information. In general, they are looking for more specific breakdowns of your income and assets. Exactly what kind of assets do you have? How liquid are they? In addition, you will often be asked about your other children's educational plans for the current year and the year to come.

While neither the FAFSA nor the PROFILE form ask income and asset information about noncustodial parents, many of the individual schools will want to know all the financial details of that parent. Some may ask the noncustodial parent to complete their own noncustodial parent form instead of the Noncustodial parent PROFILE. If you own your own business, you may need to fill out the paper College Board's Business/Farm Supplement. We'll cover both of these situations in more detail in the "Special Topics" chapter of this book.

The forms may also ask questions to determine eligibility for specific restricted scholarships and grants. In general, these scholarships are left over from a different era when private citizens funded weird scholarships in their own name. The colleges hate administering these restricted scholarships—they would much rather be allowed to give money to whomever they feel like. However, if you are a direct blood descendant of a World War I veteran, the University of Chicago may have some money for you. If you can prove that one of your ancestors traveled on the Mayflower, Harvard may have some money for you. If you are of Huguenot ancestry, Bryn Mawr may have some money for you.

# Be Careful

Take the time to be consistent. Your answers on this form may be compared to other information you've supplied elsewhere. Small differences, especially if you are estimating, are acceptable, but anything major will cause serious problems. Get out your photocopies of any previous aid forms you've completed and make sure you are not diverging.

Much as you may feel that your privacy is being invaded, do not skip any of the questions. This is the colleges' game and they get to make the rules. If you don't answer, they don't have to give you any money.

Send these forms to the schools themselves, certified mail, return receipt requested. If you are sending any supplementary information (such as tax returns) make sure that the student's name and his or her college ID # or social security number are prominently displayed on all documents. This is especially important if the student's last name is different from either of his parents'.

# The IDOC Service

Some schools may now require you to submit your income tax returns and other documents to the College Board's IDOC service. After your documents are received by the IDOC processor, they will be scanned and then made available electronically to those schools that require them in this format. If at least one of your schools is utilizing the IDOC service, you will likely receive an email notification from the College Board. Required documents can now be either uploaded online or mailed to the IDOC service. Make sure all required signatures are provided. Finally, be extra careful that you submit the tax returns (and W-2s and/or 1099s if requested) for the correct calendar year.

# Part Four

## The Offer and
## Other Financial Matters

On the day that the offers from colleges arrive there will be many dilemmas for parents. One of the most vexing is deciding whether to steam open the letters from the colleges, or wait until the student gets home from school. We can set your mind at ease about this dilemma at least. You can usually tell an acceptance letter from a rejection letter even without opening it—acceptance letters weigh more. This is because as long as you met your deadlines, you should receive financial aid packages in the same envelopes the acceptance letters came in. Most colleges will need a commitment from you before May 1. This gives you only a few weeks to sift through the offers, compare them, and—if possible—negotiate with the FAOs to improve them.

The details of an aid package will be spelled out in the award letter. This letter will tell you the total cost of one year's attendance at the college, what the college decided you could afford to pay toward that cost, and what combination of grants, loans, and work-study the college has provided to meet your "need."

On the following page you will find a sample award letter from Anytown University located in Anytown, State.

# ANYTOWN UNIVERSITY
## OFFICE OF FINANCIAL AID

FIRST NOTICE

**Academic Year**
2020-2021
**Budget Assumptions**
Resident Dependent Single
**Indentification Number**
U123456789
**Award Date**
March 20, 2020

## OFFER OF FINANCIAL AID

After careful consideration, the Financial Aid Committee has authorized this offer of financial assistance for the award period indicated at left. The decision was made after careful consideration of your application.

To accept this offer, you must complete, sign, and return the white copy of this form within four weeks of receipt. This award is subject to cancellation if you do not respond by the specified date.

If you choose to decline any part of this offer, please place a check mark in the "DECLINED" box for the corresponding part of the package.

Be sure to review the terms and conditions of the award as described in the Financial Aid booklet enclosed.

Wright Price
123 Main Street
Anytown, ST 12345

| DECLINED | | FALL 2020 | SPRING 2021 |
|---|---|---|---|
| ☐ | Anytown University Scholarship | $11,975.00 | $11,975.00 |
| ☐ | Federal SEOG Grant | $500.00 | $500.00 |
| ☐ | Estimated Federal Pell Grant | $1,720.00 | $1,720.00 |
| ☐ | Recommended Federal Direct Loan | $1,750.00 | $1,750.00 |
| ☐ | Federal Work-Study | $665.00 | $665.00 |
| | TOTAL | $16,610.00 | $16,610.00 |

| FAMILY RESOURCES | | SUMMARY | |
|---|---|---|---|
| Parent's Contribution | $980.00 | Total Estimated Budget | $36,000.00 |
| Student's Contribution | $1,800.00 | Less: Family Contribution | $2,780.00 |
| Other Resources | 0.00 | Financial Need | $33,220.00 |
| TOTAL FAMILY CONTRIBUTION | $2,780.00 | TOTAL FINANCIAL AID | $33,220.00 |

Jane Doe, Director

Note that in this case, the family contribution was set at $2,780. The total cost of attendance at Anytown for that year was $36,000. Thus, this family had a remaining "need" of roughly $33,220 which was—in this case—met in full with a mixture of grants, loans, and work-study.

The Bloggs were evidently a high-need family, and received an excellent package: $28,390 in grants (outright gift aid, which did not need to be repaid), $1,330 in work-study, and $3,500 in loans for the year.

Not all colleges will meet the entire remaining "need" of every student, and there may have been a number of reasons why the package was so good in the case of the sample student in the report above. Perhaps Joe Bloggs was a particularly bright student or the impoverished grandchild of a distinguished alumnus.

## The Different Types of Financial Aid in Detail

Let's examine the different types of financial aid that you may be offered in the award letter. An acceptance of the aid package does not commit you to attending the college, so be sure to respond by the reply date (certified mail, return receipt requested, as always). You are allowed to accept or reject any part of the package, but there are some types of aid that should never be rejected.

**Grants and Scholarships:** These should never be rejected. This money is almost always tax-free and never has to be repaid. Grants and scholarships come in different forms.

**The Federal Pell Grant:** This grant is administered by the federal government, and like all federal aid, is awarded only to U.S. citizens or eligible noncitizens. The Pell is primarily for low-income families. You automatically apply for the Pell Grant when you fill out the FAFSA. The size of the award is decided by the federal government and cannot be adjusted by the colleges. If you qualify, you will receive up to $6,195 per year, based on need.

**The Federal Supplemental Educational Opportunity Grant or SEOG:** This is a federal grant that is administered by the colleges themselves. Each year, the schools get a lump sum that they are allowed to dispense to students at their own discretion. The size of the award runs from $100 to $4,000 per year per student.

**Grants from the Schools Themselves:** The colleges themselves often award grants as well. Since this money comes out of their own pocketbook, these grants are in effect discounts off the sticker price. And because this is not taxpayer money, there are no rules about how it must be dispensed. Some schools say they award money solely based on need. Many schools also give out merit-based awards. There is no limit on the size of a grant from an individual school. It could range from a few dollars to a full scholarship. Obviously, richer schools have more money to award to their students than poorer schools.

**State Grants:** If a student is attending college in his state of legal residence, or in a state that has a reciprocal agreement with his state of legal residence, then he may qualify for a state grant as well. These grants are administered by the states themselves. The grants are based on need, as well as on the size of tuition at a particular school. Thus the same student might find that his state grant at the local state university would be smaller than his state grant at a private college. These grants vary from state to state but can go as high as $6,000 per year or more.

**Scholarships from the School:** Some schools use the words *grants* and *scholarships* more or less interchangeably, and award scholarships just like grants—in other words, based on need. Other schools give scholarships in their more traditional sense, based on merit, either academic, athletic, or artistic. Some schools give scholarships based on a combination of need and merit.

The only real difference as far as you are concerned is whether the scholarship is used to meet need or whether it may be used to reduce your family contribution. If the school wants you badly enough, you may receive a merit-based scholarship over and above the amount of your need.

**The Teacher Education Assistance for College and Higher Education (TEACH) Grant Program:** This federal grant program provides grants of up to $4,000 per year to students who intend to teach full-time in a high need field in a private elementary or secondary school that serves students from low-income families. To qualify, you must attend a school that has chosen to participate in the program and meet certain academic achievement requirements along with other requirements. It is important to note that failing to complete all of the service requirements (e.g., teaching four years within eight years of completing the program of study for which you received the grant at designated schools) will result in the amount of all TEACH grant funds received being converted to a Federal Direct Unsubsidized Stafford Loan.

**Outside Scholarships:** If you have sought out and won a scholarship from a source not affiliated with the college—a foundation, say, or a community organization—you are required to tell the colleges about this money. Often the scholarship donor will notify the colleges you applied to directly. In most cases, the schools will thank you politely and then use the outside scholarship to reduce the amount of grant money they were going to give you. In other words, winning a scholarship does not mean you will pay less money for college; your family contribution often stays exactly the same.

By notifying the colleges about an outside scholarship before getting your award letter, you ensure that the outside scholarship will be included as part of your package. This is not very satisfactory because you have effectively given away an important bargaining chip.

If you have managed to find and win one of these scholarships, you may feel that you deserve something more than thanks from the school for your initiative. By telling the FAO about an outside scholarship for the first time when you are negotiating an improved package, you may be able to use the scholarship as a bargaining chip. Some schools have specific policies on this; others are prepared to be flexible. In some cases, we have seen FAOs let the parents use *part* of that money to reduce the family contribution. In other cases, FAOs have agreed to use the scholarship to replace loan or work-study components of the package instead of grants from the school.

**Federal Work-Study:** Under this program, students are given part-time jobs (usually on campus) to help meet the family's remaining need. Many parents' first inclination is to tell the student to reject the work-study portion of the aid package. They are concerned that the student won't have time to do well in class. As we've said earlier, several studies suggest that students who work during college have as high or higher grade point averages as students who don't work.

We counsel that you at least wait to see what sort of work is being offered. The award letter will probably not specify what kind of work the student will have to do for this money. You will get another letter later in the year giving you details. In many cases these jobs consist of sitting behind a desk at the library doing homework. Since students can normally back out of work-study jobs at any time, why not wait to see how onerous the job really is? (A minuscule number of colleges do have penalties for students who fail to meet their work-study obligations, so be sure to read the work-study agreement carefully.)

While work-study wages are usually minimum wage or slightly higher, they carry the important added benefit of being exempt from the aid formulas; work-study wages do not count as part of the student's income. Other earnings, by contrast, may be assessed at a rate of up to *50 cents on the dollar*. In addition, each dollar your child earns is a dollar you won't have to borrow.

Some colleges give you the choice of having the earnings paid in cash or credited toward the next semester's bill. If your child is a spendthrift, you might consider the second option.

**Loans:** There are many different kinds of college loans, but they fall into two main categories: need-based loans, which are designed to help meet part of a family's remaining need; and non-need-based loans, which are designed to help pay part of the family contribution when the family doesn't have the cash on hand. The loans that will be offered as part of your aid package in the award letter are primarily need-based loans.

The best need-based loan, the federally-subsidized Direct Loan, is such a good deal that we feel families should always accept it if it's offered. No interest is charged while the student is in school, and repayment does not begin on Direct Loans until the student graduates, leaves college, or dips below half-time status. Even if you have the money in the bank, we would still counsel your taking the loans. Let your money earn interest in the bank. When the loans come due, you can pay them off immediately, in full if you like, without penalty. Most college loans have some kind of an origination fee and perhaps an insurance fee as well. These fees are deducted from the value of the loan itself; you will never have to pay them out of your pocket.

Here are the different types of loans in order of attractiveness.

**Federal Direct Loans:** Formerly known as Stafford Loans, there are two kinds of Direct loans. The better kind is the *subsidized* Direct loan. To get this, a student must be judged to have need by the college. The federal government then subsidizes the loan by not charging any interest until after the student graduates, leaves college, or goes below half-time attendance status.

The second kind of Direct loan is known as unsubsidized and is not based on need. From the moment a student takes out an unsubsidized Direct loan, he or she will be charged interest. Students are given the option of paying the interest while in school, or deferring the interest payments (which will continue to accrue) until repayment of principle begins. Virtually all students who fill out a FAFSA are eligible for these unsubsidized Direct loans.

In both cases, the federal government guarantees the loan, and if applicable, makes up any difference between the student's low interest rate and the prevailing market rate once repayment has begun. A dependent student may be eligible to borrow up to $5,500 for the freshman year, up to $6,500 for the sophomore year, and up to $7,500 per year for the remaining undergraduate years. However for all of these annual limits, at least $2,000 must be unsubsidized in any year.

An independent undergraduate can borrow up to $9,500 for the freshman year (of which at least $6,000 must be unsubsidized), up to $10,500 for the sophomore year (of which at least $6,000 must be unsubsidized), and up to $12,500 per year for the remaining undergraduate years (of which at least $7,000 per year must be unsubsidized).

Beginning with the 2012–2013 academic year, all Direct Loans for graduate/professional school students became unsubsidized with a maximum annual borrowing limit of $20,500 (which is even higher for certain health profession students.) Any student contemplating graduate school/ professional school in future years should be sure to refer to Chapter Eight ("Managing Your Debt").

What happens if an undergraduate student is awarded a subsidized Direct loan, but the amount is less than the maximum subsidized amount? In this case, the student can borrow up to the amount of her need as a subsidized Stafford loan and, if she wants, she can also take out an unsubsidized Direct loan for the remainder of the total annual borrowing limit.

Based on a recent deal in Congress, the interest rate for new Stafford Loans originated on or after July 1, 2013 would now be pegged to the 10-year Treasury Note rate with the rate fixed for the life of the loan. Compared to recent years, there will now be different rates for undergraduate student and graduate/profession school students. However, unlike the past few years, the fixed rate will be the same whether the loan is subsidized (available only to under-grads) or unsubsidized. This will mean the rate for these new Direct loans will be fixed at 4.53% for undergraduates and 6.08% for graduate/professional school students originated during the 2019–2020 academic year.

The rates for new Direct loans originated during subsequent academic years will be based on the last 10-year Treasury Note auction in May prior to the start of that subsequent academic year. However, there are interest rate caps for Direct Loans (that would only apply to newly-originated loans taken out in subsequent academic years) should the 10-year Treasury Note rate rise significantly.  For undergraduates the cap will be 8.25%—with a 9.5% cap on Direct Loans for graduate/professional school students.

Because the government guarantees the loans, parents are never required to cosign a Direct Loan (or Perkins) loan.

Starting in the 1994–95 academic year, under a law proposed by President Clinton, some of the Stafford loans were funded directly by the government and administered by the schools—thus eliminating the role of private lenders such as banks. This program, referred to as the William D. Ford Federal Direct Loan Program, co-existed with the Federal Family Education Loan Program (FFELP) for a number of years. The schools would decide which program they would have Stafford borrowers use to get their loan proceeds and the majority of such loans (in terms of loan volume) were originated with FFELP private lenders as the middleman. However as part of the Health Care and Education Reconciliation Act of 2010, all new Stafford loans disbursed after June 30, 2010 would be via the Direct Loan program. That is why the name changed from a Stafford Loan to a Direct Loan, though the name Stafford Loan is still some-times used.

Once you have decided on a college and accepted the aid package, the FAO will tell you how to go about obtaining the loan funds. You will have to fill out a promissory note, and because the process can take as long as six weeks, it may be necessary to apply for the loan by mid-June for the fall term.

**The College's Own Loans:** These loans vary widely in attractiveness. Some are absolutely wonderful: Princeton University offers special loans for parents at very low rates. Some are on the edge of sleazy: Numerous colleges have loan programs that require almost immediate repayment with interest rates that rival VISA and MasterCard. While these types of loans do not normally appear as part of an aid package, a few colleges try to pass them off as need-based aid to unsuspecting students and their parents. Remember that you are allowed to reject any portion of the aid package. It is a good idea to examine the terms of loans from the individual colleges extremely carefully before you accept them.

# Financial Sleight of Hand

As we've already said, there are two general types of college loans: a need-based loan (such as the subsidized Direct Loans we've just been discussing), is meant to meet a family's "remaining need"; the other kind of loan is meant to help when families don't have the cash to pay the family contribution itself.

By its very nature this second type of loan should not appear as part of your aid package. As far as the colleges are concerned, your family contribution is your business, and they don't have to help you to pay it. However, a number of schools do rather unfairly include several types of non-need-based loan in their aid package, including the unsubsidized Direct loan we just discussed, and the PLUS (Parent Loans for Undergraduate Students) which is intended to help those parents who are having trouble paying their family contribution. Administered by the government, the PLUS loan is made to parents of college children. Virtually any parent can get a PLUS loan of up to the total cost of attendance minus any financial aid received—provided the federal government thinks the parent is a good credit risk.

Thus when a college tries to meet your need with a PLUS loan, the college is engaging in financial aid sleight of hand, ostensibly meeting your need with a loan that was not designed for that purpose and which you could have gotten anyway, as long as your credit held up. If you are offered a PLUS loan as part of your need-based aid, you should realize that the college has really *not* met your need in full. An aid package that includes a PLUS loan is not as valuable as a package that truly meets a family's remaining need.

With the PLUS loans, repayment normally begins within 60 days of the date the loan was made. However, legislation now permits a PLUS loan borrower to delay repayment on a PLUS loan taken out for a student until that student graduates, leaves school, or drops below half-time status. You will need to notify the lender if you wish to defer repayment in such cases.

# Non-Need-Based Loans

While the other types of college loans won't be part of your aid package, this seems like a good place to describe a few of them, and they are certainly relevant to this discussion, for as you look at the various offers from the colleges you will probably be wondering how you are going to pay your family contribution over the next four years. Most families end up borrowing. There are so many different loans offered by banks and organizations that it would be impossible to describe them all. College bulletins usually include information about the types of loans available at the specific schools, and applications can usually be picked up at the colleges' financial aid offices or be filed online. Here's a sampling of some of the more mainstream alternatives (we'll talk about a few of the more offbeat loans in the next chapter):

**PLUS Loans:** We've already discussed some details of PLUS loans above. As credit-based loans go, the PLUS is probably the best. Parents can borrow up to the annual total cost of attendance at the college minus any financial aid received. With all PLUS loans now disbursed via the Direct Loan Program, you will apply for the PLUS loan through the financial aid office.

The recent student loan deal has also changed the way the fixed rate on any new PLUS loans will be calculated, with the new rate also based on the 10-year Treasury Note rate instead of a legislated rate.  For PLUS loans originated during the  2019–2020 academic year, the interest rate will be 7.08%—which is less than the 7.9% rate that had been charged on fixed rate Direct PLUS loans originated prior to July 1, 2013. For loans originated for the 2013–2014 academic year and beyond, there is a cap of 10.5% (that would only apply to newly-originated PLUS loans taken out in subsequent academic years should the 10-year Treasury Note rate rise significantly).

When we suggest the PLUS loans to some of our clients, their immediate response is, "There's no way we'll qualify; we don't have a good credit rating!" Before you automatically assume you won't qualify, you should realize that the credit test for the PLUS is not as stringent as it is for most other loans. You don't have to have excellent credit to qualify. You just can't have an "adverse credit history" (i.e. outstanding judgments, liens, extremely slow payments). Even if you fail the credit test, you may still be able to secure a PLUS loan provided you are able to demonstrate extenuating circumstances (determined on a case-by-case basis by the lender) or you are able to find someone (a friend or relative) who can pass the credit test, who agrees to endorse (i.e. cosign) the loan, and who promises to pay it back if you are unable to do so.

In 2014, the Department of Education relaxed the credit requirements necessary to receive the loan.

If you are rejected for the PLUS loan and are unable to get a creditworthy endorser, there is still another option available to you. In this case, dependent students can borrow extra Direct Loan funds over the normal borrowing limits. First- and second-year students can get an additional $4,000 per year, while those in the third year and beyond can get an additional $5,000 per year. In all cases, these additional Direct Loan funds must be unsubsidized. Obviously, this approach is going to put the student deeper in debt. However, if you need to borrow a few thousand dollars to cover the family contribution and are unable to get credit in your name, this strategy may be your only option.

**State Loans:** Some states offer alternative loan programs as well. The terms vary from state to state; some are available only to students, others only to parents; many are below market rate. Unlike state grants, state loans are often available to nonresidents attending approved colleges in that state.

**Lines of Credit:** Some banks offer revolving credit loans that do not start accruing interest until you write a check on the line of credit.

**CitiAssist Loans [www.studentloan.com or (800) 788-3368]:** Sponsored by Citibank, these loans to students do not have any origination fees. To make up for this, the interest rate is usually prime plus 0.50% (however this may be lower or higher at some schools). There is no minimum loan amount required. This is one of the few loan programs available to foreign students who can borrow funds by having a credit-worthy cosigner (who must be a U.S. citizen or permanent resident). Cosigners will also be required for almost all undergraduates as well as those students who do not have a positive credit history. Under certain circumstances, the cosigner can be released from the loan after 48 on-time payments are made.

**Sallie Mae Smart Option Student Loans [www.salliemae.com or (800) 695-3317]:** These cosigned private student loans require payment of interest while the student is in school and during the 6-month separation period before repayment. Cosigners may not be required after freshman year. The interest rate is pegged to the prime rate and will vary depending on the credit rating of the student (and, if applicable, the cosigner) as well as the school attended. This program offers a 0.25% interest rate reduction for students who elect to have their payments made automatically through their bank and a 0.25% interest rate reduction for students who receive all servicing communications via a valid e-mail address.

**Collegiate Loans [www.wellsfargo.com or (800) 378-5526]:** Wells Fargo Bank operates this non-need-based program for college which offers variable interest loans currently based on the prime rate and your credit history. The student is the borrower, but a parent and/or another individual usually must cosign. One can normally borrow up to the cost of education minus any financial aid.

This is only a partial listing of the different loans available. When choosing which type of loan to take out, you should consider all of the following questions:

- What is the interest rate and how is it determined?

- Is the interest rate fixed or variable, and if variable, is there a cap?

- What are the repayment options? How many years will it take to pay off the loan? Can you make interest-only payments while the child is in school? Can you repay the loan early?

- Who is the borrower—the parent or the student?

- Are there origination fees?

- Is a cosigner permitted or required?

- Will having a cosigner affect the interest rate and/or origination fees?

- Is the loan secured or unsecured? The rates on a loan secured by the home or by securities are generally lower, but you are putting your assets on the line.

- Is the interest on the loan tax-deductible?

On balance, the PLUS loan is probably the best of all these options. Unless you are able to secure more favorable terms from a state financing authority's alternative education loan program, then the only reasons to consider the other types of non-need-based loans, besides the PLUS loan, are if you prefer having the loans in the student's name or if the student is an independent student.

## Should You Turn Down Individual Parts of an Aid Package?

Some parents worry that by turning down part of the financial aid package they are endangering future aid. Clearly, by refusing a work-study job or a need-based loan, you are telling the FAOs that you can find the money elsewhere, and this *could* have an impact on the package you are offered next year. In our experience we can't remember many times when we thought it was a good idea for a family to turn down grants, scholarships, need-based loans, or work-study.

## Certainly Not Before You Compare All the Packages

Before you turn down any part of a single financial aid package, you should compare the packages as a group to determine your options.

## The Size of the Package Is Not Important

Families often get swept up by the total value of the aid packages. We've heard parents say, "This school gave us $12,000 in aid, which is much better than the school that gave us only $7,000." The real measure of an aid package is how much YOU will have to end up paying, and how much debt the student will have to take on.

Let's look at three examples:

## School A:

total cost—$30,000
family contribution—$11,000
grants and scholarships—$14,000
need-based loans—$3,000
work-study—$1,000
unmet need (what the parents will have to pay in addition to the family
    contribution)—$1,000
value of the aid package—$18,000
**money the family will have to spend—$12,000**
**need-based debt—$3,000**

## School B:

total cost—$29,000
family contribution—$11,000
grants and scholarships—$17,000
need-based loans—$500
work-study—$500
unmet need—$0
value of the aid package—$18,000
**money the family will have to spend—$11,000**
**need-based debt—$500**

## School C:

total cost—$25,000
family contribution—$10,500
grants and scholarships—$10,750
need-based loans—$3,250
work-study—$500
unmet need—$0
value of the aid package—$14,500
**money the family will have to spend—$10,500**
**need-based debt—$3,250**

School A and school B gave identical total dollar amounts in aid, but the two packages were very different. School B gave $17,000 in grants (which do not have to be repaid), while A gave only $14,000. School B would actually cost this family $11,000 with only $500 in student loans. School A would cost the family $12,000 with $3,000 in student loans. Leaving aside for the moment subjective matters such as the academic caliber of the two schools, school B was a better buy.

School C would cost this family $10,500 in cash. On the other hand, this school also asked the student to take on the largest amount of debt: $3,250.

You've probably noticed that the sticker prices of the three colleges were almost totally irrelevant to our discussion. After you've looked at the bottom line for each of the colleges that have accepted the student, you should also factor in the academic quality of the schools; perhaps it is worth a slightly higher price to send your child to a more prestigious school. You should also look at factors like location, reputation of the department your child is interested in, and the student's own idea of which school would make her happiest. In the end, you'll have to choose what price you're willing to pay for what level of quality.

## Is the Package Renewable?

An excellent question, but unfortunately this is a very difficult question to get a straight answer about. Of course there are some conditions attached to continuing to receive a good financial aid package. Students must maintain a minimum grade point average, and generally behave themselves.

It also makes sense to avoid colleges that are on the brink of bankruptcy, since poor schools may not be able to continue subsidizing students at the same level.

## Bait and Switch?

Most reputable colleges don't indulge in bait-and-switch tactics, whereby students are lured to the school with a sensational financial aid package that promptly disappears the next year.

We have found that when parents feel they have been victims of bait and switch, there has often been a misunderstanding of some kind. This might occur when parents have two children in school at the same time. If one of the children graduates, the parents are often surprised when the EFC for the child who remains in college goes up dramatically. This is not bait and switch. The family now has more available income and assets to pay for the child who is now in college alone.

Sometimes, schools minimize work-study hours during the first year so that students have a chance to get accustomed to college life. Parents are often shocked when the number of work-study hours is increased the next year, but again this is not bait and switch. It is reasonable to expect students to work more hours in their junior and senior years.

## Negotiating with the FAOs

Once you've compared financial aid packages and the relative merits of the schools that have said yes, you may want to go back to one or more of the colleges to try to improve your package.

We are not saying that every family should try to better their deal. If you can comfortably afford the amount the college says you must pay, then there is little chance that the college is going to sweeten the deal—it must be pretty good already. College FAOs know just how fair the package they have put together for you is. If you are being greedy, you will not get much sympathy. It is also a good idea to remember that the average FAO is not making a great deal of money. Parents who whine about how tough it is to survive on $200,000 a year will get even less sympathy.

However, if you are facing the real prospect of not being able to send your child to the school she really wants to attend because of money, or if two similarly ranked colleges have offered radically different packages and your son really wants to go to the school with the low package, then you should sit down and map out your strategy.

## Negotiate While You Still Have Leverage

After you've accepted the college's offer of admission, the college won't have much incentive to sweeten your deal, so you should plan to speak to the FAO while it is clear that you could still choose to go to another school. Similarly, you will not have much leverage if you show the FAO a rival offer from a much inferior college.

Try to make an objective assessment of how badly the college wants you. Believe us, the FAOs know exactly where each student fits into their scheme of things. We know of one college that keeps an actual list of prospective students in order of their desirability, which they refer to when parents call to negotiate. If a student just barely squeaked into the school, the family will not be likely to improve the package by negotiating. If a student is a shining star in one area or another, the FAOs will be much more willing to talk.

In the past few years, colleges—especially the selective ones—have become more flexible about their initial offer. Now that FAOs from the different colleges are limited in their ability to sit down together to compare offers to students, the "fudge factor" by which they are willing to improve an offer has increased. We heard one FAO urge a group of students to get in touch with her if they were considering another school. "Perhaps we overlooked something in your circumstances," she said. What she meant of course was, "Perhaps we want you so much we will be willing to increase our offer." This FAO represented one of the most selective schools in the country.

## Prepare Your Ammunition

Before you call, you should have gathered all the supporting ammunition you can in front of you. If you've received a better offer from a comparable school, have it in front of you when you call and be prepared to send a copy of the rival award letter to the school you are negotiating with. (They will probably ask to see it, which brings up another point: don't lie!)

If you feel that the school has not understood your financial circumstances, be ready to explain clearly what those special circumstances are (such as high margin debts or any other expenses that are not taken into account by the aid formula, support of an elderly relative, or unusually high unreimbursed business expenses). Any documentation you can supply will bolster your claim.

If your circumstances have changed since you filled out your need analysis form (for example, you have recently separated, divorced, been widowed, or lost your job), you should be frank and let the FAOs know. They will almost certainly make changes in your aid package.

## The Call

Unless you live within driving distance of the school, your best negotiating tool is the telephone. The FAOs will find it hard to believe that you need more money if you can afford to fly to their college just to complain to them.

If possible, try to speak with the head FAO or one of the head FAO's assistants. Make sure you write down the name of whoever speaks to you. It is unlikely that he will make a concession on the telephone, so don't be disappointed if he says he will have to get back to you or if he asks you to send him something in writing.

Some telephone tips:

- Be cordial and frank. Like everyone, FAOs do not want to be yelled at and are much more likely to help you if you are friendly, businesslike, and organized.

- Have a number in your head. What would you like to get out of this conversation? If the FAO asks you, "All right, how much can you afford?" you do not want to hem and haw.

- Be reasonable. If the family contribution you propose has no relation to your EFC, you will lose most of your credibility with the FAO.

- Avoid confrontational language. Rather than start off with, "Match my other offer or else," just ask if there is anything they can do to improve the package. Also avoid using words such as "negotiate" or "bargain". You're better off saying you wish to "appeal" the award and then present your facts. Any new information not previously presented could bolster your case, especially if you can provide supporting documentation.

- If you are near a deadline, ask for an extension and be doubly sure you know the name of the person you are speaking to. Follow up the phone call with a letter (certified mail, return receipt requested) reminding the FAO of what was discussed in the conversation.

- Parents, not students, should negotiate with the FAOs. Some colleges actually have a question on their own financial aid forms in which the parents are asked if they will allow the colleges to speak to the student rather than the parents. Colleges prefer to speak to students because they are easier to browbeat.

- Read through this book again before you speak to the FAO. You'll never know as much about financial aid as she does, but at least you'll stand a good chance of knowing if she says something that isn't true.

- If you applied "early decision" to a college and that college accepts you, you are committed to attend, and you won't have much bargaining power to improve your aid package. If you applied and are accepted "early action," you are not required to attend that school, and it is in your interest to apply to several other schools in order to improve your bargaining position. We discuss both of these options in more detail in the "Special Topics" chapter.

## The Worst They Can Say Is No

You risk nothing by trying to negotiate a better package. No matter how objectionable you are, the school cannot take back their offer of admission, and the FAOs cannot take back their aid package unless you have lied about your financial details.

## Accepting an Award

Accepting an award does not commit a student to attending that school. It merely locks in the award package in the event the student decides to attend that school. If you haven't decided between two schools, accept both packages. This will keep your options open for a little longer. Be careful not to miss the deadline to respond. Send your acceptance certified mail, return receipt requested, as always. Above all, don't reject any award until you have definitely decided which school the student is going to attend. If a school's aid package has not arrived yet, call the college to find out why it's late.

If you have been awarded state aid as part of the aid package at the school of your choice, but the award notice you received from the state agency lists the wrong college, you will have to file a form with the state agency to have the funds applied to the school you chose.

## Now That You Have Chosen a School

By the time you have chosen a college, you will already be halfway through the second base income year. Now that you understand the ins and outs of financial aid, you will be able to plan ahead to minimize the apparent size of your income and assets, and be in an even better position to fill out next year's need analysis forms. The first application for financial aid is the hardest, in part because you're dealing with a number of different schools, in part because it is a new experience. From now on, that first application will serve as a kind of template.

# Chapter Seven

## Innovative Payment Options

# Innovative Options

We've already discussed the mainstream borrowing options and methods for paying for college. Over the years, colleges, private companies, public organizations, and smart individuals have come up with some alternative ways to pay for college. These ideas range from the commonsense to the high-tech, from good deals for the family to self-serving moneymakers for the colleges and institutions that came up with them. Here is a sampling.

## Transfer in Later

Every year a few parents make an unfortunate decision: they send the student off to a college that didn't give them enough aid. After two years of tuition bills, they've spent their life savings, and the banks won't lend them any more money. The student is forced to transfer to a public university. The result? A diploma from the student's own State U. that could end up costing the family more than $175,000. The parents paid private school prices for a state school diploma.

What if they had done it the other way around? The student starts out at a state school, paying low prices. She does extremely well, compiling an outstanding academic record and soliciting recommendations from her professors. In junior year she transfers to a prestigious private college. Even if the cost were exactly the same as in the previous example, she now has a diploma from the prestigious private school, at a savings of as much as $75,000 over the regular price.

This scenario won't work without the part about the "outstanding academic record." Prestigious private colleges will almost certainly not be interested in a transfer student with a B average or less. The other thing to bear in mind is that aid packages to transfer students are generally not as generous as those given to incoming freshmen.

Both of these points must be factored into a decision to start with a public college and transfer into a select private college. However, if a student really wants a diploma from that selective private college, and the family can't afford to send her for all four years, then this is a way for her to realize her dream. Anyone interested in this tactic should be sure to consult the individual schools to see how many transfer students are accepted per year, what kind of financial aid is available to them, and how many of the credits earned at the old college will be accepted by the new college.

## Cooperative Education

Over 900 colleges let students combine a college education with a job in their field. Generally, the students spend alternate terms attending classes full-time and then working full-time at off-campus jobs with private companies or the federal government, although some students work and study at the same time. The students earn money for tuition while getting practical on-the-job experience in their areas of interest. This program differs from the Federal Work-Study Program in which the subsidized campus-based jobs are probably not within the student's area of interest, and take up only a small number of hours per week. After graduating, a high percentage of cooperative education students get hired permanently by the employers they worked for during school. Companies from every conceivable field participate in this program. The federal government is the largest employer of cooperative education students.

Getting a degree through the cooperative education program generally takes about five years, but the students who emerge from this program have a huge head start over their classmates; they already have valuable experience and a prospective employer in their field. They owe less money in student loans, and they are often paid more than a new hiree.

If you are eligible for financial aid, you should contact the financial aid office at any college you are considering to determine the effect of cooperative earnings on your financial aid package.

## Short-Term Prepayment

Recently, some colleges have been touting tuition prepayment as the answer to all the ills of higher education. In the short-term version of tuition prepayment, the parent pays the college the entire four years' worth of tuition (room and board are generally excluded) sometime shortly before the student begins freshman year. The college "locks in" the tuition rate for the entire four years. Regardless of how much tuition rises during the four years, the parent will not owe any more toward tuition.

Since most parents don't have four years of tuition in one lump sum, the colleges lend it to them. The parents pay back the loan with interest over a time period set in advance. The colleges love this arrangement, because it allows them to make a nice profit. If you pay the entire amount without borrowing, the colleges invest your money in taxable investments, which (because of their tax-exempt status) they don't have to pay taxes on. If you borrow the money from the college, they charge you interest on the money you borrow. Whatever course you pursue, the revenue the colleges earn from these prepayment plans more than make up for any tuition increases.

## Is Prepayment a Good Idea for the Parent?

While the colleges may tell you that you will save money by avoiding tuition increases each year, your savings, if any, really depend on what interest rates are doing. If you would have to borrow the money to make the prepayment, the question to ask yourself is whether your after-tax cost of borrowing will be less than the tuition increases over the four years. If so, prepayment may make sense.

If you can afford to write a check for the entire amount of the prepayment, the question to ask yourself is whether the after-tax rate of return on your investments is higher than the rate at which tuition is increasing. If so, then prepayment makes no sense.

Any prepayment plan should be examined carefully. What happens if the student drops out after one year? What happens if the program is canceled after only two years? What is the interest rate on the loan you take out? Is the loan rate fixed or variable, and, if variable, what is the cap? These are a few of the questions you should ask before you agree to prepayment.

However, unless the interest rates are extremely low—*and will remain low over the four years your child is in college*—prepayment may end up costing you more money than paying as you go.

## ROTC and the Service Academies

The Reserve Officer Training Corps has branches at many colleges. To qualify for ROTC scholarships you generally need to apply to the program early in the senior year of high school. Competition for these awards is keen, but if a student is selected he or she will receive a full or partial scholarship plus a $100-per-month allowance. The catch, of course, is that the student has to join the military for four years of active duty plus two more years on reserve. While on active duty, many students are allowed to go to graduate school on full scholarship. A student can join a ROTC program once he's entered college, but will not necessarily get a scholarship.

To qualify for the four-year scholarships, students (male and female) must have good grades, an SAT score of 1100 (out of 1600) or an ACT score of 24, they must pass a physical, and they must also impress an interviewer.

The service academies (the U.S. Military Academy at West Point and the U.S. Naval Academy at Annapolis are probably the best known) are extremely difficult to get into. Good grades are essential, as is a recommendation from a senator or a member of Congress. However, all this trouble may be worth it, for the service academies have a great reputation for the quality of their programs and they are absolutely free. Again, in exchange for this education, a student must agree to serve as an officer in the armed forces for several years.

## Outside Scholarships

Opinions are divided about outside scholarships. The companies that sell scholarship databases say there are thousands of unclaimed scholarships sponsored by foundations, corporations, and other outside organizations just waiting to be found. Critics charge that very few scholarships actually go unclaimed each year, and that the database search companies are providing lists that families could get from government agencies, the local library, or the internet for free.

Certainly it must be said that many scholarships in the search services' databases are administered by the colleges themselves. There is almost never a need to "find" this type of scholarship. The colleges know they have this money available, and will match up the awards with candidates who meet the requirements attached to the awards. It is in the colleges' interest to award these "restricted" scholarships since this frees up unrestricted funds for other students. Every year, colleges award virtually *all* the scholarship money they have at their disposal.

It must also be pointed out that when you notify a college that you have won an outside scholarship (and if you are on financial aid you are required to tell the school how much you won), the college will often say thank you very much and deduct that amount from the aid package they have put together for you. As far as the colleges are concerned, your "need" just got smaller. Thus if you hunt down an obscure scholarship for red-haired flutists, it will often not really do you any monetary good. Your family contribution (what the colleges think you can afford to pay) will stay exactly the same. The FAOs will use the outside scholarship money to reduce your aid (often your grants).

This is not to say that there aren't circumstances when outside scholarships can help pay for college, but you must be prepared to fight. If you have found outside scholarships worth any significant amount, you should talk to the FAO in person or on the phone and point out that without your initiative, the college would have had to pay far more. Negotiate with the FAO. He may be willing to let you use part of the scholarship toward your family contribution, or at least he may improve your aid package's percentage of grants versus loans.

We've talked to people who've had terrible experiences with the scholarship search companies and we've talked to other people who swear by them. Just keep in mind that this type of aid accounts for less than 5% of the financial aid in the United States. Of course, 5% of the financial aid available in the United States is still a lot of money.

We do recommend, however, that you steer clear of any scholarship search firm that promises you'll get a scholarship or your fee will be refunded. These guarantees are not worth the paper they're printed on. When you read the fine print, you'll discover that you need to send them rejection letters from each and every scholarship source they recommended to you. Many of these donors don't have the time or the resources to tell you the bad news, so you'll never get the proof you need to claim your refund. The Federal Trade Commission has closed down a number of these firms after receiving numerous complaints from students and parents who didn't get their money back.

## Innovative Loans

The very best type of loans, as we've said before, are the government-subsidized student loans. We've also already discussed home equity loans and margin loans (both of which reduce the appearance of your assets) as well as some of the more popular parent loan programs.

There is one other type of loan that can help you write the checks:

# Borrow from Your 401(k) Plan or a Pension Plan

If you are totally without resources, the IRS may allow you to make an early withdrawal of money without penalty from a 401(k) plan to pay for education. However, rather than get to this desperate situation (which will increase your income taxes and raise your income for financial aid purposes), it would make a lot more sense for you to take out a loan from your 401(k) plan or from your pension plan.

Not all plans will allow this, but some will let you borrow *tax-free* as much as half of the money in your account, up to $50,000. There are no penalties, and this way you are not irrevocably depleting your retirement fund. You're merely borrowing from yourself; in many cases, the interest you pay on the loan actually goes back into your own account. Generally, the loan must be repaid within five years. However, if you lose your job or change your employer, this loan will become due immediately, so you should exercise some caution before you proceed.

This kind of borrowing will not decrease your assets as far as the FAOs are concerned because assets in retirement provisions are not assessed anyway. However, if you've come to this point, your non-retirement assets are probably already fairly depleted.

A self-employed individual can borrow from a Keogh plan, but there will almost certainly be penalties, and the loan will be treated as a taxable distribution. Loans against IRAs are not currently permitted.

# Loans Forgiven

A few colleges have programs under which some of your student loans may be forgiven if you meet certain conditions. At Cornell University, for example, Tradition Fellows, who hold jobs while they are in college, are given awards that replace their student loans by up to $4,000 per year in acknowledgment of their work ethic. Even federal loans can be forgiven under certain circumstances. Head Start, Peace Corps, or VISTA volunteers may not have to repay all of their federal loans, for example.

## Moral Obligation Loans

Here's a novel idea: the college makes a loan to the student, and the student agrees to pay back the loan. That's it. There is no *legal* obligation to pay back the money. The student has a moral obligation to repay. Several schools have decided to try this, and the results, of course, won't be in for some time. At the moment, when a student repays the loan, the repayment is considered a tax-deductible charitable contribution. The IRS will probably have closed that loophole by the time your child is ready to take advantage of it. Nevertheless, this is a wonderful deal because it allows the student flexibility in deciding when to pay the loan back, and does not affect the child's credit rating. If your college is offering this option, grab it.

## Payment Plans and Financing Options

Many families have difficulty coming up with their Family Contribution in one lump sum each semester. There are a number of commercial organizations that will assist you with spreading the payment out over time. Some of these programs are financing plans that charge interest and involve repayment over a number of years. Others are simply payment plans in which you make 10 or 12 monthly payments during the year. These plans may require you to begin making payments in May or June prior to the start of the fall semester. A nominal fee (about $50) is usually charged for these plans. The two largest organizations that offer such budgeting plans are: Sallie Mae's Higher One TuitionPay [(800) 635-0120]; and Tuition Management Systems (TMS) [(800) 722-4867]. Many schools have developed their own deferred payment plans as well. These programs can vary tremendously from college to college.

The college financial aid office or bursar's office should be able to provide you with information regarding all your payment options, as well as the names of those commercial plans (if any) that can be used at their school. Be sure to read the fine print before you sign up for any of these programs.

## Tuition Refund Insurance

Writing that check for the first tuition bill is a sobering experience for most families. Given the large outlay of funds involved, it may make sense to take out a tuition refund insurance policy to protect yourself if the student is forced to withdraw in the middle of a term. Most colleges do give partial refunds when a student has to withdraw. How much money you get back from the college itself depends on how far into the term the student is when he/she withdraws, as well as the policies of the individual school. (There are no federal regulations governing how much money must be refunded, if any)

Tuition refund insurance—also known as tuition insurance—is designed to make up the difference. For an insurance premium of normally $150 to $400 per academic year, you can have peace of mind that any non-refunded payments for tuition and possibly room & board are not a total loss.

Bear in mind that if the student withdraws midway through the term—regardless of the reason—the school will probably not permit the student to finish the coursework after the semester is over. More than likely, the only option will be to re-enroll for the course in a future term.

For medically- related withdrawals you can often get up to 100% of what the college doesn't refund if you have taken out a tuition refund insurance policy. For mental health issues, you can often get up to 60 or 70%. Some policies also offer coverage if the student is forced to withdraw for other reasons—such as a death in the family or an employment-related relocation of the parents). Keep in mind that as the academic term progresses, you will get back less money from the school. So if there are issues that make the student's ability to complete the term unlikely, it makes sense to make a decision sooner rather than later—and to notify the school through the proper channels and withdraw relatively quickly.

Of course, if the student is at a lower-priced state school or is getting a lot of financial aid, tuition refund insurance makes less sense. But at the very least, you should carefully review the college's refund policy.  And if you are considering purchasing a policy, you should be sure to read all the fine print since some refund policies will not pay a benefit if the student withdraws due to a pre-existing medical condition that was present within a certain time period before the policy was purchased.

# National Service

One of the nontraditional methods of educational financing has been the AmeriCorps program (www.Americorps.gov). Since it was established in 1994 during the Clinton administration, more than a quarter million individuals have participated in this national service program designed to encourage young people to serve in educational, environmental, or police programs or in programs to assist the elderly or the homeless. In return for taking part in national service, a participant receives training, a living allowance at the minimum wage, health insurance, child care, and up to $5,550 per year in educational grants.

While we think this is a generally great idea, the program in its current form has a few problems from a financial aid standpoint. First, if a student joins this program after he or she has graduated, the student will not be able to use money from this program to pay college bills directly. Students would have to come up with the money in the first place. Only later could AmeriCorps grants be used to pay back loans that the student had taken out along the way. Second, with a maximum of only $5,550 per year in grant money, national service may not be the most economically efficient way for a student to pay back student loans. Unless national service appeals to you for altruistic reasons, you may be able to repay loans faster by taking a conventional job and putting yourself on a minimum wage allowance. Finally, for students who participate in the program prior to college and who demonstrate need when they apply for financial aid, the AmeriCorps grants may simply reduce those students' "need" in the aid formulas and not the family contribution. This is why many higher education organizations have criticized references to national service as a student aid program.

## Marketing Gimmicks Arrive on Campus

Some colleges have begun incentives that owe more to the world of retailing than to the world of the ivory tower. Among the offers you may find:

- discounts for bringing in a friend

- rebates for several family members attending at the same time

- discounts for older students

- reduced prices for the first semester so you can see if you like it

- option of charging your tuition on a credit card

# Chapter Eight

## Managing Your Debt

For many people, there is really no choice; if you or your child want a college education, you have to go into debt. But it turns out that there are a number of choices to make about how you go into debt and how you eventually pay it off. Most parents and students assume they have no control over the loan process. Unfortunately, this assumption may cost them thousands of dollars.

In previous chapters we've discussed the different kinds of loans that are available. Of course, the most common types of loans are Stafford and PLUS loans.

In this chapter, we'll provide more information on how to select the best loans, as well as how to pay off these loans once you are required to do so.

As usual, this advice comes with our standard caveat: We can't recommend any specific course of action since we don't know your specific situation. These strategies are only meant to steer you in the right direction. Please consult with your accountant or a financial aid planner.

# Before You Borrow

Smart financial planning dictates that you always borrow at the lowest possible cost. So the first type of loan to consider is usually the federal Perkins loan—a 5% fixed-interest rate loan made to the student; interest is subsidized while the student is in school, and during a 9-month grace period after the student leaves school, graduates or drops below half-time status. (We've already given some details on loans on pages 220–227.) The Perkins loan is available to graduate as well as undergraduate students.

For undergraduate students for the 2019–2020 academic year, an even better loan is the subsidized Direct Loan. For Direct Loans originated during the 2019–2020 school year, the rate will be fixed at 4.53% for the life of the loan. However, depending on the 10-year Treasury Note rate which will now determine the rate on any Direct Loans originated on or after July 1, 2014, the rate on the Direct Loan may be higher or lower than the 5% Perkins loan rate for new Direct Loans originated after the 2019–2020 school year.

Yet even if the Direct Loan rate exceeds the Perkins rate in subsequent years, it is still a great deal since the government pays the interest on a subsidized Direct Loans while a student is in school. And if you wish to pay off a subsidized Direct Loan before the student leaves school, graduate or drops below half-time enrollment, no interest will be charged at all.

Next in desirability is the unsubsidized Direct Loan. Unlike the Perkins and the Subsidized Direct Loan, the unsubsidized Direct Loan charges the student interest from day one. The decision whether or not to take out this type of loan depends on other factors. For example, let's say you have funds for school in a bank account that's earning 1% in a bank; in that case, it makes no sense to take out a loan in which you're paying more interest than you're earning by keeping those funds in a bank. Conversely, if you don't have the funds to pay for school, and other loans would carry a higher interest rate, then the unsubsidized Direct Loan makes sense.

And for paying the education expenses of a dependent undergraduate student, the last federal loan option available is the PLUS loan—in which one of the student's parents is the borrower. With interest charged from the time the loan funds are disbursed at a fixed rate that is higher than the fixed rate for an unsubsidized Direct Loans, this is the costliest of the federal education loan options.

There are two other types of loans available which can be broken down into two categories: the first offered by state educational financing authorities such as MEFA in Massachusetts or CHESLA in Connecticut. Depending on the eligibility criteria, some of these loans allow state residents to borrow funds for schools both in-state and out-of-state. Some also make such loans available if an out-of-state student is attending a participating school within the state that offers the loan. Most have a fixed-rate option that is sometimes lower than some federal loan options. The second category involves private alternative loans, generally offered by banks or other private lenders. While these mostly variable rate-loans can start out lower than the Federal options, if interest rates rise appreciably they can become a very costly. And unlike housing debt, in which you can convert a variable rate home equity line of credit into a fixed-rate loan before interest rates start to rise, these education loans normally cannot be refinanced with another fixed-rate education loan.

But what if you're an independent undergraduate student? The first three most attractive options offered above should be considered in the same hierarchy. Compared to most dependent under-graduate students, independent undergrads can borrow an additional $4000 for each of the first two years and an additional $5,000/year for the third year and beyond via the Direct Loan program should additional funds be needed. But that's it for federal education loans for independent undergrads, since there are officially no parents in the picture who can take out PLUS loans. Even if a parent of an independent undergraduate wants to take out a PLUS loan for their child, they cannot do so since PLUS loans are only for parents of dependent students.

What about graduate students? Beginning with the 2012–2013 academic year, graduate and professional school students are no longer be able to take out subsidized Direct Loans. They can still take out unsubsidized Direct Loan (up to $20,500 per year, and possibly even more for health profession students), but the up-to-$8,500 subsidized Stafford that existed in 2011–2012 and before is no longer available. However, all unsubsidized Direct Loans for graduate students will continue to have a fixed-interest rate—albeit at a higher rate than for undergrads. (6.08% for loans taken out in 2019–2020.)

# Graduate School Considerations

Those considering going on to graduate school, which for purposes of this chapter will include any professional school such as a law school, medical school, business school (MBA) etc., should consider borrowing the maximum amount of Perkins and subsidized Direct Loans for which they are eligible as an undergraduate. This is because unless you're fortunate enough to get a Perkins loan (and there's only a limited amount of this money available to graduate students) any money you borrow will have interest charged from the get-go. So you would be better off preserving funds in your nest egg while the student is an undergraduate, and using them instead in graduate school when the cost of borrowing is higher.

And what if you're stopping out for a few years between an undergraduate program and graduate school? With a subsidized Direct Loan no longer available to graduate students, one would be better off making minimum payments on their education loans, possibly by choosing a repayment option other than the standard one (which we'll cover shortly). Provided you have the discipline.

When you go back to school, the amount of any subsidized Stafford, Perkins, and Direct Loans that qualify for an in-school deferment will be frozen at the amount owed when you return to school until you graduate, leave school, or drop below half-time status

So you're better off stockpiling the cash for graduate school, rather than paying off these loans quickly. For two reasons: one, this will reduce your overall interest charges. And you'll also minimize or even avoid origination fees on new loans by borrowing less for graduate school or not borrowing at all. And if you are borrowing less for graduate school, the weighted average of all the loans together will ensure a lower overall rate than if you pay off lower-interest loans early and then have to take out higher-interest loans such as the 6.08% unsubsidized Stafford or 7.08% Grad-PLUS loan (which we will soon discuss).

Note: For your prior loans to again qualify for an in-school deferment, you will have to go back to the holders/servicers of your prior federal education loans and let them know you're back in school as well. You will also have to meet all other criteria based on your enrollment status. Each loan holder/servicer will send you a form to be completed by the school you will be attending, so that you'll again be eligible for the in-school deferment to suspend payments while in school and so that the government will again pay all the interest on any subsidized Stafford or Subsidized Direct Loans as well as any Perkins loans while in school.

Graduate / Professional students are eligible for three federal student loans: the Perkins loan, the Direct Loan, and the GradPLUS loan (which is a student loan that works similar to the parent PLUS in that one can borrow the total cost of attendance minus any other aid received including other student loans.) So if the Perkins and Direct Loans are not sufficient, graduate students can use the GradPLUS loans to cover their additional costs. Unlike independent undergraduate students, graduate and professional students can therefore borrow their entire cost of attendance via the federal education loan programs if no other aid is awarded. Note: Similar to a parent taking out a PLUS loan, a student borrowing through a GradPLUS loan must pass a credit test or have an eligible credit worthy cosigner to obtain the loan. Perkins and Direct Loans do not require any such credit test.

*As mentioned earlier, the Perkins loan program may be eliminated or experience changes that will make it less attractive for new loans.*

## How to Pay Off Your Loans

As soon as a student graduates, the clock starts ticking. The government gives you a six-month grace period to find a job and catch your breath—and then the bills start arriving. You might think that at least this part of the process would be straightforward: they send you a bill, you pay. But in fact, there are a bewildering number of repayment options, as well as opportunities, to postpone and defer payment.

Overriding all of this is one simple maxim: The longer you take to pay, the more it costs you. Putting it in practical terms, choosing to lower your monthly payments will stretch out the amount of time you'll be making these payments, and ultimately add thousands of dollars in interest to your bill. Sometimes this is worth it, as we'll see.

It's impossible for us to predict exactly what your monthly payments will be, since everyone owes different amounts, and borrowed on different terms. Just to give you a ballpark figure, someone who owes $15,000, at an average rate of 8% would have 120 monthly payments of about $182. Someone who owes $50,000 would have 120 monthly payments of about $607.

The only way to defer these student loan payments long-term is to stay in school. As long as you are at least a half-time student at an approved post-secondary school, you can keep those bills at bay forever. If you get a job and then later decide to go on to graduate school, your loan payments may be deferred while you are in graduate school, and resume as soon as you get out.

## Above All, Avoid Default

When all the loans come due, and a few personal crises loom as well, there's a very human urge to shove the bills in a drawer and hope for the best. This is absolutely the worst possible thing you can do.

The default rate on government guaranteed student loans is still somewhat high at the moment. This might give you the erroneous impression that a default is no big deal. You should realize that a large portion of defaulted loans comes not from college loans, but from loans made to students of "bogus" trade schools with three initials and two faces. These trade schools are often scam operations designed to fleece the federal government by preying on immigrants and poor people. A new arrival to this country may not care about or understand the importance of his credit rating, but you certainly do.

When people get into economic trouble, they tend to get very reticent, and often don't ask for help. Even though you may feel embarrassed, it is much better to call your lender and explain the situation than to miss a payment with no explanation.

As you will see, there are so many different payment options, that there is really no need for anyone ever to go into default. If you lose a job, or "encounter economic hardship," you should apply for a temporary deferment (suspension of principal and interest payments for a specified time) or something called *forbearance,* which can include temporary suspension of payments, a time extension to make payment—even a temporary reduction in the amount of monthly installments. Many lenders will draw up new repayment plans, or accept a missed payment as long as you inform them ahead of time.

Work *with* the lender. Or rather, lenders. If you have loans from more than one lender (the Perkins loans are administered separately from the Stafford or Direct Loans), one lender isn't necessarily going to know what's happening with the other, unless you tell them.

It can take years to build up a good credit rating again once you've loused it up. Meanwhile, you may not be able to get credit cards, a mortgage, or a car loan. And if you're in default, getting additional loans for graduate school can be difficult if not impossible.

## The Different Payment Plans

If you are repaying Stafford loans, Direct Loans, Supplemental Loans for Students (SLS), PLUS or Grad PLUS loans, there up to seven repayment options at present. When you pick an option, it is not for life. You can switch payment plans at any time. Here is a brief summary of the options. For more details, contact your lender(s).

**Standard repayment:** The loans must be repaid in equal installments spread out over up to 10 years. This is a good plan for people who have relatively little debt, or have enough income to afford the relatively high payments.

**Extended repayment:** The loans must be repaid in equal installments over a period that can extend up to 25 years. The increased time period reduces monthly payments, but long-term interest expenses go up dramatically.

**Graduated repayment:** Loan payments start out low and increase over time. The payments must always at least equal the monthly interest that's accruing. This is a good plan for young people whose earnings are low, but are expected to increase over time. Over the lifetime of the loan, interest expenses are much higher.

**Income-sensitive repayment:** This option allows payments that are initially low, but increase as income rises. The lender works with the borrower to establish a payment schedule that reflects the borrower's current income. The payments are adjusted annually to accommodate changes in the borrower's income. This option is available only to borrowers who took out Stafford, PLUS or Grad PLUS loans from private lenders years ago.

**Income contingent repayment:** This option is available only to borrowers with federal Direct Loans, but does not cover parent PLUS loans. In this plan, the payments are based on a combination of the borrower's level of debt and current income. With this (and the following two options), payments can be lower than the monthly interest accruing (which is called *negative amortization*). Of course, this can add substantially to the final cost of long-term interest expenses. To counter this, at the end of 25 years, the government will forgive any unpaid balance. But don't start jumping for joy: the IRS may tax you on this unpaid balance. Thus, if the government were to forgive a $10,000 remaining debt, a person in the 25 percent tax bracket would have to come up with at least $2,500 in additional taxes that year.

**Income-based repayment** and **Pay As You Earn:** Under these options, the required monthly payment will be based on your income during any period when you have a partial financial hardship. The monthly payment may be adjusted annually. The maximum repayment period under these plans may exceed 10 years. If you meet certain requirements over a specified period of time, you may qualify for cancellation of any outstanding balance. The amount of any loan canceled may be subject to income taxes. Parent PLUS Loans are not eligible. Only Direct Loans qualify for Pay As You Earn.

## Loan Consolidation

Government regulations allow you to consolidate all your education loans from different sources into one big loan—often with lower monthly payments than you were making before. As usual, the catch is that the repayment period is extended, meaning that you end up paying a lot more in interest over the increased life of the loan. However, you can always prepay your loans without penalty.

The loans that can be consolidated are: the Stafford, Direct Loans, SLS, Perkins, PLUS loans, GradPLUS loans, and loans issued by the government's programs for health-care professionals. You can't consolidate private loans from colleges or other sources in the federal consolidation program.

# How It Works

A consolidation loan can be paid back using one of the plans outlined above. In some cases, loan consolidation doesn't make sense—for example, if you are almost done paying off your loans. For the most part, student loans can be consolidated only once, and in most cases, it would be better to wait to do this until a student is completely finished with school.

You also don't have to consolidate all your loans. The rules on how your new interest rate will be calculated change constantly, so you'll need to get up-to-date information from your lender.

Before you consolidate any loans, you should also consider these factors:

- How will the interest rate be calculated?

- Are you better off excluding some loans from consolidation to get a better rate and/or to prevent the loss of some benefits with some of your loans?

- Will consolidating your loans later give you a better or a worse interest rate?

- Can you consolidate your loans(s) more than once?

- Do you have to consolidate your loans with a private lender? Do you have to consolidate your loans directly with the government? If you have a choice between the two, which consolidation plan is the best deal for you?

- If you are consolidating unsubsidized and subsidized loans together, will this affect your ability to have the government pay the interest on your subsidized loans should you go back to school?

# Loan Discharge and Cancellation

The Perkins Loan program, and to a lesser extent, the Stafford and PLUS loan programs have various provisions in which the loan can be discharged or canceled. While some provisions hopefully do not happen to you in the near future (e.g. you become permanently disabled or die), loans may also be forgiven for performing certain types of service (teaching in low-income areas, law enforcement, nursing, working with disabled or high risk children and their families in low-income communities, etc.).

One of the provisions of the College Cost Reduction and Access Act has expanded Direct Stafford loan forgiveness in exchange for public service. Borrowers who take public sector jobs in the government, the military, certain non-profit tax-exempt organizations, law enforcement, public health, or education, may be eligible—after making 120 on-time payments after October 1, 2007—to have the remaining balance of their Direct Loans forgiven.

Those with Stafford loans borrowed through banks (not borrowed through the Direct Loan program from the government through the financial office of your school) may be able to take advantage of this new provision by consolidating, or even re-consolidating, into a Direct Consolidation Loan.

Keep in mind, however, that under the current tax code, the amount of a loan that is forgiven is considered taxable income in the year in which it is forgiven. There is some talk in Washington that such public service loan forgiveness may be made exempt from such taxation through additional legislation. Of course, if this happens we will cover it in future updates.

## The Smartest Loan Strategy: Prepayment

All federally guaranteed education loans can be prepaid without any penalty. This means that by paying just a little more than your monthly payment each month, you can pay down the loan much faster than you might have thought possible, and save yourself a bundle in interest.

Obviously, if you're going to do this, try to prepay the loans with the highest interest rates first. It wouldn't make sense to prepay your 5% Perkins loan if you're paying 10% on an unsecured bank loan, or 12% on some huge credit card bill.

# Chapter Nine

## Special Topics

# Divorced or Separated Parents

The breakup of a marriage is always painful, and some parents are understandably reluctant to share their pain with strangers. We know of one set of parents who went through four years of need analysis forms without ever telling the college that they were divorced. Unfortunately, by not telling the schools about the divorce, those parents lost out on a great deal of financial aid, and put themselves through unnecessary hardships in paying for college.

No matter how painful or bizarre your personal situation is, the FAOs have heard worse, and you will find that being upfront about such problems as refusal by a former spouse to pay alimony or to supply needed financial aid data to the schools, will make the financial aid process easier. While the FAOs are quite expert at understanding the convoluted and intricate family relationships that arise out of divorce or separation, you will find that the aid formula itself tries to fit these complex relationships into a few simple categories. The result is completely baffling to most parents.

## Who Are the Custodial Parents?

The formula doesn't really care who the biological parents of a student are. Ultimately, the formula wants to know only whom the student lived with most during the first base income year. This parent, called the "custodial parent," gets the honor of completing the standardized need analysis form. And according to federal guidelines, it is this parent whose financial information will be used to determine the parents' contribution to college.

## Soap Opera Digest

Let's say that Mr. and Mrs. Jackson separated two years ago. Their only daughter Jill lives now with Mr. Jackson, and will be attending college next year. While some standardized aid forms may ask a few vague questions about Mrs. Jackson, as far as the federal financial aid formula is concerned, Mr. Jackson is the sole custodial parent and the only parent whose income and assets can be requested and analyzed by the processor. This counts as a family of two under the aid formula.

Let's say that Mr. Jackson gets a divorce from Mrs. Jackson and then marries another woman, Francine. The aid formula will now want to look at the assets and income of Mr. Jackson *and* the assets and income of his new wife as well. The instructions to the need analysis form will tell Mr. Jackson to provide information about himself as well as Francine, even if he just married her last week. Francine's income and assets will be assessed just as heavily as Mr. Jackson's, even if she didn't meet Jill until the day of the wedding, and even if they signed a prenuptial agreement stating that she would not be responsible for Jill's college expenses. This is now a family of three in the eyes of the FAOs.

What if Mr. Jackson's new wife has a 10-year-old child of her own, Denise, from a previous marriage, who will also come to live with Mr. Jackson? Now there is a family of four. Neither of the *previous* spouses will be considered for assessment by the federal formula. When it comes time for Denise's college education, Mr. Jackson's assets and income will be assessed just as heavily as Francine's.

Let's suppose that Mr. Jackson also had a son, James, from a much earlier marriage. The son has never lived with him, but Mr. Jackson provides for more than half his support. Even though the son has never lived with him, James is considered part of Mr. Jackson's "household" by the federal guidelines because Mr. Jackson provides for more than half his support. We now have a family of five for aid purposes.

If James were attending college at least half time in a degree or certificate program, he would also be included as part of the number of "household" members attending "college, graduate/ professional school, or other post-secondary school." This would help to reduce the Jackson's family contribution for Jill's college expenses.

By the way, when James (who lives with his mother, Mr. Jackson's long-ago ex) goes to college, his mother will be considered the custodial parent on *his* aid application. In effect, James can be claimed as a member of both of his natural parents' households, depending on whose aid application is being completed.

By now you may be asking why Denise (you remember Denise—Mr. Jackson's stepchild) was included as part of his household without regard to who provides the majority of her support. Since Denise would not be considered an independent student if she were to apply for federal student aid, she is automatically part of Mr. Jackson's household in the federal formula—whether or not Denise actually completes a FAFSA form for that academic year, and even whether or not she lives in the household. Even if Denise's natural father were providing all of Denise's support, Denise would still be considered a part of the Jackson's household. While this criteria applies to "other children" for the purposes of household size in the federal formula, it does not apply to the institutional formula. Of course, any child support received by Francine would have to be included as untaxed income on Jill's aid applications.

# Number of Exemptions

As you know from reading the rest of this book, the more family members you can list on the need analysis form, the lower your family contribution will be. This number will not necessarily coincide with the number of tax exemptions you claim. Let's say you have a son who lives with you, but who receives more than half support from your ex. This other parent is entitled to take the son's income tax exemption, and you are not. You will have one more member of your family than you have exemptions. The colleges are used to this situation. You may have to explain, and possibly provide documentation, but they will understand. The same situation might occur if, as part of a divorce agreement, your ex is allowed to claim the son as a tax deduction, even though the son lives with you.

In either case, when it is time for college, you'll list your son as part of your household, and your ex will not be assessed by the federal financial aid formula.

## A Quick Summary

Because parents find all this so confusing, and because the information they receive over the telephone from the college aid offices is often contradictory or misleading, we're going to summarize the key points:

1. The parent with whom the child resided most during the 12 months prior to completing the aid application is considered the "custodial parent." The custodial parent is not necessarily the parent who was initially awarded custody in the divorce agreement.

2. Siblings (including stepsiblings and half-siblings) can be considered part of the custodial parents' household provided they

   a. get more than half support from the custodial parent(s)/custodial stepparent *or*

   b. cannot be considered independent students under federal aid guidelines. (Option b does not apply in the institutional methodology.)

3. A stepparent who resides with the custodial parent will be treated by the aid formula as if he/she were the natural parent.

4. It currently doesn't matter who claims a child as a tax exemption; the number of family members is based on the rules above.

Read the instructions carefully when you complete the aid forms. If a college challenges your application by trying to disallow some members of your household, don't automatically assume that they are right and you are wrong. When you speak to the FAO, refer to the section in the instructions to the aid form on which you based your decision.

## Will an Ex-Husband or Ex-Wife's Assets and Income Ever Be Used to Determine the Family Contribution?

Parents are always concerned that the colleges will look at at the other biological or adoptive parent's income and assets and decide that the student is ineligible for aid, even if the ex-spouse refuses to help pay for college.

The vast majority of colleges will never even ask to see income or asset information from a noncustodial parent. The FAFSA has no questions about the noncustodial parent at all. While the PROFILE form asks a few questions about the noncustodial parent, the processor does not take this information into account in providing the Expected Family Contribution, and most colleges will not take the matter any further. (Of course, if you received alimony or child support from your ex, this will appear as part of *your* income.)

However, a few colleges do require that you fill out their own supplemental forms. Some schools that use the PROFILE form will require that a noncustodial parent's information be supplied by the parent with whom the student spent the least time. The colleges that ask for this information tend to be the most selective, including all the Ivy League schools. If your child applies to one of these schools, you may find that your ex-wife's or ex-husband's income and assets will indeed have a bearing on how much a college ultimately decides your family contribution ought to be.

Even if this is the case, you should not lose heart. Some types of aid must, by law, be awarded without reference to the noncustodial parent. These include the Pell Grant, the Direct Loan, and some forms of state aid.

Starting with the 2005–2006 PROFILE, some schools have required an online Noncustodial PROFILE (NCP). Details about this online form will be provided at some point at the beginning of the PROFILE process. Other schools may still choose to accept or require the traditional paper Noncustodial Parent's Statement and/or their own noncustodial parent form which, following completion, should then be sent directly to the financial aid office of any school that requires it.

To find out if you need to submit any of these supplemental forms, consult the college's own financial aid instructions.

# What If the Ex-Husband or Ex-Wife Refuses to Fill Out the Form?

The schools that require financial information about former spouses will not process your application for aid until you have supplied *all* the information they requested. If your ex refuses to supply the information you need to apply for aid, you have two options.

First, try to use reason. Your ex may be worried that merely by filling out the form, he/she is accepting legal responsibility for paying for college. Point out to your former spouse that on the form they are to complete, there is a question that asks, "How much are you willing to pay?" By writing down "0" the parent expresses a clear desire to be left out of this responsibility.

It is also worth noting that even if a college decides to assess a noncustodial parent's income or assets, this does not mean that the noncustodial parent will ever get a bill from the college. Yes, the family contribution will probably be larger, but the bill for tuition will go, as always, to the student's custodial parent. There is no legal obligation for the ex-husband or ex-wife to help pay for college unless an agreement was signed beforehand.

The second option, if the ex-spouse refuses to cooperate, is to get a waiver from the colleges. The FAOs can decide at *their* discretion not to assess a noncustodial parent if it is really clear that that individual can never be persuaded to help. You are going to have to make a strong case to get colleges to give you that waiver. This is the time to pull out all the dirty laundry—alcoholism, physical or mental abuse, chemical dependency, abandonment, chronic unemployment, and so on. Send the FAO a letter presenting your case, and include any documentation from agencies or third parties (such as an attorney, guidance counselor, or member of the clergy) that supports your case. Follow up with a phone call, and do this as soon as possible after you've decided to apply. Any information you supply will be confidential and will not go farther than the financial aid office. This will *not* jeopardize your child's chances for admission. It may, however, get you the aid you need to send your child to the school.

## Is There an Agreement Specifying a Contribution from an Ex?

You may find this question included on your need analysis form. Be very careful how you answer it. If there is an agreement, and you have every reason to expect that your ex will honor that agreement, then say yes and give the figure. However, if there is a *disagreement* as to what your ex originally agreed to provide, then it would be calamitous to say yes. The colleges will assess your ability to pay based in part on this figure. If your ex then refused to pay, you would be in bad shape. If you are not sure you can count on your ex-spouse to provide the promised money, then write "no" on the form and write a letter explaining the situation to the various colleges.

## The Noncustodial Parent's Information

You should NEVER send this data to a school unless it is required. Read the individual college's financial aid instructions carefully. Some always require it, while others want it only if you've recently divorced or separated, or if your ex has claimed the child as a tax deduction in the past few years. The information on this form should agree with that on any other forms that have already been sent in—the need analysis form and tax returns. If you and your ex still have assets held in common, make sure that your proportionate shares of these assets as reported on your need analysis forms add up to the whole. Alimony and child support figures should also agree.

# Remarriage

A stepparent's income and assets will be assessed by the FAOs just as severely as if he/she were the natural parent—even if there is a prenuptial agreement to the contrary. This being the case, it may make sense to postpone marriage plans until after your child is out of the base income years. A couple that decided just to live together while their children were in college might easily save enough money to take a round-the-world honeymoon cruise when it was all over.

*Note: a few colleges give you the option of using the financial information of either your former spouse or your new spouse to determine eligibility for the school's own grant money.*

# The Difference Between Being Divorced, Legally Separated, or Just Separated

For financial aid purposes, there is absolutely no difference. If you are not legally separated, you may be asked to provide documentation to show that you no longer live together.

# If You Are in the Process of Separating or Getting a Divorce

We have actually known of cases in which a couple separated or divorced in order to get more financial aid. This is taking the pursuit of free money way too far. We know of another couple that pretended to separate to qualify for more aid. Aside from the moral implications (you have to wonder what kind of warped view of life the children will bring away from that experience), this is also illegal.

However, if your situation has become impossible, and there is absolutely no choice but to separate, then you should try to take financial aid into account as you consider your legal options. An agreement by the soon-to-be ex-spouse to provide for your child's education could be an expensive mistake.

Let's say that a father formally agrees to pay $10,000 per college year for his daughter's education. Many colleges will say thank you very much and decrease their aid packages by $10,000. If this is an amicable separation, it might be better if no agreement were made on paper. The father could then voluntarily gift money during the year, thus preventing any loss of aid eligibility. If the separation is not amicable, and the mother is afraid she will never see the money unless there is an agreement in writing, it would be infinitely better if the father made one lump-sum payment to the mother toward college. In this way, the money becomes part of her overall assets, which can be assessed at up to only 5.65% a year.

## Avoid Acrimony

A couple in the midst of splitting up is not always in the most rational frame of mind. It is essential, however, that you try to keep your heads clear, and prevent the education of your children from becoming one more brickbat to hurl back and forth.

Cooperation is the most important part of the process. We have seen parents childishly miss financial aid deadlines just to spite their former spouse. The person who really loses out when this happens, of course, is the child.

# Transfer Students and Graduate Students

The process of applying for financial aid as a transfer student or a graduate student is very similar to applying for aid as a freshman in college. However, there are a few differences that should be discussed:

- Deadlines for transfer and graduate students are often different from the deadlines for regular undergrads. Check your applications carefully for the specific deadlines.

- If you have previously attended any colleges, you may need a financial aid transcript sent from each one of them to the schools you are applying to, especially if you are transferring during the middle of the academic year. A financial aid transcript is not the same thing as a transcript of your academic record (which you will probably need as well). You will have to send financial aid transcripts even if you received no financial aid from the previous schools.

The colleges want to look at these records in part to see what kind of a deal you were getting at your previous school, and in part to see how much you've already borrowed, for there are aggregate limits to certain types of aid. For example, an undergraduate can receive a total of only $27,500 in Perkins loans.

The best way to go about getting financial aid transcripts is to pick up blank copies from the school to which you are applying, which come already addressed, ready to be sent back to the school. You can then mail these forms to the schools you previously attended. You'll have to keep on top of the process to make sure the transcripts are sent. The records offices at colleges are often worse than the motor vehicle bureau.

- Some colleges have separate aid policies for transfer students. Often, priority is given to students who began as freshmen. This is particularly true if a student transfers in the middle of the year; the FAOs will have already committed the bulk of their funds for that school year.

- It may help if you have some kind of bargaining chip—for example, if there is another school that is also interested in you. Your *previous* school won't be much of a bargaining chip since you have probably already given them a compelling reason for why you wanted to leave.

- It will certainly help if you've maintained a high grade point average. In particular, students who are transferring to a "designer label" college from a less well-known school will need good grades and good recommendations.

# Graduate and Professional School Financial Aid Tips

Graduate and professional school aid is parceled out in much the same way as college aid but the ratio of grants to loans to work-study is unfortunately very different. Grant money has dried up in the past ten years.

Student loans, on the other hand, are somewhat easier to come by in graduate school. (For example, if you are attending law school, you can borrow up to the full cost of attendance without much trouble—which is pretty scary when you think about it.) For most students, the cap on Direct Loans rises to $20,500 per year in graduate school, though certain health profession students may be able to borrow even higher amounts. If you still need additional funds, you can borrow them using the federal GradPLUS loan or private educational loans.

The paperwork you will be asked to fill out varies widely. All schools require the FAFSA, but many schools will also require the PROFILE form or some other aid form, which asks questions similar to the PROFILE form.

Fortunately, all graduate school students will find they now meet the federal government's independent student test. If you are a graduate student, you are independent by definition for federal aid purposes—even if your parents still claim you as a dependent on their tax returns and you still live at home.

However, a few of the very selective schools will insist on seeing parent information anyway. The Harvard Law School FAOs, for example, require parents' financial data even if the student is 40 years old and the parents have long since retired to the Sun Belt. Though the schools may refuse to give you any of their own money, you can still qualify for federal loans since you meet the federal regulations for independent status.

If the school requires parental information on the PROFILE form, you will have to find out if they want parental information on the FAFSA as well. If any one of them requires parental information on the FAFSA, you will have to complete the blue and purple sections of the 2018–2019 FAFSA.

If you are planning on law school, medical school, or business school, taking on large amounts of debt is, although unpleasant, at least feasible. However, if you are planning on, say, a PhD in philosophy, you should be very cautious about borrowing large amounts of money. An alternative to borrowing is to find grant money that is not administered by the financial aid office—in graduate school, some fellowships are administered by department heads instead. In addition, students sometimes find opportunities to teach or work on professors' grant projects.

# The College's Special Needs: Academically Gifted, Minorities, Athletes, Legacies

While financial aid is based on *your* need, it is always wise to remember that it is also based to some extent on what *the colleges* need. If you fit a category a particular college is looking for, your package is going to be much better than if you don't.

Preferential packaging comes in many forms. Perhaps the FAO will decide that your expected family contribution, as computed by the need analysis computer, is a bit high. Perhaps you will be offered an athletic scholarship or a non-need-based grant.

Whatever the school chooses to call it, you are being offered a preferential package—more grant or scholarship money, less loans and work-study.

## No Time for Modesty

In many cases, these are not scholarships or grants for which you can apply. The schools themselves select the recipients, with a keen eye toward enticing high-caliber students to their programs. It is therefore crucial that the student sell herself in her application. This is no time for modesty. For example, a promising student violinist should make sure that one of her application essays is about the challenge of mastering a difficult instrument. This should be backed up by recommendations from music teachers, reviews of her performances that have appeared in newspapers, and a listing of any awards she has won. If a student is offered one or more of these merit-based grants or scholarships, it is important to find out if these awards are one-time only or whether they are renewable, based on performance. If renewable, just how good does the student's performance have to be in order to get the same package next year?

## Bargaining

Colleges are particularly likely to increase their offer if they really wanted you in the first place. Students with excellent academic records are in an especially strong position to bargain. See Part Four, "The Offer," for more details.

# Financial Aid for the Academically Gifted

Some awards come directly as a result of test scores. The National Merit Scholarship Program gives out about 1,800 nonrenewable scholarships and 2,800 renewable college-sponsored scholarships to students who score extremely well on the PSAT/NMSQT. Based on their performance on the SAT or the ACT, 120 students are designated Presidential Scholars.

At schools where all aid is based on need, a National Merit finalist will not necessarily get one penny of aid unless "need" is demonstrated. Other schools, however, automatically give National Merit finalists a four-year free ride—a full scholarship.

Some awards come as a result of the student's performance in college. These kick in during the sophomore year—an example is the Harry S. Truman Scholarship.

Merit grants based on academic performance in high school are becoming more widespread as time goes on. We believe this trend will continue as colleges begin to compete in earnest for the best students. However, most of the money awarded to students with high academic performance is less easy to see. It comes in the form of preferential packaging.

# Athletes

In general, it is up to the student to tell the colleges why the student is special through his or her application.

Athletes, however, should get in touch with the athletic department directly. When you go to visit the school, make it a point to meet the coach of the team you are interested in. Do not assume that a school is not interested in you merely because you have not been approached by a scout during the year. Get your coach to write letters to the schools you are interested in. Don't sell yourself short either—an average football player might not get a scholarship at Notre Dame, but the same applicant at Columbia might get a preferential package. Even if the school does not award athletic scholarships per se (Columbia, like the rest of the Ivy League, does not), many FAOs bend the numbers to come up with a lower family contribution for an athlete the school particularly wants.

Remember, too, that football is not the only sport in college. Schools also need swimmers, tennis players, long-distance runners, and the like.

# Minorities

Minority students now represent the fastest growing demographic on campuses across the country. While many college administrators welcome the prospect of a more diverse student body, this trend poses a challenge for the colleges, since historically many minority students have required financial aid.

While there are significant scholarship and other financial aid programs earmarked specifically for minority students, many schools now find themselves in a quandary.  How do they attract and retain what they project to be an increased number of qualified students needing financial aid at time when endowments are declining with the stock markets, fundraising campaigns are not meeting their goals due to a weak economy and financial aid budgets are already stretched tight?

Because of this anticipated increased demand for aid, it will be more important than ever for applicants to meet financial aid deadlines, to build a strong academic record in high school, and to maintain good grades in college to ensure continued funding.

Fortunately, at most schools, once on campus, students will find resources and support services designed to help them stay in school—ranging from mentors to work-study programs. The colleges have made it very clear that they remain committed to retaining the students they admit— and many will go to extraordinary lengths to keep them.  As with most facets of college life, however, students who take the initiative will be more likely to get help.

Historically Black Colleges and Universities (HBCUs) and Hispanic-Serving Institutions (HSIs) are also experiencing challenges meeting their financial needs. A number of these institutions are among  the  finest schools in the country. But minority students with high need applying to these schools need to be aware that many of them don't have the financial aid resources of other schools with larger endowments. In some cases, a minority student with high need may find that he or she will get a larger aid package elsewhere. As we mentioned earlier, it is important for all students to apply to at least one financial safety school.

## Legacies

Many colleges will go out of their way for the children of alumni. If the student's parents' circumstances are such that they cannot pay the entire cost of college, they should not be embarrassed to ask for help. At many schools it will be forthcoming.

## Running Your Own Business or Farm

As we have already mentioned, the tax benefits of running your own business or farm are considerable:  you are allowed to write off legitimate expenses, put relatives on your payroll, and possibly claim a percentage of your home for business use. The financial aid benefits are even better: your business or farm assets are assessed at a much lower rate than personal assets. This is because the colleges recognize a business's need for working capital. Thus a business's net worth (assets minus liabilities) of $50,000 will draw roughly the same assessment as a $20,000 personal asset—or even a zero assessment if it is a "family business" (see pages 112–113).

If you have been planning to start your own business, now might be a good time!

# The Four Types of Business—C Corporation, S Corporation, General Partnership, Sole Proprietor

A **C corporation**'s profits are taxed at the corporate rate. C corporations must file an IRS 1120 corporate income tax return. The profits from a C corporation owned by a parent should not be included on the standardized financial aid forms, but the assets and liabilities may need to be listed. The owner of an **S corporation** (short for subchapter S) files an 1120S corporate income tax return, but also reports profits and losses on his own personal income tax return on schedule E. On the aid forms, the owner may have to report assets and liabilities as well as profits (or losses). A parent who is part of a **general partnership** reports profits and losses to the IRS on schedule E of the 1040. For aid purposes, she reports net profits (or losses) and possibly assets and liabilities on the need analysis form.

A **sole proprietor** reports profits and losses to the IRS on schedule C of the 1040. Again, profits (or losses) and possibly assets and liabilities must also be reported on the need analysis form. A **farmer** is treated like a sole proprietor but reports profits and losses to the IRS on schedule F of the 1040. On the FAFSA form, farmers who live primarily on their farm and who can claim on schedule F of their 1040 that they "materially participated in the farm's operation" (defined as a "family farm") should not include the value of the family farm under assets and liabilities.

Keep in mind that whatever business arrangement you have, you should never report your gross revenues on the standardized aid forms. Your net income (or net loss) is what counts—gross receipts less your deductible business expenses.

## Financial Aid Strategies for Business and Farm Owners

Before the first base income year begins, it would make sense to accelerate billings, and take in as much cash as possible in advance. Try to defer expenses into the base income year. The idea, of course, is to minimize your income and maximize your expenses for the snapshot the college financial offices will be taking of your business. During the base income year itself, you might decide finally to do that remodeling or expansion you've been thinking about. In the last base income year, you will want to reverse the process you began before the first base income year: accelerate expenses and defer income, until after the colleges have taken their last snapshot.

## Starting a Business or Farm

The beginning years of a business are very often slow. Many businesses lose money in their first couple of years, until they develop their niche and find a market. Parents who dream of starting their own company often feel that they should wait until after the kids are done with college before they take on the risk of an entrepreneurial enterprise. If you always dreamed of starting your own business, but have decided to wait until after the children are done with college, think again.

The perfect time to start a business is just before your child starts college. Consider: you'll have high start-up costs (which will reduce your assets) and low sales (which will reduce your income) for the first couple of years. If you time it right, these years will coincide exactly with the base income years, which means you will be eligible for substantially increased amounts of financial aid. Any business assets will also be assessed at a lower rate than personal assets. Like many businesses, yours may well start to be profitable within four years—just as your child is finishing college.

In effect, the college will be subsidizing the start-up costs of your business. This strategy is obviously not for everyone. A business must be run with the intention of showing a profit or risk running afoul of the IRS. If you are merely indulging in a hobby, your farm or business losses may be disallowed. In addition, most schools that use the institutional methodology will disallow losses when determining eligibility for the school's own funds.

Any new business contains an element of risk, which should be carefully considered before you start. On the other hand, if you wait until your children are done with college, you may not have enough money left to start up a lemonade stand.

## Estimating Your Company's Assets and Liabilities on the Aid Form

Owners of businesses sometimes overstate the value of their assets by including intangibles such as goodwill and location. These are important elements if you were to sell the company, but irrelevant to the need analysis formula. You are being asked to list only the total value of cash, receivables, inventory, investments, and your fixed assets (such as machinery, land, and buildings).

If your net worth is negative, you will list "0" on the FAFSA for that question. On other forms you should list the total debts even if they exceed the total assets, but you will find that most colleges will not subtract a negative net worth from your total assets.

## The Business/Farm Supplement

Many schools require the owner of a business or farm to fill out a paper version of the College Board's Business/Farm Supplement. Since this statement is not analyzed by a central processor you can send signed photocopies of the completed form to any school that requests it. The form more or less mimics the IRS forms you will probably be sending the colleges anyway. Some other schools may insist on your completing their own business supplement even though such forms will look very similar to the College Board's version. If you are not the sole owner, be careful to distinguish between questions that ask for the business's total income, assets, and liabilities, and questions that ask for your proportionate share of the business's income, assets, and liabilities.

High expenses during the base income years will help to maximize financial aid. However, large business purchases cannot be deducted all at once under IRS rules. There are several different methods to depreciate your fixed assets. During the college years, accelerated depreciation probably makes the most sense, especially during the critical *first* base income year. As always, however, you should consult with your accountant, and perhaps a financial aid consultant as well.

# If You Own a Significant Percentage of the Stock of a Small Company

A parent who owns more than 5% of the stock in a small company could report this asset on the standardized need analysis form under "other investment," but it would be much more beneficial to report it under "business and farm." If you own a significant part of a small company, accountants argue that you can be said to be a part-owner of the company. Most colleges will go along with this. The advantage, of course, is that the value of the stock will be assessed less heavily as a business asset than it would have been as a personal asset.

# Selling Your Business or Farm

A huge capital gain from the sale of your business or farm will probably wipe out any chance for financial aid. On the other hand, if you are receiving a huge capital gain, you don't need aid. If possible, delay the sale until you are out of the base income years, but if the offer is good enough, take it and enjoy the feeling of never having to look at a need analysis form ever again. Oh, yes, and expect a call almost immediately from the fundraisers at your child's college. It's amazing how fast good news travels.

# Putting Your Child on the Payroll

This is a good tax move, since it shifts income to the child, who may pay tax at a reduced rate. From a financial aid standpoint, however, increasing your child's income can backfire. Each year up to 50% of the child's income gets assessed by the FAOs. Once the income reaches a certain amount (see pages 119–120), it may disqualify your family from receiving aid, or at least reduce the amount you receive.

If you are not eligible for aid, by all means consider putting your child on the payroll. A self-employed parent who hires a son or daughter does not even have to pay social security taxes on the child's earnings until the child turns 18.

# The Recently unemployed Worker

If you have been terminated, or laid off, or if you have received notice that you will be terminated, or laid off, or if you are a self-employed person who cannot make a living due to harsh economic conditions, then you should be sure to point this out to the FAO.

Many schools can use what is called "professional judgment" to increase aid for the child of a recently unemployed worker. Instead of using the base income year (when you may have been gainfully employed) they can elect to look at your projected income for next year. Since you are now unemployed, your projection will be understandably bleak. Your child's college will probably want to see some sort of documentation (e.g., termination letter from your employer, unemployment benefits certification, etc.). Taking these extra steps could be worth thousands of dollars in aid. You should also be sure to answer "Yes" to FAFSA question 84 if you qualify as a dislocated worker.

# How Do You Let the Colleges Know Your Projection for Next Year?

You will be asked on the PROFILE form to project your income for the coming year. Project conservatively. You may be out of work for a while, so assume the worst-case scenario. Do not project based on a tentative job offer; if it doesn't come through, you will be making much less than the colleges will think based on your over-optimistic projections.

If all the schools to which you are applying require the PROFILE form, then the schools will get your projected income from the College Board's analysis. Just remember to mention your work status in the "Explanations/Special Circumstances" section of the form.

Contrary to what the PROFILE instructions say, you should not list any deferred compensation—401(k), or 403(b)—or contributions to IRAs or Keoghs as part of your untaxed income in Section PR and PF. Do, however, list your gross wages, including any deferred compensation as part of your projected income from work.

The reason you should not include these items as untaxed income is that by doing so you would be overstating your income. For example, let's take married parents with projected gross wages of $30,000 (and no other income) who made a $4,000 deductible IRA contribution. If this couple followed the instructions, they would be listing a total income of $34,000 ($30,000 income earned from work, plus $4,000 untaxed income). Obviously, they should only be reporting their total income—$30,000.

If your child is applying to schools that do *not* require the PROFILE form, then you should send them a separate letter detailing your changed employment status and a projection of next year's income. When listing your projections, you should break them down into separate categories:

father's income from work (if any), mother's income from work (if any), income from unemployment benefits, and all other taxable and untaxable income.

In fact, it wouldn't be such a bad idea to send copies of this letter even to the schools that require the PROFILE form, since the FAOs at these schools sometimes miss comments written in the "Explanations/Special Circumstances" section of the form.

## If You Lose Your Job While Your Child Is in College

Call or write a letter to the FAO explaining what happened as soon as possible, and include some form of documentation. It will probably be impossible for the FAO to revise your aid package for the current semester, but this will give them warning that you will be needing more aid next semester.

# Other Disasters

If you are a nonworking parent who has been financially abandoned by a spouse, if you've had an accident that cost you a lot of money in unreimbursed medical expenses, if you lost your second job, if you received a pay cut or reduction in overtime, if you recently separated from your spouse, if your business lost its major client, if you became disabled, or had a major casualty or theft loss, you should be sure to notify the FAO immediately—even if the school year has already begun. Many schools have emergency aid funds for just these situations.

# Independent Students

If a student is judged to be independent, the need analysis companies assess only *the student's* income and assets. The income and assets of the parents do not even have to be listed on the form. Obviously, this can have a tremendous impact on financial aid. Most students have limited resources, and so the aid packages from the colleges have to increase dramatically if they are to meet the student's entire "need."

Parents often erroneously believe that by not claiming the student as a dependent on taxes, their child will be considered independent for aid purposes—but this is not the case.

It is in the school's interest to decide that a student is not independent, since independent students need so much more aid. In fact, a student is presumed to be dependent unless he meets certain criteria. The rules change from year to year (in general going from stringent to more stringent). For the 2020–2021 academic year, you are considered independent for federal aid purposes if:

A. You were born before January 1, 1997.

B. You are a veteran of the U.S. Armed Services or you are currently serving on active duty in the U.S. Armed Forces for purposes other than training.

C. When you are age 13 or older: both of your parents are deceased, You are/were in foster care, you are/were an orphan or a ward/dependent of the court, or you were a ward/dependent of the court until age 18.

D. You have children who will receive more than half their support from you between July 1, 2020 and June 30, 2021 OR you have dependents (other than your children or spouse) who live with you and receive more than half of their support from you, now and through June 30, 2021.

E. You are a graduate or professional school student in 2020–2021.

F. You are married.

G. As of the day you complete the FAFSA, you are an emancipated minor or you are in legal guardianship as determined by a court in your state of legal residence.

H. At any time on or after July 1, 2019 your high school or school district homeless liaison determine that you are an unaccompanied youth who is homeless, the director of an emergency shelter program funded by HUD determined you were an unaccompanied youth who was homeless, or the director of a runaway or homeless youth basic center or transitional living program determine that you were an unaccompanied youth who was homeless or self supporting and at risk of being homeless.

With the exception of certain health profession students whom we discuss in Part Three ("Filling Out the Standardized Forms"), meeting any one of these conditions makes you an independent student for federal aid purposes. However, the schools themselves may have their own, even tougher rules. A few schools (these tend to be the most expensive private colleges) state flat out that if the student is under 22 years old, he is automatically dependent unless both parents are dead.

These schools and others may insist that the parents fill out the parents' information section of the PROFILE form and/or the FAFSA, even if the student meets the federal rules for independence. To find out if this is the case at the schools you are interested in, consult the individual school bulletins. This will also give you an early clue as to whether a school uses the federal definition of independence, or a more rigid definition of their own.

If you don't meet the rules for independence, but have special circumstances, the FAOs have the authority to grant independent status on a case-by-case basis. To convince schools to do this requires extensive documentation. If the student has been abandoned by his parents, letters from a social service agency, court papers, or letters from a guidance counselor or member of the clergy acquainted with the situation may tip the scales.

## If You Meet the Federal Requirements, but Not the School's Requirements

A student can meet the federal requirements for independence without meeting the school's own requirements. In this case, an undergraduate student may qualify for Pell Grants, Stafford loans, and possibly some state aid based on his status as an independent student. The school's own grant money, however, will be awarded based on his status as a dependent student, taking his parents' income and assets into account.

# Independence and Graduate School

Graduate schools generally have more flexible rules about independence, and anyway, graduate students are usually no longer minors. Some graduate schools (particularly law schools and medical schools) will continue to ask for parents' financial information in awarding their own money. Even if the school will not grant independent status, virtually all students will meet the federal guidelines and be eligible for federal aid. The borrowing limits on the Direct Loans rise in graduate school, making these very worthwhile. Graduate students can borrow up to $20,500 per year and even more for certain health profession students. Graduate and professional school students are also able to borrow additional funds under the federally-sponsored GradPLUS Loan Program. This program allows such students to borrow the difference between the Cost of Attendance and any other financial aid (including loans) that have been received. Terms for the GradPLUS are somewhat similar to the PLUS loan for parents.

## Establishing Residency in a State

Establishing residency in another state is probably worthwhile only if the school you want to attend is a public university with lower in-state rates. The difference between in-state and out-of-state rates can be more than $25,000. It is true that in-state residents also may qualify for additional state grant aid available for students who attend public or private colleges, but this will generally be less than $4,000 a year—sometimes a lot less. In addition, most private colleges that meet a student's entire need will replace any money you might have gotten from the state anyway with their own funds. In this case, changing your state of residence is not worth the trouble.

Whether you will be able to pull this off at all is another story. Each state has its own residency requirements and, within those requirements, different rules that govern your eligibility for state grants and your eligibility for in-state tuition rates at a public university. These days, the requirements are usually very tough and they are getting tougher. There are some states, Michigan for example, where a student cannot be considered an in-state resident unless her parents pay taxes and maintain a primary residence in that state. Period. To find out about residency requirements for a school in a particular state, consult the financial aid office at that school.

## Planning Ahead

If you decide you need to do this, you should begin investigating residency requirements even before you apply to schools. Write to the individual state universities to ask about their rules, and set about fulfilling them before the student arrives at college. If the parents live in different states, it might be worth considering with which parent the child should spend the base income year.

# Early Decision, Early Action, Early Notification, Early Read

Some colleges allow students to apply early and find out early whether or not they have been accepted. You are allowed to apply **early decision** to only one school, because your application binds both you and the school. If they decide to admit you, you are committed to attend. The schools like early decision because it helps them to increase their "yield"—the percentage of students they accept who ultimately decide to attend. An early decision candidate must apply by as early as mid-October and will find out if he has been accepted, rejected, or deferred as early as the first week of December.

Early decision applicants may also need to apply early for aid. You should be sure to consult the college's admissions literature for early decision financial aid filing requirements. Provided that you meet your deadlines, you should receive an aid package in the same envelope with your acceptance letter.

**Early action** is an admissions option in which you are notified early of your acceptance but are not bound to attend the school. You have until the normal deadline in May to decide whether to attend. The financial aid package, however, will usually not arrive in your mailbox until April and at many (but not all) schools you usually file for aid as if you were a regular applicant. (Note: some colleges refer to this option as non-binding early decision.)

**Early notification** is offered by many colleges that use rolling admissions. As the admissions committee makes its decisions, it mails out acceptance letters. Generally, you still have until the normal deadline to let the colleges know if you are accepting their offer. You apply for aid as if you were a regular applicant. Financial aid packages may arrive with acceptances or they may come later.

Some of these schools may try to put pressure on you by giving you an early deadline to decide if you are coming. If they are just asking you to accept the financial aid package, that's fine. An acceptance of the aid package does not commit you to attend the school. However, if they are trying to force you to accept their offer of admission before you've heard from your other schools, stall. Call the school and ask for an extension. Make sure you get the name and title of the person you speak to on the phone, and send a "we spoke and you agreed" letter via certified mail to confirm.

# What Are the Financial Aid Implications of These Programs?

**Early decision:** For a high-need or moderate-need family, early decision is a big gamble, because you are effectively giving up your bargaining position. By committing to the school before you know what kind of aid package you will receive, you lose control of the process. It is a bit like agreeing to buy a house without knowing how much it costs. If the school has a good reputation for meeting a family's need in full, then this may be acceptable. However, even if the aid package they offer meets your need completely, you may not like the proportion of loans to grants. The school will have little incentive to improve the aid package since the child is already committed to attending.

If the aid you are offered is insufficient, there is a way to get out of the agreement, but this will leave you with little time to apply to other schools. We recommend that any student who applies to one school early decision should have completely filled out the applications to several other schools in the meantime. If the student is rejected or deferred by the early decision school—or if the aid package is insufficient—then there will still be time to apply to other colleges.

**Early action:** Even if a student is accepted early action, the student should probably still apply to several comparable schools. If one of these schools accepts the student as well, this will provide bargaining leverage with the FAOs, particularly if the second school's aid package is superior.

**Early notification:** The only financial aid implications of early notification occur if you are being squeezed. If a college is putting pressure on you to accept an offer of admission before you have heard from other schools, the college is also taking away your potential to negotiate an improved aid package. Fight back by asking for an extension.

## The Early Read

Some schools say that, as a courtesy, they will figure out your Expected Family Contribution for you early in the fall if you submit your financial data to them—even if you aren't applying to their school. On the face of it, this seems like an offer too good to pass up.

However, you should understand that by letting them perform this early read, you are giving up complete control over the aid process. Your financial data is now set in stone, and if your child applies to that school, there won't be much you can do to change it (in any of the ways we have set forth in this book). We think you are better off figuring out your EFC for yourself using our worksheets, or hiring a financial aid consultant (see Chapter Eleven). Letting the colleges figure out your EFC is a bit like letting the IRS figure your taxes.

# Aid for the Older Student

People who go back to school later in life often say they get more out of the experience the second time. We've found that from a financial aid standpoint, things are actually just about the same. Returnees still have to apply for aid and demonstrate need just like any incoming freshman. They are awarded aid in the same fashion.

The major difference is that they were probably employed at a full-time job during the base income year. If an older student is returning to school full-time, he should point out to the FAOs that there is no way he can earn as much money while he is in school. The first base income year is just not very representative in this case. Older students are probably independent by now, but they should not be surprised if some schools ask for their parents' financial information. Old habits die hard.

Two strategies for older students that should not be overlooked:

1. Let your company pay for it. Many companies have programs that pick up the cost of adult education.

2. Life credits! Some colleges will give you free credits for your life experience. We can't think of a better form of financial aid than that.

# International Students

For students who are not U.S. citizens or eligible noncitizens (see instructions in the standardized need analysis forms), financial aid possibilities are severely limited. No federal aid is given to nonresident aliens. However, the schools themselves are free to give their own grants and scholarships.

You should check with the individual schools to find out their filing requirements. Many colleges require that you complete special aid forms designed solely for international students—even if the student is a U.S. citizen or eligible noncitizen. Some of these colleges will also require a certificate of finance (which is issued by the family's bank certifying how much money the family has) and proof of earnings.

Because you are dealing with the vagaries of *two* separate postal systems, you should begin the application process as early as possible.

*Note: Beginning with the 2010–2011 version, the CSS PROFILE will have special questions for international students so many schools may now require international students to complete the PROFILE form as well.*

## Foreign Tax Returns

The standardized need analysis form is not equipped to deal with foreign currency, so you will have to convert to U.S. dollars, using the exchange rate in effect on the day you fill out the form. There are special instructions in the forms that apply if you fit this category. Some colleges will ask to see your actual tax return, and they will insist that it be translated into English. Believe it or not, there is someone in your country's tax service whose job it is to do this, though it may take a while for you to find him.

*Note: The filing of a foreign tax return by the custodial parent(s) will automatically make a dependent student ineligible for the Simplified Needs Test or Automatic Zero-EFC (see pages 58–61).*

## Study Abroad

There are two general types of study abroad programs:

1.  Programs run by your own college

2.  Programs run by someone else

In the former case, there is usually no problem getting your school to give you the same aid package you would normally receive. While some of these programs are a bit more expensive than a year on campus, the cost is usually not that much greater.

In the latter case, you may have more difficulty. At some schools you may be eligible only for federal aid. To avoid an unpleasant surprise, call on your FAO to find out what the aid consequences of a year abroad in another school's program would be.

# To the Professional

*A word to the guidance counselors, financial planners, stockbrokers, accountants, tax advisors, and tax preparers who may read this book:*

We spoke recently to a broker from one of the big firms who said, "We don't take financial aid into account in our investment advice because . . . well, frankly, we assume that none of our clients are eligible."

This is dangerous thinking. These days lots of people are eligible for financial aid, including (we happen to know) two of his clients. While no one can be an expert at everything, we think it would be a good thing if brokers, accountants, tax advisors, tax lawyers, and counselors knew a bit more about financial aid strategy, or were willing to admit to their client when they didn't know.

Our intent here was to give *the parent and child* an understanding of the aid process and some idea of the possibilities for controlling that process. If you can use this as a resource tool as well, we are just as happy. We would caution you, however, that this book is by no means encyclopedic, and the rules change almost constantly. To be truly on top of the situation you would have to subscribe to industry newsletters, read the *Federal Register,* attend the conventions, develop your own contacts at the colleges, and then take what those contacts tell you with a large measure of salt.

Or you could just hire a consultant to train you to become a financial aid consultant and to keep you abreast of the latest developments. For more details on such training, refer to the "About the Authors" section which follows the Glossary at the back of this book.

# Chapter Ten

## Less Taxing Matters

# The Good News

The Taxpayer Relief Act of 1997 and The Economic Growth and Tax Relief Reconciliation Act of 2001 have given middle-income families some much-needed help in raising their children and paying for the costs of higher education. Unfortunately, the regulations are truly complex and some of the goodies are mutually exclusive. While many provisions did not lapse on January 1, 2013 when they were scheduled to expire, some of these provisions still have not been made permanent. So if they expire in the future, then the old rules prior to 2002 will go back into effect. The purpose of this section is to provide you with basic information regarding some of the benefits now available for education and raising children. For more details, we recommend that you refer to the appropriate IRS publications or consult with a competent professional.

- Coverdell ESAs (formerly called Education IRAs) received an added boost under the 2001 law. Previously, the annual contribution per beneficiary (under the age of 18) was $500 from all sources. Starting in 2002, the annual limit has been increased to $2,000. Though no tax deduction will be granted for these contributions (which must be made in cash), the funds will grow tax-deferred and there will be no taxes owed on withdrawals used to pay for qualified higher education expenses. (The IRS definition of qualified expenses differs for each of the various federal tax benefits and can change from year to year, so be sure to read the fine print.) Withdrawals from Coverdells can also be made tax-free if the funds are used to pay for qualified private elementary and secondary school expenses. Prior to 2002, they could only be used for college or graduate school. The definition of "education" expenses has also been liberalized, so that since 2002 funds can be withdrawn to cover computers, internet access, and some other related expenses. While there are income limits as to who can contribute to a Coverdell, parents with higher incomes may be able to take advantage of a loophole in the law. Since the tax code states that the income limits apply to the "contributor" and does not state that the parent must be the contributor, families may be able to get someone else (whose income is below the limits) to fund the account. Prior to 2002, this benefit phased out between $150,000 and $160,000 for married couples filing jointly, and between $95,000 and $110,000 for others. Starting in 2002, the phase-out range for couples filing jointly increased to $190,000–$220,000. (The phase-out range stayed the same for others.)

- Starting in 2002, withdrawals from qualified state tuition programs (i.e., Section 529 plans which include both pre-paid plans and tuition savings accounts run by state governments) are now tax-free if the funds are used for qualified higher education expenses. This is great news! Prior to January 1, 2002, the increase in value of the plan from the time of the original contribution was subject to federal income taxes at the beneficiary's rate. The 2001 tax law also eliminates one of the major drawbacks of the old 529 plans: namely, the lack of control over how the funds were managed after you contributed to the account. Prior to 2002, once you'd set up an account, the only way to avoid early-withdrawal penalties if you wanted out of the plan was to transfer the funds to another plan AND simultaneously change the beneficiary. You can now switch to another plan once in every 12-month period.

- Since 2003, the annual tax credit parents can receive for each child under the age of 17 is $1,000. This benefit phases out gradually for single parents with an Adjusted Gross Income (AGI) above $75,000 or for married parents filing jointly with an AGI above $110,000. (For married filing separately, the threshold is $55,000.) Currently this is a "refundable credit", so you may be able to claim this benefit even if you have no federal income tax liability.

- Since 2009, parents have been eligible for a federal tax credit up to $2,500 per student per calendar year that is known as the American Opportunity (Tax) Credit or AOTC. (This credit is an expanded and renamed version of the Hope Credit which had been in existence for many years prior to 2009.) To qualify for the maximum AOTC, one must pay at least $4,000 towards qualified expenses as the credit is based on 100% of the first $2,000 in expenses paid during the tax year plus 25% of the next $2,000 in expenses paid. Up to $1,000 of the AOTC per student per year can be refundable. The income phase out ranges for the AOTC are higher than with the prior Hope Credit. For married couples filing jointly, the AOTC begins to phase out once the "Modified Adjusted Gross income" crosses the $160,000 threshold and completely phases out at $180,000. For others, the corresponding income amounts are $80,000 and $90,000 respectively. (Modified AGI is a taxpayer's AGI increased by any foreign income that was excluded.) Be aware that married parents who file separately are not eligible to claim any of the federal education tax credits which include the AOTC and the Hope Credit as well as the Lifetime Learning Credit which will be discussed shortly. The American Opportunity Credit is available for only the first four years of undergraduate postsecondary education for a given student (including any years the Hope Credit was claimed for that same student.) A student who pays for her own educational expenses may also be eligible for this credit, provided she is not claimed as a dependent on someone else's tax return. However, whether you or the student will be able to claim this credit beyond 2017 will depend if this provision of the tax code is extended.

- In addition to the AOTC, there is currently another education tax credit known as the Lifetime Learning Credit or LLC. Starting in 2003, the amount of this non-refundable credit is equal to 20% of the first $10,000 of qualified expenses paid each tax year. (Prior to 2003, the Lifetime Learning Credit was limited to 20% of the first $5,000 of educational expenses paid each tax year.) For 2016, the LLC phases out gradually for married parents filing jointly with Modified AGIs between $112,000 and $132,000, and for others with Modified AGIs between $56,000 and $65,000. (These income numbers are adjusted annually for inflation.) Unlike the 4-year American Opportunity Credit, the Lifetime Learning Credit can be claimed for an unlimited number of tax years provided one meets all the other criteria. It is therefore possible for a parent to take this credit for a few years, provided he claims the child as a dependent on his tax return. Years later, the student herself could claim the Lifetime Learning Credit on her own tax return if she goes back to school and meets the other criteria for the credit. In contrast to the AOTC, the Lifetime Learning Credit can also be used for graduate studies.

- Note: For most (but not all) taxpayers, claiming the American Opportunity Credit will result in a larger tax benefit than claiming the Lifetime Learning Credit. However, given the fine print and differing eligibility criteria, you (or your tax preparer) should still do the math and compare the results just to be sure.

- It is important to note that the above two tax benefits involve tax credits and not merely deductions against your taxable income. As such, they are much more valuable since they reduce your tax liability dollar-for-dollar. While the American Opportunity Credit can be claimed for each qualifying child in the same tax year, the maximum amount of the Lifetime Learning Credit you can take each year will not vary based upon the number of students in college. In determining the size of the credit, qualifying educational expenses will only represent "out-of-pocket" costs paid. So, for example, scholarships and grants that are awarded will reduce the amount of educational expenses used to determine the size of the credit. In many cases however, expenses paid from the proceeds of a loan will qualify as out-of-pocket expenses. This is true even if the expenses were "paid" with a student loan as the regulations focus on the amount of expenses paid but not necessarily who paid them. Unlike the LLC in which expenses are limited to tuition and mandatory fees as a condition of enrollment, for the AOTC expenses can include required "course materials" (i.e. books, supplies, and equipment) and possibly even a computer if the computer is needed as a condition of enrollment.

- There is also a waiver of the 10% penalty on withdrawals from regular IRAs and Roth IRAs prior to age 59 1/2, provided the withdrawals are used to pay qualified post-secondary education expenses. Withdrawals can cover your own educational expenses (including grad school) as well as those of your spouse, child, or grandchild. Withdrawals from traditional IRAs will, of course, still be considered part of your taxable income. The section of the tax code pertaining to withdrawals from Roth IRAs is more complicated. While there are no special provisions regarding higher education expenses, distributions of the original contributions to Roth IRAs are not subject to tax or penalty. Distributions involving the earnings in a Roth IRA are, however, subject to taxes unless other criteria are met. (For example, the distribution is made five years after the initial contribution and the taxpayer is at least 59 1/2 years of age.) It is assumed that the first dollars distributed represent the initial contribution to the Roth IRA. Because the rules regarding IRAs and Roth IRAs contain so much fine print, you should consult the appropriate IRS publications or a professional tax advisor if you are contemplating any distributions from these plans. And remember, any distributions (other than rollovers) from retirement accounts are required to be reported as income on the FAFSA and PROFILE whether taxable or not.

- The 2001 tax law also expanded the availability of the deduction of student loan interest paid on qualified educational loans. Taxpayers will still not need to itemize deductions to claim this benefit, which increased to $2,500 in 2002 and beyond. The income limits for the full deduction are currently $65,000 for single filers and $130,000 for joint returns. The maximum amount of the deduction will then gradually phase out until the income reaches the upper limits of $80,000 and $160,000, respectively. (Prior to 2002, the phase-out limits were $40,000 to $55,000 for single filers, and $60,000 to $75,000 for married filing jointly.) Since 2002, this deduction is now no longer limited to the first 60 months in which interest payments were required as it was under the prior law. These changes will mean that more taxpayers are able to claim this deduction for a longer period of time. Qualifying educational loans can be those incurred to cover your own post-secondary expenses, as well as those of your spouse or any other dependent at the time the loan was taken out. If you are claimed as a dependent on someone else's tax return for a particular year, however, you cannot claim this deduction.

And now . . .

# The Bad News

When the Economic Growth and Tax Relief Reconciliation Act of 2001 was first enacted, politicians from both sides of the aisle were patting themselves on the back. But now that the dust has settled, the truth of the matter is that the changes have been so complicated that many experts have stated that the major beneficiaries of all these changes are the tax preparers and accountants across the country.

We used to tell our clients to look before they leapt. Since 2002, we now tell them to look both ways, since the 2001 tax law and subsequent legislation are anything but tax simplification. Some of the provisions may still expire in a few years. And given the constant budget battles in Congress, there is nothing to prevent new legislation form being introduced that would impact some of these educational tax benefits.

*Note: Unlike many of the other provisions which are scheduled to sunset sometime in future, legislation was enacted in 2006 to permanently extend the provisions regarding tax-free distributions from 529 plans, provided the funds are used for qualified higher education expenses. Recent legislation has also made many provisions permanent involving Coverdell Education Savings Accounts.*

# Going . . .

Though the income restrictions on many of these benefits have been liberalized, many families are going to discover that they still don't qualify for them. Indeed, whenever news breaks about new or enhanced education tax breaks, a number of our clients will call to ask what we think already assuming the increased benefits will apply to them. We often have to burst their bubbles and tell them they won't be able to qualify because their income is too high or they do not meet all the criteria.

Many families who could qualify may also fail to get the maximum benefits simply because they don't understand all the fine print. The regulations are rather extensive and the timing of certain transactions is very important. For example, let's say your child will be graduating at the end of the 2017–2018 academic year. If you're overly eager and pay the spring 2018 tuition bill as soon as you get it in mid-December 2017 (instead of waiting until January 10, 2017 when it's due), you won't be able to claim the American Opportunity Credit or Lifetime Learning Credit in 2018 for that child simply because you paid the money too soon. That mistake might have cost you as much as $2,500 as you can only claim the credit for the tax year in which you make the payment.  If the college insists on payment before you sing "Auld Lang Syne", consider going on a payment plan for the final semester. Installment payments made after the new tax year begins may allow you to claim the credits for another tax year, provided you meet all the other criteria.

There's also the linkage among the different provisions. To prevent some tax-payers from hitting the jackpot, the benefit you receive from one of the tax benefits can often eliminate your eligibility for other goodies. For example, you can't claim both the American Opportunity Credit and the Lifetime Learning Credit during the same tax year for educational expenses paid for the same child. You can, however, claim the American Opportunity Credit for one undergraduate student and the Lifetime Learning Credit for an older sibling in graduate school on the same year's tax return (provided you meet all the other criteria). In addition for the tax year 2002 and beyond: if you claim the American Opportunity Credit or the Lifetime Learning Credit for expenses paid with funds withdrawn from a section 529 plan or Coverdell ESA, part or all of the funds withdrawn may no longer qualify for tax-free treatment unless  you forego claiming the credit. You can still withdraw funds from these plans and claim an education tax credit for the same student in the same tax year, but you'll have to pay some of the qualified expenses (as defined by the IRS for the credit you are claiming) with funds from other accounts and/or loans. Finally, many of the provisions are not available to married couples who file separate returns.

# . . . Going . . .

Then there is the impact of these provisions on financial aid. For example, the Lifetime Learning Credit and any non-refundable portion of the American Opportunity Credit will reduce your aid eligibility under the institutional methodology. Since these credits reduce your U.S. income taxes paid (an expense item in the IM formula), your available income will be higher and so your IM EFC will go up as well. While the amount of the credit will still be greater than the amount of aid that is lost, the value to you of those credits is reduced under the institutional formula for any base income year.

Other provisions are potential financial aid traps. As mentioned earlier in this book, distributions from IRAs and other retirement accounts (other than rollovers) boost your income, thereby reducing your aid eligibility. It also remains to be seen how some IRA withdrawals will impact eligibility. Will a grandmother's penalty-free withdrawal from a regular IRA to pay for her grandson's education be considered? Will the conversion of a regular IRA to a Roth IRA be considered a special circumstance taken into account by an FAO when awarding aid? Because these provisions often change from year to year, the Department of Education, the College Scholarship Service, and most college financial aid offices still have not finalized their policies as to how to handle most of these items. We will of course provide updates on our website (www.princetonreview.com/financialaidupdate) if more details become available. In the meantime, we suggest that those families who are interested in maximizing aid eligibility avoid discretionary withdrawals from retirement accounts until the rules are clarified or until they are out of the base income years.

Reminder: Most traditional financial advisors (e.g., accountants, financial planners, attorneys, stockbrokers, etc.) rarely take financial aid implications into account when making recommendations. Now more than ever before, you should investigate how such advice will affect your aid eligibility before you proceed.

# . . . Gone

Even if you qualify for these benefits and are still ahead of the game after factoring in the reduced aid, the various tax provisions may still not save you any money by the ninth inning. For the big question still remains: "Will these tax benefits save you any money in the long run?" For while many families are saving money on their taxes, many colleges have realized that fact and have just raised their tuition even higher to follow suit. So the jury is still out on how much these provisions will actually help any family or student pay for college.

# Chapter Eleven

## Looking for a Financial Aid Consulting Service

# Looking for a Financial Aid Consultant

At this point you may be rubbing your hands together and saying:

"I'm ready. Bring on those need analysis forms!" or you may be saying:

"I'd rather eat cement than ever look at those forms."

You know quite a lot about the financial aid process and you know how to take control of that process. You also know yourself, and if you don't want to get any more familiar with this subject than you already are, you can hire someone to do it for you.

## What a Financial Aid Consultant Does

A good financial aid consultant will do far more than simply fill out the forms. Anyone can throw together numbers on a paper. Principally, you hire a consultant to examine your entire financial situation ahead of time and make recommendations to increase your aid eligibility. A good consultant will know the specific rules that govern aid in your state, will be up to date on the constantly changing regulations that govern tax law and financial aid, and will assist you to complete the forms to maximize your aid eligibility.

There are several different kinds of professionals who may offer their services to guide you through the financial aid process: accountants, financial planners, tax lawyers, tax advisors, and financial aid consultants (who specialize in this field alone).

## Why Your Accountant May Say He Is Willing to Do the Form Even If He Doesn't Want To

Accountants want you to come back to see them next year. Even if your accountant hates preparing need analysis forms and even if he knows very little about the financial aid process, he will probably tell you that he'll do the forms for you. He's afraid that if he says no, you'll go to another accountant and he'll lose your regular business.

## Why You May Not Want to Let Him

At stake are tens of thousands of dollars. You do not want to be your accountant's guinea pig. If your need analysis form is his first, or even his tenth, you may not get the best aid package possible.

Of course there are accountants, tax lawyers, and financial planners who have made it their business to learn the ins and outs of financial aid. The problem is finding out whether you are dealing with one of these knowledgeable experts or a rank beginner *before* you place your child's future in his hands. How do you find a competent person?

# Ask Your Friends for Referrals

There is no licensing organization in this field, and asking your local Better Business Bureau about prospects will only reveal the most egregiously bad apples. The best way to find a good aid consultant is to ask your friends for a referral. This is far better than responding to an unsolicited sales pitch you receive in the mail or by phone. Some questions to ask your friends:

- Did the consultant give them the forms in time to meet deadlines?

- Was he available throughout the year for planning?

- Did he give them an idea of what their Expected Family Contribution would be, and was it reasonably correct?

- Did he provide them with strategies to maximize aid for the coming year?

It's always hard to know what kind of packages a family would have received had they *not* gone to a professional for help, which makes objective comparison difficult. However, if your friends came away from the experience feeling that the professional knew the process inside and out and that they had been well taken care of, then you are probably in good hands.

Fees can be expensive, but if a professional can find ways to increase your aid eligibility by thousands of dollars, even a relatively expensive fee is a bargain.

Be cautious with professionals who try to sell you financial products. They may be more interested in selling you financial investment instruments you may or may not need than in getting you the most aid. You should also be suspicious if a consultant promises that you'll receive a certain amount of aid before reviewing your situation. And pass immediately on any professional who tries to steer you toward anything illegal. Please report any unprofessional behavior to the Better Business Bureau immediately.

## Some Questions to Ask the Professional

Before you engage anyone to give you financial aid advice, you might want to ask a few of the following questions:

- What is the name of the state grants awarded here in _____?

Any professional who does financial aid consulting should certainly know the name of the state grants offered by your home state. Each state calls its grants something else, and each state has its own set of rules as to who qualifies for these grants. If the professional doesn't even know the names of the grants, he probably doesn't know the rules under which they are dispensed either.

- Should we put assets in the child's name?

A competent professional should know that student's assets are assessed at a much higher rate than parents' assets. If the family is eligible for aid, putting money in the child's name can be a very expensive mistake.

- Which year's income and assets do the colleges look at?

To determine what a family can afford to pay for college in the academic year of 2019–2020, for example, the colleges look at the income from the *prior-prior* year; in this case, 2017. They look at assets as of the day the need analysis form is completed.

- What is the difference between a Stafford loan and a PLUS loan?

Both are sponsored by the federal government, but the Stafford loan is made to students, while the PLUS loan is made to parents.

- Could you explain a couple of terms for us?

Go to the glossary and pick a few terms at random. An experienced professional should have no difficulty defining those terms.

## One Question Not to Ask:

- Could you tell us if we qualify for aid?

Of course this is the one question you really want answered, but no competent consultant could answer this question without a detailed analysis of your situation.

# Chapter Twelve

## Looking Ahead

# Future Trends in College Finance

The world of financial aid and college finance is always in flux. Making any predictions whatsoever is dangerous. However, it is safe to say that college tuitions will continue to rise at a rate faster than that of overall inflation. And now more than ever before, there is a huge difference between just applying, and applying smart. The aid is still available, but the mechanics of securing it will continue to become more complicated with more hurdles than ever before.

## The Prior-Prior Year

One of those hurdles: the decision to change the timing of the all-important "snapshot" that the FAFSA and if applicable the PROFILE, asks you to take of your finances. By changing that first snapshot from the year before the student enters college (known as the "Prior year" or PY) to two years before the student enters college (known as the "Prior-prior year" or PPY) the U.S. Department of Education as well as the school and have enhanced their ability to require more extensive documentation ensuring the validity of student and parent information. In the past, much work was spent in the aid offices resolving discrepancies between estimated PY income reported on the aid forms and the actual PY income figures on completed tax returns. So with this administrative burden sharply reduced, the U.S. Dept of Education could require college aid officers to spend more of their time verifying other data elements besides the PPY income reported on tax returns.

## Identity Theft

Another hurdle has occurred due to advances in technology. As the financial aid forms have moved online (from the paper and snail-mail route), the dangers of cyber theft and identity theft have greatly increased. Because the aid forms contain your entire financial history, dates of birth for various and social security numbers for the student and any custodial parent or stepparent required to report their finances on the FAFSA, it's important than ever to take all precautions to make sure your passwords are robust and that you keep any log-in information secure. Unfortunately, the Department of Education still uses the student's social security number as an identifier for colleges to retrieve students' processed FAFSA information. This means that prospective students using the Common Application for their admissions purposes will need to enter their social security number on the Common App if they are applying for aid at any school(s) that accepts that admissions form. Otherwise, such schools will not be able to find the student's processed FAFSA data on their system.

Because the aid forms and supporting documents contain social security number and other valuable information to identity thieves, one cannot be careful enough. To better protect yourself and your significant others, keep these following tips in mind:

Do not send copies of tax return files by email. It is more secure to send them by fax or even postal mail—unless you are uploading the documents to a school using their own secured school document system or the school is using a third party app such as the College Board's IDOC service.

Remember that neither the government, the College Board, nor the colleges will EVER ask you to provide a password in response to an email.

# The Rise of "Free" Tuition

A few states have offered free tuition for community college for some time—but in the spring of 2017, New York became the first state to offer free tuition for up to four years of college (i.e. through the first bachelor's degree). This is, of course, great news—and more states may follow. But while these announcements get a lot of headlines, it is important to understand that going to these schools is by no means free. For example, in New York, this offer only covers tuition, not room and board, books, etc. etc. And at most state universities, it turns out that room and board expenses are higher than the tuition itself. There may also be bundles of string attached to such awards. So be sure to read all the fine print about qualifying for such funds and maintaining eligibility, as well as if there are any requirements that must be met after leaving school. You should also be aware of the maximum benefit that can be awarded under the state program.

# FM and IM Divergence

Even though federal regulations have become more liberal over the last few years in terms of defining a student's "need" (for example, assessing prepaid 529 funds as assets instead of a "resource" that reduced aid dollar-for-dollar by the amount of the withdrawal, and allowing the protection of assets tied to "family businesses"), more and more colleges are becoming increasingly conservative when it comes to awarding their own funds. More and more schools are asking additional questions about the existence of (and distributions from) 529 plans that are owned by individuals other than the student's parents (such as a rich aunt, or grandparent). Even though such 529 plans do not have to be reported on the aid form as an asset, colleges want to know about them, taking the position that a student with a sizable 529 plan funded by Aunt Mary should obviously be in a position to pay more.

## The Importance of Planning Ahead

If history has taught us anything, it is that it is never too early to start planning ahead for college costs. At whatever stage you are reading this book, there are some tangible strategies you can use to help take control of the financial aid process and minimize college costs. The purpose of this book has been to show you those strategies. We hope they will make the dream of a college education a reality.

Good luck!

# Part Five

## Worksheets and Forms

# Calculating Your Expected Family Contribution

We realize that the pages of worksheets and tables that follow may seem a little intimidating. There are some books out there that claim you can calculate your EFC by consulting a single table that has been prepared by the book's author. Unfortunately, these tables ask for such vague information from the parent that they do not provide an accurate estimation in the end. The calculators on various websites are all too frequently out-of-date or use flawed logic and result in a case of "garbage in-garbage out."

When you fill out your need analysis form, you provide the processor with very specific information, but you will not be required to complete a worksheet such as this. The processor simply plugs your information into a computer program that automatically does all the calculations we are about to show you.

## So Why Should You Bother to Go Through These Worksheets at All?

There are two excellent reasons.

First, by making the calculations yourself, you will be able to see how the process works; it is amazing how small changes in the way you list your financial information can produce big changes in the final result.

Second, by having an *accurate* idea of what your Expected Family Contribution will be, you can make informed decisions about which schools to apply to, how to answer questions on the individual school aid forms like, "How much do you think you can afford to pay for college?," and what early steps you can take for next year.

## Ughhhh

If these worksheets fill you with dread, you can always hire an independent financial aid consultant to do these calculations for you. Details on how to find one are in Chapter Eleven.

## The Standard Disclaimer

While we believe that these worksheets and tables are accurate, they have not been approved by the U.S. Department of Education. In addition, the worksheets and tables regarding calculation of income have not been approved by the IRS and should not be used to calculate your tax liability for your income tax return.

# Worksheet for Calculating the Expected Family Contribution for a Dependent Student

Please note that by TAXABLE INCOME, we mean income that the IRS considers subject to possible taxation, even if the IRS does not require that a tax return be filed because the income is below a minimum level determined by them. As such, it is possible to pay no tax on a small amount of taxable income. UNTAXED INCOME or NONTAXABLE INCOME refers to income that is never subject to income tax. Some income items, such as social security benefits, can be considered either taxable income or untaxed income, depending on the taxpayer's total income.

Unless otherwise indicated, all references in this worksheet to specific IRS line numbers relate to those lines of the 2018 IRS 1040 form. To avoid confusion, we suggest that you refer to Chapter Three for more detailed descriptions of these various items. If the student's biological or adoptive parents are living apart, please consult page 167 if you are unsure whose income should be listed on this worksheet.

The worksheets and tables that follow are based on the current formula for calculating the EFC for the 2020–2021 academic year.

If you meet all of the criteria for the Simplified Needs Test (see pages 58–61), you can calculate your EFC under the simplified formula by listing zero on Line O of the Parents' Worksheet and on Line GG of the Student's Worksheet. However, we recommend that you also calculate your EFC using asset information since some schools do not use the simplified formula when awarding their own aid funds.

Some helpful tips for completing the worksheets:

1.  Round off all figures to the nearest dollar.

2.  All income/expense items relate to yearly amounts. Do not use monthly or weekly figures. All asset/liability items relate to current amounts.

3.  Since the 2020–2021 EFC will be using "prior-prior-year" income (see pages 55–56), all references to income on the Tables and Worksheets that follow should be completed using 2018 income amounts. Most likely by the time you are completing these Tables, you will have already completed the 2018 Federal income tax returns if required to file a return. If that is the case for the student's parents (or parent and stepparent) required to report information on the FAFSA, then most likely you can skip the calculations for Tables 3 and 6. Simply go to the last line of that respective Table and just list the dollar amount reported on the corresponding line of your U.S. individual income tax return(s). If separate returns were filed for 2018 by the custodial parent(s)—or the custodial parent and stepparent—reporting information on the FAFSA, list the combined dollar

amounts from both adults' tax returns (See page 167 if you are unsure which parent(s)' information is to be reported on the FAFSA.) And please remember that one's marital status for purposes of the FAFSA is the status as the date the FAFSA is filed, not the status at any time during the prior-prior year or prior year.

**Exception:** If 2018 federal tax individual income tax returns were completed as married filing jointly and the custodial parent is now separated, divorced or widowed from that other adult, then the entire Table 3 should be completed using only the custodial parent's share of the respective items to determine the custodial parent's share of the Adjusted Gross Income (AGI). To calculate the last line for Table 6: use the proportionate share of the AGI that you listed on Line C of Table 3. Divide that number by the joint AGI figure reported on the actual tax return. The number you have just calculated should then by multiplied by the combined amount of U.S. Taxes paid on the joint return (using the applicable IRS line item referenced for the last line of Table 6) to determine the custodial parent's share of the U.S. taxes paid that you will list on the last line of Table 6.

4.  Tables 1 through 7 as well as Table 9 and Table 11 (if applicable) must be completed (in order) *before* you can begin work on the Parents' Expected Contribution worksheet. The bottom lines from Tables 5 through 7 as well as Table 9 and 11 will be entered on the appropriate section of that worksheet. Table 8, Table 10, Table 12, and Table 13 should be utilized *as* you are completing that worksheet. Table 14 should be completed *before* you begin work on the Student's Expected Contribution worksheet.

5.  When completing Tables 1 and 2, be sure to enter the appropriate amounts under the proper column. Do not combine the amounts into one column, as this will give you an incorrect estimate of your Family Contribution.

6.  Any number listed in parentheses should be subtracted from the number in the same column above it.

7.  The earnings portion of any qualified withdrawals from Coverdell ESAs (Education IRAs) and Section 529 state savings accounts as well as the increase in the value of any tuition credits redeemed since the time of purchase for Section 529 prepaid plans will not be considered as part of the student's or parent's non-taxable income. Therefore, do not include any "earnings" from these accounts as part of your untaxed income in Table 4 or as part of "All other income of student and spouse" on the Student's Expected Contribution Worksheet.

8.  We suggest that you check your math. Even better, you should consider having another family member review your completed tables and worksheets for accuracy. Even if your family contribution figures are higher than the cost of attendance, you should still consider applying for aid since the FAOs may take other factors into account, you may

be eligible for state aid benefits not based on these formulas, and/or you may have made an error in your calculations when doing these worksheets.

9. Prior to the 2011 edition, we always included worksheets to calculate the expected family contribution (EFC) under both the Institutional Methodology (IM) as well as the Federal Methodology (FM). However, in a change of policy, the College Board is no longer providing anyone with the tables and formulas to calculate the EFC under the IM. However, they have agreed to provide us with calculations of the EFC using the IM for some sample case studies along with the impact that some institutional options involving the home can have on the basic IM EFC number. A comparative calculation of the EFC in the federal methodology is provided as well. However, keep in mind that small changes to one's situation can result in significant changes to the EFC in either formula. As such, these case studies should be used for informational purposes only. The EFC figures provided should not be relied on as an exact number of what your EFC will be, even if you believe your own situation is rather similar. These sample case studies and some additional comments regarding the IM appear in the Appendix of this book.

## Analyzing Your Numbers

Instead of thinking of the EFC as a definitive number for the amount you will be expected to pay towards college in a given year, you should think of the Parents' Expected Contribution on Line R (page 318) and the Student's Expected Contribution on Line JJ (page 322) as rough approximations for financial aid planning purposes. Until you receive a finalized award package from a school, it is impossible to know for certain the final number for what you will need to contribute. So instead of thinking of absolutes, it would be better to think in terms of probabilities. For example, if the EFC you calculate is quite a bit lower than the Cost of Attendance for the applicable school(s) under consideration, it would be better to focus on using those applicable strategies outlined earlier in the book to lower your EFC and complete the aid forms. This will increase the probability of your receiving more aid and will be more beneficial than trying to figure out exactly how much aid you will receive before admission and aid decisions are known. Similarly, if your EFC is significantly higher than the cost of attendance for all schools under consideration, then it is unlikely—though not certain—that you will receive any need-based funds in a given year. While you should still apply for aid (as strange things sometimes can happen with the aid process), you should also have a backup plan (i.e., applying to lower cost schools and/or to schools where there is a high probability the student will receive merit-based aid). And if in future years there will be an increase or decrease in the number of family members in college, then you should take subsequent years' aid probabilities into account based on the differing number of students attending college.

# TABLE 1
## Parents' Income Earned From Work

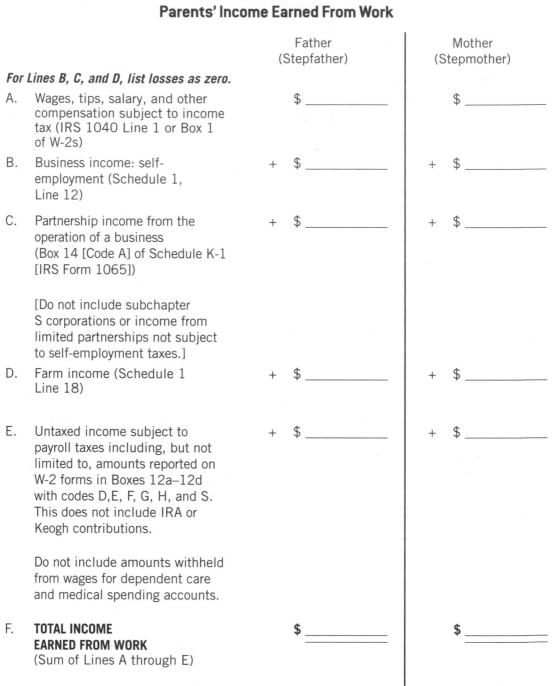

|  |  | Father (Stepfather) | Mother (Stepmother) |
|---|---|---|---|
| *For Lines B, C, and D, list losses as zero.* |  |  |  |
| A. | Wages, tips, salary, and other compensation subject to income tax (IRS 1040 Line 1 or Box 1 of W-2s) | $ _____ | $ _____ |
| B. | Business income: self-employment (Schedule 1, Line 12) | + $ _____ | + $ _____ |
| C. | Partnership income from the operation of a business (Box 14 [Code A] of Schedule K-1 [IRS Form 1065]) [Do not include subchapter S corporations or income from limited partnerships not subject to self-employment taxes.] | + $ _____ | + $ _____ |
| D. | Farm income (Schedule 1 Line 18) | + $ _____ | + $ _____ |
| E. | Untaxed income subject to payroll taxes including, but not limited to, amounts reported on W-2 forms in Boxes 12a–12d with codes D,E, F, G, H, and S. This does not include IRA or Keogh contributions. Do not include amounts withheld from wages for dependent care and medical spending accounts. | + $ _____ | + $ _____ |
| F. | **TOTAL INCOME EARNED FROM WORK** (Sum of Lines A through E) | $ _____ | $ _____ |

**Notes for servicemen and servicewomen who receive combat pay**

If you receive combat pay, you should be sure that the total amount of any combat pay received is included as part of the Total Income Earned From Work (Line F), if such pay is included in Box 3 or 5 of the W-2 form.

**If you filed or will file a tax return:** Include any taxable combat pay as part of your Adjusted Gross Income (Table 3). Include any such taxable pay that is part of your AGI on the applicable line on Table 5A.

**If you will not file a tax return:** Do not include any combat pay in Table 4.

Do not include any untaxed combat pay reported on the W-2 form in Box 12, Code Q on any Table.

## TABLE 2
## Student's (and Spouse's) Income Earned from Work

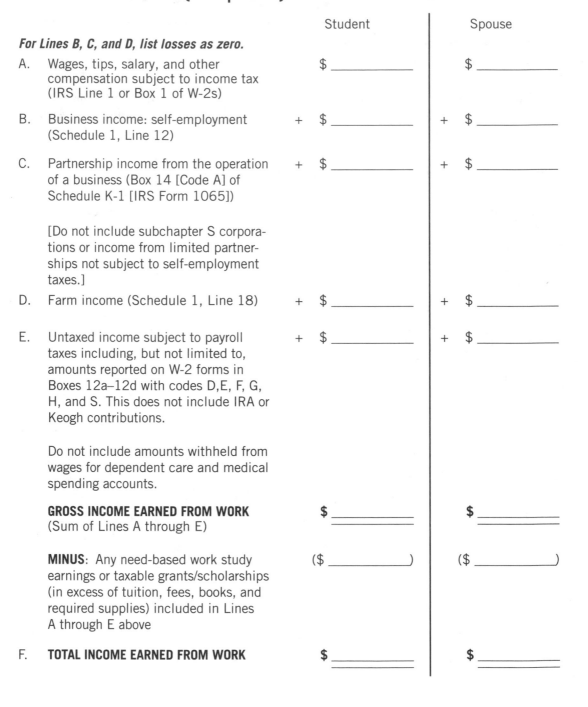

|  |  | Student | Spouse |
|---|---|---|---|
| *For Lines B, C, and D, list losses as zero.* | | | |
| A. | Wages, tips, salary, and other compensation subject to income tax (IRS Line 1 or Box 1 of W-2s) | $ _____ | $ _____ |
| B. | Business income: self-employment (Schedule 1, Line 12) | + $ _____ | + $ _____ |
| C. | Partnership income from the operation of a business (Box 14 [Code A] of Schedule K-1 [IRS Form 1065]) [Do not include subchapter S corporations or income from limited partnerships not subject to self-employment taxes.] | + $ _____ | + $ _____ |
| D. | Farm income (Schedule 1, Line 18) | + $ _____ | + $ _____ |
| E. | Untaxed income subject to payroll taxes including, but not limited to, amounts reported on W-2 forms in Boxes 12a–12d with codes D,E, F, G, H, and S. This does not include IRA or Keogh contributions. Do not include amounts withheld from wages for dependent care and medical spending accounts. | + $ _____ | + $ _____ |
| | **GROSS INCOME EARNED FROM WORK** (Sum of Lines A through E) | $ _____ | $ _____ |
| | **MINUS**: Any need-based work study earnings or taxable grants/scholarships (in excess of tuition, fees, books, and required supplies) included in Lines A through E above | ($ _____ ) | ($ _____ ) |
| F. | **TOTAL INCOME EARNED FROM WORK** | $ _____ | $ _____ |

# TABLE 3
## Adjusted Gross Income

If no parent (stepparent) in the household will file a tax return, you should do the following:

- Skip Table 3

- List the sum of both columns for Total Income Earned From Work (Table 1—Line F ) on Table 5—Line A. If no parent (stepparent) in the household had income earned from work, then list 0 (zero) for Table 5—Line A.

- Include any unearned income (i.e. any income other than income earned from work that you included in Table 1) as part of your total for Table 4.

As such  for non-filers:  your total income will be the sum of income earned from work and any other income that you received. You should make sure that you do not double-count any income.

For tax filers: refer to item 3 on page 278.

**Helpful hint:** List losses, if any, in parentheses and subtract them.

**Sum of:**

| | | |
|---|---|---|
| Father's taxable wages, tips, salary, etc. *(From Line A for Father [Stepfather] on Table 1)* | | $ _____ |
| Mother's taxable wages, tips, salary, etc. *(From Line A for Mother [Stepmother] on Table 1)* | + | $ _____ |
| Taxable interest (IRS Line 2b) | + | $ _____ |
| Dividend income (IRS Line 3b) | + | $ _____ |
| Taxable refunds of state and local income taxes, if any (Schedule 1, Line 10) | + | $ _____ |
| Alimony received (Schedule 1, Line 11) | + | $ _____ |
| Father and/or mother's income or (loss) from self-employment (Schedule 1, Line 12) | + | $ _____ |
| Capital gain or (loss) (Schedule 1, Line 13) | + | $ _____ |
| Other gains or (losses) (Schedule 1, Line 14) | + | $ _____ |
| Taxable IRA distributions, pensions, and annuities (IRS Line 4b) | + | $ _____ |
| Rents, royalties, estates, partnerships, and trusts, etc. (Schedule 1, Line 17) | + | $ _____ |
| Farm income or (loss) (Schedule 1, Line 18) | + | $ _____ |
| Unemployment compensation (Schedule 1, Line 19) | + | $ _____ |
| Taxable social security benefits (IRS Line 5b) | + | $ _____ |
| Other taxable income (Schedule 1, Line 21) | + | $ _____ |

**A. Gross Income**                    $ _____

**A. Gross Income (Line A from previous page)**     $ _____

## ADJUSTMENTS TO INCOME

**Sum of:**

Educator expenses (Schedule 1, Line 23)     $ _____

Certain business expenses for reservists, performing artists, and fee-basis government officials (Schedule 1, Line 24)     +  $ _____

Health savings account deduction (Schedule 1, Line 25)     +  $ _____

Moving expenses (Schedule 1, Line 26)     +  $ _____

Deductible part of self-employment tax (Schedule 1, Line 27)     +  $ _____

Self-employed SEP, SIMPLE, and qualified plans (Schedule 1, Line 28)     +  $ _____

Self-employed health insurance deduction (Schedule 1, Line 29)     +  $ _____

Penalty on early withdrawal of savings (Schedule 1, Line 30)     +  $ _____

Alimony paid (Schedule 1, Line 31a)     +  $ _____

IRA deductible contributions (Schedule 1, Line 32)     +  $ _____

Student loan interest deduction (Schedule 1, Line 33)     +  $ _____

Other write-in adjustments not reported on Schedule 1, Lines 23–33 (per above), but included as part of Line 36     +  $ _____

**B. Total Adjustments (Schedule 1 Line 36)**     ($ _____ )

**C. ADJUSTED GROSS INCOME**     $ _____
*(Gross Income [Line A] minus Total Adjustments [Line B])*
2018 IRS 1040, Line 7

# TABLE 4
## Parents' Untaxed Income

**Sum of:**

Payments to tax-deferred pension and savings plans (paid directly or withheld from earnings including, but not limited to, amounts reported on W-2 forms in Boxes 12a-12d with codes D, E, F, G, H, and S.) (See pages 78–79)        $ _____

Deductible IRA, SEP, SIMPLE, Keogh payments (Schedule 1, 1040, total Lines 28 and 32)        + $ _____

Child Support received for all children        + $ _____

Tax-exempt interest income (IRS 1040, Line 2a)        + $ _____

Untaxed portions of IRA, pension, and annuity distributions (IRS Line 4a minus 4b [excluding rollovers])        + $ _____

Housing, food, and other living allowances (excluding rent subsidies for low-income housing) paid to members of the military, clergy, and others (including cash payments and cash value of benefits)        + $ _____

Veterans' noneducational benefits such as death pension, and dependency and indemnity compensation (DIC), etc.        + $ _____

Untaxed workers compensation, disability        + $ _____

Deductible payments to Health Savings Accounts (Schedule 1, 1040 Line 25)        + $ _____

Any other untaxed income and benefits, such as Black Lung Benefits, Refugee Assistance, untaxed portions of Railroad Retirement benefits, or Job Training Partnership Act noneducational benefits. (See notes below.)        + $ _____

**D. TOTAL UNTAXED INCOME**        $ _____

**Do not include** extended foster care benefits, student aid, earned income credit, additional child tax credit, welfare payments, untaxed Social Security benefits, Supplemental Security Income, Workforce Investment Act educational benefits, on-base military housing or a military housing allowance, combat pay, benefits from flexible spending arrangements (e.g., cafeteria plans), foreign income exclusion, or credit for federal tax on special fuels.

# TABLE 5
## Parents' Total Income

A.  Parents' Adjusted Gross Income          $ _____
    *(From Table 3—Line C)*

B.  Parents' Total Untaxed Income        +  $ _____
    *(Appropriate column from Table 4–Line D)*

C.  **Subtotal**                            $ _____

D.  Title IV Income Exclusions           ($ _____ )
    (From Table 5A below.
    If no Exclusions, enter -0-.)

E.  **PARENTS' TOTAL INCOME**               $ _____
    *(Line C minus D)*
    (This figure will be listed at the top
    of the Parents' Expected Contribution
    Worksheet [Line G on page 317].)
    Can be a negative number.

# TABLE 5A
## Title IV Income Exclusions

**Sum of:**

Child Support PAID
Education tax credits (IRS 1040, Schedule 3, Line 50)*    $ _____

Parents' taxable earnings from need-based              +  $ _____
employment programs, such as Federal
Work-Study and need-based employment
portions of fellowships/assistanceships as
well as earnings from any co-op program

Parents' grant and scholarship aid                     +  $ _____
included in adjusted gross income.
(Include AmeriCorps benefits, as well as
grant or scholarship portions of fellowships
and assistanceships)

Taxable combat pay or special combat pay included in the AGI.  +  $ _____
(tax filers only)

**Total Exclusions**                                       $ _____
*(This figure will be listed on Line F in Table 5 above)*

* **Do not include** any refundable American Opportunity credits (IRS 1040, Line 17, item c).

# TABLE 6
## U.S. Income Taxes Paid

Adjusted Gross Income (from Table 3—Line C)                                 $ _____

**Minus:** Total Itemized Deductions                                        ($ _____ )
(same as the bottom line on Schedule A
of IRS 1040)
(If you do not/will not itemize deductions, use the following numbers based
on your tax filing status:                                                  $ _____

    Single—$12,000
    Head of Household—$18,000
    Married filing jointly or
    qualifying widow(er)—$24,000
    Married filing separately—$12,000

**Minus:** Qualified business income                                        – ($ _____ )
deduction (IRS 1040, Line 9)

**Taxable Income** (If zero or less, skip                                   $ _____
charts below and enter zero on the last
line of this table.)

Use the Taxable Income figure listed above with the appropriate chart below based on your tax filing status to calculate your U.S. Income Tax Liability. Enter the result at the end of the four tax charts. (Tax charts are based on 2018 tax rates). Then subtract any tax credits to determine a rough approximation of U.S. Income Taxes Paid.

Use if your filing status is **Single**

| If your taxable income is: Over— | But not *over*— | Income taxes paid is— | of the amount over— |
| --- | --- | --- | --- |
| $0 | $9,525 | — 10% | $0 |
| $9,525 | $38,700 | $952.50 + 12% | $9,525 |
| $38,700 | $82,500 | $4,453.50 + 22% | $38,700 |
| $82,500 | $157,500 | $14,089.50 + 24% | $82,500 |
| $157,500 | $200,000 | $32,089.50 + 32% | $157,500 |
| $200,000 | $500,000 | $45,689.50 + 35% | $200,000 |
| $500,000 | — | $150,689.00 + 37% | $500,000 |

Use if your filing status if **Married filing jointly or Qualifying widow(er)**

| If your taxable income is: Over— | But not *over—* | Income taxes paid is— | of the amount over— |
|---|---|---|---|
| $0 | $19,050 | — 10% | $0 |
| $19,050 | $77,400 | $1,905.00 + 12% | $19,050 |
| $77,400 | $165,000 | $8,907.00 + 22% | $77,400 |
| $165,000 | $315,000 | $28,179.00 + 24% | $165,000 |
| $315,000 | $400,000 | $64,179.00 + 32% | $315,000 |
| $400,000 | $600,000 | $91,379.00 + 35% | $400,000 |
| $600,000 | — | $161,379.00 + 37% | $600,000 |

Use if your filing status is **Married filing separately,**

| If your taxable income is: Over— | But not *over—* | Income taxes paid is— | of the amount over— |
|---|---|---|---|
| $0 | $9,525 | — 10% | $0 |
| $9,525 | $38,700 | $952.50 + 12% | $9,525 |
| $38,700 | $82,500 | $4,453.50 + 22% | $38,700 |
| $82,500 | $157,500 | $14,089.50 + 24% | $82,500 |
| $157,500 | $200,000 | $32,089.50 + 32% | $157,500 |
| $200,000 | $300,000 | $45,689.50 + 35% | $200,000 |
| $300,000 | — | $80,689.50 + 37% | $300,000 |

If the parents (or the custodial parent and a stepparent) are married and living together yet file separately, calculate a separate number for each parent (stepparent) and add the numbers together to determine a figure for U.S. tax liability.

Use if your filing status is **Head of the household**

| If your taxable income is: Over— | But not *over*— | *Income taxes paid is*— | *of the amount over*— |
|---|---|---|---|
| $0 | $13,600 | — 10% | $0 |
| $13,600 | $51,800 | $1,360.00 + 12% | $13,600 |
| $51,800 | $82,500 | $5,944.00 + 22% | $51,800 |
| $82,500 | $157,500 | $12,698.00 + 24% | $82,500 |
| $157,500 | $200,000 | $30,698.00 + 32% | $157,500 |
| $200,000 | $500,000 | $44,298.00 + 35% | $200,000 |
| $500,000 | — | $149,298.00 + 37% | $500,000 |

U.S. Income Tax Liability*                                            $ _____
*If you are subject to the Alternative Minimum Tax (see page 84)
you should add that additional tax to your answer.

Minus: Tax Credits (IRS 1040, Line 12)                         ($ _____ )


U.S. TAXES PAID BY PARENTS                                     $ _____
2018 IRS 1040—Line 13 minus Schedule 2, Line 46


*(This figure will be listed on the Parents' Expected Contribution Worksheet [Expenses and Allowances section].)*

# TABLE 7
## Social Security Taxes Paid

Make separate calculations for each parent (stepparent) as well as for the student (and spouse, if applicable). (Refer to the bottom line of Table 1 for father [stepfather] and mother [stepmother]; refer to the bottom line of Table 2 for student [and spouse].)

**If income earned from work is:**          Then social security taxes paid for
                                            that individual are:

**Less than $128,400**                      (Income earned from work × .0765)

**$128,400 or more**                        (The amount of income earned from work over
                                            $128,400 × .0145) + $9,822.60

        Social security taxes paid by          $ _____
        father (stepfather):

**Plus:**  Social security taxes paid by     +  $ _____
        mother (stepmother):

**Equals: SOCIAL SECURITY TAXES PAID BY**                           $ _____
**PARENTS**

*(This figure will be listed on the Parents' Expected Contribution Worksheet [Expenses & Allowances section].)*

        Social security taxes paid by the      $ _____
        student

**Plus:**  Social security taxes paid by     +  $ _____
        student's spouse (if unmarried,
        enter 0 for this line)

**Equals: SOCIAL SECURITY TAXES PAID**                              $ _____
**BY STUDENT (AND SPOUSE)**

(This figure will be listed on the Student's Expected Contribution Worksheet [Deductions Against Income section].)

An additional .9 percent (i.e., nine tenths of one percent) Medicare tax is assessed on high earning households. This additional tax will be assessed on earned income above $200,000 for individuals and above $250,000 for married couples filing jointly. As we went to press, it was still unclear if the federal methodology will be adjusted to reflect these additional taxes paid. However, given the fact that such high earners typically do not qualify for Pell Grants or demonstrate much, if any, need for other federal need-based aid programs, there is a feeling among many in the aid community that the U.S. Department of Education (DOE) will not make any adjustments to the formula to reflect the additional Medicare taxes one may be paying. As such, you should use the table above to calculate the amount of taxes paid for the purposes of these worksheets. We will, of course, post any updates to your online student tools should the DOE change their policy.

# TABLE 8
## Allowance for State and Other Taxes

| State | Parents' Income (Line E on page 317) Under $15,000 | $15,000 % up | Student's Income (Line AA on page 321) | State | Parents' Income (Line E on page 317) Under $15,000 | $15,000 % up | Student's Income (Line AA on page 321) |
|---|---|---|---|---|---|---|---|
| Alabama | 3 | 2 | 2 | Montana | 5 | 4 | 3 |
| Alaska | 2 | 1 | 0 | Nebraska | 5 | 4 | 3 |
| Arizona | 4 | 3 | 2 | Nevada | 2 | 1 | 1 |
| Arkansas | 4 | 3 | 3 | New Hampshire | 4 | 3 | 1 |
| California | 8 | 7 | 6 | New Jersey | 9 | 8 | 5 |
| Colorado | 4 | 3 | 3 | New Mexico | 3 | 2 | 2 |
| Connecticut | 9 | 8 | 5 | New York | 9 | 8 | 7 |
| Delaware | 5 | 4 | 3 | North Carolina | 5 | 4 | 3 |
| District of Columbia | 7 | 6 | 6 | North Dakota | 2 | 1 | 1 |
| Florida | 3 | 2 | 1 | Ohio | 5 | 4 | 3 |
| Georgia | 5 | 4 | 3 | Oklahoma | 3 | 2 | 2 |
| Hawaii | 5 | 4 | 4 | Oregon | 7 | 6 | 5 |
| Idaho | 5 | 4 | 3 | Pennsylvania | 5 | 4 | 3 |
| Illinois | 5 | 4 | 3 | Rhode Island | 6 | 5 | 3 |
| Indiana | 4 | 3 | 3 | South Carolina | 4 | 3 | 3 |
| Iowa | 5 | 4 | 3 | South Dakota | 2 | 1 | 1 |
| Kansas | 4 | 3 | 2 | Tennessee | 2 | 1 | 1 |
| Kentucky | 5 | 4 | 4 | Texas | 3 | 2 | 1 |
| Louisiana | 3 | 2 | 2 | Utah | 5 | 4 | 3 |
| Maine | 6 | 5 | 3 | Vermont | 6 | 5 | 3 |
| Maryland | 8 | 7 | 6 | Virginia | 6 | 5 | 4 |
| Massachusetts | 7 | 6 | 4 | Washington | 3 | 2 | 1 |
| Michigan | 4 | 3 | 3 | West Virginia | 3 | 2 | 3 |
| Minnesota | 6 | 5 | 5 | Wisconsin | 6 | 5 | 4 |
| Mississippi | 3 | 2 | 2 | Wyoming | 2 | 1 | 1 |
| Missouri | 5 | 4 | 3 | Other | 3 | 2 | 2 |

*Note for Parents' Contribution section: For Table 8 on this page, refer to the applicable state and the parents' income level from Line E on Table 5 on page 306. The tax rate in the appropriate income column for the parents listed on the table should first be multiplied by 0.01 to convert the applicable tax rate into a percentage. You will then want to take that percentage and multiply it by the Parents' Total Income (Line E on Table 5) to calculate the appropriate allowance to list for state and other taxes in the Expenses & Allowances section on page 317.*

*Note for Student's Contribution section: For Table 8 on this page, refer to the applicable state and the student's income level from Line AA on page 321. The tax rate listed in the far right column on the table should first be multiplied by 0.01 to convert the applicable tax rate into a percentage. You will then want to take that percentage and multiply it by the Student's Total Income (Line AA on page 321) to calculate the appropriate allowance to list for state and other taxes in the Deductions Against Income section on page 321.*

# TABLE 9
## Employment Allowance

To complete Table 9, refer to the bottom line on Table 1 to obtain the appropriate "Income Earned From Work" figure.

### IF A ONE-PARENT FAMILY

Total income earned from work × .35 =                                    $ _____

The maximum employment allowance is $4,000. If the number calculated above is greater than the maximum allowance, list the maximum number instead of the calculated number on the Parents' Expected Contribution Worksheet (Expenses & Allowances section).

### IF A TWO-PARENT FAMILY

Father's (stepfather's) income earned from work × .35 =            +   $ _____
(*Refer to left column, bottom line TABLE 1*)

Mother's (stepmother's) income earned from work × .35 =          +   $ _____
(*Refer to right column, bottom line TABLE 1*)

The maximum employment allowance is $4,000. Take the smaller of the two numbers. If that smaller number in the column is greater than the maximum allowance, list the maximum number instead of the calculated number on the Parents' Expected Contribution Worksheet (Expenses & Allowances section).  There is no allowance for a two-parent family in which only one parent works. If this is the case, list zero on the Parents' Expected Contribution Worksheet (Expenses & Allowances section).

# TABLE 10
## Income Protection Allowance

| Number of Family Members (Including Student) | Number in College | | | | |
|---|---|---|---|---|---|
| | 1 | 2 | 3 | 4 | 5 |
| 2 | $19,080 | $15,810 | — | — | — |
| 3 | 23,760 | 20,510 | $17,250 | — | — |
| 4 | 29,340 | 26,080 | 22,830 | $19,570 | — |
| 5 | 34,620 | 31,350 | 28,110 | 24,840 | $21,600 |
| 6 | 40,490 | 37,230 | 33,980 | 30,720 | 27,470 |

(For each additional family member above 6, add $4,570. For each additional college student above 5, subtract $3,250.)

# TABLE 11
## Business/Farm Net Worth Adjustment

Business and farm net worth for the parent(s) is somewhat sheltered in the aid formula. To determine the proper amount to list on Line K of the Parents' Expected Contribution Worksheet, first determine the net worth of the business/farm and then use the conversion rates below. **Do not include assets or liabilities for any "family business" or "family farm" in your calculations**. See pages 93–94 and 112–113. If you are a part-owner, use only your share of the net worth for the calculations.

### Net Worth (NW) = Assets minus Liabilities

If you do not have a current balance sheet available for the business and/or farm, you can use the following guidelines:

Business and/or farm assets (Include cash, investments, receivables, inventories, land and buildings, machinery and equipment net of accumulated depreciation, and other assets. Do not include the value of intangible assets such as goodwill.)    $ _____

**Minus:** Business liabilities
(Accounts payable, mortgages on land and buildings, other debts)    ($ _____)

**Net Worth** (NW) (if negative, list 0)    $ _____

Now that you have a net worth figure, use the adjustment table below to calculate the adjusted business/farm net worth.

**Helpful hint:** The ADJUSTED NET WORTH figure that you calculate should be smaller than the Net Worth figure.

| Business or Farm Adjustments | |
|---|---|
| If Net Worth (NW) | Adjusted Amount Is |
| Less than $1 | $0 |
| $1 to 135,000 | $0 + 40% of NW |
| $135,001 to 410,000 | $54,000 + 50% of NW over $135,000 |
| $410,001 to 680,000 | $191,500 + 60% of NW over $410,000 |
| $680,001 or more | $353,500 + 100% of NW over $680,000 |

ADJUSTED BUSINESS/FARM NET WORTH

(This figure will be listed on Line K of the Parents' Expected Contribution Worksheet.)    $ _____

## TABLE 12

| Asset Protection Allowance (Line O) | | |
|---|---|---|
| Age of Older Parent in Household | Two-Parent Family | One-Parent Family |
| 34 or less | $2,900 | $1,000 |
| 35–39 | $3,900 | $1,400 |
| 40–44 | $5,200 | $1,700 |
| 45–49 | $5,800 | $1,900 |
| 50–54 | $6,600 | $2,200 |
| 55–59 | $7,500 | $2,500 |
| 60–64 | $8,600 | $2,800 |
| 65 or more | $9,400 | $3,000 |

## TABLE 13

| Parent's Expected Contribution (Line S) | |
|---|---|
| Adjusted Available Income [AAI] (Line R) | Total Parents' Contribution (Line S) |
| Less than $–3,409 | $–750 |
| $–3,409 to 17,000 | 22% of AAI |
| $17,001 to 21,400 | $3,740 + 25% of AAI over $17,000 |
| $21,401 to 25,700 | $4,840 + 29% of AAI over $21,400 |
| $25,701 to 30,100 | $6,087 + 34% of AAI over $25,700 |
| $30,101 to 34,500 | $7,583 + 40% of AAI over $30,100 |
| $34,501 or more | $9,343 + 47% of AAI over $34,500 |

# PARENTS' EXPECTED CONTRIBUTION WORKSHEET

E. **PARENTS' TOTAL INCOME**                                                  $ _____
   (From Table 5—Line E)

*Expenses & Allowances*
(For explanations consult pages 79–87)

**Sum of:**

   U.S. income taxes paid *(From Table 6)*                        +   $ _____

   Social security taxes paid *(From Table 7)*                    +   $ _____

   State/other taxes *(Refer to Table 8)*                         +   $ _____

   Employment allowance *(From Table 9)*                          +   $ _____

   Income protection allowance *(From Table 10)*                  +   $ _____

F. **TOTAL EXPENSES AND ALLOWANCES**                            **($ _____)**

G. **AVAILABLE INCOME (Line E minus F)**                             $ _____
   (Can be a negative number)

**Assets & Liabilities**

(For explanations consult pages 92–98)
List only your share of assets and liabilities for this section
Do not include the home, retirement accounts, annuities, or insurance products.

For 529 Plans: Include the current value of any 529 plans (prepaid plans and/or savings plans) for the student, the student's siblings and other individuals that are owned by the custodial parent(s), as well as any 529 plans owned by the student. For Coverdell Education Savings Accounts (formerly known as Education IRAs): Include the value of any Coverdell ESAs for the student, the student's siblings, or other individuals that are owned by the custodial parent(s), as well as any Coverdells owned by the student.

# ASSETS

**Sum of:**

| | | |
|---|---|---|
| Cash, savings and checking accounts | + | $ _____ |
| 529 plans | + | $ _____ |
| Coverdell ESA (Education IRAs) | + | $ _____ |
| Investments other than real estate | + | $ _____ |
| Market value of real estate other than the home | + | $ _____ |
| **H.  TOTAL PERSONAL ASSETS** | | $ _____ |

# DEBTS

**Sum of:**

| | | |
|---|---|---|
| Debts owed on real estate other than the home (Add principal balance(s) outstanding on mortgages plus home equity line(s) of credit outstanding plus other debts against real estate.) | | $ _____ |
| Other debts against assets listed above (margin debt, passbook loan, etc.) | + | $ _____ |
| **I.  TOTAL PERSONAL DEBTS** | | ($ _____ ) |
| **J.  PERSONAL NET ASSETS** (Line H minus I) | | $ _____ |
| **K.  ADJUSTED BUSINESS/FARM NET WORTH** (From Table 11) | + | $ _____ |
| **L.  TOTAL NET ASSETS** (Line J plus K) | | $ _____ |
| **M.  ASSET ALLOWANCES** (From Table 12) | | ($ _____ ) |
| **N.  REMAINING ASSETS  (Line L minus M)** | | $ _____ |
| **O.  CONTRIBUTION FROM ASSETS** <br> If Line N is a negative number, enter -0- (zero) for that column. If Line N is a positive number, multiply Line N by .12 for your answer. | | $ _____ |
| **P.  ADJUSTED AVAILABLE INCOME (AAI)** (Line G plus Line O; if Line G is negative, subtract Line G from Line O instead.) | | $ _____ |
| **Q.  PARENTS' EXPECTED CONTRIBUTION** (Refer to Table 13; multiply the amount on Line P by the appropriate assessment rate.) | | $ _____ |
| **R.  PARENTS' EXPECTED CONTRIBUTION** <br> **PER STUDENT** *(if more than one member of the household is in college during the same academic year excluding parents)* (Divide the amount on Line Q by the number of household members in college or other postsecondary schools on at least a half-time basis, i.e., 6 credits or more a semester or the equivalent. | | $ _____ |

Paying for College

# TABLE 14
## Student's U.S. Income Taxes Paid

**For tax filers:** refer to item 3 on page 278 before performing any calculations on this page and the next.

**If the student did not and will not file a tax return:** skip to the last line on page 297 and list zero (0) as your response for the amount of U.S. TAXES PAID BY STUDENT.

**Note:** We assume that most students are listed as a dependent on the parent(s)' tax return. If this is not the case, use Table 6 as a guideline for calculating this item.

### Standard Deduction Worksheet

**Sum of:**

Student's wages, tips, salary, and other compensation subject to tax (similar to IRS 1040—Line 1) Exclude only earnings from a need based work-study job.  $ _____

**Plus:**

Student's earned income from self-employment or farming (similar to Schedule 1, Lines 12 and 18)  + $ _____

  + $ 350

**SUBTOTAL**  $ _____

**Minus:**

1/2 Self-employment tax paid (if any)  ($ _____ )

A. TOTAL  $ _____

B. Minimum amount  $ 1,050

C. Enter the larger of Line A or B  $ _____

**D. STANDARD DEDUCTION** (enter the smaller of Line C or $12,000)  $ _____

Part Five: Worksheets and Forms  319

Student's wages, tips, salary, and other compensation subject to tax (IRS 1040—Line 1)     $ _____

**Plus:**

Student's other taxable income (IRS 1040—Sum of Lines 2b, 3b, 4b, and 5b)     +  $ _____

**Minus:**

Adjustments to income (if any) (Schedule 1, Line 36)     ($ _____)

**ADJUSTED GROSS INCOME**
(IRS 1040—Line 7)     $ _____

**Minus:**     $ _____

Standard deduction (From Line D above)     ($ _____)

**E. TAXABLE INCOME**     $ _____

Use the Taxable Income figure listed above with the table below to calculate the student's U.S. Income Taxes.

| If your taxable income is: Over— | But not over— | Income taxes paid is— | of the amount over— |
|---|---|---|---|
| $0 | $9,525 | — 10% | $0 |
| $9,525 | $38,700 | $952.50 + 12% | $9,525 |
| $38,700 | $82,500 | $4,453.50 + 22% | $38,700 |
| $82,500 | $157,500 | $14,089.50 + 24% | $82,500 |
| $157,500 | $200,000 | $32,089.50 + 32% | $157,500 |
| $200,000 | $500,000 | $45,689.50 + 35% | $200,000 |
| $500,000 | — | $150,689.00 + 37% | $500,000 |

U.S. TAXES PAID BY STUDENT     $ _____
2018 IRS 1040—Line 13 minus Schedule 2, Line 46

*(This figure will be listed on the Student's Expected Contribution Worksheet [Deductions Against Income section].)*

# DEPENDENT STUDENT'S EXPECTED CONTRIBUTION WORKSHEET

## Student's Income

(Do not include any earnings from need-based work-study jobs or taxable grants/scholarships in excess of tuition, fees, books, and required supplies.)

**Sum of:**

| | |
|---|---|
| Student's wages, tips, salary, and other compensation subject to tax (From Box 5 of W-2 Form) | $ _____ |
| All other income of student (This item represents all other taxable and untaxed items such as interest, dividends, income from self-employment, capital gains, etc. Do not include social security benefits that are paid to the parent for the student or that are paid directly to the student.) | + $ _____ |

**AA.   TOTAL INCOME**                                                         $ _____

## Deductions Against Income

**Sum of:**

| | |
|---|---|
| U.S Income tax student will be expected to pay on taxable income (from Table 14 or Table 6) | $ _____ |
| Social Security Tax *(from Table 7)* | + $ _____ |
| State/other taxes *(Refer to Table 8)* | + $ _____ |
| Adjustment for Negative parent AAI [If Line P on page 295 is negative, enter that negative number as a positive amount; otherwise, enter zero(0)] | + $ _____ |
| Income Protection Allowance | + $   6,840 _____ |

**BB.   TOTAL DEDUCTIONS AGAINST INCOME**                        ($ _____ )

**CC.   AVAILABLE INCOME**                                                  $ _____
(Total Income *[Line AA]* minus Total
Deductions *[Line BB]*)
*(If Line CC is negative enter –0–.)*

## Student's Assets and Liabilities

Exclude the value of student's home and the debts on that home, as well as the net worth of the student's "family farm" and/or "family business." If the student owns a business or farm, list the full value for the net worth (assets minus liabilities equals net worth) on the appropriate line below (i.e., don't use Table 11). Don't include the business or farm debt again as part of Line EE below.

**Sum of:**

Cash, savings, and checking account $ _____

Uniform Gifts to Minors Act and custodial accounts + $ _____

Investments other than real estate + $ _____

Market value of any real estate + $ _____

Business/farm net worth + $ _____

**DD. TOTAL ASSETS** $ _____

**Minus:**

EE. TOTAL DEBTS
(Any debts against assets listed above) ($ _____)

**FF. TOTAL NET ASSETS**
(Line DD minus EE) $ _____

## Student's Contribution

**Sum of:**

GG. CONTRIBUTION FROM ASSETS
(Line FF × .20) + $ _____

HH. CONTRIBUTION FROM INCOME
(Line CC × .50) + $ _____

II. OTHER GIFTS AND SCHOLARSHIPS
RECEIVED OR AWARDED + $ _____

**JJ. STUDENT'S CONTRIBUTION** $ _____

# Sample Forms

**2020-2021**

# FAFSA®

**FREE** APPLICATION *for* FEDERAL STUDENT AID

**July 1, 2020 – June 30, 2021**

Federal **Student Aid**
*An OFFICE of the U.S. DEPARTMENT of EDUCATION*

PROUD SPONSOR *of the* AMERICAN MIND®

## Step One (Student): For questions 1-31, leave any questions that do not apply to you (the student) blank.

OMB # 1845-0001

Your full name (**exactly as it appears on your Social Security card**) If your name has a suffix, such as Jr. or III, include a space between your last name and suffix.

1. Last name

2. First name

3. Middle initial

Your permanent mailing address

4. Number and street (include apt. number)

5. City (and country if not U.S.)

6. State

7. ZIP code

8. Your Social Security Number **See Notes page 9.**

9. Your date of birth   MONTH   DAY   YEAR

10. Your telephone number   (     )

Your driver's license number and driver's license state (if you have one)

11. Driver's license number

12. Driver's license state

13. Your e-mail address. If you provide your e-mail address, we will communicate with you electronically. For example, when your FAFSA form has been processed, you will be notified by e-mail. Your e-mail address will also be shared with your state and the colleges listed on your FAFSA form to allow them to communicate with you. If you do not have an e-mail address, leave this field blank.

14. Are you a U.S. citizen? Mark only one. **See Notes page 9.**

Yes, I am a U.S. citizen (U.S. national). **Skip to question 16.** ....... ○ 1

No, but I am an eligible noncitizen. **Fill in question 15.** ........... ○ 2

No, I am not a citizen or eligible noncitizen. **Skip to question 16.** ○ 3

15. Alien Registration Number

A

16. What is your marital status as of today? **See Notes page 9.**

I am single .......... ○ 1      I am separated .......... ○ 3

I am married/remarried ○ 2      I am divorced or widowed ○ 4

17. Month and year you were married, remarried, separated, divorced or widowed. **See Notes page 9.**

MONTH   YEAR

18. What is your state of legal residence?

STATE

19. Did you become a legal resident of this state before January 1, 2015?

Yes ○ 1      No ○ 2

20. If the answer to question 19 is "No," give month and year you became a legal resident of that state.

MONTH   YEAR

21. Are you male or female? **See Notes page 9.**

Male ○ 1      Female ○ 2

22. **If female, skip to question 23.** Most male students must register with the Selective Service System to receive federal aid. If you are male, are age 18-25, and have not registered, fill in the circle and we will register you. **See Notes page 9.**

Register me ○ 1

23. Have you been convicted for the possession or sale of illegal drugs for an offense that occurred while you were receiving federal student aid (such as grants, work-study, or loans)?

Answer "No" if you have never received federal student aid or if you have never had a drug conviction for an offense that occurred while receiving federal student aid. If you have a drug conviction for an offense that occurred while you were receiving federal student aid, answer "Yes," but complete and submit this application, and we will mail you a worksheet to help you determine if your conviction affects your eligibility for aid. If you are unsure how to answer this question, call 1-800-433-3243 for help.

No ○ 1

Yes ○ 3

Some states and colleges offer aid based on the level of schooling your parents completed.

24. Highest school completed by Parent 1

Middle school/Jr. high ○ 1      High school ○ 2      College or beyond ○ 3      Other/unknown ○ 4

25. Highest school completed by Parent 2

Middle school/Jr. high ○ 1      High school ○ 2      College or beyond ○ 3      Other/unknown ○ 4

26. What will your high school completion status be when you begin college in the 2020-2021 school year?

High school diploma. **Answer question 27.** ............................. ○ 1      Homeschooled. **Skip to question 28.** .......... ○ 3

General Educational Development (GED) certificate or state certificate. **Skip to question 28.** ○ 2      None of the above. **Skip to question 28.** ........ ○ 4

*The above is a reprint of a draft of the 2020–2021 FAFSA. It is for information purposes only. Do not send in.*

27. What is the name of the high school where you received or will receive your high school diploma? Enter the complete high school name, and the city and state where the high school is located.

High School Name

High School City

STATE

28. Will you have your first bachelor's degree before you begin the 2020-2021 school year?

Yes ◯ 1    No ◯ 2

29. What will your college grade level be when you begin the 2020-2021 school year?

| | |
|---|---|
| Never attended college and 1st year undergraduate ............... | ◯ 0 |
| Attended college before and 1st year undergraduate .............. | ◯ 1 |
| 2nd year undergraduate/sophomore ............................ | ◯ 2 |
| 3rd year undergraduate/junior ................................ | ◯ 3 |
| 4th year undergraduate/senior ................................ | ◯ 4 |
| 5th year/other undergraduate................................. | ◯ 5 |
| 1st year college graduate/professional (MBA, MD, PhD, etc.) ........ | ◯ 6 |
| Continuing graduate/professional or beyond (MBA, MD, PhD, etc.) .. | ◯ 7 |

30. What college degree or certificate will you be working on when you begin the 2020-2021 school year?

| | |
|---|---|
| 1st bachelor's degree ............................................ | ◯ 1 |
| 2nd bachelor's degree ........................................... | ◯ 2 |
| Associate degree (occupational or technical program) .................... | ◯ 3 |
| Associate degree (general education or transfer program).................. | ◯ 4 |
| Certificate or diploma (occupational, technical or education program of less than two years)................. | ◯ 5 |
| Certificate or diploma (occupational, technical or education program of two or more years) .................. | ◯ 6 |
| Teaching credential (nondegree program)............................. | ◯ 7 |
| College graduate or professional degree (MBA, MD, PhD, etc.) .............. | ◯ 8 |
| Other/undecided ................................................. | ◯ 9 |

31. Are you interested in being considered for work-study?                         Yes ◯ 1  No ◯ 2  Don't know ◯ 3

**Step Two (Student):** Answer questions 32–57 about yourself (the student). If you were never married, or are separated, divorced or widowed and are not remarried, answer only about yourself. If you are married or remarried as of today, include information about your spouse.

32. For 2018, have you (the student) completed your IRS income tax return or another tax return listed in question 33?

I have already completed my return ....... ◯ 1

I will file but have not yet completed my return ..................................... ◯ 2

I'm not going to file. **Skip to question 38.** ◯ 3

33. What income tax return did you file or will you file for 2018?

IRS 1040 ..... ◯ 1

A foreign tax return, IRS 1040NR or IRS 1040NR-EZ. **See Notes page 9.** ◯ 3

A tax return with Puerto Rico, another U.S. territory, or Freely Associated State. **See Notes page 9.** ...... ◯ 4

34. For 2018, what is or will be your tax filing status according to your tax return?

Single ............................... ◯ 1

Head of household................... ◯ 4

Married—filed joint return ........... ◯ 2

Married—filed separate return ....... ◯ 3

Qualifying widow(er)................. ◯ 5

Don't know ......................... ◯ 6

35. Did (or will) you file Schedule 1 with your 2018 tax return? Answer "No" if you did not file Schedule 1 or only filed it to report an Alaska Permanent Fund dividend. **See Notes page 9 for other exceptions.**    Yes ◯ 2  No ◯ 1  Don't know ◯ 3

For questions 36–44, if the answer is zero or the question does not apply to you, enter 0. Report whole dollar amounts with no cents.

36. What was your (and spouse's) adjusted gross income for 2018? Adjusted gross income is on IRS Form 1040—line 7.  $ ⬚⬚⬚,⬚⬚⬚

37. Enter your (and spouse's) income tax for 2018. Income tax amount is the total of IRS Form 1040—line 13 minus Schedule 2—line 46. If negative, enter a zero here.  $ ⬚⬚⬚,⬚⬚⬚

Questions 38 and 39 ask about earnings (wages, salaries, tips, etc.) in 2018. Answer the questions whether or not a tax return was filed. This information may be on the W-2 forms or on the tax return selected in question 33: IRS Form 1040—line 1 + Schedule 1—lines 12 + 18 + Schedule K-1 (IRS Form 1065)—Box 14 (Code A). If any individual earning item is negative, do not include that item in your calculation.

38. How much did you earn from working in 2018?  $ ⬚⬚⬚,⬚⬚⬚

39. How much did your spouse earn from working in 2018?  $ ⬚⬚⬚,⬚⬚⬚

40. As of today, what is your (and spouse's) total current balance of cash, savings, and checking accounts? **Don't include** student financial aid.  $ ⬚⬚⬚,⬚⬚⬚

41. As of today, what is the net worth of your (and spouse's) investments, including real estate? **Don't include** the home you live in. **See Notes page 9.**  $ ⬚⬚⬚,⬚⬚⬚

42. As of today, what is the net worth of your (and spouse's) current businesses and/or investment farms? **Don't include** a family farm or family business with 100 or fewer full-time or full-time equivalent employees. **See Notes page 9.**  $ ⬚⬚⬚,⬚⬚⬚

*The above is a reprint of a draft of the 2020–2021 FAFSA. It is for information purposes only. Do not send in.*

43. **Student's 2018 Additional Financial Information** (Enter the combined amounts for you and your spouse.)

    a. Education credits (American Opportunity Tax Credit and Lifetime Learning Tax Credit) from IRS Form 1040 Schedule 3—line 50.                                                                                 $ ☐☐☐,☐☐☐

    b. Child support paid because of divorce or separation or as a result of a legal requirement. **Don't include** support for children in your household, as reported in question 93.                                   $ ☐☐☐,☐☐☐

    c. Taxable earnings from need-based employment programs, such as Federal Work-Study and need-based employment portions of fellowships and assistantships.                                                         $ ☐☐☐,☐☐☐

    d. Taxable college grant and scholarship aid **reported to the IRS as income**. Includes AmeriCorps benefits (awards, living allowances and interest accrual payments), as well as grant and scholarship portions of fellowships and assistantships.   $ ☐☐☐,☐☐☐

    e. Combat pay or special combat pay. Only enter the amount that was taxable and included in your adjusted gross income. **Don't include** untaxed combat pay.                                                      $ ☐☐☐,☐☐☐

    f. Earnings from work under a cooperative education program offered by a college.                                                                                                                                  $ ☐☐☐,☐☐☐

44. **Student's 2018 Untaxed Income** (Enter the combined amounts for you and your spouse.)

    a. Payments to tax-deferred pension and retirement savings plans (paid directly or withheld from earnings), including, but not limited to, amounts reported on the W-2 forms in Boxes 12a through 12d, codes D, E, F, G, H and S. **Don't include** amounts reported in code DD (employer contributions toward employee health benefits).   $ ☐☐☐,☐☐☐

    b. IRA deductions and payments to self-employed SEP, SIMPLE, Keogh and other qualified plans from IRS Form 1040 Schedule 1—total of lines 28 + 32.                                                                 $ ☐☐☐,☐☐☐

    c. Child support received for any of your children. **Don't include** foster care or adoption payments.                                                                                                           $ ☐☐☐,☐☐☐

    d. Tax exempt interest income from IRS Form 1040—line 2a.                                                                                                                                                         $ ☐☐☐,☐☐☐

    e. Untaxed portions of IRA distributions and pensions from IRS Form 1040—line 4a minus line 4b. **Exclude rollovers.** If negative, enter a zero here.                                                             $ ☐☐☐,☐☐☐

    f. Housing, food and other living allowances paid to members of the military, clergy and others (including cash payments and cash value of benefits). **Don't include** the value of on-base military housing or the value of a basic military allowance for housing.   $ ☐☐☐,☐☐☐

    g. Veterans noneducation benefits, such as Disability, Death Pension, or Dependency & Indemnity Compensation (DIC) and/or VA Educational Work-Study allowances.                                                    $ ☐☐☐,☐☐☐

    h. Other untaxed income not reported in items 44a through 44g, such as workers' compensation, disability benefits, untaxed foreign income, etc. Also include the untaxed portions of health savings accounts from IRS Form 1040 Schedule 1—line 25. **Don't include** extended foster care benefits, student aid, earned income credit, additional child tax credit, welfare payments, untaxed Social Security benefits, Supplemental Security Income, Workforce Innovation and Opportunity Act educational benefits, on-base military housing or a military housing allowance, combat pay, benefits from flexible spending arrangements (e.g., cafeteria plans), foreign income exclusion or credit for federal tax on special fuels.   $ ☐☐☐,☐☐☐

    i. Money received, or paid on your behalf (e.g., bills), not reported elsewhere on this form. This includes money that you received from a parent or other person whose financial information is not reported on this form and that is not part of a legal child support agreement. **See Notes page 9.**   $ ☐☐☐,☐☐☐

## Step Three (Student):

Answer the questions in this step to determine if you will need to provide parental information. Once you answer **"Yes" to any** of the questions in this step, skip Step Four and go to Step Five on page 8.

45. Were you born before January 1, 1997? .............................................................................. Yes ◯₁   No ◯₂

46. As of today, are you married? (Also answer "Yes" if you are separated but not divorced.) ................................ Yes ◯₁   No ◯₂

47. At the beginning of the 2020-2021 school year, will you be working on a master's or doctorate program (such as an MA, MBA, MD, JD, PhD, EdD, graduate certificate, etc.)? ................................................ Yes ◯₁   No ◯₂

48. Are you currently serving on active duty in the U.S. Armed Forces for purposes other than training? **See Notes page 9.** .... Yes ◯₁   No ◯₂

49. Are you a veteran of the U.S. Armed Forces? **See Notes page 9.** ......................................................... Yes ◯₁   No ◯₂

50. Do you now have or will you have children who will receive more than half of their support from you between July 1, 2020 and June 30, 2021? ...................................................................................... Yes ◯₁   No ◯₂

51. Do you have dependents (other than your children or spouse) who live with you and who receive more than half of their support from you, now and through June 30, 2021? .............................................................. Yes ◯₁   No ◯₂

52. At any time since you turned age 13, were both your parents deceased, were you in foster care or were you a dependent or ward of the court? **See Notes page 10.** ............................................................... Yes ◯₁   No ◯₂

53. As determined by a court in your state of legal residence, are you or were you an emancipated minor? **See Notes page 10.** .. Yes ◯₁   No ◯₂

54. Does someone other than your parent or stepparent have legal guardianship of you, as determined by a court in your state of legal residence? **See Notes page 10.** ............................................................ Yes ◯₁   No ◯₂

55. At any time on or after July 1, 2019, did your high school or school district homeless liaison determine that you were an unaccompanied youth who was homeless or were self-supporting and at risk of being homeless? **See Notes page 10.** ...... Yes ◯₁   No ◯₂

56. At any time on or after July 1, 2019, did the director of an emergency shelter or transitional housing program funded by the U.S. Department of Housing and Urban Development determine that you were an unaccompanied youth who was homeless or were self-supporting and at risk of being homeless? **See Notes page 10.** .................................. Yes ◯₁   No ◯₂

57. At any time on or after July 1, 2019, did the director of a runaway or homeless youth basic center or transitional living program determine that you were an unaccompanied youth who was homeless or were self-supporting and at risk of being homeless? **See Notes page 10.** ..................................................................... Yes ◯₁   No ◯₂

*The above is a reprint of a draft of the 2020–2021 FAFSA. It is for information purposes only. Do not send in.*

**2020-2021**

> If you (the student) answered "No" to every question in Step Three, go to Step Four.
> If you answered "Yes" to any question in Step Three, skip Step Four and go to Step Five on page 8.
> (Health professions and law school students: Your college may require you to complete Step Four even if you answered "Yes" to any Step Three question.)
> **If you believe that you are unable to provide parental information, see Notes page 10.**

## Step Four (Parent): Complete this step if you (the student) answered "No" to all questions in Step Three.

Answer all the questions in Step Four even if you do not live with your legal parents (biological, adoptive, or as determined by the state [for example, if the parent is listed on the birth certificate]). Grandparents, foster parents, legal guardians, widowed stepparents, aunts, uncles, and siblings are not considered parents on this form unless they have legally adopted you. If your legal parents are married to each other, or are not married to each other and **live together**, answer the questions about both of them. If your parent was never married or is remarried, divorced, separated or widowed, **see StudentAid.gov/fafsa-parent** and/or **Notes page 10** for additional instructions.

**58.** As of today, what is the marital status of your parents?

Never married........ ○ 2    Married or remarried.......... ○ 1
Unmarried and both legal parents living together.......... ○ 4    Divorced or separated.......... ○ 3    Widowed.......... ○ 5

**59.** Month and year they were married, remarried, separated, divorced or widowed.    MONTH  YEAR

What are the Social Security Numbers, names and dates of birth of the parents reporting information on this form? If your parent does not have a Social Security Number, you must enter 000-00-0000. Don't enter an Individual Taxpayer Identification Number (ITIN) in the Social Security Number field. If the name includes a suffix, such as Jr. or III, include a space between the last name and suffix. Enter two digits for each day and month (e.g., for May 31, enter 05 31).

Questions 60-63 are for Parent 1 (father/mother/stepparent)
**60.** SOCIAL SECURITY NUMBER    **61.** LAST NAME, AND    **62.** FIRST INITIAL    **63.** DATE OF BIRTH

Questions 64-67 are for Parent 2 (father/mother/stepparent)
**64.** SOCIAL SECURITY NUMBER    **65.** LASTNAME, AND    **66.** FIRST INITIAL    **67.** DATE OF BIRTH

**68. Your parents' e-mail address.** If you provide your parents' e-mail address, we will let them know your FAFSA form has been processed. This e-mail address will also be shared with your state and the colleges listed on your FAFSA form to allow them to electronically communicate with your parents.

**69.** What is your parents' state of legal residence?    STATE

**70.** Did your parents become legal residents of this state before January 1, 2015?    Yes ○ 1    No ○ 2

**71.** If the answer to question 70 is "No," give the month and year legal residency began for the parent who has lived in the state the longest.    MONTH  YEAR

**72.** How many people are in your parents' household?
Include:
- yourself, even if you don't live with your parents,
- your parents,
- your parents' other children (even if they do not live with your parents) if (a) your parents will provide more than half of their support between July 1, 2020 and June 30, 2021, or (b) the children could answer "No" to every question in Step Three on page 5 of this form, and
- other people if they now live with your parents, your parents provide more than half of their support and your parents will continue to provide more than half of their support between July 1, 2020 and June 30, 2021.

**73.** How many people in your parents' household (from question 72) will be college students between July 1, 2020 and June 30, 2021? Always count yourself as a college student. Do not include your parents. Do not include siblings who are in U.S. military service academies. You may include others only if they will attend, at least half-time in 2020-2021, a program that leads to a college degree or certificate.

At any time during 2018 or 2019, did you, your parents, or anyone in your parents' household (from question 72) receive benefits from any of the federal programs listed? Mark all that apply. Answering these questions will NOT reduce eligibility for student aid or these programs. TANF has different names in many states. Call 1-800-433-3243 to find out the name of your state's program. If you, your parents, or anyone in your household receives any of these benefits after filing the FAFSA form but before December 31, 2019, you must update your response by logging in to **fafsa.gov** and selecting "Make FAFSA Corrections."

**74.** Medicaid or Supplemental Security Income (SSI) ○
**75.** Supplemental Nutrition Assistance Program (SNAP) ○
**76.** Free or Reduced Price School Lunch ○
**77.** Temporary Assistance for Needy Families (TANF) ○
**78.** Special Supplemental Nutrition Program for Women, Infants, and Children (WIC) ○

**If your answer to question 58 was "Unmarried and both legal parents living together," contact 1-800-433-3243 for assistance with answering questions 79-92.**

**79.** For 2018, have your parents completed their IRS income tax return or another tax return listed in question 80?

My parents have already completed their return. ○ 1
My parents will file but have not yet completed their return. ○ 2
My parents are not going to file. **Skip to question 86.** ○ 3

**80.** What income tax return did your parents file or will they file for 2018?

IRS 1040.......... ○ 1
A foreign tax return, IRS 1040NR or IRS 1040NR-EZ. **See Notes page 9.**.......... ○ 3
A tax return with Puerto Rico, another U.S. territory or Freely Associated State. **See Notes page 9.**.......... ○ 4

**81.** For 2018, what is or will be your parents' tax filing status according to their tax return?

Single.......... ○ 1
Head of household.......... ○ 4
Married—filed joint return.......... ○ 2
Married—filed separate return.......... ○ 3
Qualifying widow(er).......... ○ 5
Don't know.......... ○ 6

**82.** Did (or will) your parents file Schedule 1 with their 2018 tax return? Answer "No" if they did not file Schedule 1 or only filed it to report an Alaska Permanent Fund dividend. **See Notes page 9 for other exceptions.**    Yes ○ 2    No ○ 1    Don't know ○ 3

**83.** As of today, is either of your parents a dislocated worker? **See Notes page 10.**    Yes ○ 1    No ○ 2    Don't know ○ 3

*The above is a reprint of a draft of the 2020–2021 FAFSA. It is for information purposes only. Do not send in.*

For questions 84–92, if the answer is zero or the question does not apply, enter 0. Report whole dollar amounts with no cents.

84. What was your parents' adjusted gross income for 2018? Adjusted gross income is on IRS Form 1040—line 7.     $ ☐☐☐,☐☐☐

85. Enter your parents' income tax for 2018. Income tax amount is the total of IRS Form 1040—line 13 minus Schedule 2—line 46. If negative, enter a zero here.     $ ☐☐☐,☐☐☐

Questions 86 and 87 ask about earnings (wages, salaries, tips, etc.) in 2018. Answer the questions whether or not a tax return was filed. This information may be on the W-2 forms or on the tax return selected in question 80: IRS Form 1040—line 1 + Schedule 1—lines 12 + 18 + Schedule K-1 (IRS Form 1065)—Box 14 (Code A). If any individual earning item is negative, do not include that item in your calculation. Report the information for the parent listed in questions 60-63 in question 86 and the information for the parent listed in questions 64-67 in question 87.

86. How much did Parent 1 (father/mother/stepparent) earn from working in 2018?     $ ☐☐☐,☐☐☐

87. How much did Parent 2 (father/mother/stepparent) earn from working in 2018?     $ ☐☐☐,☐☐☐

88. As of today, what is your parents' total current balance of cash, savings, and checking accounts? **Don't include** student financial aid.     $ ☐☐☐,☐☐☐

89. As of today, what is the net worth of your parents' investments, including real estate? **Don't include** the home in which your parents live. **See Notes page 9.**     $ ☐☐☐,☐☐☐

90. As of today, what is the net worth of your parents' current businesses and/or investment farms? **Don't include** a family farm or family business with 100 or fewer full-time or full-time equivalent employees. **See Notes page 9.**     $ ☐☐☐,☐☐☐

91. Parents' 2018 Additional Financial Information (Enter the amounts for your parent[s].)

    a. Education credits (American Opportunity Tax Credit and Lifetime Learning Tax Credit) from IRS Form 1040 Schedule 3—line 50.     $ ☐☐☐,☐☐☐

    b. Child support paid because of divorce or separation or as a result of a legal requirement. **Don't include** support for children in your parents' household, as reported in question 72.     $ ☐☐☐,☐☐☐

    c. Your parents' taxable earnings from need-based employment programs, such as Federal Work-Study and need-based employment portions of fellowships and assistantships.     $ ☐☐☐,☐☐☐

    d. Your parents' taxable college grant and scholarship aid **reported to the IRS as income**. Includes AmeriCorps benefits (awards, living allowances and interest accrual payments), as well as grant and scholarship portions of fellowships and assistantships.     $ ☐☐☐,☐☐☐

    e. Combat pay or special combat pay. Only enter the amount that was taxable and included in your parents' adjusted gross income. **Don't include** untaxed combat pay.     $ ☐☐☐,☐☐☐

    f. Earnings from work under a cooperative education program offered by a college.     $ ☐☐☐,☐☐☐

92. Parents' 2018 Untaxed Income (Enter the amounts for your parent[s].)

    a. Payments to tax-deferred pension and retirement savings plans (paid directly or withheld from earnings), including, but not limited to, amounts reported on the W-2 forms in Boxes 12a through 12d, codes D, E, F, G, H and S. **Don't include** amounts reported in code DD (employer contributions toward employee health benefits).     $ ☐☐☐,☐☐☐

    b. IRA deductions and payments to self-employed SEP, SIMPLE, Keogh and other qualified plans from IRS Form 1040 Schedule 1—total of lines 28 + 32.     $ ☐☐☐,☐☐☐

    c. Child support received for any of your parents' children. **Don't include** foster care or adoption payments.     $ ☐☐☐,☐☐☐

    d. Tax exempt interest income from IRS Form 1040—line 2a.     $ ☐☐☐,☐☐☐

    e. Untaxed portions of IRA distributions and pensions from IRS Form 1040—line 4a minus line 4b. **Exclude rollovers.** If negative, enter a zero here.     $ ☐☐☐,☐☐☐

    f. Housing, food and other living allowances paid to members of the military, clergy and others (including cash payments and cash value of benefits). **Don't include** the value of on-base military housing or the value of a basic military allowance for housing.     $ ☐☐☐,☐☐☐

    g. Veterans noneducation benefits, such as Disability, Death Pension, or Dependency & Indemnity Compensation (DIC) and/or VA Educational Work-Study allowances.     $ ☐☐☐,☐☐☐

    h. Other untaxed income not reported in items 92a through 92g, such as workers' compensation, disability benefits, untaxed foreign income, etc. Also include the untaxed portions of health savings accounts from IRS Form 1040 Schedule 1—line 25. **Don't include** extended foster care benefits, student aid, earned income credit, additional child tax credit, welfare payments, untaxed Social Security benefits, Supplemental Security Income, Workforce Innovation and Opportunity Act educational benefits, on-base military housing or a military housing allowance, combat pay, benefits from flexible spending arrangements (e.g., cafeteria plans), foreign income exclusion or credit for federal tax on special fuels.     $ ☐☐☐,☐☐☐

*The above is a reprint of a draft of the 2020–2021 FAFSA. It is for information purposes only. Do not send in.*

**2020-2021**

## Step Five (Student): Complete this step only if you (the student) answered "Yes" to any questions in Step Three.

93. How many people are in your household?
    Include:
    - yourself (and your spouse),
    - your children, if you will provide more than half of their support between July 1, 2020 and June 30, 2021, even if they do not live with you, and
    - other people if they now live with you, you provide more than half of their support and you will continue to provide more than half of their support between July 1, 2020 and June 30, 2021.

94. How many people in your (and your spouse's) household (from question 93) will be college students between July 1, 2020 and June 30, 2021? Always count yourself as a college student. Do not include family members who are in U.S. military service academies. Include others only if they will attend, at least half-time in 2020-2021, a program that leads to a college degree or certificate.

At any time during 2018 or 2019, did you (or your spouse) or anyone in your household (from question 93) receive benefits from any of the federal programs listed? Mark all that apply. Answering these questions will NOT reduce eligibility for student aid or these programs. TANF has different names in many states. Call 1-800-433-3243 to find out the name of your state's program. If you (or your spouse) or anyone in your household receives any of these benefits after filing the FAFSA form but before December 31, 2019, you must update your response by logging in to **fafsa.gov** and selecting "Make FAFSA Corrections."

| 95. Medicaid or Supplemental Security Income (SSI) ○ | 96. Supplemental Nutrition Assistance Program (SNAP) ○ | 97. Free or Reduced Price School Lunch ○ | 98. Temporary Assistance for Needy Families (TANF) ○ | 99. Special Supplemental Nutrition Program for Women, Infants, and Children (WIC) ○ |

100. As of today, are you (or your spouse) a dislocated worker? **See Notes page 10.**     Yes ○ 1    No ○ 2    Don't know ○ 3

## Step Six (Student): Indicate which colleges you want to receive your FAFSA information.

Enter the six-digit federal school code and your housing plans for each college or school you want to receive your FAFSA information. You can find the school codes at **fafsa.ed.gov/spa/fsc** or by calling 1-800-433-3243. If you cannot obtain a code, write in the complete name, address, city and state of the college. If you want more schools to receive your FAFSA information, read **What is the FAFSA form?** on page 2. All of the information you included on your FAFSA form, *with the exception of the list of colleges*, will be sent to each of the colleges you listed. In addition, all of your FAFSA information, *including the list of colleges*, will be sent to your state grant agency. For federal student aid purposes, it does not matter in what order you list your selected schools. However, the order in which you list schools may affect your eligibility for state aid. Consult your state agency or **StudentAid.gov/order** for details.

| | 1st FEDERAL SCHOOL CODE | OR | NAME OF COLLEGE ADDRESS AND CITY | STATE | HOUSING PLANS |
|---|---|---|---|---|---|
| 101.a | | | | | 101.b on campus ○ 1 / with parent ○ 2 / off campus ○ 3 |
| 101.c | 2ND FEDERAL SCHOOL CODE | OR | NAME OF COLLEGE ADDRESS AND CITY | STATE | 101.d on campus ○ 1 / with parent ○ 2 / off campus ○ 3 |
| 101.e | 3RD FEDERAL SCHOOL CODE | OR | NAME OF COLLEGE ADDRESS AND CITY | STATE | 101.f on campus ○ 1 / with parent ○ 2 / off campus ○ 3 |
| 101.g | 4TH FEDERAL SCHOOL CODE | OR | NAME OF COLLEGE ADDRESS AND CITY | STATE | 101.h on campus ○ 1 / with parent ○ 2 / off campus ○ 3 |

## Step Seven (Student and Parent): Read, sign and date.

If you are the student, by signing this application you certify that you (1) will use federal and/or state student financial aid only to pay the cost of attending an institution of higher education, (2) are not in default on a federal student loan or have made satisfactory arrangements to repay it, (3) do not owe money back on a federal student grant or have made satisfactory arrangements to repay it, (4) will notify your college if you default on a federal student loan and (5) will not receive a Federal Pell Grant from more than one college for the same period of time.

If you are the parent or the student, by signing this application you certify that all of the information you provided is true and complete to the best of your knowledge and you agree, if asked, to provide information that will verify the accuracy of your completed form. This information may include U.S. or state income tax forms that you filed or are required to file. Also, you certify that you understand that **the Secretary of Education has the authority to verify information reported on this application with the Internal Revenue Service and other federal agencies.** If you electronically sign any document related to the federal student aid programs using an FSA ID (username and password) and/or any other credential, you certify that you are the person identified by that username and password and/or other credential, and have not disclosed that username and password and/or other credential to anyone else. If you purposely give false or misleading information, you may be fined up to $20,000, sent to prison, or both.

102. Date this form was completed
    MONTH    DAY    2019 ○    2020 ○    2021 ○

103. Student (Sign below)

Parent (A parent from Step Four sign below.)

If a fee was paid to someone for advice or for completing this form, that person must complete this section.

Preparer's name, firm and address

104. Preparer's Social Security Number (or 105)

105. Employer ID number (or 104)

106. Preparer's signature and date

**COLLEGE USE ONLY**    FEDERAL SCHOOL CODE

D/O ○ 1    Homeless Youth Determination ○ 4

FAA Signature

DATA ENTRY USE ONLY:    ○ P    ○ *    ○ L    ○ E

*The above is a reprint of a draft of the 2020–2021 FAFSA. It is for information purposes only. Do not send in.*

Form **1040** Department of the Treasury—Internal Revenue Service (99)
**U.S. Individual Income Tax Return** 2018 OMB No. 1545-0074 | IRS Use Only—Do not write or staple in this space.

Filing status: ☐ Single ☐ Married filing jointly ☐ Married filing separately ☐ Head of household ☐ Qualifying widow(er)

| Your first name and initial | Last name | Your social security number |
|---|---|---|

Your standard deduction: ☐ Someone can claim you as a dependent ☐ You were born before January 2, 1954 ☐ You are blind

| If joint return, spouse's first name and initial | Last name | Spouse's social security number |
|---|---|---|

Spouse standard deduction: ☐ Someone can claim your spouse as a dependent ☐ Spouse was born before January 2, 1954
☐ Spouse is blind ☐ Spouse itemizes on a separate return or you were dual-status alien

Full-year health care coverage or exempt (see inst.) ☐

| Home address (number and street). If you have a P.O. box, see instructions. | Apt. no. | Presidential Election Campaign (see inst.) ☐ You ☐ Spouse |
|---|---|---|

City, town or post office, state, and ZIP code. If you have a foreign address, attach Schedule 6.

If more than four dependents, see inst. and ✓ here ▶ ☐

| **Dependents** (see instructions): | | (2) Social security number | (3) Relationship to you | (4) ✓ if qualifies for (see inst.): | |
|---|---|---|---|---|---|
| (1) First name | Last name | | | Child tax credit | Credit for other dependents |
| | | | | ☐ | ☐ |
| | | | | ☐ | ☐ |
| | | | | ☐ | ☐ |
| | | | | ☐ | ☐ |

**Sign Here**

Under penalties of perjury, I declare that I have examined this return and accompanying schedules and statements, and to the best of my knowledge and belief, they are true, correct, and complete. Declaration of preparer (other than taxpayer) is based on all information of which preparer has any knowledge.

Joint return? See instructions. Keep a copy for your records.

| Your signature | Date | Your occupation | If the IRS sent you an Identity Protection PIN, enter it here (see inst.) |
|---|---|---|---|
| Spouse's signature. If a joint return, **both** must sign. | Date | Spouse's occupation | If the IRS sent you an Identity Protection PIN, enter it here (see inst.) |

**Paid Preparer Use Only**

| Preparer's name | Preparer's signature | PTIN | Firm's EIN | Check if: ☐ 3rd Party Designee ☐ Self-employed |
|---|---|---|---|---|
| Firm's name ▶ | | Phone no. | | |
| Firm's address ▶ | | | | |

For Disclosure, Privacy Act, and Paperwork Reduction Act Notice, see separate instructions. Cat. No. 11320B Form **1040** (2018)

*The above form is a copy of the IRS Form 1040. It is for information purposes only. Do not send in.*

Form 1040 (2018)                                                                                          Page **2**

| | | | | | |
|---|---|---|---|---|---|
| | **1** | Wages, salaries, tips, etc. Attach Form(s) W-2 . . . . . . . . . . . . . . . . . | | **1** | |
| Attach Form(s) W-2. Also attach Form(s) W-2G and 1099-R if tax was withheld. | **2a** | Tax-exempt interest . . . | **2a** _____ **b** Taxable interest . . . | **2b** | |
| | **3a** | Qualified dividends . . . | **3a** _____ **b** Ordinary dividends . . . | **3b** | |
| | **4a** | IRAs, pensions, and annuities . | **4a** _____ **b** Taxable amount . . . | **4b** | |
| | **5a** | Social security benefits . | **5a** _____ **b** Taxable amount . . . | **5b** | |
| | **6** | Total income. Add lines 1 through 5. Add any amount from Schedule 1, line 22 _____ | | **6** | |
| | **7** | Adjusted gross income. If you have no adjustments to income, enter the amount from line 6; otherwise, subtract Schedule 1, line 36, from line 6 | | **7** | |
| Standard Deduction for— • Single or married filing separately, $12,000 • Married filing jointly or Qualifying widow(er), $24,000 • Head of household, $18,000 • If you checked any box under Standard deduction, see instructions. | **8** | **Standard deduction or itemized deductions** (from Schedule A) . . . . . . . . | | **8** | |
| | **9** | Qualified business income deduction (see instructions) . . . . . . . . . | | **9** | |
| | **10** | Taxable income. Subtract lines 8 and 9 from line 7. If zero or less, enter -0- . . . . | | **10** | |
| | **11** | **a** Tax (see inst.) _____ (check if any from: **1** ☐ Form(s) 8814 **2** ☐ Form 4972 **3** ☐ _____ ) | | | |
| | | **b Add** any amount from Schedule 2 and check here . . . . . . . . ▶ ☐ | | **11** | |
| | **12** | **a** Child tax credit/credit for other dependents _____ **b Add** any amount from Schedule 3 and check here ▶ ☐ | | **12** | |
| | **13** | Subtract line 12 from line 11. If zero or less, enter -0- . . . . . . . . . . | | **13** | |
| | **14** | Other taxes. Attach Schedule 4 . . . . . . . . . . . . . . . . . | | **14** | |
| | **15** | Total tax. Add lines 13 and 14 . . . . . . . . . . . . . . . . . | | **15** | |
| | **16** | Federal income tax withheld from Forms W-2 and 1099 . . . . . . . . . | | **16** | |
| | **17** | Refundable credits: **a** EIC (see inst.) _____ **b** Sch. 8812 _____ **c** Form 8863 _____ | | | |
| | | **Add** any amount from Schedule 5 _____ . . . . . . . . . . . . . | | **17** | |
| | **18** | Add lines 16 and 17. These are your total payments . . . . . . . . . . | | **18** | |
| **Refund** Direct deposit? See instructions. | **19** | If line 18 is more than line 15, subtract line 15 from line 18. This is the amount you **overpaid** . . . | | **19** | |
| | **20a** | Amount of line 19 you want **refunded to you.** If Form 8888 is attached, check here . . . ▶ ☐ | | **20a** | |
| | ▶ **b** | Routing number _____ ▶ **c** Type: ☐ Checking ☐ Savings | | | |
| | ▶ **d** | Account number _____ | | | |
| | **21** | Amount of line 19 you want **applied to your 2019 estimated tax** . ▶ | **21** _____ | | |
| **Amount You Owe** | **22** | **Amount you owe.** Subtract line 18 from line 15. For details on how to pay, see instructions . . . ▶ | | **22** | |
| | **23** | Estimated tax penalty (see instructions) . . . . . . . . ▶ | **23** _____ | | |

Go to *www.irs.gov/Form1040* for instructions and the latest information.                      Form **1040** (2018)

*The above form is a copy of the IRS Form 1040. It is for information purposes only. Do not send in.*

**SCHEDULE 1**
**(Form 1040)**

Department of the Treasury
Internal Revenue Service

# Additional Income and Adjustments to Income

▶ Attach to Form 1040.
▶ Go to *www.irs.gov/Form1040* for instructions and the latest information.

OMB No. 1545-0074

**2018**

Attachment
Sequence No. **01**

Name(s) shown on Form 1040

Your social security number

| | | | | |
|---|---|---|---|---|
| **Additional Income** | 1–9b | Reserved . . . . . . . . . . . . . . . . . . | **1–9b** | |
| | 10 | Taxable refunds, credits, or offsets of state and local income taxes . . . . . | **10** | |
| | 11 | Alimony received . . . . . . . . . . . . . . . . . | **11** | |
| | 12 | Business income or (loss). Attach Schedule C or C-EZ . . . . . . . . . | **12** | |
| | 13 | Capital gain or (loss). Attach Schedule D if required. If not required, check here ▶ ☐ | **13** | |
| | 14 | Other gains or (losses). Attach Form 4797 . . . . . . . . . . . . | **14** | |
| | 15a | Reserved . . . . . . . . . . . . . . . . . . | **15b** | |
| | 16a | Reserved . . . . . . . . . . . . . . . . . . | **16b** | |
| | 17 | Rental real estate, royalties, partnerships, S corporations, trusts, etc. Attach Schedule E | **17** | |
| | 18 | Farm income or (loss). Attach Schedule F . . . . . . . . . . . | **18** | |
| | 19 | Unemployment compensation . . . . . . . . . . . . . . | **19** | |
| | 20a | Reserved . . . . . . . . . . . . . . . . . . | **20b** | |
| | 21 | Other income. List type and amount ▶ _____ | **21** | |
| | 22 | Combine the amounts in the far right column. If you don't have any adjustments to income, enter here and include on Form 1040, line 6. Otherwise, go to line 23 . . | **22** | |

| | | | | | |
|---|---|---|---|---|---|
| **Adjustments to Income** | 23 | Educator expenses . . . . . . . . . . | **23** | | |
| | 24 | Certain business expenses of reservists, performing artists, and fee-basis government officials. Attach Form 2106 . . | **24** | | |
| | 25 | Health savings account deduction. Attach Form 8889 . | **25** | | |
| | 26 | Moving expenses for members of the Armed Forces. Attach Form 3903 . . . . . . . . . . | **26** | | |
| | 27 | Deductible part of self-employment tax. Attach Schedule SE | **27** | | |
| | 28 | Self-employed SEP, SIMPLE, and qualified plans . . | **28** | | |
| | 29 | Self-employed health insurance deduction . . . . | **29** | | |
| | 30 | Penalty on early withdrawal of savings . . . . . . | **30** | | |
| | 31a | Alimony paid **b** Recipient's SSN ▶ | **31a** | | |
| | 32 | IRA deduction . . . . . . . . . . . . | **32** | | |
| | 33 | Student loan interest deduction . . . . . . . . | **33** | | |
| | 34 | Reserved . . . . . . . . . . . . . . | **34** | | |
| | 35 | Reserved . . . . . . . . . . . . . . | **35** | | |
| | 36 | Add lines 23 through 35 . . . . . . . . . . . . . . . . . . | **36** | | |

**For Paperwork Reduction Act Notice, see your tax return instructions.** Cat. No. 71479F **Schedule 1 (Form 1040) 2018**

*The above form is a copy of Schedule 1 of the IRS 1040. It is for information purposes only. Do not send in.*

# Direct Loans
William D. Ford Federal Direct Loan Program

**Federal Direct Stafford/Ford Loan**
**Federal Direct Unsubsidized Stafford/Ford Loan**
**Master Promissory Note**
**William D. Ford Federal Direct Loan Program**

Warning: Any person who knowingly makes a false statement or misrepresentation on this form will be subject to penalties which may include fines, imprisonment, or both, under the U.S. Criminal Code and 20 U.S.C. 1097.

OMB No. 1845-0007
Form Approved
Exp. Date 05/31/2011

## SECTION A: BORROWER INFORMATION — READ THE INSTRUCTIONS IN SECTION F BEFORE COMPLETING THIS SECTION

1. Driver's License State and No.

2. Social Security No.

3. E-mail Address (optional)

4. Name and Address

5. Date of Birth
6. Area Code/Telephone No.

7. References: List two persons with different U.S. addresses who have known you for at least three years. The first reference should be a parent or legal guardian.

| | 1. | 2. |
|---|---|---|
| Name | | |
| Permanent Street Address | | |
| City, State, Zip Code | | |
| Area Code/Telephone No. | ( ) | ( ) |
| Relationship to Borrower | | |

## SECTION B: SCHOOL INFORMATION – TO BE COMPLETED BY THE SCHOOL

8. School Name and Address

9. School Code/Branch

10. Identification No.

## SECTION C: BORROWER REQUEST, CERTIFICATIONS, AUTHORIZATIONS, AND UNDERSTANDINGS – READ CAREFULLY BEFORE SIGNING BELOW

11. This is a Master Promissory Note (MPN) for one or more Federal Direct Stafford/Ford (Direct Subsidized) Loans and/or Federal Direct Unsubsidized Stafford/Ford (Direct Unsubsidized) Loans. I request a total amount of Direct Subsidized Loans and/or Direct Unsubsidized Loans under this MPN not to exceed the allowable maximums under the Act ("the Act" is defined in Section E under Governing Law). My school will notify me of the loan type and loan amount that I am eligible to receive. I may cancel a loan or request a lower amount by contacting my school. Additional information about my right to cancel a loan or request a lower amount is included in the Borrower's Rights and Responsibilities Statement and in the disclosure statements that will be provided to me.

12. Under penalty of perjury, I certify that:

A. The information I have provided on this MPN and as updated by me from time to time is true, complete, and correct to the best of my knowledge and belief and is made in good faith.

B. I will use the proceeds of loans made under this MPN for authorized educational expenses that I incur and I will immediately repay any loan proceeds that cannot be attributed to educational expenses for attendance on at least a half-time basis at the school that certified my loan eligibility.

C. If I owe an overpayment on a Federal Perkins Loan, Federal Pell Grant, Federal Supplemental Educational Opportunity Grant, Academic Competitiveness Grant (ACG), National Science or Mathematics Access to Retain Talent (SMART) Grant, or Leveraging Educational Assistance Partnership Grant, I have made satisfactory arrangements to repay the amount owed.

D. If I am in default on any loan received under the Federal Perkins Loan Program (including National Direct Student Loans), the William D. Ford Federal Direct Loan (Direct Loan) Program or the Federal Family Education Loan (FFEL) Program, I have made satisfactory repayment arrangements with the holder to repay the amount owed.

E. If I have been convicted of, or pled nolo contendere (no contest) or guilty to, a crime involving fraud in obtaining funds under title IV of the Higher Education Act of 1965 (HEA), as amended, I have completed the repayment of the funds to the U.S. Department of Education (ED) or to the loan holder in the case of a Title IV federal student loan.

13. For each Direct Subsidized Loan and Direct Unsubsidized Loan I receive under this MPN, I make the following authorizations:

A. I authorize my school to certify my eligibility for the loan.

B. I authorize my school to credit my loan proceeds to my student account at the school.

C. I authorize my school to pay to ED any refund that may be due up to the full amount of the loan.

D. I authorize ED to investigate my credit record and report information about my loan status to persons and organizations permitted by law to receive that information.

E. Unless I notify ED differently, I authorize ED to defer repayment of principal on my loan while I am enrolled at least half-time at an eligible school.

F. I authorize my school and ED to release information about my loan to the references on the loan and to members of my immediate family, unless I submit written directions otherwise.

G. I authorize my schools, lenders and guarantors, ED, and their agents to release information about my loan to each other.

H. I authorize my schools, ED, and their respective agents and contractors to contact me regarding my loan request or my loan, including repayment of my loan, at the current or any future number that I provide for my cellular telephone or other wireless device using automated dialing equipment or artificial or prerecorded voice or text messages.

14. I will be given the opportunity to pay the interest that ED charges during grace, in school, deferment, forbearance, and other periods as provided under the Act. Unless I pay the interest, I understand that ED may add unpaid interest that is charged on each loan made under this MPN to the principal balance of that loan (this is called "capitalization") at the end of the grace, deferment, forbearance, or other period. Capitalization will increase the principal balance on my loan and the total amount of interest I must pay.

15. I understand that ED has the authority to verify information reported on this MPN with other federal agencies.

## SECTION D: PROMISE TO PAY

16. I promise to pay to ED all loan amounts disbursed under the terms of this MPN, plus interest and other charges and fees that may become due as provided in this MPN. **I understand that more than one loan may be made to me under this MPN.** I understand that by accepting any disbursement issued at any time under this MPN, I agree to repay the loan associated with that disbursement. I understand that, within certain timeframes, I may cancel or reduce the amount of a loan by refusing to accept or by returning all or a portion of any disbursement that is issued. Unless I make interest payments, interest that ED charges on my loans during grace, in-school, deferment, forbearance, and other periods will be added to the principal balance of the loan as provided under the Act. If I do not make a payment on a loan made under this MPN when it is due, I will also pay reasonable collection costs, including but not limited to attorney's fees, court costs, and other fees. I will not sign this MPN before reading the entire MPN, even if I am told not to read it, or told that I am not required to read it. I am entitled to an exact copy of this MPN and the Borrower's Rights and Responsibilities Statement. My signature certifies that I have read, understand, and agree to the terms and conditions of this MPN, including the Borrower Request, Certifications, Authorizations, and Understanding in Section C, the Notice About Subsequent Loans Made Under this MPN in Section E, and the terms and conditions described in Section E of this MPN and in the Borrower's Rights and Responsibilities Statement.

**I UNDERSTAND THAT I MAY RECEIVE ONE OR MORE LOANS UNDER THIS MPN, AND THAT I MUST REPAY ALL LOANS THAT I RECEIVE UNDER THIS MPN.**

17. Borrower's Signature

18. Today's Date (mm-dd-yyyy)

Page 1 of 8

Revised 03/2009

*The above form is a draft version. It is for information purposes only. Do not send in.*

# Direct Loans
William D. Ford Federal Direct Loan Program

**Federal Direct PLUS Loan**

**Application and Master Promissory Note**

**William D. Ford Federal Direct Loan Program**

Warning: Any person who knowingly makes a false statement or misrepresentation on this form or any accompanying document is subject to penalties that may include fines, imprisonment, or both, under the U.S. Criminal Code and 20 U.S.C. 1097.

OMB No. 1845-0068
Form Approved
Exp. Date 11/30/2013

---

*SECTION A: BORROWER INFORMATION – TO BE COMPLETED BY ALL BORROWERS; READ THE INSTRUCTIONS IN SECTION G BEFORE COMPLETING THIS SECTION*

**CHECK ONE – I am a:** ☐ **Graduate or Professional Student** ☐ **Parent of a Dependent Undergraduate Student**

1. Driver's License State and No.

2. Social Security No.

3. Date of Birth (mm-dd-yyyy)

4. E-Mail Address (optional)

5. Name and Permanent Address (see instructions)

6. Area Code/Telephone No.

7. Citizenship Status (to be completed by parent borrowers only – check one)

   (1) ☐ U.S. Citizen or National

   (2) ☐ Permanent Resident/Other Eligible Non-Citizen

   If (2), Alien Registration No.

8. Employer's Name and Address

9. Work Area Code/Telephone No.
   ( )

10. References: List two persons with different U.S. addresses who do not live with you and who have known you for at least three years. If you are a parent borrower, do not list the student.

| | 1. | 2. |
|---|---|---|
| Name | | |
| Permanent Street Address | | |
| City, State, Zip Code | | |
| E-Mail Address (optional) | | |
| Area Code/Telephone No. | ( ) | ( ) |
| Relationship to Borrower | | |

*SECTION B: SCHOOL INFORMATION – TO BE COMPLETED BY THE SCHOOL*

11. School Name and Address

12. School Code/Branch

13. Identification No.

*SECTION C: DEPENDENT UNDERGRADUATE STUDENT INFORMATION – TO BE COMPLETED BY PARENT BORROWERS ONLY*

14. Dependent Undergraduate Student's Name (last, first, middle initial)

15. Social Security No.

16. Date of Birth (mm-dd-yyyy)

*SECTION D: BORROWER REQUEST, CERTIFICATIONS, AUTHORIZATIONS, AND UNDERSTANDINGS – ALL BORROWERS READ CAREFULLY BEFORE SIGNING BELOW*

17. This is an Application and Master Promissory Note (MPN) for one or more Federal Direct PLUS (Direct PLUS) Loans. I request a Direct PLUS Loan under this MPN in an amount not to exceed my or (if I am a parent borrower) the student's annual cost of attendance, minus other financial aid received for each academic year. For each loan, the school will notify me of the loan amount that I am eligible to borrow. I may cancel a loan or request a lower amount by contacting the school. Additional information about my right to cancel a loan or request a lower amount is included in the Borrower's Rights and Responsibilities Statement and in the disclosure statements that will be provided to me. If I have an adverse credit history and obtain an endorser so that I may receive a Direct PLUS Loan, only one loan may be made to me under this MPN.

18. Under penalty of perjury, I certify that:
    A. The information I have provided on this MPN and as updated by me from time to time is true, complete, and correct to the best of my knowledge and belief and is made in good faith.
    B. I am (1) a graduate or professional student, (2) the biological or adoptive parent of the student identified in Section C, or (3) the spouse of the parent and my income and assets were reported on the Free Application for Federal Student Aid (FAFSA), or would be reported if a FAFSA were filed.
    C. The proceeds of loans made under this MPN will be used for authorized educational expenses incurred by me or, if I am a parent borrower, by the student; I will immediately repay any loan proceeds that cannot be attributed to educational expenses for attendance on at least a half-time basis at the school that certified my loan eligibility.
    D. If I owe an overpayment on a Federal Perkins Loan, Federal Pell Grant, Federal Supplemental Educational Opportunity Grant, Academic Competitiveness Grant (ACG), National Science and Mathematics Access to Retain Talent (SMART) Grant, or Leveraging Educational Assistance Partnership Grant, I have made satisfactory arrangements to repay the amount owed.
    E. If I am in default on any loan received under the Federal Perkins Loan Program (including National Direct Student Loans), the William D. Ford Federal Direct Loan (Direct Loan) Program, or the Federal Family Education Loan (FFEL) Program, I have made satisfactory repayment arrangements with the holder to repay the amount owed.
    F. If I have been convicted of, or pled nolo contendere (no contest) or guilty to, a crime involving fraud in obtaining funds under Title IV of the Higher Education Act of 1965, as amended (HEA), I have completed the repayment of the funds to the U.S. Department of Education (ED) or to the loan holder in the case of a Title IV federal student loan. If I am a parent applying for a Direct PLUS

Loan for a dependent undergraduate student, and if that student has been convicted of, or pled nolo contendere or guilty to, a crime involving fraud in obtaining funds under Title IV of the HEA, the student has completed the repayment of the funds to ED, or to the loan holder in the case of a Title IV federal student loan.

19. For each Direct PLUS Loan I receive under this MPN, I make the following authorizations:
    A. I authorize the school to certify my eligibility for the loan.
    B. For each loan that I receive under this MPN, I authorize ED to investigate my credit record and report information about my loan status to persons and organizations permitted by law to receive that information.
    C. I authorize the school to credit my loan proceeds to my account at the school if I am a graduate or professional student borrower or to the student's account at the school if I am a parent borrower.
    D. I authorize the school to pay to ED any refund that may be due up to the full amount of the loan.
    E. Unless I notify ED differently, I authorize ED to defer repayment of principal on my loan if I enroll at least half time at an eligible school and, if I am a graduate or professional student, for the 6-month period after I cease to be enrolled at least half time.
    F. I authorize the school and ED to release information about my loan to the references on the loan and to members of my immediate family, unless I submit written directions otherwise.
    G. I authorize the schools, ED, and their agents to release information about my loan to each other.
    H. I authorize my schools, ED, and their respective agents and contractors to contact me regarding my loan request or my loan, including repayment of my loan, at the current or any future number that I provide for my cellular telephone or other wireless device using automated dialing equipment or artificial or prerecorded voice or text messages.

20. I will be given the opportunity to pay the interest that accrues during deferment, forbearance, and other periods as provided under the Act ("the Act" is defined in Section F under Governing Law), including during in-school deferment periods. Unless I pay the interest, I understand that ED may add unpaid interest that accrues on each loan made under the MPN to the principal balance of that loan (this is called "capitalization") at the end of the deferment, forbearance, or other period. Capitalization will increase the principal balance on my loan and the total amount of interest I must pay.

21. I understand that ED has the authority to verify information reported on this MPN with other federal agencies.

*SECTION E: PROMISE TO PAY – TO BE COMPLETED BY ALL BORROWERS*

22. I promise to pay to ED all loan amounts disbursed under the terms of this MPN, plus interest and other charges and fees that may become due as provided in this MPN. **I understand that, if I qualify, more than one loan may be made to me under this MPN for myself or for the student identified in Section C.** I understand that by accepting any disbursement issued at any time under this MPN, I agree to repay the loan associated with that disbursement. I understand that, within certain timeframes, I may cancel or reduce the amount of a loan by refusing to accept or by returning all or a portion of any disbursement that is issued. Unless I make interest payments, interest that accrues on my loan during deferment, forbearance, or other periods will be added to the principal balance of the loan as provided under the Act. If I do not make a payment on a loan made under this MPN when it is due, I will also pay any reasonable collection costs, including but not limited to attorney fees, court costs, and other fees. I will not sign this MPN before reading the entire MPN, even if I am told not to read it, or told that I am not required to read it. I am entitled to an exact copy of this MPN and the Borrower's Rights and Responsibilities Statement. My signature certifies that I have read, understand, and agree to the terms and conditions of this MPN, including the Borrower Request, Certifications, Authorizations, and Understandings in Section D, the Notice About Subsequent Loans Made Under this MPN in Section F, and the terms and conditions described in Section F of this MPN and in the Borrower's Rights and Responsibilities Statement.

**I UNDERSTAND THAT I MAY RECEIVE ONE OR MORE LOANS UNDER THIS MPN, AND THAT I MUST REPAY ALL LOANS THAT I RECEIVE UNDER THIS MPN.**

23. Borrower's Signature _____

24. Today's Date (mm-dd-yyyy) _____

*The above form is a draft version. It is for information purposes only. Do not send in.*

# Appendices

# Glossary

**ACADEMIC YEAR:** A measure of academic work to be performed by the student, subject to definition by the school.

**AGI:** Adjusted gross income. In 2017, the AGI is listed on Line 37 of the IRS 1040; Line 21 of the IRS 1040A and Line 4 of the IRS 1040EZ.

**AMERICAN COLLEGE TESTING PROGRAM (ACT):** The administrator of a group of standardized tests in English, mathematics, reading, and science reasoning.

**BASE INCOME YEAR (also known as the BASE YEAR):** The second calendar year preceding the academic year for which aid is being sought. 2017 will be the base income year for the 2019–2020 award year.

**BUSINESS/FARM SUPPLEMENT:** A supplemental aid application required by a few colleges for aid applicants whose parents own businesses or farms or who are self-employed. The individual school's aid policy will determine if this form must be completed.

**CAMPUS-BASED PROGRAMS:** Three federal student aid programs that are administered directly by the school's financial aid office (the Perkins Loan, the Supplemental Educational Opportunity Grant, and the Federal Work-Study program).

**COLLEGE BOARD:** A nonprofit association that writes and processes the CSS/Financial Aid PROFILE form.

**COOPERATIVE EDUCATION:** A college program offered at many schools that combines periods of academic study with periods of paid employment related to the student's field of study. In most cases, participation will extend the time required to obtain a bachelor's degree to five years.

**COST OF ATTENDANCE:** A figure, estimated by the school, that includes the cost of tuition, fees, room, board, books, and supplies as well as an allowance for transportation and personal expenses. This figure is compared to the Expected Family Contribution to determine a student's aid eligibility. Also known as the *student budget*.

**CSS/FINANCIAL AID PROFILE:** a need analysis application created and processed by the College Board. Also known as the CSS PROFILE or the PROFILE form.

**DEFAULT:** Failure to repay a loan according to the terms of the promissory note.

**DEPENDENT STUDENT:** A classification for aid purposes for a student who is considered to be dependent upon his or her parent(s) for financial support.

**DIRECT LOAN PROGRAM:** Formerly known as the Stafford Student Loan program, this federally funded program provides low-interest loans to undergraduate and graduate students. In most cases, repayment does not begin until six months after the student graduates or leaves school and there are no interest charges while the student is in school. For new loans disbursed after June 30, 2006, the interest rate is fixed. (Prior loans had variable rates.) There are two types of Direct loans: subsidized and unsubsidized. The subsidized Direct loan is need-based and the government pays the interest while the student is in school. The unsubsidized Direct loan is non-need-based and can be taken out by virtually all students. In many cases, students can elect to let the interest accumulate until after they graduate.

**EDUCATIONAL TESTING SERVICE:** The organization that writes the SAT exam.

**EMPLOYMENT ALLOWANCE:** A deduction against income in the federal and institutional methodologies for two-parent families in which both parents work or a single-parent family in which that parent works.

**EXPECTED FAMILY CONTRIBUTION (EFC):** The amount of money the family is expected to contribute for the year toward the student's cost of attendance. This figure is compared to the Cost of Attendance to determine a student's aid eligibility.

**FAFSA:** See Free Application for Federal Student Aid.

**FAMILY CONTRIBUTION:** Another name used to refer to the Expected Family Contribution.

**FAO:** See Financial Aid Officer.

**FEDERAL METHODOLOGY:** The generally accepted method used to calculate the family's expected contribution to college costs for federal aid purposes. Depending on the individual college's policy, the federal methodology may also be used to determine eligibility for money under the school's control.

**FEDERAL WORK-STUDY (FWS):** A federally funded aid program that provides jobs for students. Eligibility is based on need.

**FINANCIAL AID:** A general term used to refer to a variety of programs funded by the federal and state governments as well as the individual schools to assist students with their educational costs. While the names may vary, financial aid comes in three basic forms: (1) gift aid (grants and scholarships) that does not have to be paid back (2) student loans, and (3) work-study jobs.

**FINANCIAL AID OFFICER:** An administrator at each school who determines whether a student is eligible for aid and if so, the types of aid to be awarded.

**FREE APPLICATION FOR FEDERAL STUDENT AID (FAFSA):** The need analysis document written by the U.S. Department of Education. This form is required for virtually all students seeking financial aid including the unsubsidized Stafford loan.

**FSA ID:** A new personal identification system for use with U.S. Department of Education websites including the online FAFSA.

**FOTW:** FAFSA on the Web, the online version of the FAFSA.

**401(k), 403(b):** The names of two of the more popular tax-deferred retirement plans in which employees elect to defer part of their earnings until a later date.

**GIFT AID:** Financial aid, usually a grant or scholarship, that does not have to be paid back and that does not involve employment.

**GRADPLUS LOANS:** A federally sponsored educational loan program in which graduate or professional school students can borrow up to the total cost of attendance minus any financial aid received. Eligibility is not based on need.

**GRANTS:** Gift aid that is generally based on need. The programs can be funded by the federal and state governments as well as the individual schools.

**HALF-TIME STATUS:** Refers to students taking at least 6 credits per semester, or the equivalent.

**INDEPENDENT STUDENT:** A student who, for financial aid purposes, is not considered dependent on his or her parent(s) for support. Also known as a self-supporting student.

**INCOME PROTECTION ALLOWANCE:** A deduction against income in both the federal and the institutional methodologies.

**INSTITUTIONAL FORMS:** Supplemental forms required by the individual schools to determine aid eligibility.

**INSTITUTIONAL METHODOLOGY:** An alternative method used to calculate the family's expected contribution to college costs. This methodology is generally used by private and a few state schools to determine eligibility for aid funds under the school's direct control. Colleges that use the institutional methodology usually require completion of the PROFILE form.

**LONG FORM:** This generally refers to the IRS 1040 form.

**NEED:** The amount of aid a student is eligible to receive. This figure is calculated by subtracting the Expected Family Contribution from the Cost of Attendance.

**NEED ANALYSIS:** The process of analyzing the information on the aid form to calculate the amount of money the student and parent(s) can be expected to contribute toward educational costs.

**NEED ANALYSIS FORMS:** Aid applications used to calculate the expected family contribution. The most common need analysis forms are: the Free Application for Federal Student Aid (FAFSA) and the CSS/Financial Aid PROFILE form. Consult the individual school's financial aid filing requirements to determine which form(s) are required for that particular school.

**NONCUSTODIAL PARENT'S STATEMENT:** A supplemental aid application required by a few colleges for aid applicants whose parents are separated or divorced or who never married. The individual school's aid policy will determine if this form must be completed. If required, this form will be completed by the noncustodial parent. This is generally the parent with whom the child spent the least amount of time in the preceding 12 months prior to completion of the form.

**PARENTS' CONTRIBUTION:** The amount of money the parent(s) are expected to contribute for the year toward the student's Cost of Attendance.

**PARENT LOANS FOR UNDERGRADUATE STUDENTS (PLUS):** A federally sponsored educational loan program in which parents can borrow up to the total cost of attendance minus any financial aid received for each child in an undergraduate program. Eligibility is not based on need.

**PELL GRANT:** A federally funded need-based grant program for first-time undergraduate students (i.e., the student has not as yet earned a bachelor's or first professional degree). Funds from this program are generally awarded to lower- and lower-middle-income families. Years ago, this program was called the Basic Educational Opportunity Grant (BEOG).

**PERKINS LOAN PROGRAM:** This federally funded need-based program provides low interest loans to undergraduate and graduate students and is administered by the school's financial aid office. In most cases, repayment does not begin until nine months after the student graduates or leaves school and there are no interest charges while the student is in school. The fixed interest rate is currently 5%.

**PHEAA:** The Pennsylvania Higher Education Assistance Agency.

**PLUS LOANS:** See Parent Loans for Undergraduate Students.

**PREFERENTIAL PACKAGING:** The situation in which the more desired aid applicants get better aid packages, which are larger in total dollar amount and/or contain a higher percentage of grants versus loans.

**PROFILE FORM:** A need analysis document written and processed by the College Board.

**PROMISSORY NOTE:** The legal document which the borrower signs to obtain the loan proceeds and which specifies the terms of the loan, the interest rate, and the repayment provisions.

**ROTC:** The Reserve Officer Training Corps programs that are coordinated at many college campuses by the U.S. Army, Navy, and Air Force.

**SAT:** An exam, administered by the College Board, which has critical reading, math, and writing sections.

**SAR:** See Student Aid Report.

**SCHOLARSHIPS:** Gift aid that is usually based on merit or a combination of need and merit.

**SELF-HELP:** The portion of the aid package relating to student loans and/or work-study.

**SEOG:** See Supplemental Educational Opportunity Grant.

**SHORT FORMS:** This generally refers to the IRS 1040A or the 1040EZ forms.

**SIMPLIFIED NEEDS TEST:** An alternative method used to calculate the family's expected contribution to college costs for federal aid purposes, in which all assets are excluded from the federal aid formula.

**STANDARDIZED FORMS:** The generic term used in this book when referring to any of the need analysis forms that must be sent to a processing service. The two most commonly used standardized forms are the U.S. Department of Education's Free Application for Federal Student Aid (FAFSA) and the College Board's CSS/Financial Aid PROFILE form.

**STUDENT AID REPORT (SAR):** The multipage report that is issued to students who have filed a completed FAFSA.

**STUDENT BUDGET:** See Cost of Attendance.

**STUDENT'S CONTRIBUTION:** The amount of money the student is expected to contribute for the year toward his or her cost of attendance.

**SUBSIDIZED DIRECT LOAN:** See Direct Loan program.

**SUPPLEMENTAL EDUCATIONAL OPPORTUNITY GRANT (SEOG):** A federally funded need-based grant program for undergraduate students that is awarded by the school's financial aid office.

**UNSUBSIDIZED DIRECT LOAN:** See Direct Loan program.

**VERIFICATION:** A process in which the financial aid office requires additional documentation to verify the accuracy of the information reported on the aid applications.

**WORK-STUDY:** See Federal Work-Study.

# Institutional Methodology Comments and Case Studies

Prior to the 2011 edition, we included worksheets to calculate the expected family contribution (EFC) under both the Institutional Methodology (IM) as well as the Federal Methodology (FM). Beginning with the 2011–2012 award year, as a change of policy the College Board is no longer providing anyone with their proprietary tables and formulas to calculate the IM EFC. However, they have agreed to provide us with EFC amounts for the IM under some common scenarios. But before we get to those case studies, there are some additional items to note regarding the IM:

While there have been adjustments for inflation and other minor changes, we assume there have not been significant changes in the standard IM for 2020–2021.

Many colleges that use the institutional methodology often tweak the formula, for example making adjustments for the cost of living for those families residing in high cost areas. So even though one used to be able to calculate an IM EFC, that number was never written in stone— and could differ considerably from school to school. In recent years, we have found that the packages from individual schools using the institutional methodology are varying wildly based on the ways their aid policies deviate from the standard formula. As such in the past few years, the standard IM formula had been less reliable as a tool for predicting one's EFC at schools that use the IM than it had been in the distant past.

Websites that say they will give you a calculation of your EFC under the institutional methodology have not been very reliable in the recent past—and will be even less reliable this year.

For students whose parents are divorced, separated, or were never married: many schools that use the IM assess a contribution from both parents. This can result in a significantly higher family contribution than under the federal methodology which only considers the finances of the custodial parent who resides with the student.

So what's a family to do? The basic strategies outlined in Chapter 3 still apply full force; for example, high medical expenses will continue to reduce your IM EFC. At the end of this section, you will find a number of typical family situations. The College Board was kind enough to calculate the expected family contribution using the standard 2020–2021 institutional methodology for a number of common scenarios, along with a somewhat common institutional option for how home equity is treated. Along with the points below, this should give you a rough idea of what the IM EFC could be under these circumstances.

## Item One: Additional Data Elements Considered As Income

The institutional methodology includes many untaxed income elements that are not assessed in the federal formula. See pages 76–78. However except for the Earned Income Credit, pre-tax contributions withheld from wages for HSA accounts as well as for dependent care and medical spending accounts, and untaxed social security benefits for family members other than the student, most of these additional untaxed income items under the IM do not apply to most families.

## Item Two: Losses Claimed on Income Tax Return

Families who have significant losses claimed on their personal IRS 1040 tax return (for example: losses from property rental, S-corporations or partnerships, farming operations, or capital losses; or losses claimed on schedule C from self-employment) will find that their family contribution in the institutional methodology may be more than under the federal formula. Such losses can be a double-edged sword. For while these losses boost your income in the IM (compared to the FM), they also reduce the amount of U.S. taxes paid—which are a deduction under the formula.

## Item Three: Higher Allowances Against Income

In years past, for most families, the income protection allowance under the institutional formula has been greater than under the federal formula. The same is true for the deduction for state and local taxes—which has been based on a higher percentage of one's income. Combined with a somewhat higher maximum employment allowance as well as the granting of an Annual Education Saving Allowance, the IM's higher allowances will normally result in a smaller contribution from income for most families than under the federal formula. Except, of course, for family situations when Item One and/or Item Two above apply.

## Item Four: Additional Assets Assessed

The IM assesses certain assets that are excluded in the FM. For most families, this means the primary residence (i.e. your home). Yet while the standard institutional methodology considers the full equity in the home as an asset, in the past few years more and more schools have been treating one's home equity in a wide variety of ways. While some still assess the full equity, others will only consider it if your income exceeds a certain amounts (in some cases, $150,000).

Other schools that use the CSS PROFILE (Hamilton College and Bard College come to mind) exclude home equity entirely. Still others view home equity on a case-by-case basis. For example, if you bought your home recently with a large down payment, some colleges might arrive at a higher family contribution than if you bought your home 25 years ago at a modest price but have since experienced significant increases in value that cannot be readily accessed.

So having significant equity in the home can be the "wild card" in how schools using the IM calculate your EFC. Your IM EFC may be less than the federal methodology or it could be significantly more, depending on a school's policy. In the case studies that follow, we provide the IM EFC under two common ways that equity in one's primary residence is treated: a) with the full equity considered and b) with the home equity capped at two times income.

Another difference between the institutional and federal methodology is that the equity in all businesses and farms is assessed in the IM, while any "family business" or "family farm" are excluded under the Federal methodology.

For the case studies that follow, the EFCs is first calculated when only one child is in college as a freshman. The changes to the EFCs when a second child is in college are also provided.

# Case One

Typical family of four; a two-parent household living in Los Angeles, California, daughter starting freshman year, with a younger sibling age 15. The older parent is 55 years old. Both parents work. Their adjusted combined gross income is $175,000. The father's income from work is $75,000; the mother's $105,000. U.S. income tax paid in the base year: $22,850. The parents contribute $9,000 to a 401(k) plan plus $4,000 contributed pre-tax to medical spending accounts. There is no other untaxed income, and the family shows no losses on their tax return. They own a home valued at $600,000 with a mortgage of $150,000, so equity is $450,000. Excluding retirement accounts, the family has assets of $60,000 in cash, savings, checking and other investments. The family's medical expenses are $9,000 for the year. The student earned $8,000 in the base income year and has no other income. She pays $170 in U.S. income taxes, and has $1500 in a savings account.

## Results for Case One

EFC Federal methodology:
$44,879 from parents (PC) + $334 from student (SC) = $45,213 FM EFC

EFC Institutional methodology with full home equity considered:
$54,153 from parents + $3,829 from the student = $57,982 IM EFC

EFC Institutional methodology with home equity capped at two times income:
$50,453 from parents + $3,829 from the student = $54,282 IM EFC

EFC for an upperclassman with another sibling in college with full home equity considered:
PC FM: $22,860; PC IM: $33,656. (Same SC as above for FM and IM)

PC IM with home equity capped at two times income: $31,436 (2 in college)

# Case Two

Father, aged 48, is a single parent; mother is deceased. His son is starting freshman year. There is another sibling, age 16, one year behind. They currently live in Baltimore, MD. The father's income from work is $90,000. His AGI is $87,000. U.S. income taxes paid this year is $8,200. He contributes $4000 to a 401(k) and $2,000 pre-tax to a medical spending account. The father pays $3,750 for the family's medical expenses for the year. He receives $8400 per year in social security benefits per child because of the mother's death. There is no other untaxed income. Father has home equity of $260,000 ($350,000 value less $90,000 debt) and $25,000 in financial assets other than his retirement accounts. His son has no income, but has $500 in a savings account.

## Results for Case Two

EFC Federal methodology:
　　$15,422 from parent (PC) + $100 from student (SC) = $15,522 FM EFC

EFC Institutional methodology with full home equity considered:
　　$21,563 from parent + $2,325 from the student = $23,888 IM EFC

EFC Institutional methodology with home equity capped at two times income:
　　$18,703 from parents + $2,325 from the student = $21,028 IM EFC

EFC for an upperclassman with another sibling in college with full home equity considered:
　　PC FM: $8,130; PC IM: $11,885 (FM SC: $100; IM SC: $3,075)

PC IM for an upperclassman with another sibling in college with home equity capped at two times income: $9,665

# Case Three

Two parent household in Brooklyn, NY. Daughter is starting freshman year, has two siblings age 14 and 10. Father is self-employed and his income from work is $130,000. Mother works part-time for someone else and earns $10,000 in salary. Mother is 49 years old, father is 46. Their AGI is $106,400. Father contributes $6,000 to a traditional deductible IRA, with no other retirement contributions made by the family. Parents' U.S. taxes paid figure is $6,200. Home equity is $700,000 ($900,000 value less $200,000 debt). They also own a second piece of real estate with $200,000 in equity ($275,000 value less $75,000 debt) that generates a property rental loss of $5,000 in the base income year. They also claim a $3000 capital loss on their tax return. The parents have $10,000 in cash and investment equity; father has

$150,000 equity in his Schedule C business (sole proprietorship). Family has medical expenses of $10,500 (not including the self-employed health insurance deduction). The student earned $4,000 and had no other income. Therefore, there are no U.S. income taxes paid. Student's assets consist of $1,000 in a non-interest bearing checking account.

## Results for Case Three

EFC Federal methodology:
$28,973 from parents (PC) + $200 from student (SC) = $29,173 FM EFC

EFC Institutional methodology with full home equity considered:
$54,762 from parents + $2,450 from the student = $57,212 IM EFC

EFC Institutional methodology with home equity capped at two times income:
$31,802 from parents + $2,450 from the student = $34,252 IM EFC

EFC for an upperclassman with another sibling in college with full home equity considered:
PC FM: $14,931; PC IM: $33,450 (FM SC: $200; IM SC: $3,200)

PC IM for an upperclassman with another sibling in college with home equity capped at two times income: $19,674

# Key Things to Know About the IRS Data Retrieval Tool and the IRS Transcript Verification Requirement

If you've already filed a 2018 IRS 1040 personal income tax return with the IRS, the online 2020–2021 FAFSA form, known as FAFSA On The Web (FOTW), may allow you to transfer some of your financial information directly from an IRS database using an option called the IRS Data Retrieval Tool (DRT).

While this tool has been billed as a way to simplify the FAFSA, some in the aid community believe its real purpose is to more accurately verify FAFSA information and prevent fraud. The DRT can be used when you complete the original FOTW or when you're revising your FAFSA data—known as FAFSA Corrections—after your tax return has been filed. Since the DRT can be used after filing an original FAFSA, you should NEVER miss a FAFSA or other aid deadline if your taxes aren't done or you are unable to use the DRT. Be aware that it will take a number of weeks—at least three if the return was filed electronically and up to 11 if the return was mailed —before the DRT can be used.

## Determining if You Can Use the IRS Retrieval Tool

When using the interactive FOTW, the skip-logic built into the form may automatically disqualify you from using the DRT—for example if your marital status recently changed. Or (even more obviously), if your taxes aren't yet filed or you're not even required to file a return. This is no cause for alarm. Later in this section, we'll explain what to do if you're ineligible or unable to use the DRT.

But even when the FOTW tells you that you may be able to use the DRT, you'll still have a few additional hoops to jump through. Once you click "Already Completed" for FOTW questions 32 or 79, then a few more questions will appear on your screen to further determine if the DRT can be used. Certain responses to these questions will disqualify you from using the tool at that time. (If not enough time has elapsed after filing the return, you can of course try again at a later date.)

But even if you can use the DRT, there is one specific scenario when you should be extremely careful, when using the DRT. Namely, if you had a qualified rollover of funds from one retirement account into another (see pages 72–74). In this case, using the tool could significantly reduce your aid eligibility if you are not careful as income NOT REQUIRED to be reported would transfer onto the FOTW. So if you have a qualified rollover, you will want to reduce the amount transferred by the DRT by the amount of any such rollovers. (See pages 185–186).

# If You Decide to Use the IRS Retrieval Tool

If you've gotten this far and decided it is in your best interest to use the DRT, the first step is to get directed to an IRS database by using your DOE FSA ID (see pages 168–171) and then inputting your address and other information listed on your most recent tax return.

After all that, you'll be given information on how to transfer some of your tax return data onto the FOTW. Unfortunately, it is at this stage that many of our clients have reported they've had problems. So don't be surprised if the DRT doesn't work at first asking.

If you're having trouble with the DRT, here are some troubleshooting tips:

1.  If you see an error message that there is no record of your tax return, it may mean not enough time has yet elapsed. In this case, first check to be sure the return was actually filed. This is particularly applicable if you used a professional preparer. Also, IRS processing can also be delayed if you owed taxes to the IRS when you filed or were a victim of identity theft. In the latter case, you might be told you cannot use the DRT.

2.  Check that the pre-populated data on the screen is correct. For example, if you have an extremely long surname, the maximum number of characters listed for FAFSA 61 or 65 (which pre-populate on the DRT screen) are less than the number you can use on that screen—so add the additional characters. If there's any mismatch with IRS data, you may not be allowed to proceed.

3.  While you will told to use the address as it appears on the return, this may not work—since the retrieval tool uses the address in the IRS' database. "First Avenue" could easily be entered by an IRS clerk as "1st Ave". There can also to be problems if you recently switched accountants or started using new tax software and changed the way you list your address.

4.  If you live in an apartment, there is a specific question on the DRT about an apartment number on your return. But if the apartment number appears as part of your street address and not in a separate apt. # response area, entering it in the apt # response area on the DRT—instead of as a part of your street address—will likely cause problems.

5.  You may think you know the city in which you dwell, but alternate names used on your return can cause a mismatch with your IRS information. Also if the U.S. Post Office (USPS) recently changed your zip code without your moving, try the new zip code even if the old code is still on your return. (For help with the proper city and zip code, the zip code tool at www.usps.com will tell you how the feds know your city and zip code.)

6. Every character of your data must agree exactly with the IRS database. Exceptions: the symbol # and any dash in your address cannot be used.

7. If you filed a joint return with your spouse, are required to report both individual's information from the return on the FAFSA and are having trouble with the DRT: try using the other individual's FSA ID to access the tool.

Unfortunately with most of issues above, the DRT won't tell you which data element you entered is the problem. So you may need to keep trying multiple combinations of data.

And even if you do get the retrieval tool to work, it will not answer all the income questions on the FOTW. So you'll need to go back and answer those FOTW income questions that do not pre-populate. Be especially careful with FAFSA questions 43, 44, 91, and 92, since not all sub-parts of these questions pre-populate. Depending on your situation, the "income earned from work" responses may or may not transfer. Refer to pages 182–183 of this book as well the FOTW instructions for guidance about these questions on the FAFSA.

## If You Are Unable to Use the Tool...

...DON'T PANIC. You'll just have to use plan B. Here's what to do:

Go back to the FAFSA form, answering the questions based on your tax return and our line-by-line comments in Part Three, as well as information that appears on the screen. Most likely the instructions for the FOTW will tell you which specific IRS line number from your tax return correlates with a particular FAFSA question.

## Interplay between the DRT and Verification

If your aid application is selected for Verification (see pages 210–211), then federal regulations now require all tax filers whose information is reported on the FAFSA to provide the financial aid office with either a signed copy of the tax return or an official IRS Return Transcript—a document generated by the IRS which summarizes your federal tax return information. Federal regulations further stipulate that any IRS Transcript requirement can be fulfilled by using the DRT. So for tax filers, the use of the DRT when you complete the original FOTW or submit a FAFSA Correction will be much simpler and more efficient than submitting a signed copy of the entire tax return or requesting an IRS transcript. Be aware, however, that some financial aid offices may still require an official IRS transcript even if the DRT was used.

If you are not able to—or choose not to—use the DRT, you can obtain an IRS Transcript by requesting one online at www.irs.gov or calling the IRS at 800 908-9946. Be sure you request the "return" transcript for the appropriate tax year—and not your IRS "account" transcript. It will take a number of days before you receive the transcript in the mail. If you had a rollover of retirement assets, be sure to write the word "Rollover" next to the applicable line on the transcript and provide the FAO(s) with supporting documentation regarding the amount rolled over.

As with the DRT, you'll need to wait the same number of weeks after filing your return before you can request a transcript. An even longer time period will apply if an amended return was filed.

# About the Authors

KALMAN A. CHANY is the founder and president of Campus Consultants Inc., (www. CampusConsultants.com) a New York City–based firm that guides parents and students through the financial aid process. In addition to counseling thousands of families on the aid process, he has conducted workshops for corporations, schools, and other organizations. He also trains financial professionals regarding financial aid consulting. Kal is a frequent guest on television and radio shows across the country.

GEOFF MARTZ is a writer living in New York City.

# NOTES

# NOTES

# NOTES

# NOTES

**NOTES**

NOTES

# NOTES

# NOTES